"This book provides a welcome, joined-up approach to strategy development, proceeding from the visioning process to investment analysis and performance measurement. Strategic planners, dealing with complexity and uncertainty, will find the tool-kit and the many illuminating insights and examples very helpful indeed."

– John Hough, Corporate Strategy Executive with a leading global engineering company in the aerospace, defence and marine industries

"This is an important and original contribution to the strategic management literature that provides important practical tools for the practical development of strategic direction.

Set within an overall framework for the strategic development process, the book covers a range of modelling methods including visioning, problem structuring methods, system dynamics, complexity theory, real options, risk analysis, and finance and performance measurement. As well as exploring these individually the text recognises the necessity to combine different methods together to take advantage of their complementarity and synergies.

This book will be invaluable for both strategists who need practical tools and for management scientists who are interested in strategic decisions"

– John Mingers, Professor of Operational Research and Systems, Kent Business School, University of Kent, UK

"The authors see strategy formulation and implementation as inseparable activities in which every organisation engages on a continuous basis. This means that this book has the wide scope needed by a manager, from visioning through to performance measurement and financial evaluation. By bringing the range of contributors needed to cover this space, the authors have managed to provide both a conceptual framework and the detail needed by real managers who can benefit from the tools and methods described."

– Gill Ringland, CEO and Fellow, SAMI Consulting, St Andrews Management Institute

"In this unique book, management science lifts its view to take in the broader horizons of strategy. The result is a framework for strategy development, and a range of methods and models to make it operational."

– Professor Jonathan Rosenhead, London School of Economics

Supporting Strategy

Supporting Strategy
Frameworks, Methods and Models

Edited by:

Frances A. O'Brien
Robert G. Dyson

University of Warwick

John Wiley & Sons, Ltd

Other Wiley Editorial Offices

John Wiley & Sons Inc., 111 River Street, Hoboken, NJ 07030, USA

Jossey-Bass, 989 Market Street, San Francisco, CA 94103-1741, USA

Wiley-VCH Verlag GmbH, Boschstr. 12, D-69469 Weinheim, Germany

John Wiley & Sons Australia Ltd, 42 McDougall Street, Milton, Queensland 4064, Australia

John Wiley & Sons (Asia) Pte Ltd, 2 Clementi Loop #02-01, Jin Xing Distripark, Singapore 129809

John Wiley & Sons Canada Ltd, 6045 Freemont Blvd, Mississauga, ONT, L5R 4J3

Wiley also publishes its books in a variety of electronic formats. Some content that appears in print may
not be available in electronic books.

Anniversary Logo Design: Richard J. Pacifico

Library of Congress Cataloging in Publication Data

Supporting strategy : frameworks, methods, and models / edited by Frances A.
   O'Brien, Robert G. Dyson.
      p.   cm.
   Includes bibliographical references and index.
   ISBN-13: 978-0-470-05718-6 (cloth : alk. paper)
   ISBN-10: 0-470-05718-1 (cloth : alk. paper)
   ISBN-13: 978-0-470-05717-9 (pbk. : alk. paper)
   ISBN-10: 0-470-05717-3 (pbk. : alk. paper)
   1. Strategic planning—Simulation methods.   2. Management—Simulation methods.
   I. O'Brien, Frances A.   II. Dyson, Robert G.
   HD30.28.S897 2007
   658.4'012—dc22   2006036088

British Library Cataloguing in Publication Data

A catalogue record for this book is available from the British Library

ISBN: 978-0470-05718-6 (hbk)
ISBN: 978-0470-05717-9 (pbk)

Typeset in 10/12pt Palatino by Integra Software Services Pvt. Ltd, Pondicherry, India
Printed and bound in Great Britain by Antony Rowe Ltd, Chippenham, Wiltshire.
This book is printed on acid-free paper responsibly manufactured from sustainable forestry in which
at least two trees are planted for each one used for paper production.

Contents

Preface

Strategists often focus on vision and strategy formulation and all too often converge rather rapidly towards implementation. Management scientists/operational researchers are experts at analysis for evaluation and choice but may lose sight of the bigger picture. In this book we argue that successful strategic development of the organisation requires an effective and balanced strategy development process spanning direction setting, strategy creation, rehearsal, evaluation and choice, leading to a continuous process of adopting strategic initiatives.

In a changing world, there is no option to stand still; organisations need to review their direction and to create new initiatives, and crucially they need to rehearse their ideas rather than hope for the best. In many areas of everyday life, we appreciate the need for and importance of rehearsal as a means of improving the chances of a successful outcome. For example, on both stage and screen, writers, directors and actors rehearse their productions prior to public performance; sports teams practice and rehearse in the run up to the game; and students revise and rehearse prior to examinations. In the book, we value the creation of direction and the formulation of strategy, but argue that the rehearsal of strategic initiatives should be given equal prominence; it is as important to revise or abandon strategies as it is to create them.

We begin by identifying the main elements that together are required for an effective strategic development process. We then present a collection of frameworks, methods and models which alone, or in combination, actively help managers to rehearse their strategic ideas by supporting specific activities or elements within the strategic development process. The collection of frameworks, methods and models spans a range of creative and analytical approaches taken from across the strategic management and management science/operational research fields. One of the novel features of this book is that approaches from both of these fields are brought together in creating frameworks, methods and models that support activities within the strategic development process.

The book is divided into six sections, the first of which introduces the reader to the strategic development process. The remaining five sections focus on particular aspects: setting direction; creating strategic initiatives; rehearsing strategy; evaluating performance and combining approaches. Each chapter describes a different framework, method or model and is designed to introduce the reader to the topic to provide an insight into how they may use the approach in practice and to signpost future developments in the field. Many of the chapters also describe case studies of how organisations have actually used the framework, method or model being described. The collection of topics covered by the book include: drama theory, visioning, problem-structuring methods, resource-based view of strategy, SWOT/TOWS analysis, system dynamics, agent-based modelling, scenario planning, decision and risk analysis, financial evaluation, real options, robustness analysis and performance measurement. Some of the chapters also consider how methods can be combined. For example, Chapter 14 considers issues of complementarity when drama theory, system dynamics and scenario planning are applied to a single case study.

The book is aimed at three audiences. First, the book is aimed at managers and policy-makers who are looking for ways to help them support the strategic development of their organisation. Second, the book is aimed at the student of strategy, who seeks practical ways of actually creating, developing and evaluating strategic ideas. Third, the book is aimed at academics in the fields of strategic management and management science/operational research who are interested in further exploring the nature of the strategy process and means of supporting it.

The genesis of the book is a stream of research begun over 20 years ago into what constitutes effective strategic development. Two previous texts, *Strategic Development: Methods and Models* and *Strategic Planning: Models and Analytical Techniques*, arose from this stream of research. Over the past few years, we have met on a regular basis with colleagues from a number of other institutions. Through a series of meetings, seminars and workshops, held at Warwick Business School, we have learned about each others' areas of expertise and have explored opportunities for combining approaches for supporting strategy. This book has grown out of our shared experiences and represents the culmination of our explorations thus far.

Frances O'Brien and Robert Dyson
Warwick Business School

About the Contributors

Robert Berry

Bob Berry is the Boots Professor of Accounting & Finance at Nottingham University Business School. Bob worked in industry before becoming an academic. He has taught at the universities of Warwick, East Anglia and Nottingham. His research and teaching covers corporate finance and the applications of artificial intelligence to problems in accounting and finance. Bob edits the journal *Intelligent Systems in Accounting, Finance and Management*. In 1998 he was awarded the Commendation of the Chartered Institute of Management Accountants.

Jim Bryant

Jim Bryant has been Professor of Operational Research and Strategy Sciences at Sheffield Hallam University since 1990. His main research interest is the area of conflict and collaboration. With Nigel Howard he developed 'drama theory' as an approach to the successful prosecution of collaborative ventures. Jim's text *The Six Dilemmas of Collaboration* (John Wiley & Sons, 2003) is the first dealing with business applications of drama theory. Jim has acted as a consultant and trainer to both public and private sector organisations and his work on drama theory has been used notably in the health service. He has a wider interest in conflict and is presently chair of the Conflict Research Society, the interdisciplinary body for professionals working on issues of conflict and its resolution.

Adrián Caldart

Dr. Adrián Caldart is Assistant Professor in Strategic Management at Warwick Business School. He has a PhD from IESE Business School in Barcelona. Formerly in the energy sector, specialising in corporate planning and risk management, he has also been Visiting Professor in MBA and Executive programmes in Spain, Portugal and Argentina. Research interests include corporate level strategy, organisational design, strategic change and corporate governance.

Robert Dyson

Robert Dyson is Professor of Operational Research at Warwick Business School. He has served as Dean of the Business School and Pro-Vice-Chancellor of the University of Warwick. He has also been Chair of the Committee of Professors of Operational Research and President of the Operational Research Society. He researches and publishes in data envelopment analysis, performance measurement and OR and strategy, and is an Editor of the *European Journal of Operational Research*. Prior to joining Warwick he worked for Pilkington plc.

Alberto Franco

Alberto Franco is an Associate Professor in Operational Research and Systems at the University of Warwick. Alberto has an MSc in Operational Research from Lancaster University and a PhD in Operational Research from the London School of Economics and Political Science (LSE). He has been researching and consulting with problem-structuring methods for the last 10 years with a variety of organisations in the private and public sectors within and outside the UK. These include: Whitbread, Bombardier, Taylor Woodraw, Dstl, Surrey County Council,

Network Rail and Shoosmiths. He is also a Visiting Professor at the Universidad del Pacifico (Lima, Peru) and co-founder of the UK Specialist Interest Group in Problem Structuring Methods.

Giles Hindle

Giles Hindle, PhD, is an Assistant Professor at Warwick Business School and a Director of HCS Ltd, which is a provider of applied research services to public sector organizations. Giles also holds visiting posts at Lancaster University Management School and Hull University Business School. Giles has spent 15 years combining both academic and consultancy interests, and is particularly interested in strategic thinking and innovation in both the public and private sectors. Previous posts include Senior Consultant for MSA Ferndale Ltd, Secta Health Group and Tribal Consulting and Business Consultant for Lancaster University Management School. Research interests now focus on the use of Soft Systems Methodology for strategic thinking and applied research in the public sector.

Nigel Howard

Nigel Howard's work for the US government while at the University of Pennsylvania led to the theory of metagames, an extension of game theory that he applied with some success to the 1969 SALT agreement, nuclear proliferation and the Vietnam peace talks. With Jim Bryant he developed drama theory and went on to derive confrontation analysis, which he applied to defence problems in work funded by the UK Defence Evaluation and Research Agency and the US Department of Defense. Nigel is the author of two books as well as numerous articles in books and scientific journals. He is currently running a forum (www.dilemmasgalore.com) on drama theory and its applications, in which he is publishing chapters of a book being written.

Martin Kunc

Martin Kunc is Associate Professor of Strategic Management at the School of Business, Universidad Adolfo Ibañez (Santiago, Chile) where he teaches strategic management and system dynamics. His interests include the process of strategic decision-making and its effect on the dynamics of firm performance and industry evolution, as well as the use of models and simulation in strategy development. He has applied research projects for international organisations including Mars and Standard & Poor's. He has published papers in the *Journal of the Operational Research Society* among other journals. Before joining Universidad Adolfo Ibañez he was at London Business School, where he received his PhD.

Abhijit Mandal

Abhijit Mandal holds a PhD in business studies from London Business School and an MBA from the Yale School of Management. He is currently lecturing at the Warwick Business School, University of Warwick, at Coventry. His research interests are related to developing the dynamic aspect of management theories. He has sought to explore the resource-based view, strategy, mergers & acquisitions and other topics within strategic management from this angle. He has won a few best paper awards in prestigious conferences. He teaches courses related to strategy and simulation.

Maureen Meadows

Maureen Meadows is a Senior Lecturer in Management at the Open University Business School. Her research interests include the use of methods and models in strategy development, including scenario planning and visioning, and the role played by the cognitive styles of managers when they engage in strategic conversations within organisations. She holds a BA in Mathematics from the University of Oxford and an MSc in Management Science and Operational Research from the University of Warwick. She has commercial experience with National Westminster Bank, both in an internal consultancy

role with the Operational Research Group and in personal customer marketing with
responsibility for market segmentation and distribution channels.

Gilberto Montibeller

Gilberto Montibeller is Lecturer in Decision
Sciences in the Operational Research Group,
Department of Management, at the London
School of Economics. With a background in
electrical engineering, he started his career as
an executive of British and American Tobacco.
Moving back to academia, he gained a Masters
and a PhD in Production Engineering, both in the
field of Operational Research. Dr Montibeller has
been researching and providing consultancy in
Risk and Decision Analysis for the past 10 years,
and top journals of the field such as *Decision
Support Systems* and *OMEGA – The International
Journal of Management Science*. He is Assistant
Editor of the *Journal of Multi-Criteria Decision
Analysis*.

John Morecroft

John Morecroft is Adjunct Associate Professor of
Management Science and Operations at London
Business School where he teaches system
dynamics, scenario methods and strategy. He
is also an Associate Fellow at Warwick Business School. His interests include the dynamics
of firm performance and the use of models and
simulation in strategy development. He has led
applied research projects for international organisations including Royal Dutch/Shell, AT&T,
BBC World Service, Cummins Engine Company,
Harley-Davidson, Ericsson, McKinsey & Co and
Mars. He is a recipient of the Jay Wright Forrester
Award of the System Dynamics Society and a
past President of the Society. He was previously on the faculty of MIT's Sloan School
of Management where he received his PhD. He also holds degrees from Imperial
College, London and from Bristol University.

Martin Murtland

Martin is Business Champion for Factiva Insight and Text Mining at Dow Jones. Martin was Director of Content Strategy and Development at Factiva where his responsibilities include expanding the use of new content types and metadata within Factiva's products and services. Previously, Martin was responsible for Factiva's content licensing activities throughout the Americas. He has also held roles at both Factiva and Reuters in business development and marketing. Prior to joining Reuters, Martin was a product manager for Standard & Poor's marketing online analysis of the foreign exchange, bond and equity markets in Europe, the Middle East and Africa. Martin holds an MBA with Distinction from Warwick University and an MA in Marketing from Kingston University. He has spoken on numerous topics including 'Devising an Information Strategy' and 'Strategies for Intranets and Extranets'.

Fernando Oliveira

Fernando Oliveira is an Assistant Professor in the Operational Research and Information Systems Group at Warwick Business School. He was previously Assistant Professor of Management Science at Universidade do Porto and a Visiting Lecturer at Cass Business School. He holds a Licenciatura in Economics, an MSc in Artificial Intelligence, both from Universidade do Porto, and a PhD in Management Science from London Business School. His main research interests include agent-based simulation, real options and energy markets modelling.

Frances O'Brien

Frances O'Brien is an Associate Professor at Warwick Business School. Her research interests include the development and use of approaches to support strategy development, in particular scenario planning and visioning methodologies, and the practice of combining OR & strategy tools by management teams. She holds a BSc (Joint Honours) in Mathematics and Classical Studies from Surrey University and an MSc in Operational Research from Southampton University. She previously worked for the Operational Research Group of Ford of Europe as a consultant providing modelling support on simulation, manpower planning and allocation studies. She is an active member of the UK Operational Research Society for which she chairs the OR and Strategy Special Interest Group.

Efstathis Tapinos

Stathis Tapinos is currently a Lecturer in Strategic Management at Aston Business School, Aston University, UK. He earned his PhD at Warwick Business School, University of Warwick, UK, where he investigated strategy development from a process point of view and its relationship with performance measurement. His current research is engaged with strategic development processes, strategy as practice, performance measurement and the balanced scorecard. He also has an active research interest in strategic foresight and particularly the use of scenario planning. He is a member of the Operational Research Society, UK and the Strategic Management Society.

Part I

Introduction

Chapter 1

The Strategic Development Process

Robert G. Dyson, Jim Bryant, John Morecroft and Frances O'Brien

The strategic development process is defined here to embrace the management processes that inform, shape and support the strategic decisions confronting an organisation. We have adopted the term 'strategic development' for a number of reasons. Firstly, we see strategy formulation and implementation as inseparable activities in which every organisation engages on a continuous basis, so the idea of ongoing development is central to our thinking. Secondly, the widely used term 'strategic planning' has become debased by association with the creation of deterministic, one-shot 5- and 10-year plans: for us this suggests an unhelpful rigidity in thinking about the future. Thirdly, 'strategic management' is too loose a term to describe the emphasis that we wish to place here upon reflective engagement and analytical questioning that characterises the approaches introduced in this book: nor does that term suggest the same focus upon the development of the organisation.

Strategic decisions, the focus of the strategic development process, do not form a distinct category at one extreme of some imagined spectrum leading from tactical, through operational to strategic decisions. Rather, there is a set of characteristics that lead towards a decision being labelled as 'strategic'. These characteristics include the following:

- Breadth of scope and therefore of implications right across and beyond the organisation.
- Complexity and inter-relatedness of decision-making context, demanding integrated treatment.
- Enduring effects, possibly of an irreversible nature, with little or no scope for trial and error.
- Significant time lag before impact, with widening uncertainty over the timescale involved.
- Disagreement about the motivation for, and the direction and nature of, development.
- Challenging the status quo, creating a politicised setting where change is contested.

ORGANISATIONAL DEVELOPMENT

To set the strategic development process in a practical context, it is helpful to think about the categories of strategic decisions through which organisations evolve and develop. Such categories might include vertical integration, diversification/reputation, retrenchment/re-focus, opportunism, market development, product/process development and e-strategy. Specific examples of each are shown in Figure 1.1.

A vertically integrated organisation is one that owns and controls all aspects of the supply chain from the raw material through to the sales of the final product. The PIMS studies (Profit Impact for Market Strategy; Schoeffler, Buzzell & Heany, 1974) of the 1960s and 1970s indicated that vertical integration was a key driver of profitability and as a result became a focus for strategic development for many organisations at that time. The clearest examples would be the oil companies, which encompass exploration, drilling, refining, distribution and finally filling stations (often franchised). This strategy by the major oil companies effectively drove the small independent garage/filling station out of business, giving the major companies a considerable competitive advantage. This advantage has been challenged at the downstream end by the major supermarket chains.

Diversification/reputation strategies typically involve a portfolio of businesses producing a range of products or services. There may be minimal synergy between some of the elements of the portfolio, apart of course from financial synergy through cash movements and the risk-reduction benefits of portfolios. Richard Branson's Virgin brand has retained its reputation associated with airlines, mega-stores, mobile phones and rail companies, and the reputation has been retained despite the difficulties with the West Coast mainline railway in the UK. Tesco has diversified from supermarket food retailing to general retailing, local stores and financial services, whilst Mitsubishi (like Virgin) has a broad portfolio of companies. The University of Warwick (UW) was one of the first UK universities to respond to the cutbacks in government spending in the early 1980s. The University diversified into post-experience education through the Warwick Business School and Warwick Manufacturing Group, into the overseas student market and executive education centres, and

Vertical Integration	Shell
Diversification/Reputation	Tesco, Virgin, Mitsubishi, BA, UW
Retrenchment/Re-focus	Sainsbury's, BA
Market Development	VW, UW
Product/Process Development	Sony, Phillips, Pilkington, UW
Opportunism	Group 4, Stagecoach, Jarvis
e-Strategy	Prudential/Egg, e-Bay, Tesco
Mergers and Acquisitions	IBM, GlaxoSmithKline

Figure 1.1. Classes of Strategic Decisions

generally diversified its revenue base. British Airways (BA) diversified into low-cost air travel by establishing the company Go, although it was later divested at a time when such airlines were becoming increasingly popular. It was finally sold by its financial backers to easyJet – a rather pointless set of strategic moves in terms of business development.

In recent years the interest in retrenchment and re-focus strategies has predominated, in contrast to the earlier vertical integration and diversification strategies. Sainsbury's set up Homebase to build on their retailing skills but later divested it. BT divested its mobile phone business. BA divested Go just as low-cost airlines were 'taking off'. The fashion for retrenchment and re-focus has been fuelled by outsourcing as a strategy. These strategies lose any benefits of vertical integration and the risk-reduction benefits of a portfolio. BA also outsourced catering to Gate Gourmet, on the grounds that it was not core business. However, the difficulties that the company experienced in 2005 suggest perhaps that the concept of core business should not be drawn too tightly (you can't travel long haul without food on board). In contrast to the move to outsourcing, the motor racing Formula 1 company BAR (now Honda), which required quality of the highest order, produced every part of their car and engine in-house in order to retain complete control over the quality system.

Market development strategies involve targeting new geographical markets, possibly through mergers or acquisitions. VW, for example, made an early and significant impact on the Chinese automobile market. Product and process development is a key strategy in the fast-moving electronics business, whilst a classic example of process development was the invention of float glass by Pilkington in the 1950s. The new process was such an improvement on the previous sheet and plate glass processes that every company in the world had to adopt the process within a few years, giving considerable licence fees to the inventor. (Pilkington was taken over by Nippon Sheet Glass in 2006.) Many strategies arise out of the resources, competencies and capabilities of the organisation but that may not be the case for opportunistic strategies when they arise. The opportunities arising from the retrenchment of the government under the Thatcher administration in the UK allowed Stagecoach to invent itself, starting with two buses in the north of England and moving rapidly to become a global enterprise. Group 4, a security company, won the contract to organise the inspection system for nursery schools. Jarvis took advantage of the private finance initiatives but found the opportunities not so rewarding. The arrival of the internet allowed e-strategies, which could range from completely new businesses such as e-Bay through to a reinvention of grocery delivery by Tesco Online. Many organisations see acquisitions as a way to develop, such as IBM taking over the consultancy arm of PriceWaterhouseCoopers or GlaxoSmithKline seeing acquisitions as a way of extending their product range; merger activity is also evident in the names of the companies just cited.

Each of these forms of strategic development demonstrates to different degrees the characteristics indicated earlier. The richness of possible developments is clear from these varied histories, but also the fact that even the high level of expertise in many company boards cannot guarantee sound strategic direction and guidance. An argument here, expanded in detail in the chapters that follow, is that explicit rehearsal of strategy is essential to augment and improve strategic thinking.

MANAGEMENT AS CONTROL

We begin our development of an organising framework to represent the strategic development process from a most basic – indeed some might think most unpromising – foundation. This is the simple control system model shown in Figure 1.2. We chose this model, not because we are wedded to some mechanistic metaphor about the behaviour of people or the systems that they create, but because it offers a clear insight into the concept of feedback, a concept that lies at the very heart of the model that we shall go on to develop.

Consider then a situation that we wish to manage. Further, suppose that this management activity is essentially about the achievement of some target state, and that it involves the manipulation of a range of resources that can be drawn upon to obtain the requisite performance. Then the managerial task is centrally concerned with adjusting those factors that are controllable within a situation that is in continual flux, and being buffeted by external forces. Figure 1.2 shows this process as a 'control procedure' that can inject a 'resource' in order to adjust the realised performance (captured through 'performance measurement') to meet the 'target': but though the procedure is implemented in the 'system', further 'uncontrolled inputs' lead to perturbations, which in turn demand subsequent adjustments.

The diagram could describe the operation of an air-conditioning system: the target is a set room temperature that is monitored, and the resource is a device for heating/cooling the incoming air. So feedback based upon the actual state of the ambient air is used to establish the necessary control action. A more pertinent example for our purposes in this book might be the meeting of a sales target by a product division. Any monitored shortfall (e.g. variance from budgeted figures) would most probably lead to an injection of effort into promoting the product to achieve the hoped-for sales revenue.

The control system is a poor model from the strategic development perspective as it is likely to be narrow in scope. The effects of the decision are likely to be short term and there is typically the opportunity for repeated decision-making. Nevertheless, it has some attractive features. It highlights the need for a sense of purpose through the target, it introduces a concept of feedback of performance and the system contains a number of essential elements, all of which need to be in place and effective for the system to work effectively. For example, if the resource is inadequate then it will

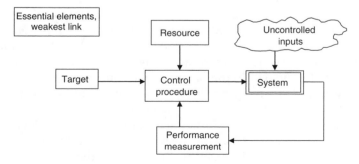

Figure 1.2. A Simple Single-Loop Control System

not be possible to achieve the target; if there is no target then there is no rationale for development; and if there is no measurement of performance and feedback then control cannot be achieved. The system is only as effective as its weakest link.

Nevertheless, a simple control system is surprisingly good at mimicking purposeful behaviour. Consider a car fitted with cruise control. In this case the control process regulates the speed of the car and replaces the normal thinking, judgement and reaction of the driver, albeit in a limited way. It is an uncanny experience to drive such a vehicle because the accelerator pedal seems to have a mind of its own. As the terrain changes the pedal presses itself down or eases off exactly as a person would move it. The control procedure is shown in Figure 1.3. A target speed is set and compared with the measured speed of the car on the motorway. When the car encounters a hill its measured speed declines and the cruise control depresses the accelerator, thereby drawing more engine power and increasing the car's speed until it reaches the target speed. When dipping into a valley the reverse happens, and the pedal moves up to reduce power. On the flat the accelerator pedal setting remains fixed with target speed and measured speed equal, with just enough engine power to overcome the road surface and wind resistance.

The striking similarity between the reaction of a cruise controller and a normal driver demonstrates vividly that feedback and intelligent adaptation are more closely related than is commonly thought. Indeed, control processes that incorporate additional feedback channels and more information can replicate quite sophisticated processes of adaptation. Imagine, for example, a system capable of delivering a car safely to a chosen destination in a specified time. Skilful taxi drivers routinely accomplish this task, so what kind of feedback describes their behaviour? Cruise control alone is obviously not enough. Simultaneous speed *and* distance control are important to maintain a target speed without hitting the car in front. Also, the car should not drift off the road, so there is a need to monitor and control positioning. In other words, intelligent adaptation is characterised by multiple goals, with corresponding performance measures and priorities to be managed. But then there is what taxi drivers call 'the knowledge', where to go and which road to take. Destination and route also belong in the control model to help plan the journey and take an overview. Nowadays, satellite navigation systems make it possible to chart the best route to a given destination. This capability to look ahead, coupled with multiple

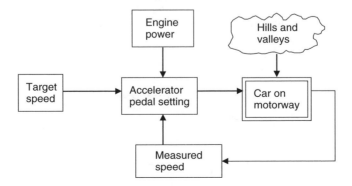

Figure 1.3. A Car on Cruise Control, Slightly Intelligent Adaptation

feedback control processes, contains the necessary intelligence and information to complete the journey and indeed to outdo the taxi driver.

DIRECTION-DRIVEN STRATEGIC DEVELOPMENT

Strategy-making is about the crafting of deliberate actions to shape an organisation's future. This implies intentionality steered by an explicit sense of direction. The implications of a lack of sense of direction are nicely illustrated by the Cat in *Alice in Wonderland*. 'Would you tell me please which way I ought to go from here?' said Alice. 'That depends a good deal on where you want to get to' said the Cat. 'I don't care much where' said Alice. 'Then it doesn't matter which way you go' said the Cat.

Eden and Ackermann (1998) view strategy as 'a coherent set of individual discrete actions in support of a system of goals, and which are supported as a portfolio by a self-sustaining critical mass, or momentum of opinion in an organisation'. We see 'desired direction' as a key driver of strategic development, which may be articulated through a mission or vision statement, a set of strategic objectives or goals supported by performance measures and possibly targets. A well 'articulated direction' will stimulate behavioural responses in the organisation, shaping change (hopefully) in the direction in which we wish to see strategic development. Ideally, this leads to the virtuous circle shown in Figure 1.4, where the solid lines denote the direction of desired influence and the dotted lines denote the components of the articulated direction that together influence behaviour.

There may, however, be many pitfalls and unintended consequences along the way that result in the 'realised direction' being different from the 'desired direction'. For instance, the use of share options as incentives may lead to senior management focusing on improving the share price in the short term, which may not be in the longer-term interest of shareholders; targets for waiting lists in hospitals may lead to easy operations being prioritised to the detriment of patients with more serious conditions, or to faster throughput at the expense of hygiene; school league tables may lead schools to seek to improve the quality of their intake as much as the educational process; targets for train punctuality may mean that the schedule time

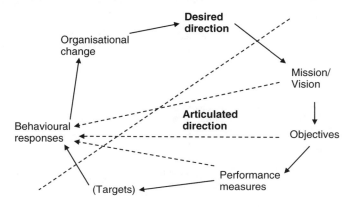

Figure 1.4. Direction-Driven Organisational Change

is unnecessarily long. Furthermore, the mission or vision itself may be unrealistic or misguided: for example, Marconi (previously known as GEC), a cash-rich diversified company, developed and pursued the vision of converting itself into a focused telecoms company overnight. Unfortunately, profitable businesses were divested as they did not fit the vision, the cash mountain was spent on a series of overpriced acquisitions and the company was brought to its knees. So, a major programme of organisational change can have benefits that fall far short of the original intentions.

At the same time, unexpected events and changed circumstances can lead to hurriedly changed actions. Contingency plans may need to be put in place to deal with foreseeable emerging challenges, which can disrupt or even overturn plans. Unforeseeable events may require unplanned emergency actions. Each of these situations may again result in the organisation's realised direction being different from its desired direction. This is especially the case in today's global business environment, where the shockwaves of local events can be amplified and promulgated in quite unanticipated ways. Oil price hikes have obvious impacts across all sectors: more insidious changes – consider, for example, the fallout from a successful computer virus attack – have differential and destabilising consequences. Such threats (or opportunities) provide the stimulus for creative strategy development: making up strategy 'on the hoof'. More subtle strategy-making can be seen in the aggregation of small-scale responses to localised situations. So independent, uncoordinated reactions by front-line staff to customer demands may share some common pattern (e.g. stemming from an organisational culture in which customers are seen as 'a nuisance') that retrospectively can be characterised as a de facto strategy. Such emergent strategies may be 'unauthorised' and even unwanted, but they can be as potent as any deliberate plan if undetected by management.

These enhancements of the 'ideal' model of direction-driven organisational change lead to the more realistic picture shown in Figure 1.5. Here the notions of deliberate,

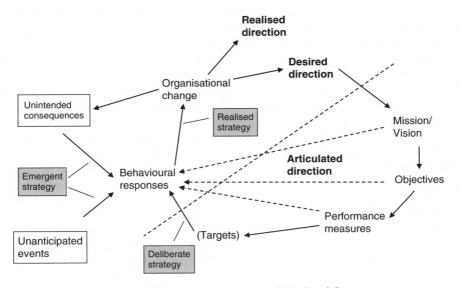

Figure 1.5. Deliberate, Emergent and Realised Strategy

emergent and realised strategy correspond to those distinguished by Mintzberg *et al.* (2003). In practice, it is quite likely that the realised direction differs from the desired direction for a variety of reasons that have been explored above. One of the key tasks of strategic development is to minimise the gap between what is experienced in terms of the realised direction of the organisation and what is actually desired.

STRATEGY REHEARSAL

A simple single-loop control system of the kind introduced earlier is inadequate to the task represented in Figure 1.5. Quite apart from the infeasibility of handling the unexpected (whether derived from the unintended consequences of organisational actions or from the occurrence of unforeseen events), the sheer variety of possibilities would overwhelm any simple homeostat. Furthermore, reactive control only adjusts strategy once an undesirable change has been detected, and given the likelihood of delay occurring before the effects of strategic action become apparent, this means that an organisation could find itself on the path to irrecoverable decline. An effective strategic development process therefore needs to be pro-active and to possess a learning mechanism that involves looking ahead. Such a mechanism involves anticipating possible futures, developing strategic options and testing out their possible future impact by considering their projected performance along with the organisation's current performance; such a combination forms the corporate equivalent of satellite navigation with multiple feedback control.

Our enhanced representation of the strategic development process has, as a principal feature, the creation and use in strategic discussions of models of the organisation that can explore future performance and be used to test and evaluate alternative strategic options. This future performance can then be fed back to be compared with the desired future direction of the organisation. The future performance will also, of course, be influenced by external uncontrollable factors and the evaluation needs a way of capturing this uncertainty. The rationale behind evaluation is, of course, that we should adopt a critical stance to strategic initiatives. The more that a strategic option is tested and shown to be valid then the more likely it is that it will operate well in practice. There is a danger that this approach is seen as over-elaborate, and key decision-makers may well prefer the 'hunch and hope' approach augmented by a search for supporting evidence. There is nothing wrong with hunches, but hoping for the best without testing and evaluating the hunches can be a high-risk way of managing an organisation. Nevertheless, the testing and evaluation of strategic options must be timely; a balance must be struck between thorough testing and timely actions.

Modelling to support decision-making is the focus of the discipline of operational research. Workers in this field have used models for rehearsal – to test strategic initiatives for their future impact before rolling them out in the organisation. Additionally, rather than passively awaiting feedback signals that implementation is off course, models can be used to anticipate what might go wrong and fix hidden inconsistencies in strategy. This implies that instead of hunch and hope we are proposing something more formal involving the ingredients shown in Figure 1.6.

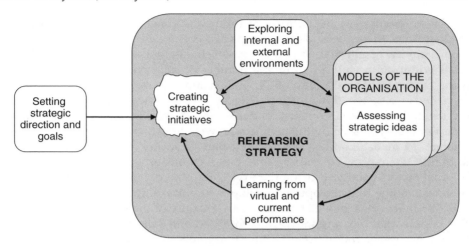

Figure 1.6. The Strategy Rehearsal Process

Here strategic initiatives are fed into a model, or models, of the organisation for assessing strategic ideas and the effects of uncertainty. The use of the models by the management team leads to an imagined outcome and *virtual* performance, for comparison with strategic direction and goals. The introduction of fast-acting 'virtual feedback' also provides a learning opportunity with which to adjust strategic initiatives to anticipate and avoid implementation problems, or with which to redesign and create new future direction and goals; we call this learning opportunity 'strategy rehearsal'. The situations that can be imagined (and how vividly) depends on the modelling approaches and the effort expended. Some models are particularly good at investigating the likely actions and reactions of competitors, while others are helpful for assessing strengths and weaknesses of the firm itself. Some models reveal problems of coordination between functions, while others point to internal political barriers that may block initiatives.

Some models take the form of simple diagrams and maps, while others involve simulations. Some, perhaps the most common, focus on the financial impact of initiatives. The models envisaged here are not perfect replicas of the real organisation in all its complexity; rather, they contain judiciously chosen simplifications of organisational reality so that managers can test vital aspects of strategy development. The rehearsal process itself will involve the evaluation of specific strategic options but also search for the most appropriate overall strategy given the uncertainties faced by the organisation.

To give an immediate and familiar example, the common tool of 'SWOT analysis' is a simple framework that focuses managerial attention upon the internal resources (strengths and weaknesses) and the external context (opportunities and threats) of an organisation that is exploring its strategic potential. The focus that SWOT creates is neither inevitable nor in any sense complete, but it has been found to be useful and, when employed effectively (usually within a structured group process), insightful in strategy formation. But SWOT analysis does not produce a *model* in the sense that is often understood by the term. Consider a different example: if we recognise and seek to specify, say in the form of a demand function, the price elasticity of a product, then this *is* a model of the market concerned and can be used to test the profitability of alternative strategies which might be suggested by different factions within an organisation. Link a number of such relational models together and the more complex response of a dynamic and uncertain marketplace could be represented by a system dynamics model. Nor have all models to be quantifiable. We subscribe to Pidd's description of a model as 'an external and explicit representation of a part of reality as seen by the people who wish to use that model to understand, to change, to manage and to control that part of reality' (Pidd, 2003). Returning then to SWOT analysis, we can say that a map capturing the interconnectedness of individual factors produced using the SWOT framework, particularly in relation to how they combine to drive option development, for example, using the framework of a TOWS matrix, is a model. One distinctive feature of the models that we refer to in this book is that they are individual, localised and purpose-built. Each situation is treated as special, and a model is built that refers to it alone.

THE STRATEGIC DEVELOPMENT PROCESS MODEL

Figure 1.7 shows the whole strategic development process. A vital component of strategic development is the feedback control model described earlier, but added are

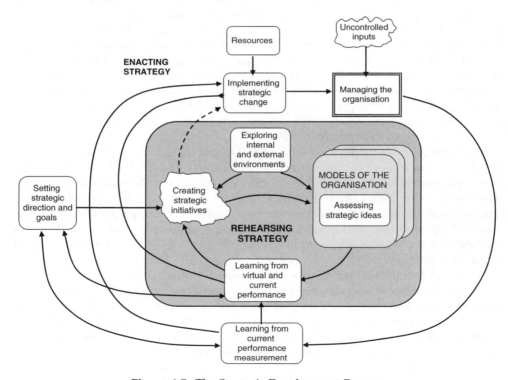

Figure 1.7. The Strategic Development Process

the processes for setting strategic direction, for creating strategic initiatives and for rehearsing strategy that transform myopic corrective action into purposeful action with foresight. One way to interpret the feedback loops of the diagram is to imagine that a new strategic initiative forms inside the organisation within the cloud-like symbol labelled 'creating strategic initiatives'. The initiative can be taken forward in one of two ways. It can be taken straight into the organisation (represented by the dashed arrow) as the basis for implementing strategic change. This route of taking strategic initiatives *directly* to implementation is the route of hunch and hope and emergent strategy, with all its limitations. Incremental corrective action used reactively when unintended consequences arise corresponds to 'single-loop learning' (Argyris & Schon, 1978), since such action encourages the manipulation of present policies in the pursuit of current objectives.

Alternatively, the initiative can be cycled around the inner loop of rehearsing strategy where strategy can be tested, modified and refined. Here, aspects of the real world are replicated to enable learning from virtual performance. The advantage of this inner loop is the feedback it provides about the desirability and feasibility of strategic initiatives. We are suggesting that management teams conduct complementary tests to rehearse strategy in the inner loop, both before and during implementation. Tests that reveal unsatisfactory virtual performance may suggest pre-emptive tactical adjustments in implementation. Such tests may also lead to fundamental changes in strategic initiatives or even call into question the organisation's strategic goals and the strategic direction that lies behind them. Once sufficient testing has been carried out, the initiative can be abandoned or moved towards implementation in the real world. The addition of the inner loop to the strategic development process creates an opportunity for 'double-loop learning', since the strategic rehearsal of initiatives prior to implementation facilitates the modification of the direction and goals that lie behind them. The outer loop involves learning from current performance, a routine management role, which may lead directly to adjusting implemented strategies or may lead to further strategy creation and rehearsal. The direct links from learning to implementation may also involve testing in the real world through the use of small-scale or pilot projects. This approach is adopted in the public sector in the UK, where funding is made available on a short-term basis to improve services to citizens. The pilots are developed for their plausibility and if successful the intention is that they are incorporated into the mainstream delivery of the service.

The outer and inner learning loops combine to address a core organisational learning dilemma identified by Senge (1990): 'We learn best from experience but we never directly experience the consequences of many of our most important decisions. The most critical decisions made in organisations have system-wide consequences that stretch over years or decades. These are exactly the types of decisions where there is the least opportunity for trial and error learning.' The strategic development process resolves this dilemma by allowing fast experimentation around the inner loop that also sharpens management's ability to recognise vital early clues for corrective action from current performance.

A key message from the original control model was that all the elements of the system need to be in place and effective for the entire process to operate effectively.

From Figure 1.7 we can see that the equivalent essential elements for strategic development are:

- Setting strategic direction – encompassing a vision, mission, strategic objectives and goals.
- Designing a performance measurement system aligned to the strategic direction.
- Sense-making – exploring the internal and external environments and assessing the uncertainties.
- Creating strategic initiatives informed by strategic direction, strategic goals, the internal and external environments and learning from virtual performance.
- Evaluating strategic options using models of the organisation, taking account of future uncertainties.
- Rehearsing strategy in a virtual feedback process that incorporates learning from virtual performance.
- Selecting and enacting strategy in a real feedback process that incorporates learning from virtual and/or current performance.

These elements can be broadly categorised to cover direction, creation, rehearsal, evaluation and choice. **Direction** encompasses setting the vision/mission, strategic objectives, performance measures and targets. **Creation** may encompass sense-making, visioning and strategic initiative/option development. **Rehearsal, evaluation and choice** would cover exploring, testing, revising and selection leading to the enacting of strategy.

The feedback paths in strategic development can be viewed as learning processes. Whenever the outcome of an initiative does not work out as intended, it suggests that there was something faulty about people's original expectations. To discover such inconsistency from real-world experience usually requires timely performance measurement for two reasons. Firstly, performance measures provide a signal that something is wrong and corrective action is needed. Secondly, they provide information that facilitates a review of the very process or strategy that produced the inconsistency in the first place (Tapinos, 2005). In other words, performance measurement is an important component of the feedback path that enables people to learn about the actual success or failure of their initiatives when compared with the desired organisational direction they want to head towards. Even so, this real-world feedback cannot easily challenge people's strategic misconceptions because the relevant performance information is not available until implementation is well underway, and for one-off strategic decisions that is often too late. Virtual feedback overcomes this learning deficiency by allowing timely, repeated experiments in a representation of the real world where the fear of consequences is removed.

STRATEGIC DEVELOPMENT AT THE UNIVERSITY OF WARWICK

The strategic development of an organisation and its strategic development process can be illustrated by the case of the University of Warwick (UW), a UK university founded in 1965 on a green-field site in central England on the boundaries of the

City of Coventry and the County of Warwickshire, some six miles from the town of Warwick. The University had a difficult period in the late 1960s but then developed strongly to become the largest and arguably the leading UK university of those founded in the 1960s and a rival to the longer-standing universities, being recognised for its quality and entrepreneurship (see, for example, the Lambert Review; HM Treasury, 2003).

The campus developed from a green-field site in 1965 to a comprehensive university campus of some 16 000 students and a turnover approaching £300 m 30 years later. Figures 1.8 and 1.9 show the physical development achieved between 1968 and 2005.

The successful development of the University stems from the initial support of the local communities and businesses of Coventry and Warwickshire, the entrepreneurial stance of its first vice-chancellor and his senior officers, the commitment to quality research and teaching of the founding academics, and the adherence to these principles by their successors. But it is the subsequent management of the strategic development process that is of greatest interest here, for we argue that this has contributed significantly to the present outcome.

A good example of the way that strategic development has been managed at UW is the handling of the reduction in government support to universities in the early 1980s [which included the removal of funding for non-European Union (EU) students] and the continuing reduction in the funding per student through the 1980s and 1990s. This is illustrated in Figure 1.10.

The reduction in funding in 1980 caused many universities to close departments. The Warwick response was to adopt a make-half, save-half policy, and in particular

Figure 1.8. The Warwick Campus 1968
Source: Dales and Fletcher, Coventry, 1968.

Figure 1.9. The Warwick Campus 2005
Source: Warwick University 2005. Reproduced by permission of Warwick University.

STUDENTS AND FUNDING: 1976–2000

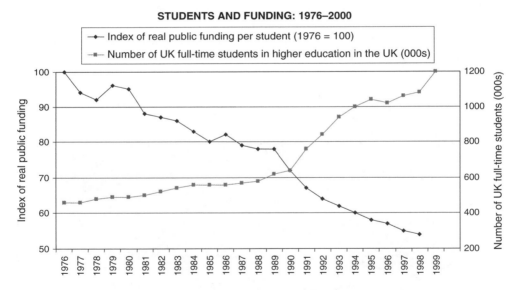

Figure 1.10. Students and Funding

to diversify its activities and its sources of income. This led to a strong period of development from the early 1980s, which continued at least until the time of writing. This diversification and development is illustrated in Figure 1.11. In particular, the graph shows the change in balance of funding from government-based [Higher Education Funding Council for England (HEFCE) grants and Home & EU fees] to business turnover, which includes research grants.

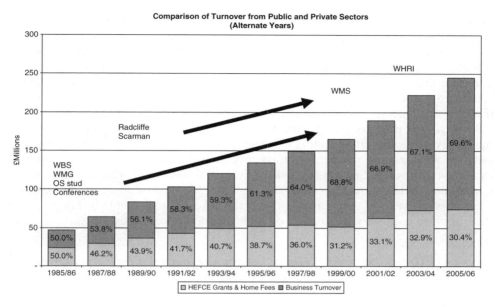

Figure 1.11. Diversification and Development at the University of Warwick

UW had a conference activity using its mainstream teaching and residential accommodation more or less from its founding; the diversification involved a development of this business. The Warwick Manufacturing Group (WMG) was founded in 1980 and developed strongly, initially with residential modular masters programmes for people in industry, with residential accommodation in a converted hall of residence (Arden House). The Warwick Business School (WBS) started a period of strong growth, particularly with the expansion of the Warwick MBA from just a full-time course to a programme with evening, residential modular and distance learning versions. The University built two residential teaching centres (Radcliffe and Scarman Houses) for use by both internal and external users, which provided both a valuable facility and an additional source of income. A strong and successful recruitment drive for overseas students (OS) was launched. In the late 1990s the Warwick Medical School (WMS) was founded, initially as a joint school with Leicester University but later the joint school became a collaborative arrangement giving autonomy to WMS. In the early 2000s the University took over a government research establishment, which became the Warwick Horticultural Research Institute (WHRI).

Direction setting at UW is largely the responsibility of the governing body, the University Council, which includes senior members of the University and lay (external) members. This is supported by the Strategy Committee, a subcommittee of Council, and the Steering Committee, the senior management committee of the University. It is in these bodies that debates take place about the general direction of the University, formalised in the University's corporate plan which includes a mission statement and a set of strategic objectives that change relatively slowly over time. Strategic initiatives can be top down with the Strategy Committee at the hub, such as the decision to secure a medical school, or bottom up such as the development of courses for business in WMG and WBS. Away-days and work-shops have been used intermittently at both corporate and departmental levels to stimulate the search for new initiatives. Strategy rehearsal is enacted through the use of a 5-year financial planning model to test the financial viability of proposals, with non-financial aspects being considered qualitatively. A rolling financial plan is constructed annually but is also used during the year and updated appropriately if a new strategy is adopted or circumstances change significantly (e.g. under- or over-recruitment of students). Uncertainty is accounted for in strategy rehearsal mainly by including safety factors in forecast income streams – perhaps an appropri-ately risk-adverse approach for a university. In a recent evaluation of a large-scale project (a campus in Singapore), risk analysis was also used. The various strategic bodies also review current performance using academic and financial databases on a continuous basis so that learning does take place. The elements of Figure 1.7 are thus in place with varying degrees of sophistication and effectiveness.

FRAMEWORKS, METHODS AND MODELS FOR STRATEGIC DEVELOPMENT

Faced with the genuine complexity of strategic development, it is not unsurprising that studies show (Isenberg, 1984) that many managers retreat into a 'hunch and hope' approach, perhaps accompanied by a search for corroborating (sometimes retrospective) evidence for their decisions. They certainly tend to bypass rigorous, analytical planning and when they do use analysis it is always in conjunction with intuition. As Isenberg says, 'being "rational" does not best describe what the manager presiding over the decision-making process thinks about nor *how* he or she thinks'. But neither is 'intuition' the opposite of rationality: it may best be thought of as the use of well-tried scripts based upon experience, and so is neither arbitrary nor irrational. In practice, executives seem to work on issues from both sides, seeking a match between 'gut' and 'head' and so using accumulated experience to 'act think-ingly' (as Weick, 1979 so cogently puts it) in the hurly-burly of organisational life.

What support does mainstream strategic management offer to the beleaguered executive? A review of the academic literature and the popular 'trade press' quickly reveals the prevalence of short-lived fads, usually stressing the need to focus on one or other facet of the arena of strategy. Almost universally these provide strictly generic advice, often as mantras – 'be agile and responsive', 'promote organisational learning', 'achieve transformational leadership' – and baulk at sullying their pristine concepts with the grit of data, opinion and belief. Yet understanding and working with the particularity of situations is a distinctive skill of high-performing managers, and is a key requirement if feelings of surprise are to be taken seriously in novel situations rather than ignored in the manner of an indifferent executive.

Bringing these requirements together – for coping with variety, for managing complexity, for respecting intuition and for taking notice of specificity – shapes the form of the strategic development process in Figure 1.7 that we contend is needed to enhance managerial performance. At its heart lies explicit representations, or models, of the experienced world-to-be-managed that can be used to develop and rehearse strategy. These representations are not a direct, feature-by-feature replica of the organisation in its strategic context, but a deliberate simplification that nevertheless aims to capture the essence of what the strategist feels is going on; or rather, what the strategist feels is important in what is going on. And this latter statement points to a rather different prerequisite for creating a model: we need some guidance on which aspects of a 'situation' should, or may most profitably, be attended to. Following Goffmann (1986) we use the term 'framing' to refer to the process of deliberately and systematically isolating certain features from the slices of organisational activity that characterise strategic development.

Models, methods and frameworks appear throughout the book. In Part II the focus is on direction setting, and visioning techniques are covered in Chapter 2. Drama theory and stakeholder analysis is the concern of Chapter 3, with the focus on the actors involved in strategic development. The ubiquitous problem structuring methods are considered in Chapter 4. The latter methods, including cognitive mapping, strategic framing and soft systems methodology, are particularly valuable for direction setting and strategy creation but also have been used for qualitative evaluation.

In Part III the focus moves from direction setting to the overlapping activity of creating strategic initiatives. Here the resourced-based view (RBV) of strategy creation is developed (Chapter 5), and in Chapter 6 a range of methods and models, including five forces, product portfolio matrices and scenarios, are discussed with the long-standing SWOT framework used to connect internal (RBV) and external (scenarios, five forces) perspectives.

The creation of alternative strategic initiatives leads naturally to methods for rehearsing strategy, which is the focus of Part IV. A key modelling approach for rehearsal is system dynamics as described in Chapter 7, which is a valuable tool for understanding the development of strategy through time. In Chapter 8 agent-based models are introduced, which can give insights into issues of complexity and their resolution. Finally, scenario planning appears here (Chapter 9) as its primary rationale is to capture the uncertainty of the future to enable strategies to be tested against alternative futures. However, the scenario development process also provides an external perspective for strategy creation.

Rehearsing strategies leads into the requirement for choice (Part V) as a creative organisation will generate more alternatives than it can move to implementation. Scenarios can assist in the choice process as indicated in the previous section, but if a quantitative representation of uncertainty is required then decision and risk analysis can be applied (Chapter 10). Although the qualitative and quantitative approaches to incorporating uncertainty appear to be alternatives, they are in fact complementary with scenarios being valuable in evaluating broad strategies and decision and risk analysis being applied to specific strategic projects. Chapter 11 considers the design of the performance measurement systems, for both public and private sectors, necessary for evaluation (but also important in articulating the direction of the organisation) and the most popular framework, the balanced scorecard, is reviewed. Chapter 12 covers the important financial aspects of strategic investments. Finally, the issue of flexibility in strategic development is raised (Chapter 13) and the approaches of robustness analysis and real options are introduced. Again, they appear to be alternative approaches to evaluating the flexibility of strategic options but it is argued that they can be seen as complementary.

	Direction	Creation	Rehearsal	Evaluation	Choice
Visioning	X	X			
Stakeholder analysis	X	X			
Drama theory	X	X			
Problem structuring methods	X	X		X	X
Resource-based view		X			
SWOT analysis		X			
Five forces		X			
Product portfolio matrices		X			
PIMS		X	X	X	
System dynamics			X	X	
Agent-based models			X	X	
Scenario planning		X		X	X
Decision/risk analysis				X	X
Balanced scorecard		X	X	X	X
Financial summary measures				X	X
Robustness analysis		X		X	X
Real options		X		X	X

Figure 1.12. The Methods/Process Matrix

Throughout the book the use of multiple methods to support strategic development is either implicit or explicit, and Part VI (Chapter 14) presents a case demonstrating how drama theory, system dynamics and scenario planning can be combined to generate complementary insights. It has also been indicated that there is no simple one-to-one relationship between methods and process parts or elements; some methods can support multiple parts of the process, as Figure 1.12 shows.

THE STRATEGIC DEVELOPMENT PROCESS MODEL AS A DIAGNOSTIC TOOL

The key concept of the process model proposed here is that if organisations wish to be successful in the long term then they need an effective process in place as in general it is too late to see if untested actions lead to successful outcomes. The process model explored in this chapter consists of a number of essential activities or process elements, which together contribute to effective organisational strategic development. The concept of a set of essential process elements was previously explored by Dyson and Foster (1980, 1983), where they developed a set of attributes of effectiveness for successful strategic planning. An early version of the process model appeared in Tomlinson and Dyson (1983), and a later development appeared in Dyson (2000). Dyson and Foster (1980) proposed that the process orientation and their set of attributes of effectiveness lead naturally to the concept of a diagnostic tool for assessing the strategic development process (or strategic planning process in their case). Carrying this concept over to the strategic development process of Figure 1.7 leads to the diagnostic tool shown in Figure 1.13.

Setting strategic direction		
Implicit from current situation only	Set explicitly but projection only	Exploration of desirable directions leading to aspirational, clearly articulated futures
Designing the performance measurement system		
Financial measures only	Broader set of measures developed	Aligned and balanced set of measures developed with appropriate communication mechanisms
Sense-making		
Minimal internal and external exploration	Some environmental scanning and internal appraisal	Rich exploration of internal and external environments
Creating strategic initiatives		
Incremental proposals only	Wider search for alternatives	Creative direction-driven search for initiatives
Evaluating strategic options		
Simple financial evaluation only	Assessment on a limited set of measures	Multi-dimensional assessment incorporating risk and uncertainty
Rehearsing strategy		
Limited reflection on initiatives – hunch and hope	Wider impact of initiatives assessed	Search for appropriate overall strategy
Selecting and enacting strategy		
Initiative choice made in isolation	Impact on organisation considered	Search for coherent, flexible and robust strategy with action plan
Feedback, learning and communication		
Process elements developed in isolation	Some connectedness recognised	Feedback of real and virtual performance connecting process elements leading to organisational learning
Participation of stakeholders		
Senior management team only	Wider internal participation	Broad internal and appropriate external involvement

Increasing effectiveness

Figure 1.13. Strategic Development Process Diagnostic

The diagnostic tool consists of nine dimensions, seven of which directly correspond to the activities that we believe are essential to effective strategic development; the remaining two relate to the process as a whole. Each dimension consists of a range of evaluative comments indicating the extent to which the activity is undertaken; at one end the suggestion is that superficial attention is paid to the activity, whilst the other end describes how effective engagement in the activity should appear. The middle ground on the evaluative range indicates partial engagement with the activity. It should be noted that the descriptors used in the evaluative range focus on the quality of the activity rather than on the use of specific frameworks, methods and models; this is in keeping with the notion that various frameworks, methods and models can be used to support different activities.

The diagnostic tool serves a number of purposes – first it can be used descriptively to provide an overview of the state of the current strategic development process. Such a description may be a useful activity in its own right. Alternatively, the diagnostic tool can be used prescriptively to explore, benchmark and revise the various dimensions of the tool which directly correspond to particular aspects and components of the process. In this way, the strategic development process can be evaluated on each of the dimensions and where the process is found to be inadequate, consideration can be given to employing appropriate frameworks, methods or models. Let us consider the example of setting direction. If this activity was evaluated as being 'implicit from current situation only', then the organisation could consider the use of visioning approaches to improve this dimension. Similarly, scenario development could be deployed if the process was deemed not to capture uncertainty adequately. Although the book covers a wide range of methods, there is no suggestion that all should be used in all contexts. Rather, they should be used selectively following an assessment of the efficacy of the process.

In summary, the diagnostic tool proposed here may be used descriptively to capture the current state of strategic development within an organisation, or prescriptively to facilitate the design of an effective strategic development process.

CONCLUDING REMARKS

A major theme developed throughout this chapter is that the long-term success of an organisation and the existence of an effective strategic development process are inextricably linked. In this chapter we have identified the key elements or activities that together form such a process; we have also highlighted the important role that rehearsing strategy contributes in making this process an effective one. A key contribution of this book is the collection of frameworks, methods and models, which used individually or in combination, support the different elements of the strategic development process.

To position the contribution that this book makes to the wider body of knowledge, it is worth saying a little about the management context in which we see frameworks, methods and models being developed and used. Our approach here is in line with Isenberg's (1984) finding that 'the primary focus of on-line managerial thinking is on organisational and interpersonal processes'. Our approach is also consistent with de Geus' (1997) view that planning and strategic decision-making are essentially learning processes. We also note that our approach spans a number of the 10 schools that form Mintzberg, Ahlstrand and Lampel's (1998) strategy safari, something which is in keeping with their notion that strategy formation combines various aspects of their different schools. In the concluding section of their book they note: 'Strategy formation is judgemental designing, intuitive visioning, and emergent learning; it is about transformation as well as perpetuation; it must involve individual cognition and social interaction, cooperation as well as conflict; it has to include analyzing before and programming after as well as negotiating during; and all of this must be in response to what can be a demanding environment. Just try to leave any of this out and watch what happens.'

This book sets out some productive, effective and rounded frameworks of enquiry, each of which is best used to fuel a debate within an organisation about its strategic direction, its strategic potential, its strategic options or its strategic achievement. So, when models are generated – and each framework contributes to shaping a model (or at least some organised evidence) of what is happening or could happen or did happen – they are intended to be treated as simulators (or playthings or toys, to use Eden's, 1993 simile). Our frameworks and models are therefore created specifically to help managers to *develop and rehearse* their ideas: to test them out both in the structured context of the model and in the unstructured and possibly combative debate about appropriate strategy that goes on in and across any organisation.

REFERENCES

Argyris, C. & Schon, D.A. (1978) *Organisational Learning: A theory of action perspective*. Addison-Wesley: Reading, MA.

de Geus, A. (1997) *The Living Company*. Harvard Business School Press: Boston, MA.

Dyson, R.G. (2000) 'Strategy, performance and operational research', *Journal of the Operational Research Society*, **51**, 5–11.

Dyson, R.G. & Foster, M.J. (1980) 'Effectiveness in strategic planning', *European Journal of Operational Research*, **5**(3), 163–170.

Dyson, R.G. & Foster, M.J. (1983) 'Effectiveness in strategic planning revisited', *European Journal of Operational Research*, **12**, 146–158.

Eden, C. (1993) 'From the playpen to the bombsite: the changing nature of management science', *Omega*, **21**(2), 139–154.

Eden, C. & Ackermann, F. (1998) *StrategyMaking: The Journey of Strategic Management*. Sage: London.

Goffmann, E. (1986) *Frame Analysis: An essay on the organisation of experience*. Northeastern University Press: Boston, MA.

HM Treasury (2003) Lambert Review of Business – University collaboration. HMSO: London.

Isenberg, D.J. (1984) 'How senior managers think', *Harvard Business Review*, **Nov/Dec**, 81–90.

Mintzberg, H., Ahlstrand, B. & Lampel, J. (1998) *Strategy Safari*. Prentice-Hall: Harlow, Essex.

Mintzberg, H., Lampel, J., Quinn, J.B. & Ghoshal, S. (2003) *The Strategy Process: Concepts, Contexts, Cases*. Prentice-Hall: Harlow, Essex.

Pidd, M. (2003) *Tools for Thinking: Modelling in Management Science*. John Wiley & Sons: Chichester, UK.

Schoeffler, S., Buzzell, R.D. & Heany, D.F. (1974) 'Impact of strategic planning on profit performance', *Harvard Business Review*, **Mar/Apr**, 137–145.

Senge, P. (1990) *The Fifth Discipline: The art and practice of the learning organisation*. Doubleday: New York.

Tapinos, E. (2005) Strategic development process: investigating the relationship between organisational direction and performance measurement. PhD Thesis, Warwick Business School.

Tomlinson, R.C. & Dyson, R.G. (1983) 'Some systems aspects of strategic planning', *Journal of the Operational Research Society*, **34**, 765–778.

Weick, K.E. (1979) *The Social Psychology of Organizing*. Addison-Wesley: Reading, MA.

Part II

Setting Direction

Chapter 2

Visioning: A Process for Strategic Development

Maureen Meadows and Frances O'Brien

INTRODUCTION

The importance of a clear corporate vision and strategy for organisations faced with conditions of increasing change and uncertainty has been demonstrated by empirical research (Coulson-Thomas, 1992): 72% of companies participating in the Bain 2005 Management Tool Survey reported that they made use of 'mission and vision statements' (Rigby & Bilodeau, 2005). More than 90% of respondents to a survey of UK-based organisations reported that they had a vision statement in place, or were currently developing one (O'Brien & Meadows, 2000).

This chapter consists of four main sections. We begin with an introduction to visioning, and its place in a process of strategic development. This introduction is structured around the following questions:

- What is a vision?
- Why have a vision?
- Who develops a vision?

The next section considers the question of how to undertake visioning, drawing on the advice of a range of relevant literature. Then, we address in more detail the question of how effective visioning processes can be undertaken, and this is illustrated with three examples of visioning exercises undertaken by the authors. The final section of the chapter discusses the characteristics of effective visioning processes, and reflects on recent and future directions in the field of visioning.

AN INTRODUCTION TO VISIONING

What is a Vision?

Parikh and Neubauer (1993) define vision as 'an image of a desired future state of an organisation'. Kouzes and Posner (1996) go further in describing four attributes of vision: ideality, uniqueness, future orientation and imagery. For Nanus (1996), a vision is a carefully formulated and clearly articulated statement of intentions that defines a destination or future state of affairs that an individual or group finds desirable. Ackoff (1993) notes that 'corporate visions are usually descriptions of what their executives would like their organizations to be at some time in the future. Corporate visions have seldom been formulated by a cross section of corporate stakeholders'.

Lipton (1996) defines vision as a combination of mission, strategy and culture, where mission is defined as the purpose of the organisation, strategy as the basic approach to achieving the mission, and culture as the values of the organisation that support the purpose and the strategy. Collins and Porras (1998) define two components to vision: 'core identity' that consists of core values and core purpose, and 'envisioned future' that consists of a vivid description of the organisation, and a 'Big Hairy Audacious Goal'.

Schoemaker (1992) defines strategic vision as 'the shared understanding of what the firm should be and how it must change'. Kotter (1990) argues that 'what is crucial about a vision is not its originality but how well it serves the interests of important constituencies – customers, stockholders, employees – and how easily it can be translated into a realistic competitive strategy'.

An example of a vision statement is given in Box 2.1. It is taken from the Strategic Plan of the University Library, at the University of Warwick, UK, and it is chosen because of its links with the case studies to be presented later in this chapter.

Box 2.1.   Mission, Vision and Values Statement for the University Library, University of Warwick, UK

The Library Mission

The library's mission is to deliver best fit with the institutional mission, and to provide strategic leadership and innovation to support the University information environment. It will deliver outstanding information resources and services as an integral element of the University's achievement of excellence in research, teaching and the student learning experience.

The Library Vision: Delivering Excellence and Innovation in Information Services

The library has a unique part to play in supporting the institutional mission and will adopt a pro-active role in the rapidly changing environment in which it operates. It will provide a first class range of resources, supported by innovative, high quality and distinctive services. It will position itself as a major information resource provider to support the University's various communities and the continuing success of the institution. It will work in creative partnerships with others to assist delivery of the institutional mission and will act as the catalyst for a range of initiatives.

The library will exist both as a physical and virtual entity, enabling researchers, teachers and students to research anywhere, anytime. Library staff will work with academic staff, students and other service providers to underpin effective teaching, learning and research. The library will become easier to use, removing the barriers (both real and perceived) between the user and the information they require. It will support users to be increasingly self-sufficient in obtaining the information and services they need.

However, the library is no longer a separate entity consisting primarily of its physical or virtual collections. It is responding to a growing interdependence and blurring of roles, particularly amongst academic support units. 'The library' will increasingly become a diffuse service within the University, part of the fabric of the institution, working with others to offer a holistic range of support for the institution's various endeavours.

The Library's Values

The library supports and delivers the broad values and principles that shape and reinforce the University's work. In addition, the library values:

– User-focused services.
– Consultative partnerships with stakeholders.
– Participation in decision-making.
– Flexibility, innovation and responsiveness.
– Forward thinking and planning.
– Reflection and self-evaluation.
– Individual and team contributions from staff.
– Acceptance of appropriate personal responsibility.
– Commitment to the personal development of its staff.

Why have a Vision?

Kotter (1990) draws a distinction between management (which he describes as coping with complexity) and leadership (coping with change). He argues that setting the direction of change is fundamental to leadership, and that the direction-setting aspect of leadership does not produce plans (planning is a management task), it creates visions.

A common motivation for engaging in a visioning process is an awareness of dissatisfaction with the way things currently are, or the direction in which things are heading (see, for instance, Walker, 1996; Ziegler, 1991). For example, a driving force behind the Peruvian twenty-first century study was a general sense of dissatisfaction with the country's social and economic problems (Garland, 1990). Another example is when a company's management is convinced that the status quo is totally unacceptable, perhaps due to new competitor activities (Kotter, 1995). There is evidence of visioning exercises being triggered by changing circumstances, whether external to the organisation (e.g. increasing competition) or internal (such as a change of personnel at the top of the organisation). High levels of interest in visioning in a particular industry sector (for example, the financial services industry in the UK, and utilities companies in the UK) have coincided with turbulent periods in the history of those sectors (Meadows & O'Brien, 2006; O'Brien & Meadows, 2003). Walker (1996) argues that visions underpin and promote change, and that effective agendas for action usually *follow* the creation of the vision, not vice versa. A vision is a necessary pre-condition for strategic planning, and provides the key criteria against which all strategic options should be evaluated (Hadridge, 1995; Nanus, 1996) – we return to this point later in the chapter in our discussion of Figure 2.1. The role of performance measurement in strategic development – in monitoring and control, and enhancing organisational learning – is discussed more fully in Chapter 11.

Who has a Vision?

It is, of course, important to consider the practice of visioning in its context, i.e. embedded in a range of organisations of different types. While vision statements are already accepted practice amongst large private firms in a diverse set of industry sectors (see, for instance, Meadows & O'Brien, 2006; O'Brien & Meadows, 2003 for examples of visioning in the utilities and financial services sectors, respectively), evidence of their use by an even wider range of organisations is growing. For instance, Marshall and McKay (2002) consider the problems facing SMEs (small and medium-sized enterprises) engaging in electronic commerce, and propose a framework to guide and structure strategic thinking which begins with an 'e-vision'.

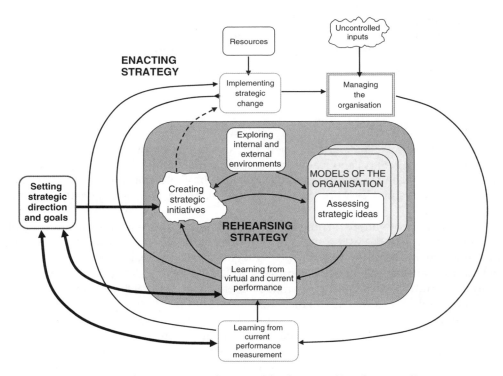

Figure 2.1. Where Visioning Supports the Strategic Development Process

Examples of visioning for public services (e.g. libraries, local government, land use planning) are becoming increasingly common in the literature (Boone, 2001, 2002; Boyle, 2001; Peel & Lloyd, 2005). Enthusiasm for visioning amongst third-sector organisations also appears to have increased; for example, Kilpatrick and Silverman (2005) advocate visioning to leaders of non-profit organisations, and Winistorfer *et al.* (2004) give an account of a visioning exercise for such an organisation.

One striking difference between the types of organisation mentioned above (which might include multi-national corporations, small businesses, public sector bodies, large and small charities, for instance) is the range of different stakeholders that each organisation has to consider, including employees, shareholders, customers, taxpayers, donors, volunteers, and so forth. This must raise questions about the desirability and practicality of stakeholder involvement in visioning – and whether different visioning exercises will require different processes to ensure an effective outcome. It has been argued on a number of occasions that there are benefits to be gained from wide participation in the visioning process (see, for instance, Ackoff, 1993; Stewart, 1993; Wilson, 1992). O'Brien and Meadows (1998) note that partici-pation brings different opinions and values to the process, and these can help the development of a robust vision. Lucas (1998) also calls for widespread input into the visioning process, and notes that 'we have to know who we are before we can decide where we want to go'. We will return to the question of variety in visioning processes in the sections that follow.

HOW TO DEVELOP VISIONS

A vision is something that is created. Some visions are created deliberately through controlled conscious thought. Others emerge through a less conscious learning process. Some visions appear suddenly, while others build up gradually over time in an incremental process (Westley & Mintzberg, 1989). Visions tend to be regularly reviewed and updated (O'Brien & Meadows, 2000), for instance as part of an annual planning process.

The literature on vision development typically advocates a process of internal and external analysis that culminates in the development of a vision statement. The exact sequence and combination of steps differ from author to author, but the following elements are usually present (see, for instance, Stewart, 1993; Wilson, 1992).

Analysis of the current situation of the organisation (internal): e.g. Raynor (1998) suggests that a 'mission statement' should be constructed, which describes concisely the customers and core competencies of the organisation.

Analysis of the organisation's external environment: e.g. Schoemaker (1992) recommends a twofold analysis involving broad scenarios of possible futures that your firm may encounter, and a competitive analysis of the industry and its strategic segments.

Identification of the desired future state(s), or vision(s): e.g. Kouzes and Posner (1996) suggest that you should first identify what you want to accomplish, and why (e.g. how would I like to change the world for myself and my organisation?). You should then write an article – based at a point in the future, when you are being recognised for your accomplishments – about 'how you've made a difference', for instance, what am I most proud of? What's my greatest contribution?

Connection of the future vision to the present state of the organisation (seeking contrasts): e.g. Parikh and Neubauer (1993) argue that the vision should be contrasted with the current reality, and that the discrepancies tend to lead to creative tensions which move participants towards detailed action planning.

Test for robustness of the vision: e.g. Frisch (1998) proposes using risk profiles and business cases for several visions, to facilitate the selection of one that is robust.

Schoemaker (1992), van der Heijden (2004) and Wilson (1992) explicitly mention the development of external scenarios as a means of analysing the company's future environment. Dale (2002) sees methods such as visioning and scenario planning as part of 'issue recognition' – suggesting that a strategy-formation process should be driven by problems, opportunities, uncertainties and controversies.

For Lucas (1998), other critical components of a successful visioning process include a description of the vision that is sufficiently detailed to allow account-ability, and strong support for the implementation of the vision. Longman and Mullins (2004) also choose to focus on implementation, and highlight the role of effective project management in moving from high-level strategic statements to the operationalisation of strategy.

While most managers would agree that a clear organisational vision, accepted and understood by all stakeholders, is a desirable goal, many organisations appear to struggle to achieve this aim. The next section presents three examples of a successful process for vision development, adapted for different situations and purposes. The aim is to take a detailed look at a suggested process for visioning, and at how a group of diverse participants have worked with the process described.

VISIONING IN ACTION: THREE CASE STUDIES

Developing an e-Learning Vision for the University of Warwick

An example of a participative visioning process is provided by a workshop run in 2002 at the University of Warwick. The aim of the workshop was to clarify a vision for the University in the area of e-teaching and e-learning, encompassing the University's many teaching departments, and the support teams involved in helping to deliver the vision. Twenty-one members of staff attended the workshop, including library staff, IT staff and academics from the full range of disciplines represented at the University.

The background to the exercise was that the authors were asked to plan and facilitate a visioning workshop by the Chair of the University's e-Learning Steering Group. He was responsible for developing an 'e-learning strategy' for the University, and reporting back to the University's IT Policy Committee. While various docu-ments and plans on the subject of e-learning already existed, there was a recognised need to pull together existing strands of thought, to inject fresh ideas, to increase consultation and participation in strategy development, and to aid communication and 'buy-in' in a large organisation with thousands of students and thousands of staff.

The workshop was entitled 'The Future of Teaching and Learning', and participants were told that the event aimed to draw out their ideas of a desirable future for teaching and learning at the University – and how that future could be supported by technology. Due to diary constraints, the workshop was planned to last just 3 hours. Therefore the authors were required to design a process that could achieve some useful output within these tight timescales. However, it was also agreed that further communication, discussion and action planning should take place after the workshop itself, as a further injection into a continuing process of strategic development.

The planned process for the 3-hour workshop (plus follow-up activity, as discussed later) can be summarised as follows:

Step 1   Identify the values that underpin teaching and learning at the University of Warwick.

Step 2   List potential mechanisms for delivering and supporting teaching and learning.

Step 3   Consider the desirability and feasibility of the potential mechanisms listed above.

Step 4   Develop and describe preferred future visions of teaching and learning at the University of Warwick.

The participants were divided into three groups of roughly equal size. One group consisted entirely of academic staff, one group consisted entirely of 'technical specialists' involved in IT support and library-based roles, and the third was a 'mixed' group of staff in different roles. The intention behind the group selection was to ensure that a full range of opinions were heard during the workshop, and to promote in-depth discussion.

The aim of Step 1 was to consider the past and present of teaching and learning at the University, before moving on to explicitly consider the future. Past experience of visioning exercises indicates that many participants find it difficult to consider their future visions without first discussing the foundations on which that future will be built, i.e. where are we coming from, as an organisation? What issues have we faced in the past, and what do we currently face? Each group was therefore asked to identify the values that underpin teaching and learning at the University.

Examples of the values generated by the groups included:

– We are an international community.
– We want access for all – no 'digital divide'.
– We want to be innovative, and explore new technology.
– We want to encourage diversity; teachers and learners should have autonomy and choice in their use of IT.

Having had a plenary discussion of the values generated by each of the three groups, the facilitators moved the workshop onto Step 2, where participants were asked (working in the same three groups) to identify mechanisms for delivery and support that they would like to see in place at the University. After some consideration, a timescale of 5 years in the future was chosen; it was felt that a shorter time horizon would discourage visionary thinking, but a very long time horizon would not lead participants to engage seriously with the conversation. Participants were asked to 'suspend their disbelief' and identify a range of ideas for supporting teaching and learning that they felt would support the values listed in Step 1.

Examples of delivery mechanisms were:

– We want a network that is 100% available and reliable!
– We want our administrative systems to be fully integrated.
– We want to be excellent at delivering on-line resources and web-based publishing.
– We want excellent training – and time to develop new ideas.

The list of delivery/support mechanisms generated was turned into a questionnaire, and – after a short break – participants were asked to consider the desirability and feasibility of the mechanisms generated. Participants (working individually) completed the questionnaire, which asked them to rate each idea (mechanism) on scales of 1 to 5, for both desirability and feasibility. These answers were analysed for each of the three groups, and for the group of participants as a whole.

The workshop ended with a plenary discussion of progress made towards a vision for e-learning at Warwick. To complete Step 4, each participant was asked to write their own vision, and submit it to the facilitators after the event. This activity produced a range of responses, e.g. a detailed description of how some current teaching modules could be delivered in very different ways in 5 years' time, a 'day in the life' of a Warwick student in 5 years' time, and more general descriptions of the range of activities that might make up teaching and learning in the future.

The authors synthesised all of the above material into a document containing a summary of values, a single overview vision statement and a sample of individual visions. The 'client' (Chair of the e-Learning Steering Group) was then the main author of an e-learning strategy for the University, which was used to identify priority areas for action, and express an intention to bid for resources. Future work focused on the detail of action planning, including budgets and timescales.

Feedback suggested that the workshop had been a successful event. The structured process for the activities was clear to the participants, and the majority of people present engaged with the planned activity with enthusiasm. The 'client' found the data generated (such as ideas for mechanisms, and their ranking on desirability and feasibility) extremely useful; it gave an indication of what staff wanted to see happen, and these perceptions could be validated with a larger sample of people. The workshop had endorsed some aspects of existing e-learning activities and plans, and pointed to areas where further work was necessary.

Developing a Vision for the West Midlands Research Libraries Network

A second example of visioning for strategic development is given by a one-day workshop run by the authors in 2004, to support a strategic conversation amongst representatives of higher education libraries in the West Midlands of the UK. The group wanted to set a collaborative agenda for research support between their institutions (e.g. to encourage greater sharing of materials that are of value to researchers, rather than duplication across institutions), and hence the workshop was attended by 10 people representing university libraries in the region.

The authors were asked to plan and facilitate the visioning workshop by the Librarian at the University of Warwick, who had agreed to host the meeting.

The planned process for the day can be summarised as follows:

Step 1a Exploring foundations: the past and present.
Step 1b Exploring foundations: values that underpin research support.
Step 2a Creating a desired future.
Step 2b Achieving the desired future: goals and targets.
Step 3a Supporting the desired future: potential mechanisms.
Step 3b Supporting the desired future: desirability and feasibility.

Participants were divided into two groups of equal size. In Step 1a, each group was asked to consider the history of each participant's institution and library, and how research is supported at those institutions. As in the previous example, the rationale behind this step was to 'surface' issues about the past and present that had to be acknowledged before the participants could move on to talk about the future.

Examples of issues raised at this stage included:

– The range of institutions represented by people in the room; for instance, although the day's conversation was to be about supporting research, some of the universities represented were primarily teaching institutions with relatively poor research records, while others saw themselves as 'research-led' institutions.
– The level of frustration felt by some library staff; they were very enthusiastic about supporting research, but felt that they were hampered by a lack of engagement on the part of many users, and by a lack of resources in some instances.

The two groups pooled and discussed their ideas, before moving on to Step 1b, where participants described the values that underpinned their experience of supporting research activities. The list of values generated by the two groups included:

– 'Customer focus': we need a better knowledge of what researchers want!
– The library should be 'first choice' as a source of research support (for content, advice, etc.).
– The library should be considered part of research activity (e.g. included in funding bids; research should be properly costed).
– Research should 'add value' to the institution; the library should be 'part of the bigger picture' of the institution.

Again, ideas generated in Step 1b by each group were shared and debated. As an introduction to Step 2, where participants were asked to design their desirable future, the facilitators introduced an exercise to enhance creativity. Participants were asked to imagine an event – a grand celebration – some years hence (the year 2010 was chosen), where members of their network are being honoured for their contribution to research support. Each group had to describe such an event, including the venue, the guest list and the nature of the contribution for which they were being honoured. One group chose to celebrate the role of research support in a fuel technology project (given the proud history of the automotive industry in their region of the UK), which had driven the region's economy forward; attendees included government ministers and key people in the automotive industry. The second group chose to celebrate their role in information gathering in an international context; their celebration, held in the USA with many high-profile guests from the public and private sector, acknowledged a varied set of achievements that had contributed to intelligence gathering, peace-keeping and democracy.

This light-hearted exercise led to the generation of a number of concepts that would feed into the group's desirable vision of the future; they saw research support as:

– A hub.
– A portal for information and innovation.
– An incubator for research.
– A facility for knowledge management and knowledge transfer.
– Able to add value via search strategies, and via information packaging.
– Able to break down barriers.
– Supporting self-learning by researchers.

One important aim of the creativity exercise was to help the groups to move smoothly and naturally into Step 2a, where they were asked to identify key elements of their preferred future. Some of the key elements generated were:

– We provide a linking activity between different centres of research expertise.
– Academics understand what we offer, and how to access it.
– We are an integrated element of research activity, in and across our institutions.
– We are fully engaged in developing and delivering our institutions' strategies for research, and teaching/learning.
– We fully understand the range of research support skills available across our members, and we advertise them to our customers.
– We are committed to further develop our research support skills in ways that add value to new research areas.
– Knowledge is managed and transferred between ourselves in the network.
– Our network is seen as having a better overview of research support needs and services than anyone else in our region.
– We develop and promote innovative research support mechanisms.
– We understand what academics need to develop their research to its full potential.

It is worthy of comment that a major theme emerging at this stage was around better understanding between the library staff and their users, such as researchers, other academic staff and students. However, the decision had been made that no library users were to be included in this initial meeting. Its main purpose was to 'build bridges' between a diverse set of institutions – which was seen as an important and possibly delicate task in itself. The need to involve other stakeholders was acknowledged, but not addressed on this occasion – the desire was expressed to hold future meetings to continue the discussion.

When the list of possible elements had been shared and discussed, each group selected the elements of the vision that they considered to be key, or of the highest priority. In Step 2b, each group was asked to identify three 'stretch goals' for the elements of their vision that they had chosen, and to identify a number of targets associated with the goal (short, medium and long term). Examples of two of the goals set (and associated targets generated) are given below.

Goal: Academics understand what we offer, and we understand what they need from us.

Targets: Short term: Conduct an audit of current support services (across the institutions represented).
Medium term: Conduct an audit of researchers' needs.
Long term: Develop and promote a 'portfolio' of research support services.

Goal: To be demonstrably indispensable to researchers.

Targets: Short term: At a local level, identify opportunities for increasing engagement in research activity; create a shared knowledge base.
Medium term: To be involved in every major research bid (at a key stage).
Long term: Develop indicators to demonstrate added value/a distinctive contribution.

Step 3a concerned the generation of ideas for potential mechanisms to support the vision. The two groups worked to list a range of ways of supporting research that they would like to see in place by, say, 2010 (which was 6 years hence). Examples of potential mechanisms are:

– Develop (a template for) a researcher e-literacy programme (noting that such a programme would need a champion, shared electronic space and evidence of demand for skills).
– Establish a taskforce to coordinate research support in the region.
– Explore sources of funding, e.g. to buy staff time.

Finally, in Step 3b, each individual was required to vote on the desirability and feasibility of each potential support mechanism, so that priorities for action could be identified.

It was agreed that the Warwick representative who hosted the meeting should report back to the wider West Midlands Higher Education network. At their next meeting, in response to a document describing the visioning workshop and its outputs, the network established a group to audit current practice on research support, and explore best practice.

Developing a Vision for Newcastle University Library

Over the past couple of years, staff at Newcastle University Library have engaged in a process of strategy development for the library services offered across the

University and to the wider community. As part of this process a great deal of analytical work had already been undertaken and documented. It was felt that help was needed to bring the work together. The Librarian, based at the Robinson Library, had previously experienced a strategy workshop facilitated by the authors. He invited the authors to lead a workshop for himself and his senior colleagues from the three libraries of the University, to support them in developing strategy, particularly focusing on the development of a vision and identification of strategic priorities.

The workshop was entitled 'Developing Strategy: Vision and Priorities' and involved five participants who were librarians and sub-librarians of the three Newcastle University libraries and their services. The team were aware that the exercise would not include representation from the library's various stakeholder groups, e.g. students, academics and researchers, but felt that initially they needed to undertake the exercise for themselves to gain a better understanding of their own perspective on the future prior to seeking wider involvement through participation or consultation.

The workshop was scheduled to run over 1 day and was split into four steps:

Step 1   Exploring foundations, including the past and present, current strengths and weaknesses and values that underpin our priorities.
Step 2   Developing a desired future vision for Newcastle University Library.
Step 3   Exploring the external environment and identifying future opportunities and threats.
Step 4   Exploring the robustness of the vision through TOWS analysis and identifying future strategic priorities.

The design of the four steps of this visioning process was influenced by SWOT/TOWS analysis (Weihrich, 1993), which takes a balanced perspective of internal issues (in the form of strengths and weaknesses) along with external issues (in the form of opportunities and threats) to provide a framework for facilitating the generation of strategic options. Here the internal appraisal conducted in Step 1 was used to provide a historic and current perspective, whilst the external appraisal in Step 3 was used to encourage consideration of possible future issues that could occur in the external environment. Thus, the purpose of Step 1 was to explore the past and present upon which the future vision needed to be built. Participants were asked to reflect upon two questions: 'What is the history of my institution and its library?' and 'What are the current priorities of my institution and its library?' Both questions acknowledged that the library was part of a larger organisation which can influence its activities and priorities. Nevertheless, the library has a certain level of autonomy in determining its own future, thus it is not simply a question of implementing someone else's priorities and plans. The library has a role to play in determining its own future direction and activities.

During Step 1, participants typically described historical developments, not only in terms of their library and the wider institution of the University, but also in terms of the wider external environment. Developments that characterised the University's past and present included its change of status from a college to a university in the later 1960s, along with historical restructuring that had taken place to reduce the number of faculties from seven to three. Developments that characterised the library's past and present included the formation of one central library, the opening of the Robinson Library where the working environment changed, and the belief that the library had been technologically innovative in the delivery of its services, for example, they had been an early adopter of the OPAC cataloguing system.

A set of issues that came through quite clearly at this stage concerned the nature of the relationship between the library and the wider university. In particular, visibility and understanding of the library's role and potential with relation to the central university were seen as key issues. This was illustrated by comments such as 'we're expected to cope and do', or 'we're left to do our own thing'.

Developments that characterised the past and present external environment included technological change in the way that libraries work: e.g. the introduction of the OPAC (on-line public access catalogue), CD-ROM network and, more recently, computer-driven services; increasing numbers of overseas students wanting to study in the UK; and changes in the way universities are funded, e.g. the Research Assessment Exercise (RAE), which is a national exercise in the UK to assess the quality of UK research and to inform the selective distribution of public funds for research by the four UK higher education funding bodies.

The group identified a number of values including:

- Being aligned with the University's values.
- Making sure the user gets what they need/want.
- Good working environment – physical and cultural.
- Pride in our profession – believing in what we do.
- Collaborative style of working within the library and the wider University.
- Willingness to explore technological innovation.

The library's key strength, as identified by the group, was staff culture, in terms of commitment to their role and way of working, self-belief, willingness to change and experiment, and sense of humour. Other strengths included: the overall quality of existing services, the library's reputation outside the University, IT innovation and infrastructure, and collaborative working within the library itself and across the University.

The most prominent weakness identified was that of materials resourcing, particularly the inflexibility of resource purchasing models and resourcing journal subscriptions. Lack of time for staff to start new initiatives as well as complete their current roles was also seen as a key weakness. Other perceived weaknesses included a risk-averse culture, the library's profile and presence within the wider University, the location of the Robinson Library with respect to the central campus, and the characteristically slow decision-making processes within the library that meant it took 'too long to get things done'.

An important part of Step 1 was to agree a timescale for the exercise. Participants were invited to reflect on what caused change and how frequently change occurred within their environment. The group identified the natural cycles of academic life, for example, many undergraduate courses lasting for 3 years, however, this was felt to be too short a horizon for a vision. The recent environmental scanning exercises that the group had undertaken had looked 8 to 10 years ahead. The group felt that this was too far into the future for a vision, as the world may have changed radically within such a timescale. The group settled on a 5-year horizon for their visioning exercise as this was felt to be far enough into the future to see some cycles of change within the University environment but not too far into the future to be unachievable. For the part of the exercise that considered the external environment, the group agreed to use a timescale of 8–10 years, as this had been used for their previous environmental scanning work.

The aim of Step 2 of the process was to create a vision for the future of Newcastle University Library. This was undertaken using a creative role-play visioning exercise that aims to draw on deeply held values and to help the group elicit what really matters about their desired future. Thus the group was given the following setting for a scene 5 years in the future:

'It is 2011, representatives from Newcastle University Library are to be honoured at a grand celebration . . .'

Given this scene setting, the group were required to decide upon the venue, the reason for the honour and the guest list. They were then asked to role-play themselves in their created scene by visualising and verbalising what was happening. The group chose to celebrate 'Excellence and innovation in information service provision', a national award made to Newcastle University Library by the UK Prime Minister. The award was the culmination of a national competition where users voted for the 'best' information service provision that they had experienced. The event was to take place at The Sage, Gateshead, a purpose-built music and arts centre on the banks of the River Tyne. Included in the guest list were all library staff, representatives from Ex Libris (a worldwide supplier of software solutions for libraries), Herbert Van de Sampel (a key figure in developments affecting the automation of library services), the Head of the British Library and Laurie Taylor (broadcaster, columnist and ex-librarian).

To capture the essence of their vision of the future, the following statement was produced by the participants: 'Newcastle University Library is known and recognised for excellence and innovation in information service provision to the University and its wider community.'

The key elements underpinning this vision were:

– Stronger engagement with the University.
– Stronger profile and trust within the University.
– User-focused, responsive and reflective service.
– Pro-active in developing and applying knowledge of the changing information environment to the University's needs and use of information.
– Measurement of excellence and value for money.

To demonstrate to the group how they could use the material from Steps 1 and 2 in the construction of a vision statement, the following sample vision statement was produced by the authors:

Newcastle University Library's vision is to be known, respected and recognised for its excellence in innovation in information service provision to the University and its wider community. The library will be highly visible, have a strong profile and be trusted across the University and further afield. The library will demonstrate its ongoing commitment to collaboration, by forming strong links both within and external to the University. Library staff will form a highly motivated, committed and appropriately skilled team who take pride in providing a responsive and reflective service in support of both research and learning. Library staff will continue to be pro-active and innovative in developing and applying knowledge of the changing information environment to the University's needs and use of information.

Step 3 of the process required participants to explore the external environment and identify key opportunities and threats facing the library. Participants were invited to brainstorm factors within their external environment, which varied within the timescale of 8–10 years and were important to the library, but difficult to control. The participants used post-it notes to record individual factors, which were then placed on a workspace constructed on a wall.

The factors were clustered into groups of related concepts, for example, the success of the RAE in 2008, the future size and make-up of the student population, the existence of alternative access points to information (e.g. Google), the sophistication of IT tools and levels of funding for higher education. Each factor was then given a range of values over which it might vary given the time horizon for the exercise (8 years). Thus, the RAE may be a success or a failure, student numbers may increase or decrease, as could levels of funding. The sophistication of IT tools and the existence of alternative access points to information were both considered to be factors that would take on a particular value in the future, namely increasing – these may be thought of as certainties or predetermined factors.

Next, participants considered each key factor (within its range of values) in turn and decided whether the factor, taking a particular value, posed an opportunity or a threat over the future time horizon. Participants then voted on which opportunities were not to be missed and which threats should be taken seriously.

A key opportunity not to be missed was perceived to be a successful RAE, as this would enable the library to become more embedded in a research enterprise. Another opportunity not to be missed was the increasing sophistication of IT tools, as this could lead to improved services and better integration of technology, giving the users better value. Increasing student numbers were also seen as an opportunity, since this would result in greater demand for library services.

A significant threat was perceived alternative access points as this may lead users to prefer alternatives to the library, e.g. Google Scholar. Another key threat was the increasing student numbers as the library might not be able to cope with escalating demand for resources and access to expertise. Another perceived threat was the reduced levels of funding, which may lead to service cuts.

Step 4 brought together the work of the previous three steps. Firstly, potential strategic options were generated by comparing the opportunities and threats from Step 3 with the strengths and weaknesses of Step 1.

For example, considering the strength 'IT innovation and infrastructure' along with the opportunities of 'Increasing sophistication of IT tools' and 'More alternative access points' led to the generation of the following strategic options:

- Increase knowledge of IT development.
- Identify relevant IT development for use in these areas.
- Develop staff IT skills.

Considering the key weakness 'Materials resourcing' with all threats led to the generation of the following strategic options:

- Clearly articulate the need for resourcing.
- Use arguments to influence funders.
- Demonstrate link between student numbers and resources, e.g. per capita spend.
- Get more resources on a recurring basis.
- Develop services so that physical marginalisation becomes not so important.

Next, the complete set of potential options were considered in the light of the vision created in Step 2 to check the goodness-of-fit between those options that might be prioritised and the vision, the implication being that either might need revising in the light of such an analysis. It should be emphasised that the purpose of this step was not to come up with a set of prioritised strategies for implementation, rather it was to select a list of candidate options that would require further testing, for example for their feasibility and resource implications.

By the end of the workshop, Step 4 had not been completed. The team took the process forward to a subsequent meeting where they completed the exercise. Despite this, the client feedback was very positive; the process gave a boost to the strategy development work that the group was engaging in. The process had been designed for a single day, but both the client and facilitator felt that with hindsight this was too ambitious. Such exercises require a great deal of mental activity and draw on an individual's emotional energy to such an extent that participants are often both physically and mentally tired by the end of the day. Future visioning workshops could be split over 2 days, each consisting of two steps. Such an arrangement is not only less tiring, but also provides the opportunity for reflection before moving on through the process.

VISIONING PAST, PRESENT AND FUTURE: A DISCUSSION AND SOME REFLECTIONS

Table 2.1 summarises the visioning designs discussed previously into a single generic structure, with five broad stages. Each stage is made up of a number of possible steps or 'building blocks', which can be selected or de-emphasised according to the needs of the client organisation or group undertaking the visioning exercise, and the precise purpose of the particular visioning session being designed (this is discussed further below).

Table 2.1. The Five Generic Stages of a Visioning Exercise, with Typical 'Building Blocks'

Stages	Building blocks
1: Defining the project	Identify a focus for the exercise, e.g. what's driving the need for change. Conduct stakeholder analysis (see, for example, Mitchell, Agle & Wood, 1997). Establish a participant list or project team.
2: Exploring the organisation's (or group's) external environment	Identify future trends, e.g. PEST analysis, and conduct competitor analysis (see, for instance, McGee, Thomas & Wilson, 2005). Identify opportunities and threats for the organisation/group (for SWOT/TOWS analysis, see Weihrich, 1993).
3: Exploring the organisation's (or group's) internal environment	Explore foundations: the past and present of the organisation/group. Clarify values that will underpin the vision. Identify strengths and weaknesses of the organisation/group (again, for SWOT/TOWS analysis, see Weihrich, 1993). Analyse resources and competencies of the organisation/group (see, for instance, Prahalad & Hamel, 1990).
4: Creating the desired future	Develop preferred vision, or visions, for the organisation/group. Identify objectives, goals and targets associated with the preferred vision(s).
5: Supporting the desired future	Contrast the vision with the present state. Identify options for action/mechanisms to move the organisation/group closer to its preferred vision(s). Consider the desirability and feasibility of the actions/mechanisms identified.

Note that in the above we have adopted a multi-methodological perspective, i.e. drawing on a range of approaches such as stakeholder analysis, PEST, SWOT/TOWS analysis, and so forth. For a fuller discussion of SWOT/TOWS analysis (Weihrich, 1993), see Chapter 6. Multi-methodology is discussed further in Chapter 14.

Comparing and Contrasting the Three Case Studies

The structure of the first case study can be summarised as follows:

- Planning the visioning exercise: discussing the background and purpose of the session, and listing attendees (Stage 1 – carried out prior to the meeting via discussions between the client and the facilitators).
- Identifying values (Stage 3).

- Identifying mechanisms to support the vision, and their desirability and feasibility (Stage 5).
- Developing the visions themselves (Stage 4).
- Follow-up activity, e.g. more detailed action planning and bidding for resources (Stage 5).

Diagrammatically the steps involved in the first case study can be shown as follows:

1: Defining the project	3: Exploring the internal environment	5: Supporting the desired future	4: Creating the desired future	Follow-up activity

The structure of the second case study contains some of the same steps but with some important differences:

- Planning the visioning exercise: discussing the background and purpose of the session, and listing attendees (Stage 1 – carried out prior to the meeting via discussions between the client and the facilitators).
- Exploring foundations: the past and present of the institutions represented (Stage 3).
- Identifying values (Stage 3).
- Developing visions (Stage 4).
- Listing goals and targets to achieve the vision (Stage 4).
- Identifying mechanisms to support the vision, and their desirability and feasibility (Stage 5).
- Follow-up activity – reporting back to committee to plan the way forward, considering resources required, etc. (Stage 5).

Diagrammatically the steps involved in the second case study can be shown as follows:

1: Defining the project	3: Exploring the internal environment	4: Creating the desired future	5: Supporting the desired future	Follow-up activity

The structure of the third case study again contains some of the same steps as the previous two, but with some important differences:

- Planning the visioning exercise: discussing the background and purpose of the session, and listing attendees (Stage 1 – carried out prior to the meeting via discussions between the client and the facilitators).

- Exploring foundations: the past and present of the institutions represented (Stage 3).
- Identifying values (Stage 3).
- Identifying strengths and weaknesses of the organisation/group (Stage 3).
- Developing visions (Stage 4).
- Identifying future trends (Stage 5).
- Identifying opportunities and threats for the organisation/group (Stage 5).
- Identifying options for action/mechanisms to move the organisation/group closer to its preferred vision(s) (Stage 5).
- Follow-up activity, e.g. more detailed action planning and bidding for resources (Stage 5).

Diagrammatically the steps involved in the third case study can be shown as follows:

1: Defining the project	3: Exploring the internal environment	4: Creating the desired future	2: Exploring the external environment	5: Supporting the desired future

Comparing the three case studies diagrammatically we see the following:

Case 1	1: Defining the project	3: Exploring the internal environment	5: Supporting the desired future	4: Creating the desired future	Follow-up activity
Case 2	1: Defining the project	3: Exploring the internal environment	4: Creating the desired future	5: Supporting the desired future	Follow-up activity
Case 3	1: Defining the project	3: Exploring the internal environment	4: Creating the desired future	2: Exploring the external environment	5: Supporting the desired future

Each of the five stages of Table 2.1 will now be considered, in the light of this comparison.

Stage 1: Defining the project. For all three visioning exercises, 'Stage 1' activities around project definition took place some weeks or months before the visioning event was due to take place. The authors/facilitators held discussions with the 'clients', via telephone and e-mail and, in some instances, on a face-to-face basis. These discussions covered the perceived need for, and potential benefits of, the visioning exercise that the client was requesting; relevant background information to the visioning exercise, e.g. particular issues that the organisation or group were currently facing; and hence what the focus of the exercise should be. On this basis, the authors planned the visioning events and prepared materials as necessary. It is important to note that these early conversations also discussed who should attend the visioning events that were being planned, and typically the client was then tasked with ensuring the right attendance on the day. Such decisions are clearly crucial to the success of visioning exercises, and the authors would support the participation of a broad range of stakeholders to enhance the quality of dialogue and increase the chances of successful implementation of ideas emerging (see, for instance, Mitchell, Agle & Wood, 1997 for a discussion of stakeholder identification). However, once again, the three exercises described were subject to practical constraints on attendance due to tight timescales and other issues, and some compromises were made on the breadth of attendance in each case. For example, the first exercise ('Developing an e-learning vision for the University of Warwick', where great care was taken to include a full range of University staff in terms of role and academic discipline) did not involve any students in the meeting, because the decision was made to involve other stakeholders such as students at a later stage in the visioning process. Similarly, as mentioned earlier, the second exercise ('Developing a vision for the West Midlands Research Libraries Network') was attended by library staff from across the region, but did not involve any researchers; the initial aim was to 'build bridges' between a diverse set of institutions, before involving other stakeholders. Finally, the third exercise ('Developing a vision for Newcastle University Library') did not involve any library users, either staff or students of the University. This emphasises the point that a single visioning meeting is rarely an end in itself. In any complex situation, there are likely to be numerous stakeholders, and a series of events may be required before all of the relevant issues can be raised and debated. Visioning should be seen as a staged and iterative activity embedded within a larger process of strategic development, which can support interested parties in their desire to have a fruitful strategic conversation and to identify positive courses of action for their organisation or group.

Stage 2: Exploring the external environment. A number of activities from Table 2.1 were not included in all of the visioning sessions. For example, in the first two case studies, the authors chose not to emphasise the 'Stage 2' activities where participants analyse the external environment of their organisation or group. Again, practical concerns such as limited time will always influence the design of a visioning event. However, more importantly, the authors felt (having consulted with the 'clients' of these exercises) that these activities were less valuable in these particular instances, because these clients were not private sector firms in highly competitive and rapidly changing industries, for example, and already appeared to have a good awareness of their external environments. With more time, it would have been possible to address 'Stage 2' activities for these clients; for example, scenario planning could have been undertaken, to generate scenarios for e-learning (perhaps at a national or international level) or for research support. However, this could not have been done in a single meeting.

In the third case study (Newcastle University Library), we have seen that the decision was made to include some tasks around 'exploring the external environment' in the day's activities. Participants were asked to brainstorm key factors in their external environment, and to select those factors that were most important and most uncertain to their organisation for further consideration. Each factor was allocated a range of possible values that it might take over the timescale under discussion, and participants identified the potential opportunities and threats that the factors might present to their organisation, before voting on the most important ones. These tasks bear a striking resemblance to elements of the scenario planning process described in Chapter 9; however, in a 1-day workshop where the focus was to generate a robust vision, the group did not proceed to writing scenarios for their organisation. The Newcastle University Library case demonstrates that in situations where time constraints do not allow a full-blown scenario planning exercise to take place, some of the steps that are typically used in a scenario planning exercise to underpin a structured exploration of the key issues in an organisation's external environment can also be used as part of a visioning exercise to serve a similar purpose. Further comments linking scenario planning and visioning will be made in the final section of this chapter.

Stage 3: Exploring the internal environment. In addition, the planned activities in the three case studies did not explicitly address some aspects of the clients' internal environments (Stage 3 activities), such as core capabilities or competencies. This did not appear to be the most appropriate use of valuable time for a number of reasons. For example, the participants for the second case study were representatives of a relatively informal network of diverse institutions – certainly not a typical traditional organisation with a clearly defined focus and resource base.

Some other differences emerge between the three examples presented. For instance, the second case study has a more explicit emphasis than the first case study on exploring the foundations (past and present) of the organisation as perceived by the participants at the visioning session. This design change was due to an increasing awareness, on the part of the authors and facilitators, of the importance of 'Stage 3' activities around exploring foundations and clarifying organisational values. It is our experience that many individuals find it hard to move straight into activities where they are asked to envision their ideal futures, without first discussing issues that have been important to their situation in the past, and any issues that are particularly important to their organisation or group today. These 'Stage 3' activities are, in our view, an essential part of the visioning process.

Stage 4: Creating the desired future. In terms of differences between the three cases, it is also notable that the first example moves from values into mechanisms before coming back to visions (i.e. moving from Stage 3 to Stage 5 before coming back to Stage 4), while the second flows (perhaps more logically) from values, to visions, to goals and targets, and finally to mechanisms (addressing Stages 3, 4 and 5 in order). A very practical concern around time constraints comes into play here. When planning the first case study, only a half-day session was available for bringing the participants together. The authors were therefore concerned that, if the session moved from the Stage 3 activity around values into the Stage 4 activity around visions, then there would be little or no remaining time to address the Stage 5 activity around mechanisms to support the vision. It was decided that, given the particular circumstances of the first case study, discussing the mechanisms to support any desired future was essential (as the aim of the exercise was to move towards an e-learning strategy for the University, and hence to advise the University on what mechanisms to put in place), but arriving at consensus on a single vision was not so important – as long as a range of mechanisms are provided for people to choose from. In fact, in this instance, a plurality of visions was desirable, as it was essential to allow individual academics from a range of disciplines to have heterogeneous visions for their own teaching modules, for example. It therefore seemed appropriate to allow the detailed visioning (describing desirable futures to be created, such as individual taught courses) to take place as individual activity after the meeting itself had finished.

The circumstances of the second case study were, however, rather different. Encouraging representatives of diverse institutions to move towards a single agreed future was very important – in fact this was really the main goal of the exercise. Hence the authors chose to spend a significant part of the day on creating alternative visions and debating them.

Stage 5: Supporting the desired future. In all case studies, the focus on action planning – to ensure a set of positive outcomes after the visioning event – would ideally have been even stronger. However, in the first two instances, the 'real decision-makers' were not in the room at the time of the visioning session itself. The clients of these exercises were tasked with making recommendations, but did not, for instance, have the power to decide 'on the spot' how scarce resources would be allocated. In addition, once again, time was tight, and detailed action planning would have required a second meeting in both cases.

In the third case study (Newcastle University Library), some different issues emerged that hampered the development of a comprehensive action plan. Key decision-makers, such as the Librarian, were indeed present. However, the intention of the authors and the client, to achieve wide participation from library staff, was only partially successful. Some staff were not present, largely due to the practical difficulties around ensuring high levels of attendance from a single department on a single day when the department's typical day-to-day activities must continue as normal. Hence, action planning to support the desired future was not completed on the day of the workshop; instead, future activities to widen participation even further, and to take action planning to the next level of detail, were undertaken.

Variety in Visioning

The above discussion indicates that the design of an individual visioning exercise needs to be tailored to suit the needs of each particular situation. Consideration should be given to the aims of the exercise (for instance, how important is it to achieve consensus on a single desirable picture of the future?), as well as to practical issues such as time constraints. Facilitators can draw from the building blocks listed in Table 2.1, and make choices about which of the activities to emphasise (and which to minimise) in order to achieve the goals of the visioning event.

It is also important to compare Table 2.1 with our other established visioning approaches. O'Brien and Meadows (1998) describe a visioning process for the city of Bristol in the UK, which was based on an approach known as CHOICES. In that instance, the organisers of the visioning process prepared (after extensive research and consultation) a set of discussion materials, which outlined three alternative visions for the city. These discussion materials, including the three CHOICES for Bristol, were made publicly available (e.g. via newspapers), and used as a starting point for an estimated 400 (or more) discussion groups and meetings across the city. The CHOICES approach is summarised in Table 2.2 (O'Brien & Meadows, 2007).

Table 2.2. The CHOICES approach

Phase	Some key tasks
1: Project definition	Establish project team. Establish drivers for change.
2: Issue exploration	Identify stakeholder concerns.
3: Preparing discussion materials	Project team summarise history of the organisation; current key issues; overview of project process and timescales; a set of visioning scenarios.
4: Dialogue and idea generation	Promote dialogue via dissemination of discussion materials; generate ideas for action.
5: Producing the vision	Analyse and consolidate ideas for action. Encourage participation in vision generation.
6: Planning for action	Build commitment to action.

A comparison of Table 2.1 with Table 2.2 reveals some strong similarities between the CHOICES-based approach to visioning and the more general structure of a visioning exercise presented earlier. CHOICES can be viewed as a special case of the generalised visioning design summarised in Table 2.1. The question therefore arises as to the circumstances in which a CHOICES-based exercise might be most appropriate. To answer this, we need to consider the advantages that a CHOICES-based approach might offer to an organisation or group wishing to undertake visioning. In a visioning exercise with multiple group meetings, the discussion materials with alternative visions ensure that each group has a common starting point, and that key issues (contained in the materials) are brought to the attention of all participants. Moreover, if more than one facilitator is to lead the multiple groups, having shared materials can help to provide consistency of facilitation across the group meetings. However, a CHOICES approach also has a number of disadvantages. In particular, the production of the discussion materials with a set of alternative future visions is a time-consuming and skilled process, requiring a good knowledge of the complex problem area under discussion, and the ability to articulate and discuss the issues of concern in a balanced and fair manner. Such activity may not be justified for a single visioning event, for instance.

Some Conclusions and Reflections

A review of the literature on visioning (see, for instance, the many references given in the second section of this chapter) from the perspective of a practitioner intending to run a visioning exercise tends to reveal a range of descriptive accounts of visioning based (at best) on a single case study. The reader is frequently given little information on how to undertake a particular step in the recommended visioning process. In particular, when the reader is concerned with moving towards action and implementation in the later stages of a visioning exercise, little detailed advice is typically given on how to progress to action planning, for instance what to do with the vision when you have developed it; how to use it to generate strategies, goals and options for action; how to contrast the vision with the present state of the organisation, and so on.

The intention of the authors of this chapter has been, first, to add some detail to these later stages in the process, for instance by suggesting activities where participants brainstorm possible mechanisms to support the vision, and vote on the desirability and feasibility of the mechanisms. Our aim has also been to support the recommendations made with multiple case studies, and to propose a visioning process that is highly flexible to allow for variety in both the particular needs of the organisation or group engaging in visioning, and in their particular context or external environment. As previously stated, the choice of building blocks (from Table 2.1) to be used in a particular visioning exercise will depend upon the identity of the organisation or group that is the 'client' for the exercise (e.g. a private firm in a highly competitive industry sector may place particular emphasis on Stage 2), the purpose of the visioning exercise (e.g. the importance of working towards consensus on a single, clearly articulated picture of the desired future by the end of the session, versus allowing a range of options to stay in play) and the identities and roles of the individuals participating in the visioning session (e.g. their power to take action following the meeting).

While the case studies presented here were designed to support the participants in a strategic conversation about setting direction for their organisation or group, it was not the intention of the authors to run a workshop that would address the entire process of strategic development in a single day. Returning to the model of the strategic development process presented in Chapter 1 (see Figure 2.1), visioning is primarily an activity that supports direction setting in the first instance. Figure 2.1 highlights the linkages between the activity labelled **'setting strategic direction and goals'** and a number of other essential activities; for instance, visioning can lead us to generate new ideas for possible strategic projects (**'creating strategic initiatives'**). Crucially, a vision statement provides us with goals and targets that we can measure our progress against (see Chapter 11 for further discussion of performance measurement in relation to strategic development); and when rehearsing strategy, virtual performance measures can be tested back against the vision to gain valuable insights into whether potential strategic initiatives are desirable. Hence, visioning supports **'learning from virtual and current performance'**.

It should be emphasised that the visioning process recommended in this chapter is not designed to provide adequate coverage of the entire process of strategic development, nor does it emphasise the iterative nature of strategic thinking that is highlighted by Figure 2.1. The model advocated in Chapter 1 stresses the importance of strategy rehearsal, including strategy evaluation and performance measurement; these vital dimensions of strategic development are not fully addressed by typical visioning activities alone, but by a combination of methods and models described in the remaining chapters of this book.

Readers who go on to read Chapter 9 may be struck by apparent similarities between scenario planning and visioning. We have already noted that if we wish to incorporate an exploration of external uncertainties into a visioning workshop, some of the stages outlined in Chapter 9 as part of a scenario planning process will serve this purpose very well; indeed, if time allowed, scenario planning could be undertaken as part of Stage 2 of a visioning workshop (see Table 2.1). However, it is important to stress key differences between visioning and scenario planning. The aim of visioning, discussed in this chapter, is to paint rich pictures of our desirable future, e.g. where do we (say, our organisation) want to be in 10 years' time? These pictures focus on our organisation's *internal* world. The aim of scenario planning, discussed in Chapter 9, is to paint rich pictures of the *external* environment that our organisation may be inhabiting in, say, 10 years' time, and hence to persuade us to consider robust strategies to deal with the range of opportunities and threats that may exist at that point. In other words, visioning is a creative process that encourages us to dream about what might be possible and to invent our ideal organisation, while scenario planning focuses us on the external environment and how it might constrain our dreams as well as supporting them. The two methods are focused, then, on different stages in the strategic development process; in Figure 2.1, visioning primarily supports **'setting strategic direction and goals'**, while scenario planning focuses in the first instance on **'exploration of the external environment'**. The authors have considered (O'Brien & Meadows, 2001) the question of the order in which these steps in the strategic development process should be undertaken, i.e. does it make a difference whether we undertake 'blue sky' thinking first, before considering constraints in 'the real world'? Preliminary results suggested that the introduction of a set of scenarios into the strategic development process, *following* a visioning exercise, did increase the participants' awareness of the differing degrees of success that a vision might achieve in different external environments, thus supporting the development of a more robust vision. Further work is required to demonstrate conclusively whether reversing the order of the activities, i.e. undertaking scenario planning *before* visioning, significantly inhibits the creativity of the participants in the visioning exercise.

The case studies described here raise a broad range of issues concerning the future of visioning that demand further research. For instance, consider the following.

Facilitation: the authors have discussed elsewhere (O'Brien & Meadows, 2007) a number of concerns around the facilitation of visioning workshops, such as the need for two facilitators to help manage the process and the content of the sessions, the simultaneous facilitation of multiple groups and the level of facilitation ('hands-on' versus 'hands-off') that is appropriate.

Software: as software for group decision support becomes more widely available, what is the impact of its use (e.g. for electronic brainstorming and electronic voting) on the process and content of a visioning workshop?

Content analysis: comparing the content of vision statements; what makes a 'good' vision statement?

In conclusion, when considering the role of visioning in strategic development, it is clear that a vision can motivate a process of strategic development. However, it is also clear that a visioning exercise is rarely an end in itself; rather, it can act as a focal point for strategic development, a prompt for a strategic conversation, an opportunity to get people thinking and talking, and a catalyst that supports further strategic thought and activity.

REFERENCES

Ackoff, R.I. (1993) 'Idealized design: creative corporate visioning', *Omega*, **21**, 401–410.

Boone, M.D. (2001) 'Steering the cybrary into the twenty-first century: who is the leader?', *Library Hi Tech*, **19**(3), 286–289.

Boone, M.D. (2002) 'Taking FLITE: how new libraries are visioning their way into the future', *Library Hi Tech*, **20**(4), 464–468.

Boyle, P. (2001) 'From strategic planning to visioning: tools for navigating the future', *Public Management*, **83**(4), 23–27.

Collins, J.C. & Porras, J.I. (1998) *Built to Last: Successful Habits of Visionary Companies*. Century Press: London.

Coulson-Thomas, C. (1992) 'Strategic vision or strategic con?: rhetoric or reality', *Long Range Planning*, **25**, 81–91.

Dale, M.W. (2002) 'Issue-driven strategy formation', *Strategic Change*, **11**(3), 131–142.

Frisch, B. (1998) 'A pragmatic approach to vision', *Journal of Business Strategy*, **Jul/Aug**, 12–15.

Garland, G.H. (1990) 'Peru in the 21st century: challenges and possibilities', *Futures*, **May**, 374–395.

Hadridge, P. (1995) 'Tomorrow's world', *Health Service Journal*, **5th Jan**, 18–20.

Kilpatrick, A. & Silverman, L. (2005) 'The power of vision', *Strategy & Leadership*, **33**(2), 24–26.

Kotter, J.P. (1990) 'What leaders really do', *Harvard Business Review*, **May/Jun**, 103–111.

Kotter, J.P. (1995) 'Leading change: why transformation efforts fail', *Harvard Business Review*, **Mar/Apr**, 59–67.

Kouzes, J.M. & Posner, B.Z. (1996) 'Envisioning your future: imagining ideal scenarios', *The Futurist*, **May/Jun**, 14–19.

Lipton, M. (1996) 'Demystifying the development of an organizational vision', *Sloan Management Review*, **Summer**, 83–92.

Longman, A. & Mullins, J. (2004) 'Project management: key tool for implementing strategy', *Journal of Business Strategy*, **25**(5), 54–60.

Lucas, J.R. (1998) 'Anatomy of a vision statement', *Management Review*, **87**(2), 22–26.

Marshall, P. & McKay, J. (2002) 'An emergent framework to support visioning and strategy formulation for electronic commerce', *INFOR*, **40**(1), 3–22.

McGee, J., Thomas, H. & Wilson, D. (2005) *Strategy: Analysis and Practice*. McGraw-Hill: London.

Meadows, M. & O'Brien, F.A. (2006) 'Under pressure: visioning in a regulated environment', *Systemic Practice and Action Research*, **19**(6), **Dec**, 537–551.

Mitchell, R.K., Agle, B.R. & Wood, D.J. (1997) 'Towards a theory of stakeholder identification and salience: defining the principle of who and what really counts', *Academy of Management Review*, **22**(4), 853–886.

Nanus, B. (1996) 'Leading the vision team', *The Futurist*, **May/Jun**, 21–23.

O'Brien, F.A. & Meadows, M. (1998) 'Future visioning: a case study of a scenario based approach'. In: Dyson, R.G. & O'Brien, F.A. (eds), *Strategic Development: Methods and Model*. John Wiley & Sons: Chichester, pp. 39–54.

O'Brien, F.A. & Meadows, M. (2000) 'Corporate visioning: a survey of UK practice', *Journal of the Operational Research Society*, **51**(1), 36–44.

O'Brien, F.A. & Meadows, M. (2001) 'How to develop visions: a literature review, and a revised CHOICES approach for an uncertain world', *Journal of Systemic Practice and Action Research*, **14**(4), 495–515.

O'Brien, F.A. & Meadows, M. (2003) 'Exploring the current practice of visioning: case studies from the UK financial services sector', *Management Decision*, **41**(5&6), 488–497.

O'Brien, F.A. & Meadows, M. (2007) 'Developing a visioning methodology: visioning choices for the future of operational research', *Journal of the Operational Research Society* (forthcoming), available online October 2006.

Parikh, J. & Neubauer, F. (1993) 'Corporate visioning'. In: Hussey, D.E. (ed.), *International Review of Strategic Management*, Vol. 4. John Wiley & Sons: Chichester.

Peel, D. & Lloyd, G. (2005) 'City-visions: visioning and delivering Scotland's economic future', *Local Economy*, **20**(1), 40–52.

Prahalad, C.K. & Hamel, G. (1990) 'The core competence of the corporation', *Harvard Business Review*, **May/Jun**, 79–91.

Raynor, M.E. (1998) 'That vision thing: do we need it?', Long Range Planning, **31**(3), 368–376.

Rigby, D. & Bilodeau, B. (2005) 'The Bain 2005 management tool survey', *Strategy & Leadership*, **33**(4), 4–12.

Schoemaker, P.J.H. (1992) 'How to link strategic vision to core capabilities', *Sloan Management Review*, **Fall**, 67–81.

Stewart, J.M. (1993) 'Future state visioning – a powerful leadership process', *Long Range Planning*, **26**, 89–98.

van der Heijden, K. (2004) *Scenarios: The art of strategic conversation* (2nd edn). John Wiley & Sons: Chichester.

Walker, P. (1996) *Creating Community Visions*. The Local Government Management Board: London.

Weihrich, H. (1993) 'Daimler-Benz's move towards the next century with the TOWS matrix', *European Business Review*, **95**, 4–11.

Westley, F. & Mintzberg, H. (1989) 'Visionary leadership and strategic management', *Strategic Management Journal*, **10**, 17–32.

Wilson, I. (1992) 'Realizing the power of strategic vision', *Long Range Planning*, **25**, 18–28.

Winistorfer, P.M., de la Roche, I., Ramsay Smith, W., Kutscha, N. & Brauner, A.B. (2004) 'Visioning for the future of the forest products society', *Forest Products Journal*, **54**(7/8), 8–17.

Ziegler, W. (1991) 'Envisioning the future', *Futures*, **June**, 516–527.

Chapter 3

Achieving Strategy Coherence
Jim Bryant and Nigel Howard

INTRODUCTION

'War', states Rupert Smith, the general who commanded Britain's armoured division in the first Gulf War, 'no longer exists. Confrontation, combat and conflict undoubtedly exist . . . War as cognitively known to most non-combatants, war as battle in a field between men and machinery, war as a massive deciding event . . . no longer exists' (Smith, 2005). Instead, the principal task of the Western military is to confront parties that resist the dictates of the New World Order (Bush, 1991) and to get them – or, when dealing with 'extremists', those that actively or passively support them – to comply or collaborate. The task, albeit necessarily carried out by warriors trained to kill and destroy, is the cultural–political one of 'changing hearts and minds'. Smith points out that the shift to this 'new paradigm' is so vast that it is not yet properly recognised or understood by the military, let alone by the civilians who fund them. Billions continue to be wasted on inappropriate weapons and training. Traditional military doctrine, training, organisation, methods and systems await needed transformation. As demarcations blur between the roles of military and politicians, soldiers find themselves working in uneasy partnership with civilian agencies (aid agencies, local political leaders, the civilian police, government departments, community groups) with quite different cultures, attitudes to society and hierarchies of command. Orders cannot be issued to them; their agreement must be reached through persuasion and mutual respect. Working with such unfamiliar allies, the military must somehow influence the basic objectives and attitudes of populations with even more divergent customs, cultures and beliefs. This problem, first brought into focus in operations in Bosnia and Kosovo, became pressing with the wars in Iraq and Afghanistan.

One response by the USA, the UK and NATO has been to develop military concepts based upon ideas introduced by ourselves and others in the early 1990s – the ideas of drama theory (Howard, 1994, 1999; Bryant, 2003). A new paradigm is proposed, under which a new task is defined for commanders at all levels. The task: to conduct a sequence of 'confrontations' leading on to 'collaborations' with parties, such as mentioned above, whose cooperation is needed for a campaign to meet its objectives. A campaign is seen as won, not just, as in the traditional view, through a sequence of engagements leading to victory, but more through a sequence of confrontations leading to collaboration and cooperation. Arguably, this view can be seen as implicit in past campaigns. In any case, it is arguably vital for winning current 'asymmetrical' wars (Howard, 1999; Murray-Jones & Howard, 1999; Howard & Murray-Jones, 2001).

This military concept is known as 'confrontation and collaboration analysis'. Being based upon drama theory, which was originally conceived of as applying to business and politics, it is a concept of operations that transfers at once to non-military interactions. The military focus on killing people and destroying assets finds a parallel in a business focus on crushing competition by technical superiority. Now, while technical competence remains vital in business, just as the capacity to out-escalate the enemy remains vital for the military, neither superior weaponry on the battlefield nor superior technology in business is enough on its own. The military need to 'win hearts and minds'; businesses need to share information, to work flexibly to a common end, and to collaborate not only with suppliers, customers and regulators but even with competitors. Many old distinctions between manufacturer, supplier and distributor have dissolved, and there is a new imperative to work with a volatile mix of local agents, global networks, independent specialists and potential allies. The strategic thinking of even the largest businesses cannot ignore the impact of 'weak' or non-traditional players: empowered by the internet and access to the media, consumer activists, pressure groups and single-issue campaigners can wreak havoc with the best-laid plans. And political forces, health and safety directives or equal opportunities legislation can utterly change a company's competitive circumstances.

In both military and civilian life, pressures in today's complex, multi-party environments force commanders and managers to act on ambiguous, incomplete yet over-abundant information within settings where their decisions will rarely be uncritically accepted. Ideally, their actions should support alliance or company objectives while providing a platform from which subordinates can work productively. Often, they do not. Hasty, ill-considered managerial choices made in the face of conflict often fail to align with agreed partnership goals or with declared corporate vision and simultaneously cramp local direction. Piecemeal, inconsistent decision-making leads to a state of organisational schizophrenia, with a disconnect between mission statements, espoused values and actions. This creates major problems for customers, suppliers and others who are unable to make sense of what they experience as an organisation's strategy, and so find it hard to establish and maintain appropriate relationships with the organisation to which this incoherent strategy attaches.

We shall now briefly consider two examples. The first is a strategic alliance between businesses, the second an example from the military.

Airline Alliance

Negotiation of a collaborative strategy takes place at the highest level. At successive levels below this, managers are tasked with handling local interactions with counterparts in partner organisations. These take place under the guiding principles of top-level agreements, but may nevertheless involve competition for resources or customers, since the qualities that make another organisation a promising partner may also make it a likely competitor. Such relationships induce schizophrenic attitudes. An example – to which we return briefly at the end of this chapter – was found in an intervention by one of us in the sales function of a major airline that had recently joined a global alliance. The Board was frustrated by lack of headway in exploiting the alliance's business opportunities. At sales-force level, over-protective company loyalties were getting in the way of selling alliance products that were part of the portfolio offered to customers. This was despite public commitments made at company level to the alliance. There was a fundamental dislocation between the ways strategy was being implemented at different levels within the organisation. Interactions between sales agents and customers needed to be handled in a way consistent with the messages being sent between middle-level managers in the two companies and with messages they received from their respective company boards. In this case – typical of many alliances – greater coherence across levels within the organisation was needed to ensure that the benefits of collaborative strategy were realised in practice.

The Military and 'Client Experience'

Next, consider how the military find the need to manage what in business is called the 'client experience'. Take a patrol dealing with civilians suspected of involvement with terrorism. Do it wrong and front-page news is created. A sergeant's mistake can spell disaster for a whole mission. But to be effective, the patrol needs to coordinate not only with high-level strategy but also with non-military actors such as aid agency workers. In general, there is a need for coordination at all levels of command between the military and other members of the international community in the vital task of influencing 'swing voters' – i.e. parties such as ethnic or religious communities that may choose either to collaborate with the military or with terrorists irreconcilably opposed to stabilisation and reconstruction. Suppose, moving to theatre level, that the theatre commander in Iraq or Afghanistan meets with a national religious leader and reaches an understanding with him as to anti-terrorist cooperation in a certain area. Word passes down from the religious leader to local sheiks; suppose, however, that local military commanders are not informed. When a local sheik meets with the local company commander he will be disenchanted (though often not surprised) to find that the company commander knows nothing about this agreement. The soldier's tone remains suspicious and intransigent, just as if no high-level understanding existed. Clearly, the company commander would do a better job of getting the sheik to tell him about terrorist actions such as planting of IEDs (the Improvised Explosive Devices that regularly blow up convoys) if he were able to march in, shake the sheik's hand, and say, 'I understand we are now working together . . . '

In the civilian sector, where many organisations aspire to the label 'client first', the equivalent requirement is that there will be consistency in customers' distinct encounters with different facets of the organisation. Errors here damage the entire credibility of a business campaign. Nothing is more damaging for service relationships or more likely to undermine belief in management than a mismatch between the experience of service delivery and the rhetoric of policy declarations. This is especially evident in public services, where everyday shortcomings overwhelm government claims about improvements and 'joined-up working' easily becomes a joke. In either case, how can senior management make sure that values, intentions, direction and behaviour reinforce each other – i.e. that their organisation has a coherent strategy and that staff at each level 'sing from the same hymn sheet'?

This chapter will argue that the military idea of a system for 'command and control of confrontation and collaboration', developed on the basis of drama theory, can help to answer such questions. The military have always had a penchant for analysing, rationalising and giving adequate training in each task they undertake. The task we have identified is just as vital for non-military organisations as it is for the military. We should therefore see if and how their proposed way of doing it can be applied generally. First, however, we need to review the differing attitudes of military and civilian organisations to internal and external conflict, as these attitudes have important consequences for the use of drama-theoretic methods.

EXTERNAL AND INTERNAL CONFLICT: MILITARY AND CIVILIAN PERSPECTIVES

The military deal, ultimately, with killing and being killed. From this arise certain systemic differences between military and non-military organisations. In particular, military and non-military have different attitudes towards internal and external conflict – differences which are relevant to the question: how and when can we build explicit models of conflicts between parties?

It is easier for any organisation to be frank and open about conflicts between 'us' and 'them' than to acknowledge conflicts within 'us'. But in the military, loyalty between fellow-warriors is a supreme value, while the 'outsider' you are dealing with may be out to kill you. For this reason, the 'us–them' distinction is stronger than elsewhere. It is quite impossible to set up official, formal systems that recognise and deal frankly with conflicts within a military force, within its chain of command or between a force and its military allies. All such tensions are dealt with indirectly, by recognising and taking as pre-eminent only a common interest in fulfilling the common military mission. Of course, this official stance has to be imposed upon the reality it refuses to recognise – the reality of intra-organisational and personal conflicts that exist in the human system. To reconcile these two realities, the military rely on the personal leadership qualities of commanders, the sanctions of military discipline and a general emphasis on 'morale'-building.

In business, the 'us–them' distinction is far less clear-cut. Allies, suppliers, customers, even competitors – all may fall on either side of this psychological barrier. Hence, it is both easier to talk about internal conflicts than it is in the military and, at the same time, less easy to talk about any kind of conflict in the frank, strategising kind of way in which the military address external conflicts.

This fact is important when using drama-theoretic methods that essentially use a kind of scalpel to reveal the naked truth about conflict and cooperation. Drama theory is a theory about the communication (in particular, the exchange of threats and promises) that takes place between parties trying to reach agreement with each other as to how they will act. It posits that such communication involves a mixture of emotion and reason, leading parties to change their values, objectives and beliefs. The theory can be used to build models of the conflicts that exist between organisations or between parties in an organisation. Conflict in organisations can, however, be highly sensitive, and building explicit models of it can be dangerous.

To see the difficulties that arise, consider the concept of 'political feasibility' developed by organisational theorists. In a changing world, organisations need the ability to build and develop new strategies to meet new situations. Now, achieving sustainable strategic change is considered to be absolutely dependent upon creating the political will inside the organisation for it to take place. This is political feasibility. One widely used process for building such a political will is the JOURNEY-making approach of Eden and Ackermann (1998). This is a team-based methodology that centres upon creating a structured discussion about strategic intentions and opportunities and involves the creation of explicit models – in the form of cognitive maps – of the group's thinking about possible actions. For Eden and Ackermann, 'strategy making and its realization together create a sequence of platforms for strategic change and organizational achievement'. They define effective strategy as 'a coherent set of individual discrete actions which are supported as a portfolio by a self-sustaining critical mass, or momentum, of opinion in the organization'. They claim that this underpinning coherence can be achieved through a designed conversational process that interacts continuously with strategy in action, confirming or suggesting redesigns of strategy as reflection and understanding inform renegotiation and implementation. In their view, coherence is especially important when strategic change is seen as the accumulation of 'small wins' rather than as a 'grand slam' outcome, since coherent thinking provides a consistent context for individual local actions that add up to an overall strategy.

But what if managers frustrate coherence by deliberately opposing each other? It becomes necessary to do more than force or persuade them to eliminate perceived inconsistencies between strategy elements – though even this is often left undone. To resolve conflicts and coordinate policies while encouraging innovation, there is a need to develop shared values and beliefs across an organisation without imposing a perceptual frame that hampers creativity, ownership or achievement. Eden and Ackermann make central use of causal maps representing how a group thinks about strategy and strategic predicaments, both to stimulate debate and sum up its results. In using such a method, they are more frank about conflicts between managers than the military would be about conflicts between its own officers. But still they do not expose the tactics – the combinations of threats and promises – by which managers are secretly planning to get their way in the battleground of internal politics.

So what would we, as drama theorists, propose? Drama theory allows us to model the rational–emotional process by which parties with different yet interdependent objectives move from confrontation to collaboration or vice versa, and in doing so change, to a greater or lesser extent, their fundamental objectives, attitudes, motivations, values and beliefs. But in order to analyse how parties switch from foe to friend or friend to foe, we need to analyse friend-to-friend conflicts in the same way as friend-to-foe. Yet such an approach is bound to raise questions. Every manager knows that confrontations occur in their organisation. It is a fact of life that managers pursue individual and group interests that lead to confrontation. Yet many doubt that this fact of life can profitably be modelled, particularly when conflicts are internal. Will not modelling confrontation encourage confrontation, contrary to our aim of collaboration?

We do not dodge this problem. It is real and must be faced. Drama theory makes two points that are relevant. First, parties trying to achieve collaboration on a set of issues *always* face a possible or actual confrontation – that which threatens if they fail to collaborate. The threatened confrontation may involve various levels of conflict, from violent (a riot or a war), antagonistic (a strike), suboptimal (a standoff between production and marketing) to a simple end to any relationship ('no deal' between a buyer and seller). But the threat always exists. Moreover, the parties are conscious of it – at some level – and it strongly influences their behaviour. That is why there is a need to analyse it, and why the parties involved can profit from such analysis. At the same time, however, drama theory asserts that parties in the process of moving into or maintaining collaboration cannot mention this possible confrontation to one another – because to do so is to be confrontational. Put simply: for a party to describe, model or point to the possible confrontation that shadows its collaboration with another is, in effect, to move into that confrontation. For a party trying to move towards or maintain collaboration, this is generally (though perhaps not always) a bad move.

It follows, therefore, that what we shall call a CC model (a drama-theoretic model of 'Confrontation' leading to 'Collaboration') can never be shared between the parties involved. Each must make its own, separate CC model of their interaction, a model not meant for the other's eyes. This is not necessarily because the models contain confidential information. They may not, in which case one party may take a peek at the other's analysis without harm, *provided it knows the other did not mean to show it*. It is the intentional pointing to a confrontation that is confrontational.

Models like those of Eden and Ackermann, designed to summarise common information and meanings between would-be collaborating parties, are strictly complementary to CC models. They depict a negotiated, shared view held by a strategy-making team; CC models can peer behind this façade and expose the internal machinations afoot. But they are also complementary in helping to manage relationships with external parties. The overall JOURNEY-making process includes an explicit focus upon stakeholder analysis and management. However, it generally fails to move much beyond the identification of stakeholders and a rather superficial consideration of their power and interest in a situation. The dynamics of interactions between an organisation and other stakeholders is dealt with, if at all, by a loose technique called 'role-think'. In contrast, CC models of 'external' interactions provide a much more structured and explicit picture to support strategic thinking about stakeholder management.

Used in these ways, CC modelling requires a clear distinction between 'us' and 'them' of the kind that the military find easy but that civilians sometimes find problematic. When, however, this distinction can be made, we argue that civilian organisations can make effective, profitable use of the kind of command-and-control systems for confrontation and collaboration that have been developed for the military. Note that a simple rule applies to the CC models used by such systems. Because 'official', authorised information is generally shared within an organisation, official CC models must always represent the organisation as a single, unified party in confrontation with external parties, although this single party may be represented by a number of different 'agents' (internal parties that represent the organisation in different ways at different levels). A collection of such CC models can be built into a multi-level system for conducting the organisation's interactions with external parties, thereby coordinating its policies and providing an accounting system for its relationships. This is what is meant by command and control of confrontation and collaboration.

Such a system will also help internal cohesion by building a shared view of the organisation's objectives and strategy in relation to the outside world. In addition, individuals trained in CC modelling within an organisation can use their knowledge in a private, implicit way to improve their interactions with other internal parties.

But there is another way that CC modelling can help build internal cohesion. Paralleling the military's use of fictionalised scenarios for training, we argue that there are great benefits from using drama theory to build a fictionalised version of the organisation and its internal and external conflicts, within which personnel can role-play their internal confrontations with each other. CC models can be used to produce briefings for role-players of an accuracy and quality equal to the best film or stage direction – particularly in relation to the all-important emotional factors. It can also give clear, unambiguous results: 'This is where you have ended up.' Role-play followed by discussion ('Can you see how you might have done better?') can be transformative experiences for participants, with great benefits for the organisation.

In sum, we argue for two uses of CC modelling to enhance strategic coherence: one, in setting up a system for effective command, control and coordination of interactions with outside parties; the other, in improving internal cohesion through role-playing internal problems in a fictionalised setting. From the outset, we emphasise the complementary relationship between our approach and others we have mentioned. As suggested earlier, methods such as Eden and Ackermann's JOURNEY-making (1998) are well suited to developing within-group dialogue and shared understanding, for instance between internal factions in an organisation, or between partners in a collaboration. Such methodologies help to achieve resolution of differences between parties. The construction of CC models complements them by providing a ruthlessly honest understanding of the internal and external relationships of an organisation, to be used for conducting external confrontations and collaborations and for fictionalised role-playing of internal ones. Among the many applications of such an approach might be to help a company explore ways of managing its supply chain or help a consortium to see how it could operate more effectively in a global marketplace.

OVERVIEW OF THE CHAPTER

We begin our account of CC modelling in the next section, by introducing some basic theoretical concepts and a useful notation – the 'options board'. This is illustrated in the following section through an example drawn from the vehicle manufacturing industry. We then go on to present our general conception of the overall development of any interaction between parties. This enables us, in the next section, to give an outline of the process of CC modelling. We include here a comparison of our drama theory concepts with the influential, prescriptive approach of Fisher and Ury (1981).

Drama theory is founded on the principle that the future is created (in part) by interactions between stakeholders. The next section therefore looks at a key stage in CC model-building: identifying stakeholders. From this we move on to what is conceptually the most ambitious section of the chapter, where we outline a model initially developed for the military (Murray-Jones & Howard, 1999) for a multi-level CC system to handle relationships with external parties. We show, by using an example drawn from the engineering industry, how such a system might be transferred into a civilian context.

In our final sections, we look at how to get around the fact that such an 'official' system cannot be used to manage internal relationships. We first discuss how to use CC models to build a role-playing system (a so-called 'immersive drama') that lets members of an organisation practice collaboration within a fictionalised version of their corporate world. Finally, we discuss extending this system to create what is effectively a fictionalised version of the multi-level CC system that can be used as a powerful tool for organisational learning.

Our general contention is that strategy coherence can be helped by building a system of explicit models of interactions with external parties, coupled with a fictionalised role-playing system that allows internal parties to play out and analyse the emotional dynamics of conflicts between themselves. The chapter concludes by placing CC modelling within the strategic development process considered in the first chapter of this book.

ANALYSING AN INTERACTION AT A 'MOMENT OF TRUTH'

In our view, strategy is necessarily designed and achieved between parties: it is negotiated. It must be, for were an organisation to try to impose its view on another it would inevitably generate a reaction – of opposition or approval – that through a feedback process would modify its subsequent direction. The same applies to direction of parties and groups within an organisation, though here it may be less obvious, due to the influence of an erroneous idea about command – the idea that people can or should 'just follow orders'. Interestingly, this idea is openly rejected in British military doctrine, where it is replaced by the idea of 'mission command' – that a subordinate commander should not normally be told what to do, but instead *what objective to reach*, and should even disobey orders when knowledge of local conditions tells him they would not achieve his superior's intent.

We therefore see strategy implementation as the enacted summation of actions taken by individuals and groups across an organisation, both in response to external demands and internal pressures and in concert with other stakeholders in the organisation's future. Now these strategic actions, taken by internal as much as external parties, represent deliberate – possibly reluctant, but still deliberate – choices emerging from consideration – often inadequate – of possible outcomes of interaction with other parties. It follows that achieving strategic coherence requires the orchestration and improvement of sets of interlinked confrontations-leading-to-collaboration among interacting parties at all levels. This is why a model of interaction forms the building block for the strategy support systems we recommend.

How then do we analyse a basic interaction? For simplicity, consider a two-person situation, although our theory applies to any number of parties. Two parties that need to accommodate each other in some area will each come to the situation with a view as to how it should be resolved. We term these advocated solutions the 'positions' of the parties; they state what actions the parties would have themselves and others undertake. If the positions advanced by parties are compatible (i.e. they are not in disagreement; each is at least willing to accommodate the other in matters where it doesn't assert a view), then they are already collaborating. Note that this does not mean that all their problems are solved. In general, they will still have *dilemmas of collaboration* – whether to believe each other's promises, or be believed. As they go into the details of their planned cooperation, more such dilemmas may appear as they uncover differing understandings of their 'agreement'. They have, however, reached the second stage of conflict resolution. They have left behind the first stage – confrontation – though as we look into the dilemmas of collaboration we will see that they may fall back into it. Confrontation is always the ghost of the collaboration feast.

If, on the other hand, positions are not compatible, then each party is bound to use inducements – threats and promises – to encourage others to accept its proposals. Why are they bound to? Because each will ask itself a very serious question, and assess others' intentions in an attempt to answer it: 'What is going to happen if we can't agree?' Having estimated an answer to this question, it will see as 'threats' the intentions of others that happen to be contrary to its own position and as 'promises' the proposals of others that meet its position. And provided the interaction is important enough to awaken its sensitivity and intelligence, it will see that others are similarly assessing its own 'threats' and 'promises', and will start to see its own intentions and proposals in this light.

The result: the parties' communicated or understood intentions constitute a third possible future, additional to the parties' positions – the so-called 'fallback' or 'threat-ened future'. This is the 'BATNA' (Best Alternative To a Negotiated Agreement) defined by Fisher and Ury (1981), with one important difference. In the real world, a party may communicate an intention that is not its 'best' alternative to an agree-ment. In other words, it may make an incredible threat – incredible because against its own preferences. It then has what we call a 'threat dilemma', one result of which may be that a party becomes angry enough to cause its preferences to change so that it prefers to carry out its hitherto incredible threat. Fisher and Ury (who regard emotions in general as dysfunctional) assume away this possibility: we analyse it.

Our next step will be to formally model parties' positions and stated intentions using a so-called 'options board'. A sequence of such boards will model just how an organisation gets others to 'buy into' and implement a solution in line with its objectives. In doing so, of course, it generally finds that its objectives change in response to others' pressure. Thus, CC modelling does not show a party how it can set a unilateral objective and procure its achievement – that is both logically impossible (since if it were possible, all parties could do it) and contrary to real-life observation (consider the implications of the military term, 'mission creep'). Instead, it can help a party explore collaborative advantage and home in on a solution that benefits all parties – as well as understand how an interaction may escalate and go from confrontation into conflict. Importantly, it shows exactly how collaboration and conflict are both driven by emotion and creativity as well as by reason. Though based upon drama theory (Howard, 1994), which is an extension of game theory, CC modelling does not require mathematical knowledge, but gives simple models understandable by users. (Our models were produced using Confrontation Manager™ software, obtainable from Idea Sciences, Inc., at www.ideasciences.com.)

At what point do we model the interaction, given that an options board model is a snapshot taken at a particular moment? In any interaction, it is the moment before parties commit to action of some kind that is critical. This is the so-called 'moment of truth' when they communicate 'final' intentions to each other – i.e. intentions they propose to act upon. Until then, their intentions are taken to be tentative, as intentions are if not ready to be acted on. It is also the time when they most convincingly use emotion and rational argument in an effort to cajole, persuade or influence others to adopt their particular cooperative solution. At a moment of truth, drama theory asserts that parties find themselves facing one or more of six dilemmas, from each of which there is a repertoire of escapes, consisting of ways of sending messages that change the situation. Dilemmas arouse specific emotions, which in turn give rise to rationalisations to justify desired changes in the interaction. As a result, parties may postpone the action they were about to take and reassess what to do, the situation having changed.

Note the important fact that because we analyse a model of an interaction for dilemmas (rather than for solutions), CC modelling directs the modeller to look at the real-world context in order to find ways in which, through the use of reason directed by emotion, the interaction itself may be redefined. Dilemmas point to something 'wrong' with the model – i.e. to ways in which the parties themselves will look outside the model for ways of redefining their situation. Thus, the modeller is directed to look 'outside the box', rather than remain trapped within the model he or she has built.

Four 'confrontational' dilemmas relate to the challenge of reaching agreement; two dilemmas of collaboration relate to the challenge of keeping it. Drama theory provides a mathematical proof (Howard & Murray-Jones, 2001) that if they face none of these six dilemmas, parties must agree on a single solution that they fully trust each other to carry out.

ILLUSTRATING CC MODELLING: A VEHICLE MANUFACTURING EXAMPLE

To illustrate these concepts, consider a confrontation between a vehicle manufacturer and one of its component suppliers. Under increasing pressure in the motor market, the manufacturer must secure a better deal from the supplier. The unstated but implicit threat is that if a price reduction cannot be achieved then a replacement supplier will be sought. Figure 3.1 shows an options board that captures the consequent moment of truth.

At the left side, the two parties and the options available to each are listed as we have described them. The body of the table is organised into columns, each of

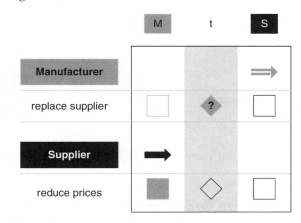

Figure 3.1. Options Board for Motor Supply Management

which summarises a possible outcome: a shaded symbol indicates that the corresponding option is taken; an unshaded one that it is not. The leftmost column gives the manufacturer's position (i.e. that the supplier is not replaced, but complies by reducing price), while the supplier's position is at the right: between them is the threatened future. To these previously stated outcomes we have added and shown in the figure some assessments by parties of each other's actual or putative preferences or intentions. The arrow in the supplier's row denotes the manufacturer's view that it (the supplier) would rather be replaced than reduce its prices: it points in the direction of the supplier's preferences between columns 'M' and 't'. The weakened arrow in the manufacturer's row means that the supplier believes the manufacturer might not replace it if it stands firm. The question mark in the threatened future column signifies a doubt on the part of the supplier that, if it came to the crunch, the manufacturer would replace it. These assessments give rise to three dilemmas of confrontation for the manufacturer (but, as it happens, none for the supplier).

- A persuasion dilemma (implied by arrow in supplier row): manufacturer doubts that supplier would agree to reduce prices rather than be replaced – so how can supplier be **persuaded** to comply?
- A rejection dilemma (implied by arrow in manufacturer row): supplier suspects that manufacturer would rather put up with the status quo than get another supplier – so how can manufacturer credibly **reject** supplier's intransigence?
- A threat dilemma (implied by question mark in column 't'): supplier doubts that manufacturer would carry out its **threat** to replace it.

These dilemmas place the manufacturer under pressure to concede, as indicated by the fact that both arrows point to the supplier's position. They can be more directly summed up in a graphic called a 'tug of war' (Figure 3.2). Positions are shown by ovals and stated intentions (the threatened future) by a box; positions and intentions are given snappy titles signalling what they mean. Horizontal arrows show each party's preferences between the threatened future and the other's position, while

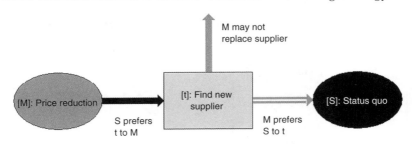

Figure 3.2. Tug of War between Manufacturer and Supplier

vertical arrows show question marks – doubts whether an intention or proposal would actually be carried out. From this diagram it is clear that the manufacturer is losing the tug of war. It is being pulled towards the supplier's position, while the pivot of action, the threatened future, has an instability (the vertical arrow) unfavourable to the manufacturer.

What can the manufacturer do? Escaping its dilemmas requires changing the assumptions we have made to construct the model. An emotional response (one that contradicts its own preferences) might be to come to prefer finding another supplier. Negative emotion towards the current supplier will prompt this *preference change*, emotion that will prompt rationalisations such as 'if they can't find a way to drop prices then they aren't good enough to supply us and we'd have to replace them sooner or later anyway'. Note that, by assumption, this is not the manufacturer's initial, 'objective' assessment; the point is that emotion prompts a reassessment to see if the emotional response can be justified. On a methodological point, when we talk of an organisation feeling emotion, we mean individuals feeling emotion on its behalf: emotion is of course an individual feeling.

Rationalisation along these lines may succeed, eliminating the manufacturer's rejection and threat dilemmas, which both arise from the latter's formerly supine attitude. However, the manufacturer's persuasion dilemma, stemming from the supplier's view that it simply can't afford to drop prices, still remains, and if it is left when the others are eliminated, will lead to the conflict outcome [t]: an end to the relationship. To eliminate this dilemma, the supplier's preference must change – whereas to eliminate the rejection and threat dilemmas it was the supplier's view of the manufacturer's preference that was required to change.

However, rationalisation to eliminate rejection and threat dilemmas may also fail. It depends on there existing an alternative source of supply that can be switched in to fill the manufacturer's need: not necessarily a likely situation. Realising this, the manufacturer may feel a more positive emotion towards the present supplier, prompting it to rationalise a *change of position* to meet both parties' needs. Could a low-price deal between supplier and manufacturer be identified by a task-force of members of the two organisations, familiar with the constraints on both sides, whose established relationship should provide a good foundation for frank and full discussions? Thinking so, the manufacturer might shift its position to the coopera-tive solution in Figure 3.3. Provided the supplier can be persuaded of the realism of the manufacturer's proposals – notice the question mark signifying a potential

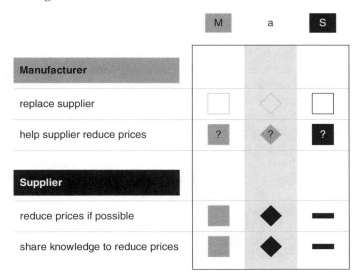

Figure 3.3. Collaborative Options Board for Motor Supply Management

doubt – the parties might agree on this solution, creating the collaborative options board shown. (Collaboration is marked by the fact that the 'stated intentions' column in the middle is headed 'a' for 'agreement'.) Notice that in this options board the supplier does not itself propose either to 'reduce prices if possible' or to 'share knowledge'; it is, however, willing to accept the manufacturer's suggestion that it do so, giving rise to the collaborative intentions shown.

What dilemmas does this board throw up? The supplier has a trust dilemma: how can it **trust** the manufacturer to help it reduce prices? This dilemma creates emotions and rationalisations that are positive but mistrustful: cooperative scepticism. The manufacturer has a corresponding cooperation dilemma: how to persuade the supplier that it can and wants to **cooperate**? This dilemma creates exclusively positive emotion and rationalisations aimed at making its promise credible – in this case, by actually finding cost-reduction measures. In sum, the emotion evoked by this options board is generally positive (i.e. goodwill), whereas Figure 3.1 was dominated by the negative emotion required to underpin the manufacturer's incredible threat – though at the final moment of truth, positive emotion was evoked by the manufacturer's need to accommodate the supplier's position.

In general, collaboration evokes positive emotion. Negative emotion characterises confrontation – which, however, can also generate the positive emotion needed to transform it into collaboration. The positive emotion generated by collaboration itself dissolves, however, once all dilemmas of collaboration have been resolved – i.e. once parties can and do fully trust each other to carry out an agreed plan. No emotion is then felt over an operation that has become prescribed and predictable.

The reader may wonder what is the sixth dilemma: we have discussed five. Briefly, it is the positioning dilemma facing a party that prefers another's position to its own. Usually this is because it considers the other's position to be desirable but unrealistic, typically due to opposition from a third party. The corresponding emotion is irritation, leading to sometimes quite active hostility to a party whose position one actually prefers. Peacekeepers in Bosnia felt this kind of irritation with the Bosnian government for rejecting the demands of the Bosnian Serbs.

Our example illustrates key features of analysing an interaction at a moment of truth. First, the focus on declared positions of the parties and the sanctions available to them. Second, systematic consideration of doubts/uncertainties that detract from the credibility of promises and threats. Third, identification of specific dilemmas faced by each party and exploration of the rational–emotional routes (emotion leading to rationalisation) by which they may be removed. The routes are specified generically. Specific ways of following them require looking outside the model at the real-world environment for factors not present in the current model. Fourth, discovery, through research and exploration, of dilemma-resolution strategies for each party that incorporate these new factors and transform the situation. The emotionally inspired aim of parties will be to bring about changes in positions, preferences, intentions or beliefs that, to be believable, must be supported by adequate reason and evidence (rationalisation).

An options board model of a particular moment of truth is not, however, a model of the whole interaction. It is like the mathematical derivative of a curve in calculus, showing its direction at a particular point in time. The whole curve, if we follow this metaphor, consists of the progress of an interaction from its beginning to where it ends in either conflict or cooperation. In this section we have shown this, in part, by displaying two options boards, one following the other. In the next section we describe in general how an interaction builds up to successive moments of truth and ends in either conflict or cooperation.

GOING FROM CONFRONTATION TO COLLABORATION – OR CONFLICT

Figure 3.4 shows the phases by which cooperation is achieved, either by going from scene-setting (top left) straight across to collaboration (top right) and straight down through a cooperative decision to a cooperative dénouement (bottom right), or by deviating through confrontation – i.e. turning right at the build-up before turning left up to collaboration. Alternatively, the diagram shows how collaboration may never occur, or may break down into confrontation, which then escalates into conflict. To see this, either turn right at the build-up and go from confrontation to a conflictual decision followed by a conflictual dénouement, or deviate by first going straight across to a collaboration that, through a right-hand turn, breaks down into confrontation and ends in the same bad way.

What do the phases mean? At the beginning is **scene-setting**. This means that previous interactions, together with their unintended consequences, have set the context of an interaction – i.e. the environment within which certain issues must be decided by certain parties. Next is **build-up**. Here, parties interact in a tentative manner until they have created a 'common reference frame' – i.e. they have established sufficient mutual understanding to allow them to communicate over the

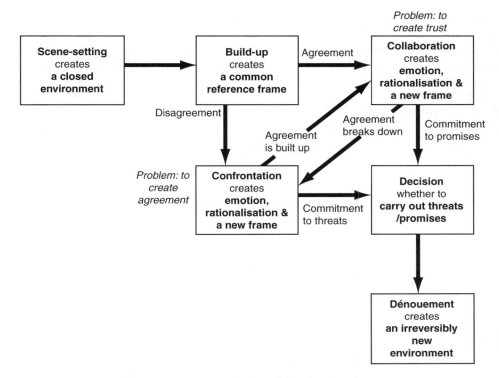

Figure 3.4. The Six Phases of Conflict Resolution

issues. This includes common knowledge of positions and intentions, without which communication is ambiguous.

At this point, parties' communicated intentions may be compatible with everyone's position, leading to **collaboration**. If not, there is **confrontation**. This may, as we've seen, lead to a **conflictual decision** (e.g. following their impasse, the manufacturer must decide whether actually to replace the supplier) or to an agreement (e.g. the joint study of cost reduction) on which to collaborate. Collaboration may lead to a **cooperative decision** (a decision whether to carry out the agreement reached), but is always in danger of breaking back down into confrontation as parties' efforts to get and give commitments lead to incompatible positions. Either type of decision (conflictual or cooperative) is taken separately by each party as they decide whether to carry out their threats or promises and, at the same time, whether to believe or disbelieve each other's. The result is a (possibly flunked) conflict or a (possibly failed) resolution. Alternatively, a party may recoil from this hard choice and try to reopen discussions with the others (note that it may be possible for parties to go back to previous phases – a possibility not shown in the diagram). **Dénouement** occurs when irreversible actions are taken, either in fulfilment of threats and promises or reneging on them. In any case, it generally turns out differently than parties expected, due to unforeseen consequences.

Observe that the build-up is driven by parties anticipating the collaborations or confrontations that their tentative positions and intentions may lead them into and making adjustments accordingly. It ends when they state positions or intentions they regard as 'final'. Observe too that the dénouement leads, in general, to new interactions, foreseen or unforeseen – i.e. it often coincides with a new scene-setting.

Clearly, the phases in Figure 3.4 may be gone through a number of times before the issues are settled or end in conflict. To model what happens requires a sequence of options boards, the nth transforming into the $(n+1)$th. An interaction over a set of issues will be modelled by such a sequence, not by the snapshot given by a single board.

OUTLINE OF THE PROCESS OF CC MODELLING

Having reviewed the basics of CC modelling, let us ask how it would be used by an organisation to prepare for a specific interaction. Note that since we are describing an official, formal process, we must assume that the organisation is preparing to interact with an external party – 'them' against 'us'.

People, at present, use their intuition. We show in Figure 3.5 how they could improve on this – while strengthening, not neglecting, intuition. The diagram outlines the four essential phases of the process that would be followed by a party (whether an individual, a group or an organisation) as it uses CC modelling to help manage its confrontations with others.

First, REGARD what is going on in a non-judgemental manner. This means picking out salient features and making basic judgements as to who is involved, over what issues. Next, choose a specific focus round which to build a model to

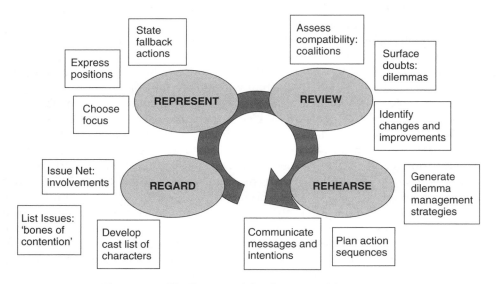

Figure 3.5. The Process of Confrontation Management

REPRESENT parties' positions and intentions at a particular moment of truth – a point when each party will claim to have taken its 'final' stand. Note, however, that it may be appropriate to analyse a 'virtual' moment of truth that never actually occurs, but exercises a decisive influence through being foreseen by the parties. Foreseeing, during the build-up phase, that one is heading towards a particularly fatal moment of truth may be enough to cause a party to change tack. This is a subtle point, but an important one.

Having modelled a moment of truth, dilemma analysis follows, with a REVIEW of rational–emotional changes by which we and others may try to dissipate dilemmas – noting that dilemmas necessarily exist unless and until we all fully agree and trust each other. Whilst, of course, such complete, accustomed trust occurs in all walks of life, it simply means that our interaction no longer presents any problems – i.e. is routine and boring. It will be unlikely, in fact, to register as an interaction.

Your REVIEW must, we know, look outside the current model, within which dilemmas are hard-wired. Thus, the analysis is inherently dynamic, with each current model leading to suggestions that we build another – or we will not be modelling parties' thinking. But a party cannot make credible (i.e. get others to accept) a new model without persuading them by sending messages. The REHEARSAL phase consists of simulating or imagining the exchange of messages that will arise from the current model as each tries to persuade the other of the changes it is provoked to make. Role-play, if affordable, is the best way to do it. This phase may lead to action – initiating communication with other parties or exploring the environment to check out possible methods of dilemma-elimination – or to a new model, based on insights gained. In fact, it will generally lead to a new model anyhow, since both communication with other parties and research into possibilities will change the reality we face or our perception of it.

This four-phase process, carried out with the organisation modelled as a single, unitary party, is how CC modelling should be used in the 'rehearsing strategy' phase of the overall strategic development process introduced in Chapter 1. The 'models of the organisation' produced are options boards and tug of war diagrams, used to assist managerial thinking and reflection on strategy. Strategic initiatives are stimulated by learning gained from dilemma analysis; for example, our car manufacturer would be stimulated to do research on and see the value of supply-chain collaboration, as opposed to exerting economic pressure on suppliers.

Internal conflicts that threaten strategic coherence (such as between newly merged companies) are not, however, addressed directly by this process. They are ameliorated. People work better together after analysing and rehearsing their organisation's interactions with external parties. But this effect is indirect. Our suggestion, elaborated below, is that internal conflicts be addressed directly by building fictionalised versions of internal conflicts and getting people to role-play them using the four-phase process.

We end this section with a comment on the widely followed 'principled negotiation' approach of Fisher and Ury (1981). The assumption behind this – if stated in our terminology – is that parties have no dilemmas other than rejection dilemmas (i.e. they prefer each other's positions to 'no deal') so that their utilities inhabit a Pareto-bounded, positive quadrant with 'no deal' at the origin. To keep them there, parties are assumed to be able to trust each other once they have a deal, to make only credible threats and never to prefer the stalemate of 'no deal' to what some party is proposing. The authors' reason for these unrealistic assumptions is that they take preferences as fixed and given – as economists, game theorists and decision theorists generally do. Given fixed preferences, their assumptions are necessary or a deal would not be possible between parties. Paradoxically, however, they also advise against 'position-taking'. This is paradoxical since the existence of rejection dilemmas implies conflicting positions. Our explanation is that in the process of Figure 3.4 they advise staying in the build-up phase, where positions and intentions are stated tentatively in an exploratory mode, until parties can find a way into collaboration without ever encountering a dilemma. This will work if parties can pretend convincingly enough that their problems stem from misunderstanding each other (i.e. inability to communicate), not disagreement. Under the special assumptions that Fisher and Ury make, their advice to 'principled negotiators' is well-judged and entirely drama-theoretic; its one flaw is that it rejects any positive role for emotion.

STAKEHOLDER ANALYSIS

Being alert to stakeholder interests is increasingly seen as vital for strategists. The World Bank (1992), for example, regards stakeholder analysis as essential to managing an enterprise on sustainable development principles. Stakeholders – those with a declared or potential interest in a change process – range from employees, partners and customers to regulators overseeing performance or acting as custodians of the environment for future generations. The view that the future results from interactions between stakeholders (rather than, for example, from abstract trends or developments) is essentially drama-theoretic.

For successful CC modelling of a set of issues, it is important to scope a situation broadly before homing in on key interactions. To do this a 'long list' of stakeholders is developed first, using imagination to go beyond those conventionally seen as relevant. Breadth is enhanced by using checklists. Mason and Mitroff (1981), for example, suggest these criteria for inclusion:

- Imperatives. Those that reveal an interest through demands, slogans or acts of defiance (e.g. strikes).
- Position. Those that affect outcomes through their placement in administrative or power structures.
- Reputation. Those seen by others in the broad system as influential, regardless of their formal position.
- Participation. Those taking part in activities related to the core issue (e.g. through membership, attendance or voting).
- Opinion-leadership. Those that influence or seek to influence the views of others (e.g. directors, journalists, politicians).
- Demography. Individuals that may be treated as a distinct group by virtue of shared characteristics such as age, income, religion or disability.
- Relationship. Those that have an important relationship with the system (e.g. suppliers, customers, regulators or competitors).

'Short lists' of key stakeholders can then be drawn from the long list to capture those most affected by a strategy and most involved in making it. To assess who is 'key', stakeholder mapping can be used (Johnson, Scholes & Whittington, 2005); this means assessing each stakeholder in terms of its *interest* and *power*. Results are presented as in Figure 3.6. 'Smiley' faces like those shown can represent stakeholder attitudes (supportive, hostile or apathetic), values (commercial or ethical) or affiliations, and have been effective in workshop-based interventions such as the airline alliance work cited earlier. Arrows in the diagram show possible movements of stakeholders across the grid as a result of internal or external factors – for example, stakeholder management policies informed by interaction analysis.

The 'cast list' of parties in a CC interaction is normally a subset of the players in the stakeholder grid, since interactions are framed around particular 'bones of contention', of which there will usually be a number. Resolution of an interaction may involve additional stakeholders, as a party may deliberately involve a hitherto uninvolved stakeholder (e.g. a context-setter).

How does one decide whether to admit a stakeholder to the list of those involved in an interaction? Quite simply, those involved in the 'common reference frame' are those that those involved see as involved! This may seem simplistic, but is soundly based, for (while the cast may always change) only those involved in the interaction determine its development, and they are by definition uninfluenced by those they see as uninvolved. Likewise, the actions included in a CC model are just those proposed or threatened by the parties involved – which may actually require listing options that are known by some to be infeasible, yet appear in the list because they are demanded by others. The result is a 'requisite' model (Phillips, 1984): one that is sufficient to capture and understand the issue at hand and represents the social reality shared by the cast.

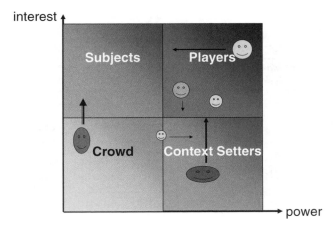

Figure 3.6. A Dynamic Power–Interest Stakeholder Grid

A MULTI-LEVEL CC SYSTEM FOR HANDLING RELATIONSHIPS WITH EXTERNAL PARTIES

What we have described so far is a system for handling a particular CC interaction in order to settle a particular set of issues. Now an organisation has to handle many interactions with external parties at many levels of delegation, from staff handling customers up through managers handling suppliers right up to the company board handling top-level relationships. To maximise effectiveness, the organisation needs to coordinate the messages it sends, so that superiors support subordinates, subordinates support superiors, colleagues on the same level support each other and messages sent now support and are supported by messages sent later. In other words, it must carry out command and control of confrontation and collaboration in the manner envisaged by the military.

A system for doing this, based on work for the military, is shown in Figure 3.7. This simply shows that the mission our superior delegates to us is, from our superior's viewpoint, a delegated mission, while to us it is our superior's mission. We analyse it and derive from it a number of own-level missions we ourselves must carry out to fulfil our superior's intent. Many of these we actually carry out through our subordinates – e.g. the UK government carries out a mission of invading Iraq through its subordinate, the UK armed forces; the UK Ministry of Defence plans this mission, along with others, and delegates it to be carried out by a general in command of a UK invading force; the commander of this force carries out various own-level missions and at the same time delegates missions to be carried out by his subordinate commanders; and so on. Thus, we derive from our own-level missions various delegated missions to be carried out by our subordinates. To us, these are delegated missions; to our subordinates, they are their superior's mission.

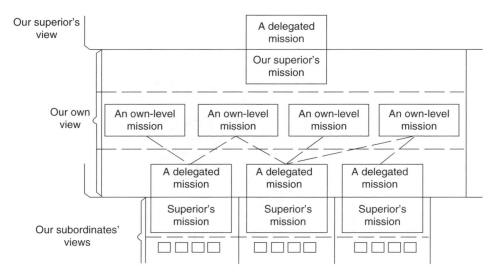

Figure 3.7. Diagram of a Multi-level Confrontation/Collaboration System

This, in outline, is a system set up to coordinate interactions with external parties. Each leader of an organisational unit (each commander, in military terms) has in view three types of mission – where a mission is defined as a set of inter-related interactions undertaken to confront/collaborate with external parties. The first type is the mission handed down by the leader's superior, comprising a set of interactions in which the options wielded by the superior are actually implemented by the unit leader we are considering, so that in effect the superior acts through this leader. Having received this superior's mission, the leader must plan and initiate a number of own-level missions (sets of interactions with parties at the leader's own level) in order to fulfil it. This is the second type of mission the leader must have in view. Some of these own-level missions include options actually implemented by the leader's subordinates; the leader must therefore pick out sets of interactions (missions) to be delegated as missions to subordinates. Such delegated missions are the third type of mission the leader must have in view. To each subordinate, the set of interactions it receives as a mission is, of course, a mission of the first type – a superior's mission; and so on.

Note that the principle of 'mission command' (not to give orders, but instead to assign objectives) is implemented under this system. Each subordinate knows from their superior's mission what their superior is trying to achieve in interaction with external parties, and from this plans own-level missions. Planning and implementing these may lead subordinates to suggest changes in their superior's mission, to be assessed by their superior in light of its knowledge of higher-level missions and simultaneous missions being carried out by colleagues. Vice versa, developments in higher-level missions (the superior's 'own-level' missions) may warrant changes to the missions it delegates. The system helps to alleviate the problem identified by a US general: 'If only my captains knew what I need to know, so that they can pass it up to me.' A similar problem in industry might be: 'If only my sales managers knew what I need to know . . . '

To provide an example, consider a situation that we encountered recently involving a major engineering conglomerate – let's call it Founders – and its relationship with a smaller company – Shapers – in the same industry. Founders has learnt that one of its main competitors, Western Engineering, intends entering an emerging market in which Shapers is a key player; with Western's massive resources it could quickly dominate this market and undermine Shapers' position. In the wider and long-standing rivalry between Founders and Western this development would be unwelcome. Founders has therefore decided to offer to supply Shapers with technology that will enable it to see off the threat; but it would expect to charge a premium price for it. Meanwhile a fourth company, Cutters, can supply Shapers an alternative, cheaper but inferior technology that might possibly counter the threat it faces. Working with one of Founders' senior managers, the options board shown in Figure 3.8 was created.

A first observation is that no other party has a stance on Western's options (dashes in Western's option rows) and Western has no stance on theirs (dashes in Western's position column). In other words, Western is acting quite independently and autonomously. In a similar way, others have no committed view on Cutters' action, but the parallel is not complete as Cutters does have a view about theirs, or at least about Shapers' actions: Cutters thinks Shapers should team up with

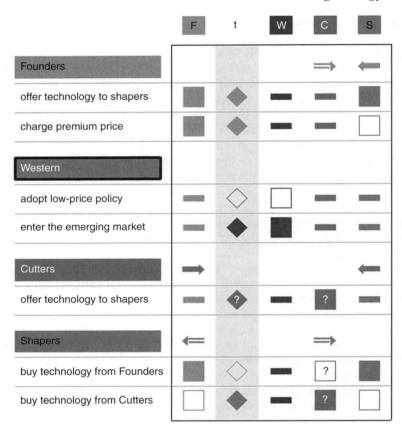

Figure 3.8. Options Board Showing a Moment in a Four-Person Interaction

it. The implication is that if Founders can reach a deal with Shapers, then they needn't worry about the others: not about Western because it will do what it wants regardless; not about Cutters because it can do nothing to undermine their accord.

The tug of war in Figure 3.9 therefore focuses on the relationship between Founders and Shapers. Both the F and S arrows point towards Founders, signifying that at the moment of truth its position is preferred by both these parties. This creates a rejection dilemma for Shapers (they prefer Founders' proposal to the threatened future). Shapers also face a threat dilemma (buying technology from Cutters isn't credible) and a persuasion dilemma (Founders, not believing that Shapers would implement its threat, prefers the fallback to Shapers' position). In contrast, Founders faces no dilemmas.

How could this situation be resolved? Shapers, moved by anger at Founders' 'unfair' demand, might overcome its rejection dilemma by determinedly refusing to pay a premium price on the pretence that Cutters' technology is adequate. To counter this, Founders might request Shapers to justify its pretence, but must be careful not to make Shapers angrier still, anger being Shapers' weapon. Face-saving

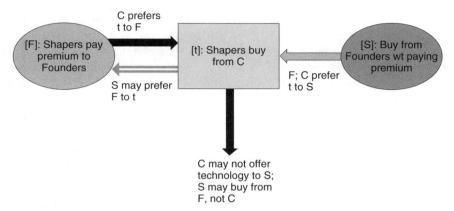

Figure 3.9. Tug of War between Founders and Shapers

methods (e.g. a 'token' price reduction) may be needed to help Shapers retreat from its position. If the critique of Shapers' pretence fails, whether due to inadequate rationale or inappropriate emotional tone, Founders may have to offer a genuine compromise on price. This would have the advantage of creating the basis for a stable alliance.

Returning to the concept of a multi-level system, let us now ask how this inter-action might support and be supported by interactions at higher and lower levels in Founders' organisation. Consider the view of the Founders division (call it ShapeTech) that owns the technology being offered to Shapers. Assume that the top management of Founders has, in pursuit of its overall strategy, taken the position that Founders should offer this technology – i.e. the F column in Figure 3.8 is the position of top management. Then the superior mission it delegates to ShapeTech would contain (among others) the interaction shown in Figure 3.8. ShapeTech now decides (or is directed) to open technical discussions with Shapers about what is involved in the technology and how it could be transferred. Having this model (Figures 3.8 and 3.9) in its view will enable ShapeTech to conduct these discussions in such a way as to support the position of top management and be ready to relay to them any new facts or nuances that might help top management in its negotiations.

In light of its superior mission, ShapeTech will build own-level models to assist in its interaction with Shapers' scientists and technologists. ShapeTech's position in a typical one of these models will consist, no doubt, of scientific/technological assertions about ShapeTech's technology that show (without asserting) that its cost-reducing, quality-enhancing properties make it worth its admittedly high price. Shapers' position will consist of denials of these assertions. The alternative tech-nology possibly being offered by Cutters may not be considered explicitly, but ShapeTech, guided by its superior's intent, will assert a position that shows how inferior this technology is. Emotions generated by the dilemmas of its interaction with Shapers' technologists will motivate ShapeTech to find rationalisations in the shape of sound, verifiable, scientific evidence and arguments that justify its posi-tion. Note that in our paradigm there is no contradiction between strong emotion driving one to prefer a certain result and the finding of rational evidence to prove it. On the contrary, it is the scientist's strong emotion, generated by dilemmas, that drives him or her to find the evidence – if it exists. And if it does not exist? Then the emotion serves another valuable purpose – that of finding a weakness in the current technology that will have to be corrected sooner or later. Moreover, the emotion generated by the current confrontation will drive the scientist to seek a way of correcting it in time to resolve the present interaction satisfactorily.

These benefits, of course, depend on those involved having strong scientific consciences, supported by the culture of Founders. They must not cheat. As it is clearly in Founders' interest that this be so, there will or should be policies in place to ensure it. These should be made operational through the mission delegated from top management to Founders' personnel department: part of this mission should be to make it pay an employee to have a strong scientific conscience.

As for the lower managerial levels that ShapeTech will delegate missions to, these might consist of the teams that make the actual, physical transfer of technology and train Shapers' staff in using it. Note that if the transfer is simple, this 'lower managerial level' may comprise the same people as those involved in the own-level mission. Often one person may operate on different managerial levels at different times. Whether this is so or not, knowing the reason why the mission has been delegated – i.e. having in view the superior's mission that has been delegated to them – will enable those doing the transfer to do it in such a way that Shapers feel they are getting what they bargained for, thus enhancing prospects for the alliance. There will, of course, be interactions between parties (confrontations avoided in the interests of collaboration) during transfer and training, just as in all human interaction that is not routine.

Let us now ask – if not a hierarchy of people, what is the hierarchy of levels we are talking about? It is a hierarchy of functions, not necessarily of status, pay or prestige. To see what these functions are, we will consider five distinct yet complementary ways of defining strategy that are inspired by – though somewhat different from – those presented in a seminal paper by Mintzberg (1987). Strategy, we assert, can be seen as a *plan* to guide action, a *ploy* to outwit others, a *pattern* of conscious or unconscious behaviour, a *perspective* governing the organisation's view of the world, and a *position* that defines the organisation's aimed-for relation to its environment. In these terms, the first function of strategic management is to monitor the *pattern* of the organisation's behaviour. Is it satisfactory? The major determinant of this, for a commercial organisation, would be projected profit; members of the organisation might have different criteria. If the pattern is unsatisfactory, the *perspective* of certain parties, inside or outside the organisation, must change. They need to take on different attitudes or objectives. Management needs to take a *position* on what changes it proposes, but should recognise that it is impossible to change such fundamentals of behaviour in the one-sided, instrumentally rational manner envisaged in decision theory, game theory or economics. To change others' objectives you must make it possible for them to change your own objectives. In the words of a British general to one of us, 'To win a confrontation I must bet myself.'

The next step is to form a *plan* for bringing about these changes – a plan that must be drama-theoretic in looking forward to a rational–emotional fray in the course of which both sides undergo change. In other words, those involved must look forward to mutual learning. The superior must learn from the subordinate and vice versa; colleague must learn from colleague, expert from client, etc. Finally, the plan involves the use of *ploys* in the form of dilemma-eliminating courses of action or messages. As the term suggests, the reasoning behind these 'ploys' is not shared between the parties involved; as we have emphasised, no drama-theoretic model can be shared between parties trying to collaborate because it acknowledges the existence of actual or potential confrontation – and to acknowledge this is to confront, and thereby to move away from collaboration.

In the second section of this chapter, on external and internal conflict as seen by the military and by civilians, we gave this as the reason why drama theory cannot be used explicitly for interactions within the organisation, only for interactions with external parties, as in the above example. Internally, its use must be implicit, or at least not officially mentioned. A number of examples of explicit (albeit unofficial) analysis of internal interactions may be found on the drama-theoretic website Dilemmas Galore (www.dilemmasgalore.com): see the Business Strategy forum. For example, one forum member initiated a discussion thread that developed into a 'live' account of how drama-theoretic analysis was helping a sales manager to give effective leadership to an underperforming and discontented sales team. It described, stage by stage, how the manager built a CC model prior to each new development in the situation and updated this model after interacting with her subordinates. The account illustrates the many benefits that come from a clear view and sound explanation of the emotional complexities of one's interactions with others. A particular benefit is a much healthier attitude – a movement 'from bitterness and resentment to self-awareness and self-confidence'.

But, as said, it is impossible for such analysis to be explicit and official. In the next section we discuss our proposal for getting around this: we use CC modelling to construct a fictionalised version of the organisation within which people can play out their own and each others' roles, thus improving mutual understanding, learning and the effective handling of relationships.

Let us meanwhile sum up this section as follows. Five definitions of strategy apply at all levels in an organisation. At every level, patterns are observed, needs are felt to change perspectives, positions are taken, plans are made to change others' positions and ploys are adopted. In other words, each internal party has criticisms, from within its own view, of the perspectives of superiors, subordinates and colleagues. The dynamics of organisational strategy formation consist of their acting upon these criticisms. There is a need to orchestrate and conduct the resulting process of drama-theoretic change. That is what a multi-level system for conducting external relationships is for.

IMMERSIVE DRAMA

Managing change within and across organisations is a preoccupation of today's leaders, especially in the public service. Not only must they garner and mobilise resources, they must also gain the commitment and support of diverse stakeholders.

One of us came across a typical example in a Community Safety Partnership (CSP). Such partnerships were established as a result of a statutory duty placed upon local authorities and the police to work with named 'cooperating bodies' (e.g.

the Probation Service, Health Trusts) and 'participating' groups (e.g. the voluntary sector, Chambers of Commerce) in locally based multi-agency teams to tackle crime in a community context. However CSPs, like other 'imposed' partnerships, have inbuilt biases (e.g. lead bodies seldom successfully power-share) and their cultural diversity presents problems.

One of the most contentious issues in the specific CSP with which we worked was agenda-setting: the lead bodies preferred to set the agenda, drawing in community partners as and when appropriate; the latter sought a jointly defined agenda. A corresponding options board is shown in Figure 3.10.

Under the assumptions made by CSP managers, the lead bodies faced a rejection dilemma (they found it hard credibly to resist adopting a jointly defined agenda, which they preferred to collapse of the partnership), while the community partners faced rejection, threat and trust dilemmas (respectively: they also would prefer to sacrifice their role in agenda-setting than lose the partnership; their threat to exit the CSP was suspected as a bluff; and, they could not trust the lead bodies not to renege on an agenda-sharing deal).

Now in this instance, as often in such community-based partnerships, the community partners had not recognised the real power they possessed in their threat of exit. In many such situations it is a mandatory requirement that such bodies be engaged in the process, making this sanction a powerful weapon. Reflecting on the model, the CSP managers realised that if the community partners became more aware of this power that they unknowingly possessed then the interaction would be transformed. In drama-theoretic terms, they would be inspired to eliminate their rejection and threat dilemmas (i.e. realizing the power conferred by their ability to exit, they would prefer to do so rather than submit to agendas defined for them). The lead bodies would then face a persuasion dilemma (if they insisted on defining the agenda alone, they would not be able to encourage the community partners to stay in the partnership) and a threat dilemma (it would therefore become incredible that they would so insist). This knowledge became a potent tool for the managers to put pressure on the lead bodies to rebalance the CSP.

Managing such relationships between partners in today's networks and alliances is a key aspect of strategy. However, many managers have little training for such

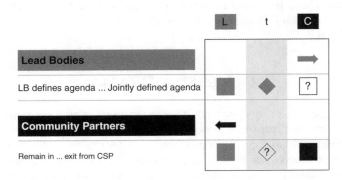

Figure 3.10. Interactions in a Community Safety Partnership

situations and too few 'safe' opportunities to acquire the necessary experience. Explicit use of drama theory by one side carried, as usual, the danger that it might arouse suspicion and antagonism from the other. With this in mind, drama-theoretic analysis was used to help design role-play-based training simulations for executives, specifically tailored to inter-organisational working. The CSP study above, for example, was used to shape an extended exercise on public sector partnerships undertaken by students on the Masters in Public Administration programme at the University of Warwick. The 20 or so students in the class were divided into groups of 4/5 people, each taking on the role of one of the 'characters' (e.g. police force, local authority, council for voluntary services, etc.) in a CSP based in a fictitious local community. Each group was supplied with a short briefing on its role, comprising:

- Its character's background, values and aspirations.
- How its character sees other characters.
- What 'bones of contention' exist involving it and other characters; and what positions are held and sanctions available.

The task in the simulation was to shape a collective response to an imagined government review of CSPs, which required them to put forward clear and comprehensive proposals for the evaluation of their achievements. Role-players in such 'immersive dramas' are entirely free to decide with whom they meet and talk and how they progress the shared task – but must do so 'authentically'. In other words, they should no more make frivolous policy choices or arbitrary changes of position than they would in reality. A redefinition of the interaction such as is required to eliminate dilemmas – e.g. changing one's position, introducing new options (for oneself or another) or changing preferences (one's own or another's) – must be made credible by advancing relevant evidence and presenting it in an emotionally consistent way (e.g. with goodwill to underpin a conciliatory change).

CC modelling is fundamental to the detailed design of such exercises, as it is used to embed specific dilemmas in the relationships between role-players. This is done by basing briefing materials upon options board models, in turn based upon analysis of relevant 'live' interactions. Exercises are thereby created that present specific challenges to those taking part, and so can deliver carefully tailored personal development experiences. A further illustration of the creation of an immersive drama is given in Chapter 14, where the earlier stages of 'backroom' analysis are presented in more detail.

An example drawn from consultancy rather than education is provided by a major study (Bryant & Darwin, 2004) that one of us undertook with a colleague for the UK Department of Health. The Department was keen to understand the tensions that might arise between agencies working within a new framework for the delivery of primary health care. Basing our simulation on an imagined community and populating it with characters such as GPs, acute hospitals, social service workers, pharmacists and so on, we created a role-play that was used to safely examine the framework for possible 'hot' points. This half-day simulation, the creation of which had involved a concentrated, month-long programme of interviews and discussions with health service managers, provided useful insights into the difficulties that might be faced in the new system.

How effective was it in forming a collaborative strategy? The collective response of the role-players did comprise an emergent collaboration between elements of the primary care delivery system. However, a familiar problem loomed. The lessons learned by participants, when taken back to their own internal group, were bound to prompt dissent and divisions within the organisation – the familiar 'ghosts at a negotiation' that present a 're-entry' problem for delegates going back to their constituencies.

Clearly, it is insufficient merely to involve staff in a single 'away-day' exercise. In order to build effective collaboration between organisations, it is necessary to create an ongoing, all-embracing role-playing system – a 'mirror' into which people in each organisation can enter to work out their problems in fictional mode. The time invested will be saved many times over through improved cooperation. We discuss such a system in the next section.

A FICTIONALISED VERSION OF THE MULTI-LEVEL CC SYSTEM

To overcome the problem of linked confrontations and permit the resolution of one confrontation realistically to impact upon others, we propose creating a multi-level, cross-issue 'confrontation/collaboration database' for an organisation or web of organisations – a network of the interactions, represented at any one moment by linked options boards, in which the organisation, its members, its partners and its context are engaged. These boards would be linked hierarchically and non-hierarchically, so that choices made in one would constrain or enable choices in others. Everything in the database would be fictionalised, and the whole used for role-playing. The seemingly magical effect of fictionalisation – even transparent fictionalisation – is to defuse the confrontational effect of drama-theoretic analysis. Analysis no longer sends a confrontational message.

Consider doing this in the case of the airline discussed earlier. The need there was for sales staff to act in a manner consistent with their newly shaped alliance. Our proposed database would contain interactions (among others) over:

- Merging functions between airlines ('being a good partner').
- Customer service delivery by each airline ('putting the customer first').
- Incentivising sales people ('a motivated sales force').

An options board for the service delivery interaction would concern cooperation between departments to achieve the best possible customer experience. One issue might be a difference of view between the sales function, requiring a new IT support system to operate effectively in the alliance market, and an intransigent IT function unwilling to accommodate such needs in the aftermath of a recent major rethink of corporate information systems – all in the context of a wider interaction between alliance partner airlines keen to demonstrate to each other how seriously they have taken on board the primacy of cooperative working. The sales vs. IT conflict may itself provide the environment within which sales force team leaders are seeking greater autonomy for their staff, but are hampered by the lack of reliable data from the IT system on which to base bonus and incentive schemes. Clearly these three levels of interaction inter-relate – but there is necessarily no explicit link-up between the confrontations and collaborations that are going on, since to model these is to make them more confrontational.

Not so if the parties role-play themselves and each other in a fictionalised (but otherwise identical) version of reality that lets them vent their spleen or experiment with cooperation – and afterwards learn from the experience by analysing it. Our proposed system is shown schematically in Figure 3.11. Options boards representing what is going on at each level would be developed in confidential sessions with relevant staff. As situations are reframed, tackled and resolved in the fictional system, so the corresponding boards would be updated and made available both to those for whom the changes provide a strategic context (subordinate levels) and those that provide the context for them, who need this information for their own interactions. In addition to being able to access options boards for the own-level confrontations in which they are involved, individuals would be able to access those delegated to them in their superior's mission.

This, in short, is the recursive process modelled in Figure 3.7, with each level solving strategic challenges at its own level and delegating to autonomous lower levels the task of achieving implied strategic objectives at their levels. The process is also two-way, with outcomes of lower-level confrontations constantly fed back to the managers with ultimate authority and responsibility.

What, then, is the difference between the fictionalised system and the real-world one modelled in Figure 3.7? Simply that in the real-world system, all parties belonging to the organisation that operates the system are modelled as agents of one party – the organisation itself. They take a single, unified position and never have differing preferences. This is achieved by ironing out differences prior to input into the model, using management tools that, in accordance with standard system-theoretic and decision-theoretic paradigms, overcome differences by assuming collaboration. Differing positions and explicit lack of trust appear only in models of relations with external parties.

In contrast, the fictionalised model used for role-playing represents internal differences explicitly and dramatically in order to provide briefings to role-players and to structure the simulation – as well as to help role-players analyse their own behaviour after each role-playing session. This enables explicit (albeit fictional) awareness of differences and how to handle them. Importantly, however, both the role-playing itself and the analysis that follows make participants aware of the danger of making basic differences explicit in real life. This, of course, parallels and reinforces what we all learn from processes of socialisation in our personal lives.

External interactions are modelled the same way in both systems. The fictionalised system, however, allows our people to role-play outsiders and learn from the experience of doing so, leading to more effective handling of customers, suppliers, regulators and other external parties.

To take a different example, consider briefly the UW case of Chapter 1. Warwick University has long-term strategic paths (e.g. growth through business diversification), medium-term developments (e.g. the evolution of the Warwick MBA) and short-term changes (e.g. managing conference activities), each involving the cycle of rehearsal, implementation, managing and learning, and each embedded within

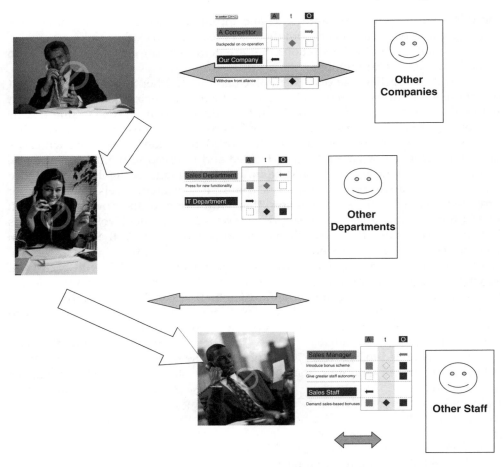

Figure 3.11. A Fictionalised Enterprise Confrontation/Collaboration System Photos: Photo Disc, Inc.

processes at the next higher level. We can imagine the improvement in strategic coherence that would be brought about by an externally orientated, real-world system like that in Figure 3.7. Indirectly, this would also improve internal coherence by focusing people's attention on common external friends or foes; but this effect is indirect.

Other tools discussed in this book, based on the assumption of collaboration, also tackle internal coherence by turning a Nelsonian blind eye to basic internal differences arising from differing interests, values, objectives and attitudes, rather than merely from different information. In this section we have shown how these internal differences can be tackled explicitly within a fictionalised version of the organisation, used for training. In general, the drama-theoretic tools outlined in this chapter may be used consciously or unconsciously, explicitly or implicitly. We assert, however, that they directly tackle obstacles to coherence by their effect in 'changing hearts and minds'.

CC MODELLING WITHIN THE STRATEGIC DEVELOPMENT PROCESS

As this chapter has demonstrated, CC modelling provides a language for exploring and mapping out a broad strategic direction for an organisation. This is done by using explicit, bespoke models to represent what is and what might be going on in an organisation's interactions with others – interactions defined at any level. Alternative futures are sketched out (the columns in an options board) and the pressures that each presents to the parties involved are made clear. This provides strategic guidance. However, it has also been shown how CC modelling is used by organisations literally to 'rehearse strategy' and provide individuals with relevant training through role-play-based simulations.

How does this fit into the strategic development process used in this book? It is clear that CC modelling can contribute in several areas, depending on how it is applied. However, the prime emphasis in this chapter has been upon the contribution that it can make in building consistency in strategy across an organisation or between collaborating organisations. In this sense it supports **'setting strategic direction and goals'** as highlighted in Figure 3.12.

CC models also summarise ongoing interactions (**'current performance'** in the sense that the quality of relationships is performance) and so create a **'model of the organisation'** in its 'political' environment. By shaping **'learning from virtual and current performance'**, they help in **'setting strategic direction and goals'**. Usually

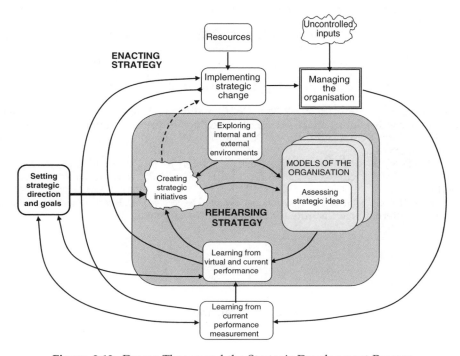

Figure 3.12. Drama Theory and the Strategic Development Process

the models challenge thinking and so lead to **'creating strategic initiatives'**. The models are then used to test and refine these initiatives. As mentioned earlier, the rehearsal 'cycle' may itself be played out by a management team through formal role-play based upon CC modelling. However, the treatment here has focused upon how the creation of coherence of strategy in an enterprise may be achieved in principle and in practice.

REFERENCES

Bryant, J. (2003) *The Six Dilemmas of Collaboration: Inter-organisational relationships as drama.* John Wiley & Sons: Chichester.

Bryant, J.W. & Darwin, J. (2004) 'Exploring inter-organisational relationships in the health service: an immersive drama approach', *European Journal of Operational Research*, **152**, 655–666.

Bush, W. (1991) Speech to congress, March 6th. Extracts at www.al-bab.com/arab/docs/pal/pal10.htm.

Eden, C. & Ackermann, F. (1998) *Making Strategy: The journey of strategic management.* Sage: London.

Fisher, R. & Ury, W. (1981) *Getting To Yes: Negotiating Agreement Without Giving In.* Hutchinson: London.

Howard, N. (1994) 'Drama theory and its relationship to game theory', *Group Decision and Negotiation*, **3**, 187–206 and 207–253.

Howard, N. (1999) *Confrontation Analysis: How to Win Operations Other than War.* CCRP, Department of Defense: Washington, DC.

Howard, N. & Murray-Jones, P. (2001) 'Co-ordinated positions in a drama-theoretic confrontation: mathematical foundations for a PO decision support system', CCRTS Symposium, 2001; available from www.dodccrp.org.

Johnson, G., Scholes, K. & Whittington, R. (2005) *Exploring Corporate Strategy: Text and cases* (7th edn). Prentice-Hall: London.

Mason, R. & Mitroff, I.I. (1981) *Challenging Strategic Planning Assumptions.* John Wiley & Sons: New York.

Minzberg, H. (1987) 'The strategy concept 1: five Ps for strategy', *California Management Review*, **30**(1), 11–24.

Murray-Jones, P. & Howard, N. (1999) 'Confrontation analysis: a command and control system for conflicts other than war'. In: Proceedings of Command and Control Research and Technology Symposium. CCRP Publications: Washington, DC. Downloadable from www.dodccrp.org.

Phillips, L. (1984) 'A theory of requisite decision models', *Acta Psychologica*, **56**, 29–48.

Smith, R. (2005) *The Utility of Force: The Art of War in the Modern World.* Allen Lane: London.

World Bank (1992) *Business Strategy for Sustainable Development: Leadership and accountability for the 90s.* International Institute for Sustainable Development.

Chapter 4

Problem Structuring and the Building and Negotiation of Strategic Agendas

Alberto Franco, Jim Bryant and Giles Hindle

INTRODUCTION

Why do organisations perceive some issues as strategic and not others? What is the process by which issues reach an organisation's strategic agenda, and how can such a process be effectively supported? The purpose of this chapter is to address these questions by focusing on the building and negotiation of strategic agendas as a means to understand how organisations determine when, why and how to respond to or anticipate changes in their internal and external environments.

The chapter will focus on the early stages of the strategic development process, when strategic issues are first paid attention to and debated by managers. It will pay particular attention to the problem-structuring processes that shape the set of issues which top management perceives as strategic, and review a number of modelling approaches that can effectively support such processes. Such modelling approaches, also known as problem-structuring methods (Rosenhead & Mingers, 2001), play a significant role in the 'creating strategic initiatives' element of the strategic development process discussed in Chapter 1. It is important to note, however, that problem structuring and strategic agenda building and negotiation are in practice a significant part of everyday organisational life and thus present throughout the activities constituting the strategic development process model advocated in this book.

STRATEGIC AGENDA BUILDING IN ORGANISATIONS

All organisations, at any point in time, have a strategic issue agenda. Dutton (1997) defines a strategic issue agenda as the set of issues that demands top management's attention. Issues that are part of the strategic issue agenda include those events, developments or trends that are perceived by decision-makers to have the potential to affect organisational performance (Ansoff, 1980) – e.g. the advent of new technological developments, gaps in organisational performance, changes in an industry's regulatory frameworks, etc. The exact form and content of issues vary across organisations in terms of size, variety or range and turnover rate, depending on an organisation's carrying capacity for dealing with them (Dutton, 1997; Dutton & Duncan, 1987a; Hilgartner & Bosk, 1988).

The notion of strategic agendas assumes that attention is a limited and scarce organisational resource (March & Shapira, 1982). It involves the investment of an organisation's information processing capacity to an issue (Dutton, 1988), which is allocated through either formal or informal means. Examples of the former are the formation of a management team organised around the issue, or the incorporation of the issue as part of the formal organisational planning system cycle; informal means may include, for example, the existence of issue-based conversations or the collection of issue-related information (Dutton, 1997).

From an organisational point of view, the building of strategic issue agendas is an important mechanism by which issues emanating from the organisation's internal and external environments activate and direct top management's attention, beginning the strategic development process (see Chapter 1). As such, strategic agenda building can be seen as the means by which organisations adapt to internally or externally induced changes (Dutton, 1997). In addition, it has been argued that the processes of strategic agenda building are subject to managers' concerns and reactions to the meaning implied by their affiliation with an issue before, during and after it has been placed on the strategic agenda (Dutton & Duncan, 1987b). Therefore, strategic agenda building is also significant from an individual perspective, because it is a process by which organisational actors can acquire and build their sense of who they are and what they stand for (Dutton *et al.*, 1997, 2001).

The remainder of this chapter is organised as follows. In the next section we describe our perspective of the strategic agenda-building process, and present a model of strategic agenda building as an issue construction process that takes place within management teams' meetings.[1] The model builds upon a social constructionist perspective (Berger & Luckmann, 1966), and it is intended to serve the function of deriving a clear role for the type of analytical assistance that this book is concerned with. Next we present a family of problem-structuring methods as a particular form of assistance which can be available to support the strategic agenda-building and negotiation process. We conclude this chapter by discussing some of the modelling and process skills required to deploy these methods in practice.

STRATEGIC AGENDA BUILDING AS AN ISSUE CONSTRUCTION PROCESS

We subscribe to the view of organisations as 'systems of distributed management attention' (Ocasio, 1997). Within this view, an organisation is seen as a pluralistic marketplace of issues where motivated managers build strategic agendas through issue-selling or coalition-mobilising processes (Dutton & Ashford, 1993; Dutton *et al.*, 1997, 2001). Within such processes, issues are neither objectively strategic nor pre-packaged. Rather, they are open to interpretation, ambiguous and contested, and

---

[1] Strategic agenda building is not confined to meetings and can certainly take place within less formal settings. Nevertheless, we narrow our focus to such a setting because it represents the typical forum where strategic issues are appreciated and debated in organisations.

will only reach the strategic agenda when decision-makers see them as important, legitimate and feasible to resolve (Dutton, 1997). Furthermore, strategic issues are defined through a social interaction process which creates meaning for them (Berger & Luckmann, 1966; Dutton & Duncan, 1987a; Dutton, Fahey & Narayanan, 1983; Eden & Ackermann, 1998; Eden *et al.*, 1981), and the way these meanings are interpreted depends on the decision-makers' personal and organisational frames of reference (Shrivastava & Schneider, 1984; Thomas & McDaniel, 1990; Thomas, Shankster & Mathieu, 1994).

Within the context of creating strategic agendas in the boardroom, we can conceptualise such processes as involving two main activities: structuring the issue and making sense of the issue. *Structuring* is the process by which decision-makers explicitly articulate a framework of the various factors that they perceive to be implicated in the issue and how they inter-relate. This activity can be carried out in a more or less detailed and sophisticated fashion, but it is likely to include some or all of the following: labelling of issues into categories such as threats or opportunities, the definition of an issue's causality, the identification of interdependencies, the articulation of different issue attributes such as novelty, urgency and feasibility, and the development of issue-related commitments (Dutton, 1993; Dutton & Duncan, 1987a; Jackson & Dutton, 1988; Rochefort & Cobb, 1994; Smith, 1994). *Sense-making* is fundamentally an individual mental activity which involves the interpretation and understanding of what this articulated framework, and the actions that seem to be suggested by it, mean for an individual in relation to the world in which he/she acts (Eden, 1982, 1986; Milliken, 1990; Thomas & McDaniel, 1990; Thomas, Clark & Gioia, 1993; Weick, 1995).

The structuring and sense-making activities operate cyclically: as the problem is being structured, decision-makers try to make sense of the issue and may change their understanding of it; and as changed understanding is achieved by decision-makers, they may engage in further issue structuring. Throughout this cycle of structuring and sense-making, the opportunity for negotiation with regards to the strategic issue definition will be created (Eden, 1982, 1986). The effectiveness of managers in negotiating the entrance of a particular issue in top management's strategic agenda will have a significant effect on the issue-related commitments that are likely to be achieved during the agenda-building process.

Seeing strategic agenda building as an issue construction process assumes that agenda building is significantly shaped by both the subjective interpretation and the intentions of organisational actors (Eden, 1992b; Pitt *et al.*, 1997). Furthermore, success in the building of strategic agendas will depend on managers actively participating in the negotiation and the management of meanings about the issues (Eden, 1992b). This implies that processes of psychological and social negotiation will be central to the building of strategic agendas by decision-makers (Eden, 1992b; Eden & Ackermann, 1998).

The way in which strategic issues are structured and defined has important implications for the strategic development process as a whole; for it limits the potential nature and outcome of strategic decision-making and plays an important role in determining who participates in the strategic development process. For example, the successful placement of a particular issue on the strategic agenda may lead managers to engage in coalition mobilising so that certain individuals are included

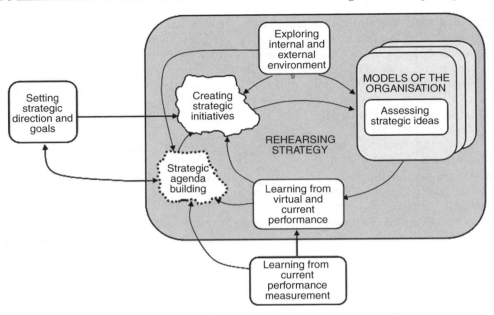

Figure 4.1. Strategic Agenda Building and the Strategic Development Process

or excluded from the strategic development process. The process by which an issue is structured and defined as strategic, therefore, represents a significant mechanism through which managers can influence the strategic development process. This is shown in Figure 4.1, which depicts how strategic agenda building influences specific elements of the strategic development process model proposed in Chapter 1.

If we are to effectively support the strategic development process from its early stages, then there is a need for approaches which can be used to facilitate the building and negotiation of strategic agendas. Some scholars have suggested that the modelling methods available within the management science field can be useful mechanisms in helping managers participating in strategic development activities (e.g. Dyson, 2000; Pidd, 2004). In particular, it has been argued that problem-structuring methods (Rosenhead & Mingers, 2001) can play an important role in negotiating strategic agendas by supporting the structuring and sense-making of issues (Eden, 1992b; Eden & Ackermann, 1998, 2001a). The following sections will first describe problem-structuring methods, and then explore how they can assist the strategic agenda-building process.

THE ROLE OF PROBLEM-STRUCTURING METHODS IN THE CONSTRUCTION AND NEGOTIATION OF STRATEGIC ISSUES

Problem-Structuring Methods (PSMs) are a family of participatory and interactive methods developed within the discipline of Management Science/Operational

Research (MS/OR), whose purpose is to assist management teams gain a better understanding of organisational issues characterised by high levels of complexity, uncertainty and conflict. This is achieved through the explorations of different perceptions, using modelling and facilitation to support social and psychological negotiation, with a view to generating consensus on issue structure and defini- tion, and usually, on initial commitments to consequential action (Rosenhead, 1996; Rosenhead & Mingers, 2001).

The key word in PSMs is 'structuring'. Within the PSM field, structuring is used in the sense of identifying concepts and activities that are relevant to the problem situation, of clarifying the relationships between them and of focusing on key areas and excluding others, at least temporarily. (Some PSMs also generate and evaluate alternative options but this will not be our focus here.) It can be observed that this notion of structuring is very similar to our definition of the strategic issue-structuring activity elaborated in the previous section in its emphasis on generating changed understandings of the issue by and between participants, so that they can reach agreement both on the strategic nature of the issue and on commitments which will address it.

Table 4.1 gives an overview of four PSMs designed to support the structuring and negotiation of strategic issues: Strategic Options Development and Analysis (Eden, 1992b); Soft Systems Methodology (Checkland, 1981; Checkland & Scholes, 1990); Strategic Choice Approach (Friend & Hickling, 2005); and Drama Theory (Bennett, Bryant & Howard, 2001). The list is not exhaustive, and the reader is referred to Rosenhead and Mingers (2001) for a more detailed presentation of these and other methods. Before we clarify the potential role that PSMs may play in the analysis of strategic issues and the formation of strategic agendas, a more detailed characterisation of the processes of applying PSMs, their available technology and their intended products is needed. These characteristics are summarised in Table 4.2.

The orientation of PSMs is to aid management teams in agreeing the nature of the complex, strategic issues they face so that a strategic agenda can be jointly built and a cycle of the strategic development process can be initiated. This focus on teams is because, in changing internal and external environments, there is a plurality of organisational actors with different interests who will need to engage in formal agenda building if the issues they perceive as strategic are to be paid attention to by top management.

Consequently, when individuals participate in a PSM process, they engage in strategic conversations (van der Heijden, 1996) to exchange and increase their under- standing of the issues which are being structured (Ford & Ford, 1995; Franco, 2006). The PSM process is therefore claimed to be *participative* in the sense that participants are able to jointly construct the issue, make sense of it, arrive at a shared issue defi- nition and develop a portfolio of options relevant to the issue so defined (Rosenhead & Mingers, 2001). In addition, this participatory process is typically *facilitated* by an individual or a team (Ackermann, 1996; Phillips & Phillips, 1993).

The PSM process is also *interactive* (Rosenhead, 1996; Rosenhead & Mingers, 2001), both in the sense that it requires interaction between participants, and in the sense that they interact with the analysis. This latter interaction reshapes the analysis, and the analysis reshapes the discussion. The PSM process is also thought to be *iterative* (Rosenhead, 1996; Rosenhead & Mingers, 2001), because the process is repeated until

Table 4.1. Problem-Structuring Methods

Name	Focus	Purpose	Modelling
Strategic Options Development and Analysis (SODA)	Representation of individuals' perceptions of a situation in their own language.	Develop shared understanding of the problem situation leading to commitment to consequential actions.	Psychological constructs and their inter-relations captured and analysed through cognitive/cause mapping.
Soft Systems Methodology (SSM)	Exploration of different world views relevant to a situation and contrast their implications in a process of debate.	Learn about and improve a problematic situation by gaining agreement on feasible and desirable changes.	Models of 'ideal' human activity systems developed through the use of rich pictures, root definitions and systems models.
Strategic Choice Approach (SCA)	Recognition of key uncertainties influencing a set of interconnected choices, and the management of commitments.	Make incremental progress by committing to a set of priority decisions, explorations and contingency plans.	Decision graphs and option graphs are used to develop a feasible set of interconnected options, which are then evaluated against a set of comparison areas that bring key uncertainties to the surface.
Drama Theory	Representation of a conflictive situation involving different players and their interacting decisions.	Clarify the competitive structure of a situation and identify possibilities for cooperation, and scenarios that will be stable.	A set of players, their options and possible strategies are captured by developing a 'card table' and exploring the stability of solutions by analysing the different potential dilemmas faced by the players.

Source: Based on Rosenhead and Mingers (2001).

the issue or issues are satisfactorily structured so that participants feel sufficiently confident in making commitments.

Built into the different PSMs are features whose purpose is to enable participants to distance themselves from previous positions during the PSM process, effectively providing them with a certain degree of ambiguity or 'equivocality' regarding their own positions (Eden, 1992a; Eden & Ackermann, 1998, 2004). This, it is argued, allows participants to change their positions in response to what they have learned about the issue without destroying the social order in the management team (Eden, 1992a). Changing positions imply individuals 'changing their minds', i.e. changed beliefs, changed values and changes in the salience of particular issues or values (Eden, 1986). The consequence of this *adaptability* is that it becomes easier for participants to reconcile the position they eventually take both with principles and with past words and actions during the strategic agenda building process.

Most PSMs are organised into stages or modes and thus are *phased*. This 'phasedness' makes it possible for the users of the method to conclude without passing through all the modes that compose it, and still have a visible product which can be of use to them. Furthermore, the phases of the different PSMs do not have to be followed in a linear sequence. Instead, PSMs tend to operate in a *non-linear* fashion which makes it possible for the participants to cycle between the phases. As Eden (1986, 1992a) argues, the characteristic non-linearity of the PSM process is a direct consequence of acknowledging that participants in a group decision-making process will consider the practicality of possible actions at the same time as the problem is formulated.

Thus far we have looked at the characteristics of the PSM process. As we have seen, PSMs offer flexibility in their application and can be responsive to group dynamics and/or the particularities of the issues at hand (Rosenhead, 1996; Rosenhead & Mingers, 2001). In practice, this flexibility has allowed the possibility of their combined use, as well as of their use in combination with other strategic modelling methods such as visioning (Chapter 2), scenario planning (Chapter 9), system dynamics (Chapter 7) and decision and risk analysis (Chapter 10).

The technology available with PSMs is *model-based*. Modelling is the defining characteristic of these methods which gives them their unambiguous management science identity. As Eden (1986, 1988) argues, PSM models provide actors with a 'transitional object' (De Geus, 1988), which can be used to increase their multiple understandings of the issues and negotiate future courses of action.

The type of models built with PSMs are said to be *requisite* (Phillips, 1984). This means that they contain sufficient knowledge and information to help participants find a way forward. Furthermore, PSM models are expressed in visual, *diagrammatical form* and mostly use participants' own *language* rather than mathematics or quantitative data to represent the problem. PSM proponents argue that only language has the degree of richness and transparency suitable for the modelling of complex problems (Checkland, 1981; Eden, Jones & Sims, 1983; Rosenhead, 1996; Rosenhead & Mingers, 2001). These models are thus characterised by *reduced quantitative data requirements*.

It has been claimed that diagrammatical methods are of particular value in representing structural, cognitive and behavioural complexity (Eden & Ackermann, 2004; Rosenhead, 1996; Rosenhead & Mingers, 2001). In PSM models there is supposed to be nothing hidden, which makes them *transparent* (i.e. easy to understand) and *accessible* (i.e. simple to use).

Indeed, these attributes of transparency and accessibility have made it possible for some PSM scholars to promote PSMs as *low-technology* approaches (e.g. Friend & Hickling, 2005). This characteristic is aptly expressed in the settings and tools used for building PSM models: a room spacious enough for participants to move around freely and with movable chairs laid out in a horseshoe fashion; large sheets of paper attached around the walls of the room; a simple, non-permanent means of sticking papers to these walls; and a good supply of marker pens with contrasting colours are all that is usually needed for a PSM modelling session (Eden, 1990; Friend & Hickling, 1997; Hickling, 1990; Huxham, 1990). This suggests that PSM modelling is technically a relatively unsophisticated activity conducted in a workshop format, and one which does not necessarily require software to support it (Ackermann & Eden, 1994). Some PSMs do, however, use software to support their modelling processes (Ackermann, 1990; Ackermann & Eden, 1994, 2001; Eden, 1992a; Eden & Radford, 1990; Phillips, 1989).

Models in PSMs are used to graphically represent, among other things, relationships between concepts, activities or stakeholders, relationships of similarity or influence, and relationships between options. Especially significant is the modelling of *cause and effect relationships* through which the different elements that make up the issues are identified. By modelling cause and effect relationships, PSM models are thought to help participants to 'look beneath the surface' to establish issue structure.

Several products have been claimed to be the result of the use by management teams of PSMs processes and technology. Some of these products, shown in Table 4.2, are tangible outcomes of the PSM process, whilst others will be less visible but valuable in their own right (Friend & Hickling, 2005).

The most visible PSM product is obviously the model built during the PSM process and which contains the *issue structure*. On the other hand, the PSM model is thought to facilitate the achievement of a number of invisible products. First, it is argued that by allowing the mutual exploration of the structure of the issue as portrayed by the model, PSMs enable the *accommodation of multiple and differing positions* (Checkland, 1981, 1999). The argument is based on the notion that issues characterised by complexity, uncertainty and conflict will commonly require participants to adjust their positions and/or expectations to take into consideration the possible objectives and strategies of others (Rosenhead, 1996; Rosenhead & Mingers, 2001). Accommodations between actors may also require issue selling or coalition forming (Dutton & Ashford, 1993; Dutton *et al.*, 2001; Eden, 1986, 1996; Eden & Ackerman, 2001b), which may produce a *shift in power relations* during the PSM process (Eden, 1992a).

Second, the analysis of cause and effect relationships embedded in the PSM model is thought to give participants an *increased understanding* of the issues, of organisational processes and culture, and of others' beliefs and values. Such increased understanding is taken to be conducive to *learning* (Checkland, 1981, 1999; Eden & Ackermann, 1998; Friend & Hickling, 1997). Third, it is argued that actors' active participation in the analysis and modelling process produces strong *ownership* of the strategic agenda, and of the actions to be taken, as well as acceptance of respon-

Table 4.2. PSM Process, Technology and Products

Process
Group-based
Facilitated
Participative
Interactive
Iterative
Adaptable
Phased
Non-linear
Combinable with other modelling approaches
Technology
Model-based
Requisite
Diagrammatic/language-based
Reduced quantitative data requirements
Transparent/accessible
Low technology
Products
Issue structure
Increased understanding
Accommodations of multiple positions and in power relations
Ownership of strategic agenda and of consequence of planned actions
Partial commitments
Learning

Source: Based on Rosenhead and Mingers (2001).

sibility for the consequences of the actions taken (Rosenhead, 1996; Rosenhead & Mingers, 2001).

What have been described in the preceding sections are the typical characteristics of the family of PSMs as a whole, though individual methods may vary with respect to these in certain respects. In the following section, we illustrate their potential by presenting three vignettes describing three applications of PSMs to support a management team engaged in the structuring and negotiation of strategic issues supported by PSMs.

PROBLEM STRUCTURING AND STRATEGIC ISSUE BUILDING AND NEGOTIATION IN PRACTICE

Vignette 1: The Alliance Challenge Case

Entering a business alliance is a major strategic decision for any organisation, but is all the more challenging when the partner organisations are international competitors. This was the case for the airline, referred to here as Aerfly, that forms the subject of the present vignette. One of the authors with a colleague was called upon by Aerfly's worldwide sales function to review issues emerging from the new dynamics and inter-relationships created by Aerfly's membership of a major airline alliance. This recent development had added many fresh and some rather unexpected issues to the strategic agenda and the General Manager (Sales) was looking for ways of best achieving the benefits of collaboration.

Our initial meeting with the client revealed a large number of aspects of alliance working with implications for the sales function. However, the major focus identified could be summed up in the question, 'How to sell together?' Collaboration meant that organisations having different cultures, structures and perceived markets were seeking to work together in attracting and selling to customers. Furthermore, sales staff incentive structures and product pricing were predicated upon a competitive rather than a cooperative business model so that local tensions were created. The task was seen in part as educational. This involved helping sales staff at all levels to keep the alliance 'front of mind', while showing them how they could leverage the framework to drive incremental revenue. However, there was also a motivational aspect: encouraging staff loyalty to shift from Aerfly products alone to the wider portfolio offered by the alliance.

The top managers of the sales function were clear that they sought a fresh look at the issues and solutions. They wanted to involve a group of senior managers in an exploration for potential strategies and in shaping up a project plan. It was decided that involving them in a 1-day workshop to build a strategic agenda offered several benefits: notably, it would help to build commitment to initiating a programme of planned change to exploit the opportunities of an alliance environment.

The workshop structure comprised three main elements. In the first part, the participants would begin working together on shared issues (moving beyond 'motherhood'), identifying the key players and establishing the leverage that they possessed. The second stage would be to surface future challenges, especially for Aerfly, in the alliance context and to develop ways of handling these. The final part of the day would be devoted to action planning, working towards the creation of a commitment package that would help the group to deliver necessary change and manage the transition. Overall then the day would contribute to Aerfly's strategic agenda by providing thinking space within which the participants could identify, review, explore and develop agenda items to be injected into the ongoing strategy development process for the sales function.

We were fortunate that the workshop participants – about a dozen in all – brought into the room a remarkable range of experience and perspectives. Most of them had made their careers in the airline industry, but their service with Aerfly ranged from a few months to two decades: this meant that 'critical outsider' views were present to disrupt any parochial complacency. Furthermore, the participants were functionally and culturally diverse, between them having worked in most aspects of sales and marketing and having often done so in partner or competitor airlines in other countries. For all of them the challenges of the alliance agenda were central to their own present responsibilities, though the latter varied from a focus on IT systems to revenue management and sales force leadership.

Our starting point, following introductory remarks, was to examine how the 'new world' of partnership was populated: specifically, we identified stakeholders around the notion of 'leveraging the alliance environment'. We placed clear emphasis upon the exploitation of alliance working through sales force activities for the benefit of Aerfly, their customers and themselves as our clients quite rightly demanded focused outputs: this was not an academic exercise.

Following a short period of individual brainstorming, a list was built up using a 'round robin' method in plenary mode by inviting participants to contribute parties (sectors, organisations, individuals, etc.) who should be added to a list built up on a flipchart. Subsequently, the items were arranged according to the perceived power and interest of the parties with respect to alliance working. This approach to stakeholder management was described earlier (Chapter 3) in this book. It produced a shared appreciation of 'who matters' and the power–interest (P–I) plot (see the anonymised version in Figure 4.2) generated a good deal of discussion and some mild surprises for a number of the workshop attendees: for example, the signif-icance of corporate customers, the roles of three key individuals and the essential contribution of the Human Resources department were all recognised. This decep-tively simple process was a vital first step in the negotiation of meaning discussed in the first part of this chapter. Although we made use of software for interactive on-screen revision of the P–I grid, this technology was in no way essential.

At this point it would have been possible to embark upon a dynamic analysis of the main interactions between stakeholders, for example using the drama theory framework presented in Chapter 3: indeed such an approach was considered during pre-planning for the workshop. However, our client had expressed a strong wish that the emphasis should be upon the 'how' (rather than the 'what' and 'why') of alliance working and with a view to exploring the necessary sales force behaviours, rather than opening up wider questions about the rationale of the alliance decision, we decided that the workshop should take a different route.

Accordingly, the next stage was to use oval mapping, a technique that forms part of the SODA and JOURNEY-making (Eden & Ackermann, 1998) problem-structuring methodologies (see Table 4.1), to create a jointly owned picture of the beliefs and aspirations of the group. This complemented the broader, contextual view provided by the stakeholder work, by encouraging participants to think about what they wanted to see, and to see changed in the 'brave new world' of alliance working.

The Oval Mapping Technique (OMT) has developed over a period of more than 30 years as a powerful means of enabling groups to surface issues and to represent individual and collective beliefs and assumptions about a shared field of concern. The intention is to create a jointly owned picture of what is going on, with the intention of developing commitment to joint action plans in order to effect change. OMT is a facilitated, workshop-based approach, typically used with groups of up to a dozen members. The usual physical setting is a spacious, uncluttered room, with one unbroken wall that can be used as a workspace to which 'ovals' (ideally custom-made oval Post-Its™ are used) can be affixed. Participants are each given a pack of blank ovals and a marker pen, and are asked to respond initially to a 'trigger question', writing each response as a short phrase (7–10 words). Contribu-tions are not 'answers' to the question, but should exploit in a more general sense the deep knowledge brought into the room by participants and will usually open up fresh uncertainties and questions. Assertions, statements, issues and all other contributions must all be written up, even if first voiced.

As material is generated it is added to the 'dump' on the wall; here it is gently organised spatially by the facilitator, who will be better placed to notice clusters

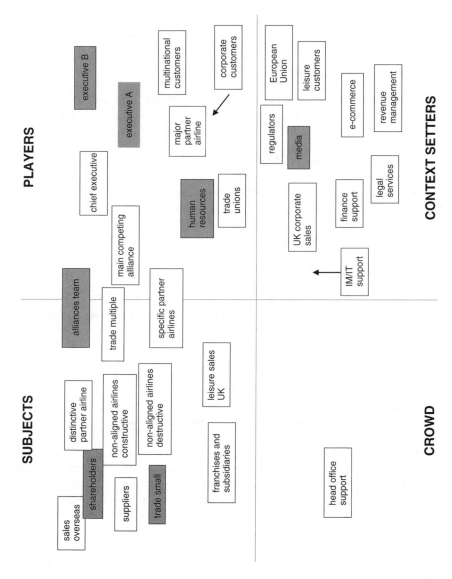

SUBJECTS

sales overseas

shareholders

suppliers

trade small

distinctive partner airline

non-aligned airlines constructive

non-aligned airlines destructive

franchises and subsidiaries

leisure sales UK

PLAYERS

alliances team

trade multiple

main competing alliance

specific partner airlines

chief executive

executive B

executive A

human resources

trade unions

multinational customers

corporate customers

major partner airline

CROWD

head office support

CONTEXT SETTERS

IM/IT support

UK corporate sales

finance support

legal services

regulators

media

European Union

leisure customers

e-commerce

revenue management

Figure 4.2. Power–Interest Stakeholders Grid

Source: Based on Eden and Ackermann (1998).

of ideas or areas of controversy. Participants are forbidden from removing others' contributions, no matter how much they may disagree with them! The facilitator may also prompt the group by pointing out emerging issues, by asking for clarifications or by encouraging fuller participation. The whole process is fast-moving and energetic: breaking up and moving clusters around is normal. 'Piggy-backing' of ideas off others is expected. As the pace slows, the facilitator will encourage 'laddering' of concepts, contributors thereby explaining, using further ovals, how or why they would achieve some of the statements appearing in the 'map'. Normally, with further elaboration and reorganisation of the materials, this will result in a map that includes both strategic ends and means.

The final stage is for the facilitator to work with the group to insert tentative links between areas of the map or between individual items, such links showing relationships – and especially assumed causality. The eventual picture can then be shaped into a wall picture that contains (conventionally at the top) goals and aspirations as well as desired outcomes and means (in the middle) and options, issues and specific actions (conventionally at the bottom): linking arrows tend to point upwards, demonstrating how actions ladder up to goals. Software tools (Decision Explorer™ is the most widely used application) can be employed to help manage and manipulate what is usually a very extensive and rich display. A summary of the OMT process is depicted in Figure 4.3.

---

1. Create a suitable environment for interactive group working. This usually requires obtaining a large, well-lit, level workspace within which (typically a dozen) participants can readily move as well as having good sight of a shared workspace (usually flipcharts on a wall) managed by the facilitator.

2. Explain the aim of the process to participants, explaining that it is a way for them to contribute their ideas, beliefs, views and knowledge to a pool of shared concerns around the subject of the session, and then to examine the implications of these materials for future decisions.

3. Provide each participant with materials for the OMT. At its simplest these would consist of a pad of Post-Its ['ovals'] and a felt-tip pen for each person. Ask them to write their contributions, one to each 'oval' and stick them 'onto the wall'. Statements on the ovals should be brief but self-contained, and ideally have an action orientation (e.g. 'ensure that alliance benefits are Aerfly benefits').

4. Tell participants that they should continue generating material (including 'piggy-backing' on others' ideas) in this manner. Amending others' contributions is not allowed, but developing them (e.g. providing supporting evidence) or making a critique (i.e. advancing opposing views) is permitted.

5. The facilitator gently drives the process by prompting to encourage elaboration of ideas. Once the process is under way the facilitator also begins to organise the material, drawing together tentative clusters and marking up relationships (as lines or arrows) between groups of ovals.

6. Reorganising and inviting additional material often continues for some time (maybe 3–4 hours), the facilitator frequently taking a lead role in this. As the overall picture grows in detail and complexity, specialist software may be introduced to capture and display the whole map for later work.

7. Subsequent work with the oval map produced varies according to the needs of the group. For example, emergent goal systems (organised hierarchies of issues showing how potential actions contribute to desired – or undesired – outcomes) may form the basis for strategic agendas.

Figure 4.3. Oval Mapping Technique (OMT) Process Steps

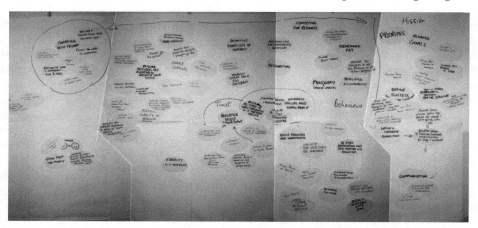

Figure 4.4. The Beginnings of Airfly's Oval Map
Note: The purpose of this figure is not that its content should be readable, but that it should
provide an indication of what an oval map looks like.

We shall now see how this process was particularised for the Aerfly sales team. The trigger question used to establish practical focus here was 'How can we keep the alliance "front of mind" and leverage its potential as a sales tool?' In little over half an hour the group generated close to 100 ideas, each written on an oval-shaped card and organised thematically on a public wall space as shown in Figure 4.4. Some important clusters appeared including, for example, designing recognition/rewards, trust-building, creating transparent customer benefits, evaluating value-added, sharing learning, changing the Aerfly mindset. As tentative links were inserted between the ovals, overall structures also became evident: so the way that behaviours contributed to the corporate mission and were underpinned by mutual understanding and a learning culture was apparent. This stage of the workshop enabled participants to get their gnawing concerns 'onto the wall' and in their own terms, rather than spending time discussing some idealised model of partnership activities.

Conventionally, the ideas in an oval map are prioritised and then understood by disclosing the implicit goal system that informs the prioritisation, with a view to shaping strategy within the bounds of available resources. However here we (and our clients) were keen to gain a firmer grasp of Aerfly's organisational culture, as this understanding seemed to be a prerequisite for developing any programme of change. We made use here of the familiar framework of the 'cultural web' (Johnson, Scholes & Whittington, 2005) and dividing the participants into three subgroups, invited them to create flipcharts that answered questions about Aerfly's stories and myths, rituals and routines, symbols, power structures, control systems and organisational structures. A 'sanitised' version of one of these is shown in Table 4.3.

Subgroup working helped to draw out the diversity of perspectives within the group, and enabled more intensive contribution and sharing. As the groups presented their work the sense emerged of an exhaustingly energetic, competitively macho, moderately arrogant team, suspicious of partner airlines and frustrated by the turgid bureaucracy of the rest of the Aerfly organisation. With a critical eye,

Table 4.3. Cultural Web for Airline Alliance Case

STORIES AND MYTHS	Stories relate to: successes, persistence, thinking outside of the box, bravado, creativity. Story themes: nobody likes us; we're too expensive/too slow to react; morale is always at an all-time low; rivalry between business and leisure. Myths: real salespeople are on the road; 'Nobody works as hard as us'. Hero[in]es: high performers [revenue]/mavericks. Villains: people who stop you selling [e.g. rev mgt]; Richard Branson; senior management. Atmosphere: macho, competitive, jokey/sarcastic.
RITUALS AND ROUTINES	Clinching (embracing the difficult) and renewing deals. Sales force effectiveness studies: sales awards; sales targets/forecasts. Excuse management. Consensus building to create standardisation. 'High flyers'/fast track. Firefighting. Routines: budgets/reports/forward bookings. Liquid team building; entertaining; family trips. Training programmes: producing professionalism and consistency.
SYMBOLS	Acronyms: all internal and inaccessible. Complex reporting systems. Laptops. Company car. Head office. Flashy clothes and suits. Mobile phones. Flashy clothes.
POWER STRUCTURES	Revenue at any cost. Direct and on-line sales – with a passion. Efficiency might mean talking yourself out of a job. Political patronage; kingdoms and empires; power centres. Arrogance; 'my solution is best'. Lobbying. Core beliefs: evangelical view of motivating the sales force and giving them tools and support. Blockages to change: history. History. Mistrust of other airlines: looking at negative aspects of alliance agreement vs. opportunities. The competition is within not outside the alliance!
CONTROL SYSTEMS	Costs and revenue. Reward. Fear culture. Budgets and targets. Failure not punished: generous pay-offs; unclear accountability. Changing measures. Career development. Internal audit.

Table 4.4. Continued

	Peer pressure.
	Headcount resources.
ORGANISATIONAL STRUCTURES	Flexible and flatter structure to encourage cooperation.
	Who 'owns' the revenue → who owns the cost budget.
	Networked hierarchical structures but informal contacts encouraged.
	Constantly changing [both structure and people].
	New managers always restructure.
	Power structures: don't try it in my patch!
OVERALL	Very reactionary.
	No stability.
	Change is possible with leadership from above.

they saw their sales function as having a very reactive, short-termist regime, lacking stability and driven by a (widely disliked) revenue-chasing ethos.

A short period remained before the scheduled lunch break for a review of the morning's achievements. Reviews are important in enabling participants to recognise the 'invisible products' of their work as well as for consolidating agreements. In the present case achieving consensus within the group was not a major concern – it was largely already present – but there had been a real need to share experiences, to escape from routinised and time-pressured rituals and to take a broader look at how value could be created in the alliance context.

The workshop resumed after lunch with some input from ourselves, presenting some lessons from partnership work in other industries and settings. This was something that our client had specifically requested, since there was no desire to 'reinvent the wheel'. Most organisations regard their own problems as unique, and while this is literally true – the whole model-based approach that is advocated in this book is predicated upon the need to create specific models of specific situations – there are nonetheless generic issues (e.g. trust-building, conflicting loyalties, unequal commitments, power imbalances) in working with others that must be successfully managed. We set out for scrutiny some metaphors for partnership (e.g. as marriage, as diplomacy) against which participants could set their experiences. We also summarised some of the main findings from research and practice in the field and led an animated discussion on the implications for Aerfly sales. There was much critical debate about the value of the alliance: did it just represent the 'lowest common denominator'? Would access to alliance networks just make Aerfly better able to compete with its partners? Was the alliance a business proposition or a cultural proposition?

To take these and the material from the morning sessions forward we used a highly foreshortened version of the process used in 'whole systems' events (Weisbord & Janoff, 2000). This is a design that we have used extensively elsewhere and found most effective for enabling a group to reach clear commitments to agreed actions. The overall framework is split into five steps: focus question, present situation, underlying contradictions, strategic directions and systematic actions, as explained next.

The starting point was the focus question 'Looking back from 5 years hence, what would you want to say that the alliance has achieved?' The backward-looking stance frees participants from the inevitable urge to forecast trends and encourages them to think about goals. Once again (since by this time attendees were familiar with the technology) we used ovals to capture people's answers to the trigger question. We then teased out in discussion the underlying contradictions that might prove to be barriers in realising this vision. It became apparent that some arenas of activity would help to resolve these contradictions and release the practical vision and we sketched these out. We next drew explicitly upon two elements from the morning – the stakeholder analysis and the cultural audit – and so working in two subgroups designed some actions that would set Aerfly on the right path. The first group sought ways in which stakeholders could best be managed to achieve the vision; the second group found ways that the culture needed to be altered to attain the desired outcome.

To illustrate the actual outputs this process generated, the 5-year aspirations included:

- Devolved decision-making (within a framework).
- All alliance airlines benefited financially from the relationship.
- Higher service standards (highest common denominator).
- Value and new products for the customer.
- Systems designed for the alliance rather than shoehorned into the alliance.

The output of the two subgroups each produced almost 20 very specific actions, against every one of which one or more of the participants made a personal commitment. To give a flavour of their content, they covered such things as:

- Switch focus towards team targets.
- Ensure the PR front is pushed to get more messages to the media.
- Work with ArcticLine to develop e-commerce.
- Extend smart performance data across the board.
- Indicate alliance implementation plans on key performance indicators.

Direct linkage into the ongoing business development process was thereby supported. Consolidating these action plans and a final period of reflection concluded the workshop. The latter was also an important part of the day, since one of the aims had been to expose the participants to a range of previously unfamiliar tools, techniques and methods that they could use directly for themselves 'back at the office'.

Vignette 2: The Turf Science Ltd Case

Turf Science Ltd (TS) is a UK-based company that produces specialist turf fertiliser for golf courses and football clubs around the world. The company employs 30 people and has a turnover of £5 million. Key activities of the company include securing and maintaining accounts with turf managers, soil testing to determine fertiliser requirements, designing bespoke fertiliser solutions and delivering fertiliser orders around the world.

The following case describes how Soft Systems Methodology (SSM) (Checkland, 1981, 1999) was used during a consultancy project to facilitate strategic agenda building within the company. The project was run over a 2-month period and included three half-day workshops, which were fully documented by the facilitator (one of the authors). The workshops were delivered in a large meeting room with whiteboard and flipcharts.

The first workshop involved a general mapping of the problem situation as a whole. This session involved the senior management team of the company – managing director, sales director, UK sales manager, general administrator and operations manager – and the SSM facilitator. The purpose of the workshop was to enable the senior team to step back from their day-to-day activities, consider the organisation's situation as a whole and identify key strategic issues.

The technique used in the first workshop was rich picturing. A rich picture is a simple cartoon-like representation of the situation as a whole (Checkland & Scholes, 1990). The picture enables participants to capture key features of the situation and express points of view in a relatively relaxed environment. In this particular workshop, the facilitator took the lead in drawing the picture on the whiteboard, whilst the participants contributed with information, explanations and general discussion and opinion. The role of the facilitator was to ask open questions of the participants that would enable a comprehensive picture to be developed and ensure good overall participation within the team.

A draft rich picture was developed after approximately 90 minutes (see Figure 4.5 for the documented version). More importantly, all participants had been given the opportunity to express their points of view without explicit evaluation by the team. Differing points of view were simply recorded on the picture as being a factual part of the problem situation. After a break for coffee, the team was then encouraged to list issues they perceived in the problem situation. This list of issues was recorded on a flipchart and centred on the need to improve the sales system of TS.

By this point in the session participants had a good overall feel for the situation and could appreciate the existence of differing points of view within the team. The issue generation process was therefore synchronously affected by participants' own position in the company and a sense of the overall situation of the company. Hence, for example, whilst the operations manager expressed concerns over the issue of a new contract for the supply of raw materials, he was also seen to express concerns over the recruitment and training of new sales staff.

The workshop was terminated without conclusions or the action planning of subsequent workshops. This was to enable participants to receive documentation on the workshop and allow them (and the facilitator) to reflect on the session. The subsequent documentation included a copy of the rich picture, descriptive text concerning the situation, a comprehensive list of issues and suggestions for further work (suggested by the facilitator, on reflection).

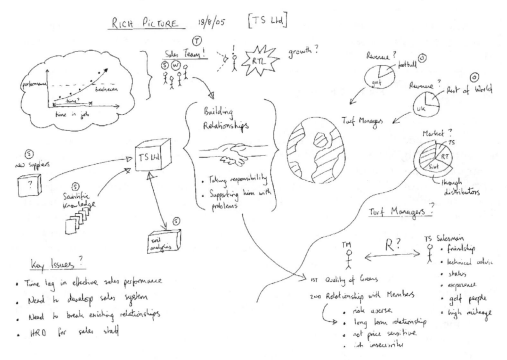

Figure 4.5. Rich Picture of Turf Science's Situation

The key strategic issues identified in the workshop related to factors limiting the growth of the company; in particular, human resource issues relating to the sales team and the design of the sales system itself. Essentially, the company was struggling to recruit sales staff who could match the performance of existing sales staff, and the deployment of human resources in general appeared suboptimal. In order to explore these issues in greater depth, a second workshop was designed to specifically address the sales system of TS.

The second workshop was another half-day session, but split into two subsessions, and involved senior management and sales staff. The first half of the workshop involved another rich picture session specifically addressing the nature of the existing sales approach adopted by TS. The second half of the workshop involved a modelling session inviting the participants to explore the notion of an 'ideal' sales system for TS.

The purpose of the modelling session was to encourage participants to step back from current arrangements for sales within TS and allow new ideas and alternative methods to be surfaced and discussed. The technique in SSM used for this type of 'ideal' modelling is called Human Activity System (HAS) modelling, although it is not normally feasible to make this modelling language fully explicit to participants due to time and capability constraints.

Participants were invited to imagine an ideal sales system – a perfect system that would achieve an agreed set of operational and strategic purposes. It was

> A system to (a) secure new accounts and (b) maintain existing relationships with turf managers by operating a sales system utilising field sales staff $+$ a central support team in order to support the profitable growth of TS.

Figure 4.6. Root Definition of Ideal Sales System

agreed the operational purpose of the ideal sales system was to (a) secure new accounts and (b) maintain profitable relationships with turf managers in specific geographical areas; and the strategic purpose of the ideal sales system was to support the profitable growth of Turf Science Ltd. Once these purposes (expressed in a 'root definition' in SSM terminology – see Figure 4.6) were agreed, the participants were asked to brainstorm activities which such a system would need to perform. As the purpose of the sales system was considered relatively uncontroversial (although the recognition of the dual purposes of securing new accounts and maintaining relationships was regarded as an important development), it was this part of the workshop that was particularly beneficial to the company. Here participants could think creatively about how to achieve the objectives of the system without restraint; assumptions could be surfaced and challenged, new ideas could be entertained.

It is worth noting that only the documentation of the second workshop included the final versions of the root definition and HAS model (see Figure 4.7 for the final model developed). It was not feasible time-wise or desirable quality-wise to try to finish these within the workshop session. Rather, the facilitator was able to write up the session in his own time over the following few days. This approach enables reflection and learning to occur on the part of the facilitator and avoids technical difficulties impinging upon the valuable workshop time with participants. The documentation also included a simplistic description of the modelling process in order to ensure participants could follow the logic of the session in retrospect, interpret the model successfully and (hopefully) enable them to use the method themselves in future in-house sessions.

Essentially, the modelling technique attempts to link activities together through logical dependencies. For example, it is clear that designing a programme of communication and events for turf managers is logically dependent upon appreciating turf managers' characteristics; i.e. we would want to appreciate the nature of turf managers before we designed the programme. The activities as a whole then constitute the systems system – for more details on conceptual model building, see Checkland and Poulter (2006).

The final workshop in the programme involved a review of the first two workshops and, in particular, a careful examination of the ideal system design created in the second workshop. Comparison of the model with existing arrangements, reflection and discussion led to action planning in terms of further work and also the implementation of strategic initiatives. These included new definitions for the role of sales staff, a new personal development system for sales staff involving external mentoring and the creation of a new centrally operated system for securing new accounts with turf managers.

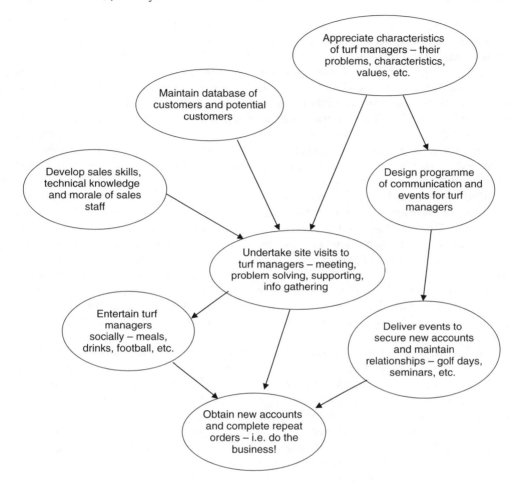

Figure 4.7. Ideal Model of TS Sales System

Vignette 3: The LeCo Learning Case

In the late 1990s a major player in the UK leisure sector, referred to here as LeCo, had initiated a large number of renovation and estates projects within its hotels division. After mixed experiences with the first few projects, LeCo was keen to get better value for their investment by capitalising upon the potential for learning from issues arising during projects and their resolution which could be shared by members of a project team and transferred to future situations or projects within LeCo. It was this background that led one of the authors to become involved in the design and running of three post-completion project review workshops for LeCo.

Before the workshops took place, it became evident that LeCo and their preferred suppliers (e.g. contractors, architects, designers, etc.) had different agendas about how to use their learning from the projects. LeCo wanted to ensure that their 'learning to provide higher value' agenda was taken up seriously by their suppliers.

However, the suppliers felt unable to implement such an agenda unless a number of issues regarding LeCo's organisational processes, routines and responsiveness to their needs were improved.

Over an 18-month period, two redevelopment projects and one design and new build project were reviewed. Overall, each of the workshops involved seven to nine participants representing a number of stakeholders including senior managers from LeCo's property division and operational management, as well as senior representatives of LeCo's service providers in charge of delivering different parts of the projects (e.g. contractors, designers, architects, etc.). A different set of service providers was involved in each workshop and only one company other than LeCo was involved in more than one workshop.

Before the workshops, expectations were running high for LeCo, as they were keen to put their agenda on the table, and ensure that their service providers would support it. On the other hand, responses to a pre-workshop questionnaire suggested that LeCo's service providers had issues with LeCo's behaviour throughout the projects, which had a negative impact on the actual return they had obtained for their work. Specifically, LeCo was perceived to be unable to provide well-defined project briefs, and slow and inefficient in their responses to the needs of their service providers. The latter's agenda was, therefore, one of persuading the client that to get better value they must first understand the impact of their actions on the project.

The layout of the rooms for the workshops was similar to that associated with a typical PSM workshop. That is, the room was arranged in a horseshoe layout without tables. In addition, the workshops were 'recorded' using large flipcharts fixed to the walls with 'blu-tack'. The purpose of recording the sessions in this manner was to enable as much of the work as possible to be exhibited at the same time so as to allow participants to make easy reference to previous work. Furthermore, the resulting visual representation of the workshop's progress lent itself to recording with a digital camera for speedy distribution to participants after the workshops.

The workshops were conducted using a particular PSM, namely, the Strategic Choice Approach (SCA) (Friend & Hickling, 2005). SCA aims to support the negotiation of strategic agendas by focusing on the issues faced by a management team in terms of 'decisions' to be made in a particular situation. It is an incremental approach that recognises the need for an explicit balance between choices to be made now and those left open until specified points in the future.

The approach presents a view of any process of strategic choice in terms of a dynamic balance between four modes of working: shaping, designing, comparing and choosing. In the *shaping* mode, individual agendas are structured in terms of decision areas, i.e. any area of choice over which participants can exercise at least some influence; comparison areas, i.e. a set of criteria which is sufficient to represent all the main dimensions of concern (economic, environmental, social or political); and uncertainty areas, i.e. any areas of doubt or disagreement which affect the comparison of alternative courses of action. During the *designing* mode, choices are explored in terms of their interconnectedness, and a set of decision portfolios are developed. In the *comparing* mode such portfolios are assessed using a relevant set of comparison areas. Finally, work in the *choosing* mode produces a negotiated and agreed agenda for action comprising a set of immediate and deferred decisions, together with different types of explorations for managing uncertainty.

During the first workshop, there were different views between the participants about the areas where decisions needed to be made. After a facilitated discussion, the development of an effective and efficient briefing process was agreed to be the main area of concern. This area was seen as strategic and crucial for future projects. During the workshop, however, the discussion moved away from strategic issues and concentrated on operational aspects of the project under review. In particular, 'snagging' (i.e. the process of identifying defects in the resulting product) was specified as the most urgent area to address. This area represented an operational issue related to the handover of the project which was part of the hotel operator's own agenda. The issue was addressed, and the discussion returned to the initial focus.

During the latter part of the workshop, participants engaged in the development and prioritisation of options for action. Participants were encouraged by the facilitator to focus on options which they could effectively act upon. All the options surfaced were then discussed within the group to compare and evaluate in terms of their feasibility and consequences. All participants voiced their opinions and concerns about the options surfaced. This discussion gave rise to agreements regarding actions to be implemented, together with their responsible actors and tentative deadlines.

The second workshop followed a similar format to that of the first one. Developing the right level of detail in the project brief was the main concern expressed by participants. Figure 4.8 reproduces the beginnings of the development of the 'decision graph' built during the workshop and containing areas where participants believed there were some choices available.

A link between two decision areas indicates that workshop participants expressed a belief that it could make a difference to consider this pair of decisions jointly instead of separately. For example, any choices regarding the level of detail in the project brief (labelled as 'BRIEF?' in Figure 4.8) will have an impact on the choices available for the management of the interface between LeCo and their service providers (labelled as 'INTERFACE?' in Figure 4.8). The discussion leading up to the development of the decision graph in Figure 4.8 helped workshop participants to become aware of their diverse points of view about the strategic issues confronting them, and to clarify how these issues were inter-related.

Finally, the last workshop mainly focused on developing improved ways of managing project changes. This focus can be explained by the fact that the hotel under review was a new design and build project, which represented a particularly complex and expensive venture for LeCo, a scale of project they had never attempted before. Some of the actions that resulted from the three workshops included: sign off completed specifications of units; development of roles, accountabilities and responsibilities matrix; development of project briefing process and manual; development of snagging process and handover plan for projects; development of Client Contractor Customer Satisfaction survey; and review of cross-organisational processes and agreements.

Post-workshop interviews indicated that participants viewed SCA as a highly participatory and effective problem-structuring process that allowed them to

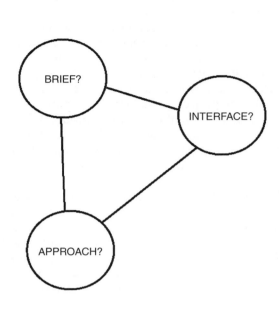

Decision Area	Label
What level of detail specifications should be provided in the project brief	BRIEF?
How can the interface between LeCo and their service providers be managed?	INTERFACE?
What approach to design/build should be adopted	APPROACH?

Comparison Area	Label
Flexibility of partners to manage situations	FLEXI:
Speed of decision making when things go wrong	SPEED:
Profitability	PROFIT:

Uncertainty Area	Label
Planning constraints	?CONSTRNT
Accuracy of assumptions in cost plan	?ASSUMPN
LeCo decision on model bedrooms	?DECISION

Figure 4.8. Beginning of a Decision Graph for LeCo

develop a better understanding of each others' agendas, and negotiate issues long considered to be major obstacles to the efficiency of the business relationship so that an agreed strategic agenda was jointly produced. As a result, mutual adjustments in the relationship between LeCo and their service providers ensued. In particular, there was evidence that SCA may have contributed to high levels of commitment to continue doing future business together.

CONCLUSIONS

This chapter was aimed at introducing the idea of building and negotiating strategic agendas as an issue construction process, and using model-driven approaches such as Problem-Structuring Methods (PSMs) to support that process. The short case descriptions have illustrated how successful strategic agenda building and nego-tiation depends heavily on having a transparent, highly participative and flexible problem-structuring process that facilitates good strategic conversations among a variety of stakeholders. Indeed, the role of PSMs within conversations is an area of current research within the PSM field (e.g. Franco, 2006).

PSMs place particular demands on those wishing to use them to facilitate the negotiation of strategic agendas; for it would require both group facilitation and modelling skills. The issue of transferability of PSMs for strategic development has already been raised elsewhere (e.g. Keys, 2006; Westcombe, Franco & Shaw, 2006) and there is already some 'how-to-do' literature available to potential users of these methods (e.g. Ackermann & Eden, 2005; Checkland & Poulter, 2006). A possible way to gain experience with the methods is to first try them in small-scale, low-risk projects before moving on to larger strategic ones.

The vignettes have illustrated how PSMs can be used flexibly and in combination with conventional complementary strategy tools (e.g. the cultural web) to deliver value to management teams. Their explicit and transparent representation of the particular features of the business that these teams are managing is in contrast to the vaguer prescriptions of much of the strategic management literature. Furthermore, it is this structuring activity and its associated visible (i.e. explicit model representation of the issues) and invisible (e.g. shared understanding) products that enables the construction and negotiation of bespoke strategic agendas for action. It is also possible, as in the stories told above, to inject a fresh 'outsider' view into the workshop mix, and so help participants to break 'out of the box' in thinking strategically about their issues.

REFERENCES

Ackermann, F. (1990) 'The role of computers in group decision support'. In: Eden, C. & Radford, J. (eds), *Tackling Strategic Problems: The role of group decision support*. Sage: London.

Ackermann, F. (1996) 'Participant's perceptions on the role of facilitators using group decision support systems', *Group Decision and Negotiation*, **5**, 93–112.

Ackermann, F. & Eden, C. (1994) 'Issues in computer and non-computer supported GDSSs', *Decision Support Systems*, **12**, 381–390.

Ackermann, F. & Eden, C. (2001) 'Contrasting single user and networked group decision support systems for strategy making', *Group Decision and Negotiation*, **10**, 47–66.

Ackermann, F. & Eden, C. (2005) *The Practice of Strategy Making: A step-by-step guide*. Sage: London.

Ansoff, H.L. (1980) 'Strategic issue management', *Strategic Management Journal*, **1**, 131–148.

Bennett, P., Bryant, J. & Howard, N. (2001) 'Drama theory and confrontation analysis'. In: Rosenhead, J. & Mingers, J. (eds), *Rational Analysis for a Problematic World Revisited: Problem structuring methods for complexity, uncertainty and conflict*. John Wiley & Sons: Chichester.

Berger, P.L. & Luckmann, T. (1966) *The Social Construction of Reality: A treatise in the sociology of knowledge*. Doubleday: New York.

Checkland, P. (1981) *Systems Thinking, Systems Practice*. John Wiley & Sons: Chichester.

Checkland, P. (1999) *Soft Systems Methodology: A 30-year retrospective*. John Wiley & Sons: Chichester.

Checkland, P. & Poulter, J. (2006) *Learning for Action: A short definitive account of Soft Systems Methodology, and its use for practitioners, teachers and students*. John Wiley & Sons: Chichester.

Checkland, P. & Scholes, J. (1990) *Soft Systems Methodology in Action*. John Wiley & Sons: Chichester.

De Geus, A. (1988) 'Planning as learning', *Harvard Business Review*, **66**, 70–74.

Dutton, J.E. (1988) 'Understanding strategic agenda building and its implications for management change'. In: Pondy, L., Boland, R. & Thomas, H. (eds), *Managing Ambiguity and Change*. John Wiley & Sons: Chichester.

Dutton, J.E. (1993) 'Interpretations on automatic: a different view of strategic issue diagnosis', *Journal of Management Studies*, **30**, 329–357.

Dutton, J.E. (1997) 'Strategic agenda building in organizations'. In: Shapira, Z. (ed.), *Organizational Decision Making*. Cambridge University Press: Cambridge.

Dutton, J.E. & Ashford, S.J. (1993) 'Selling issues to top management', *Academy of Management Journal*, **18**, 397–429.

Dutton, J.E. & Duncan, R.B. (1987a) 'The creation of momentum for change through the process of strategic issue diagnosis', *Strategic Management Journal*, **8**, 279–295.

Dutton, J.E. & Duncan, R.B. (1987b) 'The influence of strategic planning on strategic change', *Strategic Management Journal*, **8**, 103–116.

Dutton, J.E., Fahey, L. & Narayanan, V.K. (1983) 'Toward understanding strategic issue diagnosis', *Strategic Management Journal*, **12**, 307–323.

Dutton, J.E., Ashford, S.J., O'Neill, R., Hayes, E. & Wierba, E. (1997) 'Reading the wind: how middle managers assess the context for selling issues to top managers', *Strategic Management Journal*, **18**, 407–425.

Dutton, J.E., Ashford, S.J., O'Neill, R. & Lawrence, K. (2001) 'Moves that matter: issue selling and organizational change', *Academy of Management Journal*, **44**, 716–736.

Dyson, R. (2000) 'Strategy, performance and operational research', *Journal of the Operational Research Society*, **51**, 5–11.

Eden, C. (1982) 'Problem construction and the influence of OR', *Interfaces*, **12**, 50–60.

Eden, C. (1986) 'Problem solving or problem finishing'. In: Jackson, M. & Keys, P. (eds), *New Directions in Management Science*. Gower: Aldershot.

Eden, C. (1988) 'Cognitive mapping: a review', *European Journal of Operational Research*, **36**, 1–13.

Eden, C. (1990) 'Managing the environment as a means to managing complexity'. In: Eden, C. & Radford, J. (eds), *Tackling Strategic Problems: The role of group decision support*. Sage: London.

Eden, C. (1992a) 'A framework for thinking about group decision support systems', *Group Decision and Negotiation*, **1**, 199–218.

Eden, C. (1992b) 'Strategy development as a social process', *The Journal of Management Studies*, **29**, 799–811.

Eden, C. (1996) 'The stakeholder/collaborator strategy workshop'. In: Huxham, C. (ed.), *Collaborative Advantage*. Sage: London.

Eden, C. & Ackermann, F. (1998) *Strategy Making: The journey of strategic planning*. Sage: London.

Eden, C. & Ackermann, F. (2001a) 'SODA: the principles'. In: Rosenhead, J. & Mingers, J. (eds), *Rational Analysis for a Problematic World Revisited: Problem structuring methods for complexity, uncertainty and conflict*. John Wiley & Sons: Chichester.

Eden, C. & Ackermann, F. (2001b) 'Group decision and negotiation in strategy making', *Group Decision and Negotiation*, **10**, 119–140.

Eden, C. & Ackermann, F. (2004) 'Use of "Soft OR" models by clients: what do they want from them?' In: Pidd, M. (ed.), *Systems Modelling: Theory and practice*. John Wiley & Sons: Chichester.

Eden, C. & Radford, K.J. (1990) *Tackling Strategic Problems: The role of group decision support*. Sage: London.

Eden, C., Jones, S. & Sims, D. (1983) *Messing about in Problems: An informal structured approach to their identification and management*. Pergamon: Oxford.

Eden, C., Jones, S., Sims, D. & Smithin, T. (1981) 'The intersubjectivity of issues and issues of intersubjectivity', *The Journal of Management Studies*, **18**, 37–47.

Ford, J.D. & Ford, L.W. (1995) 'The role of conversations in producing intentional change in organizations', *Academy of Management Review*, **20**, 541–570.

Franco, L.A. (2006) 'Forms of conversation and problem structuring methods: a conceptual development', *Journal of the Operational Research Society*, **57**, 813–821.

Friend, J. & Hickling, A. (1997) *Planning under Pressure: The strategic choice approach*. Butterworth-Heinemann: Oxford.

Friend, J. & Hickling, A. (2005) *Planning under Pressure: The strategic choice approach*. Elsevier: Oxford.

Hickling, A. (1990) 'Decision spaces: a scenario about designing appropriate rooms for group decision management'. In: Eden, C. & Radford, J. (eds), *Tackling Strategic Problems: The role of group decision support*. Sage: London.

Hilgartner, S. & Bosk, C.L. (1988) 'The rise and fall of social problems: a public arenas model', *American Journal of Sociology*, **94**, 53–78.

Huxham, C. (1990) 'On trivialities in process'. In: Eden, C. & Radford, J. (eds), *Tackling Strategic Problems: The role of group decision support*. Sage: London.

Jackson, S.J. & Dutton, J.E. (1988) 'Discerning threats and opportunities', *Administrative Science Quarterly*, **33**, 370–387.

Johnson, G., Scholes, K. & Whittington, R. (2005) *Exploring Corporate Strategy: Text and cases*. Prentice-Hall: London.

Keys, P. (2006) 'On becoming expert in the use of problem structuring methods', *Journal of the Operational Research Society*, **57**, 822–829.

March, J.G. & Shapira, Z. (1982) 'Behavioral decision theory and organizational decision theory'. In: Ungson, G.R. & Braunstein, D.N. (eds), *Decision Making: An interdisciplinary inquiry*. Oxford University Press: New York.

Milliken, F.J. (1990) 'Perceiving and interpreting environmental change: an example of college administrators' interpretations of changing demographics', *Academy of Management Journal*, **33**, 42–63.

Ocasio, W. (1997) 'Toward an attention-based view of the firm', *Strategic Management Journal*, **18**, 187–206.

Phillips, L. (1984) 'A theory of requisite decision models', *Acta Psychologica*, **56**, 29–48.

Phillips, L. (1989) 'People-centred group decision support'. In: Doukidis, G., Land, F. & Miller, G. (eds), *Knowledge-based Management Support Systems*. Ellis-Horwood: Chichester.

Phillips, L. & Phillips, M. (1993) 'Facilitated work groups: theory and practice', *Journal of Operational Research Society*, **44**, 533–549.

Pidd, M. (2004) 'Contemporary OR/MS in strategy development and policy-making: some reflections', *Journal of the Operational Research Society*, **55**, 791–800.

Pitt, M., McAulay, L., Dowds, N. & Sims, D. (1997) 'Horse races, governance and the chance to fight: on the formation of organizational agendas', *British Journal of Management*, **8**, S19–S30.

Rochefort, D.A. & Cobb, R.W. (1994) 'Problem definition: an emerging perspective'. In: Rochefort, D.A. & Cobb, R.W. (eds), *The Politics of Problem Definition*. University of Kansas Press: Lawrence, KA.

Rosenhead, J. (1996) 'What's the problem? An introduction to problem structuring methods', *Interfaces*, **29**, 117–131.

Rosenhead, J. & Mingers, J. (eds) (2001) *Rational Analysis for a Problematic World Revisited: Problem structuring methods for complexity, uncertainty and conflict*. John Wiley & Sons: Chichester.

Shrivastava, P. & Schneider, S.C. (1984) 'Organizational frames of reference', *Human Relations*, **37**, 795–809.

Smith, G.F. (1994) 'Classifying managerial problems: an empirical study of definitional content', *Journal of Management Studies*, **32**, 679–706.

Thomas, J.B. & McDaniel, R.R. (1990) Interpreting Strategic Issues: effects of strategy and the information processing structure of top management teams. *Academy of Management Journal*, **33**.

Thomas, J.B., Clark, S.M. & Gioia, D.A. (1993) 'Strategic sensemaking and organizational performance: linkages among scanning, interpretation, action and outcomes', *Academy of Management Journal*, **36**, 239–270.

Thomas, J.B., Shankster, L.J. & Mathieu, J.E. (1994) 'Antecedents to organizational issue interpretation: the role of single-level, cross-level and content cues', *Academy of Management Journal*, **37**, 1252–1284.

van der Heijden, K. (1996) *Scenarios: The art of strategic conversation*. John Wiley & Sons: Chichester.

Weick, K.E. (1995) *Sense Making in Organizations*. Sage: Thousand Oaks, CA.

Weisbord, M. & Janoff, S. (2000) *Future Search: An action guide to find common ground in organizations and communities*. Berrett-Koehler Publishers: San Francisco, CA.

Westcombe, M., Franco, L.A. & Shaw, D. (2006) 'Where next for PSMs – a grassroots revolution?' *Journal of the Operational Research Society*, **57**, 776–778.

Part III

Creating Strategic Initiatives

Chapter 5

Strategy Creation – The Resource-Based View

Abhijit Mandal

This chapter provides an introduction to the resource-based view and the major developments in that perspective that brought it prominence in the strategic management literature.

The opening section of this chapter traces the antecedents and the origins of the resource-based view from a certain part of the literature in economics that concerns itself about differentiated products, which in turn facilitates the concept of differentiated firms as realistic subjects for study in the disciplines of economic and strategic management. The next two sections follow the major developments of the resource-based view that occurred in the decade from the mid-1980s; it is extended to include the competence literature. The subsequent section links resources and capabilities to strategy generation. The next two sections explore the shortcomings in the presented material, followed by a section that explores the nature of resource heterogeneity. Consequently, a dynamic perspective is developed in the two sections that follow. The last section concludes.

ORIGINS IN INDUSTRIAL ORGANISATION

E.H. Chamberlin was an economist who addressed the mechanism of value creation in firms, before most others. The ideas which originated in his doctoral thesis were later enhanced, developed and published in the book *The Theory of Monopolistic Competition* (1933). He attempted to achieve a more realistic approach to the theory of the firm, though he did not actually come up with such a theory. His central idea was that a producer (or a firm) had the power to differentiate its product as part of its competitive strategy. A supporting assumption was that the ability to exercise the power would depend on the prevailing market structure. In other words, every firm in an industry has a monopoly of its own variety but its monopoly power is limited by the offerings of its competitors.

Chamberlin pursued this idea in the direction that he thought management would seek to exploit it – that is, to differentiate their firm's product to customers and thereby obtain more freedom in pricing and production. Hence his attention to tools such as advertising and R&D expenditure; these would presumably be utilised by managers to prove to customers that the product was indeed different from the similar offerings of its competitors. The implication of this idea is that the market can exist in a state of disequilibrium, as price competition would be limited by variety that was in the interest of customers. The premise that the firm can influence the behaviour of the customer has been well studied in the field of marketing. Nevertheless, how management rhetoric influences the long-term behaviour of stakeholders who are external to the firm is not yet so widespread in strategic management literature.

Chamberlin's ideas clearly influenced the industrial organisation school as well, but with a twist. This school focused on the supporting assumption that the ability to exercise monopoly power would depend on the prevailing market structure. Hence, the famous SCP paradigm: the *(industry) Structure → (firm) Conduct → Performance* model, which is based on the work of Mason (1939) and Bain (1956, 1959). Here the emphasis is on tangible features like the magnitude of industry concentration, economies of scale and scope, and the strength of entry barriers in the belief that they constrain behaviour and thereby influence performance. The inference is that the key factors cited above, which are external to the firm, would determine the extent of the impact that the firm's actions (undertaken by management) had on firm profitability (e.g. in promoting product differentiation through advertising or after-sales services).

Some contributors, including Caves (1972, 1980), later applied this model to strategy, treating market structure as an exogenous, stable variable (Bain, 1972). Finally, Porter (1980, 1985) adapted this particular approach to strategy into the 'five-forces' model for understanding competitive advantage by classifying the whole gamut of external factors that affect a firm into five categories. His original recommendations (Porter, 1980) of low cost, differentiation and focus correspond to the three main avenues of firm action from Chamberlinian economics for improving profitability: lowering the price in order to sell more, differentiating the product to enlarge the sphere of the limited monopoly power and advertising, when the differentiation is intangible to objective assessment.

Later, game theory exponents such as Nash (1951, 1953), Schelling (1960) and Nalebuff and Dixit (1991) introduced new analytic methods, but these were based on many of the assumptions of the industrial organisation theory. To summarise the industrial organisation approach as it is seen now, industrial or market structure is the largest single factor in determining profits for firms. The industrial organisation understanding accommodates various factors that are *exogenous to the firm,* such as the influence of customer preferences, fixed costs and the role of entry barriers as key determinants of performance. Competitive advantage and sustainable competitive advantage derive from the accrual and protection of monopolistic rents,[1] based on privileged market positions.

---

[1] Rents are the extra profits earned by a firm that can successfully exploit special resources belonging to them. Rent from a particular resource implies the ability to exploit and appropriate that particular resource.

These approaches view the firm simply as a supplier in the product market. Further, as explained by Porter (1981), there is assumed to be one ideal position in the industry or the strategic group that, in successful outcomes, best resists market forces and yields monopoly power-based extra profits. This implies that an industry-level view of firms is taken, where firms (in the same industry or in the same strategic group) perceive objectives and bases of competition in identical fashions. These theories are weak in some aspects such as the process of competition, the dynamic aspect of change in the market forces (e.g. firm performances like bankruptcy and mergers can eventually determine the structure of the industry) and the creation of industry structure.

In such an industry-based view, there is relatively little for the manager of the firm to do. The more homogenous the nature of the industry, the more he needs to focus on the minimising cost. As far as strategic behaviour is concerned, it is limited to changing the overall industry conditions – whose modalities point to the limited applicability of this framework in real life. Moreover, it is extremely difficult to derive implications for non-profit firms such as public sector organisations, who may not have a direct incentive for minimising costs.

Such severe limitations have prompted a logical move to consider other drivers of firm profitability. Here we point to the studies carried out by Schmalensee (1985), Rumelt (1991) and McGahan and Porter (1997) among others, which effectively showed that industry effects accounted less than firm effects in explaining the variance of firm profitability. One of the most important theories that opted to use firm-level explicators to explain variations in the profits of firms has been the resource-based view.

RESOURCE-BASED VIEW: PRINCIPALS AND ORIGIN

The main exponents of the initial expansion in the Resource-Based View (RBV) literature, which has occurred over the last two decades, have been Wernerfelt (1984, 1995), Barney (1986a–c, 1989, 1991), Grant (1991) and Peteraf (1993). In their view it is the firm, rather than the industry, that should occupy the centre of attention. They took the view that the most significant part of inter-firm differences in performance could be accounted for by 'Ricardian' rents.[2] They postulated that these extra profits arise from the heterogeneity of resources in firms (i.e. heterogeneous resource positions), which are sustained by resource position barriers (Wernerfelt, 1984). This kind of heterogeneity results from the imperfections in strategic factor markets (Barney, 1986b, 1989); these imperfections allow the managers of a specific firm, or some firms, acquisition of heterogeneous resources at lower than their fair price. These positions are represented in Figures 5.1 and 5.2.

The most important difference with the industrial organisation school was that they shifted the search about the drivers responsible for competitive advantage from factors *outside* the firm to factors *inside* the firm. This implied that managers of firms had a relatively more active role to play in the performance of their firms

_____

[2] Ricardian rents arise from limited or insufficient supply of certain resources. In the remaining part of this chapter, the term 'rent' may be substituted by 'extra profits'.

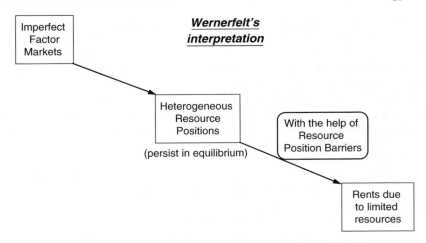

Figure 5.1. Wernerfelt's Interpretation

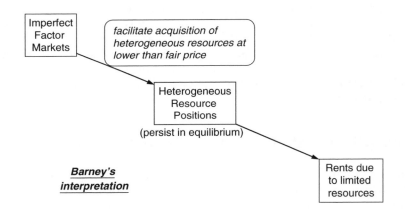

Figure 5.2. Barney's Interpretation

than was permitted according to the scope of the industrial organisation school. Naturally, the power implied by RBV was more acceptable to management and was one of the reasons that the resource-based view subsequently overshadowed the industrial organisation school. Grant (1991) outlines for managers a procedure to use the strategic planning process for utilising resources, and how the status of resources can shape the strategic planning task. Our book extends these approaches: it discusses various tools and processes that managers could use to execute their role in the strategic planning process.

This outlook is very comfortable with steady state; after the 'unique' or the 'different' resource is somehow acquired and employed, the firm and the industry (assumed to be at steady state) would still sustain a differential advantage with respect to other firms regarding profits (or rent). The extra profit could then be attributed to that special factor of production. Of late, the Chicago school of economics-based idea that such extra profits could also be attributed to greater efficiency in exploitation of the resource has been put forward (Peteraf & Barney, 2003).

The principal outcome of the efforts of Wernerfelt, Barney and Peteraf was to produce a compact framework that stated the special properties that resources must have, to be in a position to produce extra profits. These were the characteristics of: valuableness, rarity, inimitability and non-substitutability (Barney, 1991); ex post limits to competition; ex ante limits to competition, immobility and heterogeneity (Peteraf, 1993). While the first two characteristics of each were supposed to be responsible for the differential in extra profits earned due to uncertainty, the remaining two characteristics were supposed to be responsible for the sustainability of those extra profits due to limits on imitation.

The ideas enshrined in these works created a significant impact in the academic and management communities, resulting in two kinds of reactions. First, the number of papers published that tried to apply the resource-based framework in specific aspects of business and management saw tremendous growth in the 1990s. A second reaction was the development of a critique of the implications of the framework. The critique was along two lines – a sceptical line that pointed to the theory's shortcomings as it was while the other line wanted to bring in more dimensions from real life. The sceptics doubted whether RBV qualified as a theory and pointed to the tautological aspects in the definition of value (Priem & Butler, 2001). This is explored in more detail after the next section of this chapter. This second line of criticism towards RBV was along two implicit dimensions – time and complexity – both of which are relevant to managers.

The temporal critique questions the assumption of steady state because it downplays the inherent dynamics of resources. This is a significant deviation from real life, where managers know that there is no steady state, particularly when considering an extended period of time. One of the first pointers in this direction was the insight that it takes time for resources to accumulate (Dierickx & Cool, 1989). The other dimension, complexity, is based on an analysis of the nature of empirical work carried out to test the propositions of RBV (Bromiley & Fleming, 2002; Priem & Butler, 2001).

An important aspect of such work is that the dependent variable is called competitive advantage while the independent variables are called resources. This is based on the presumption that the fundamental construct of the theory is limited to 'resources'. This complexity critique resulted in a development of theory that moved away from 'stand-alone' resources to focus on the basic links amongst resources, since resources are not necessarily valuable by themselves, but only in combination with others (Black & Boal, 1994). It was developed to some extent in the literature on competences which is described in the next section. The complexity critique is based to some extent also on the distinction between resources and services (Penrose, 1959).

An implicit assumption in RBV attributed the origin of differential performance of the firm to differences in at least one of the factors of production, whether intangible or tangible. The typical implied mechanism of the extra profits was a combination of acquisition of the resource below fair price (either due to luck or private information) with subsequent appropriation of those extra profits arising from its value-creating characteristics, through isolating mechanisms (Rumelt, 1984). These isolating mechanisms are usually firm-level investments and are analogous to entry barriers at the industry level and mobility barriers among strategic groups (Caves & Porter, 1977; McGee & Thomas, 1986). An extensive list of isolating mechanisms is presented by Mahoney and Pandian (1992, Table 1). Isolating mechanisms may explain why other firms do not catch up with the leader – but only after the lead has been established.

As an example of the mechanisms displayed in Figures 5.1 and 5.2, consider a typical large research-based pharmaceutical firm in the profit sector. Such a firm will seek to maximise the number of patents it holds, and further, try to increase the remaining length of life of those patents. The logic behind this is that the patents are protected from imitation by law; hence, significantly higher prices can be charged for those chemicals protected by active patents. Firms that have strong brands follow a typically similar strategy when they charge a premium. For an example in the non-profit sector, consider the prominent business schools in London and away from London. Those who have established premises in the mega-polis can more easily fill large class sizes in finance-related subjects, due to their proximity to the financial centre of Europe. This advantage is not available to those even an hour's commute away from the capital.

A consequence of such an implicit assumption was that management's strategic role was largely limited to acquisition and appropriation. Their rich and vital role in the dynamic stewardship of resources was not given the recognition that is due. Another related consequence was academic inattention to the processes that managers executed vis-à-vis the firm's resources. The best way that managerial ability could be accommodated here was to assume that the extra profit-earning resources were the product of greater efficiency in exploitation. For example, when considering resources that embody knowledge, this narrow perspective would limit management to considering whether such resources can be acquired at less than fair cost, and how can these resources be exploited while minimising operating costs.

However, efficiency is a function of productivity. Productivity is relevant only with reference to services extracted from resources. The idea of services is also implicitly associated with combinations of resources, since at least one other kind of resource is needed to exploit a given resource in an efficient manner. Thus, it is important to consider the linkages among the various contributing elements (Levinthal, 1995). This kind of resource combination is characteristic of competences: the two principal dimensions here are the modifiers of the principal resource being exploited, which are typically exogenous to it, as well as the nature of service extracted from the principal resource.

THE COMPETENCE LITERATURE

The earlier works in the resource-based view focused on the term 'resources' as the basis for conceptualising what was important inside the firm. As mentioned above, the particular contributors in this regard were Wernerfelt, Barney and Peteraf. Later, a word called 'competence' was used to convey a concept more sophisticated than 'resource'. In fact, Selznick (1957) had earlier defined the term *distinctive competence*' as a conceptual response to dynamic adaptation, associating it with effectiveness rather than efficiency. This term was used to underline the crux of senior management objectives for the firm.

In other words, when an organisation is faced with a serious or significant problem, management may respond by deciding that the organisation should develop skills previously unavailable to it; it might even decide to develop unique skills that nobody else has – the motivation behind this is to make the organisation distinct from its competitors. Hofer and Schendel (1978) built upon these ideas to propose *'distinctive competencies'* as the unique pattern of resource deployments and skill dependencies. These responses are based on the basic idea that a given set of resources may be managed in different ways to meet different objectives. Figure 5.3 is a schematic representation of their idea.

Continuing in that tradition, Hamel and Prahalad (1990) specified three characteristics of *'core competencies'* that are necessary towards obtaining a competitive advantage.[3] These characteristics are in parallel to the qualities of resources specified by Barney (1986a) and Peteraf (1993) that are necessary to sustain competitive advantage. In the context of a corporate organisation, core competencies are conceptualised as flexible consolidations of technologies and skills that are drawn from the whole organisation, rather than the business unit, to empower business-level adaptation of the firm to the competitive market environment.

Some time later, Teece, Pisano and Shuen (1997) introduced the concept of *dynamic capabilities* into the literature. 'Dynamic' refers to the capacity to renew competencies so as to achieve congruence with the changing business environment. 'Capabilities' emphasises the key role of strategic management in appropriately adapting, integrating and reconfiguring internal and external organisational skills, resources and functional competencies to match the requirements of a changing environment.

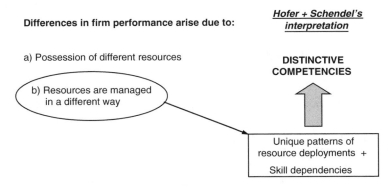

Figure 5.3. Hofer and Schendel's Interpretation

---

[3] The three characteristics are: A core competence provides potential access to a wide variety of markets. It should make a significant contribution to the perceived customer benefits of the end products. It should be difficult for competitors to imitate.

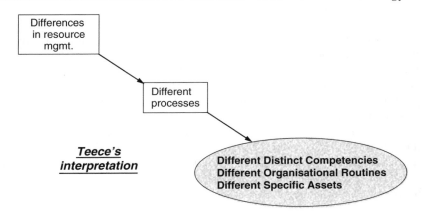

Figure 5.4. Teece's Interpretation

Hence the concept of dynamic capabilities: it is the firm's ability to integrate, build and reconfigure internally oriented and externally oriented competencies to address rapidly changing environments. It can be seen as an emerging and potentially integrative approach to understanding the sources of competitive advantage. Competitive advantage of firms is seen as resting on distinctive processes, shaped by the firm's (specific) asset positions, and the evolution paths it has adopted or inherited. As indicated in Figure 5.4, this conceptualisation implies that the utilisation of dynamic capabilities requires a change in the way resources are managed from previous practices; the implication is that it would lead to the creation of new (and therefore different) kinds of processes, which in turn would lead to the formation of new distinct competencies, new organisational routines and new specific assets. One can appreciate that this interpretation based on capabilities stands closer to the intentions of Penrose than those interpretations based solely on resources.

LINKING RESOURCES AND CAPABILITIES TO STRATEGY

Lengnick-Hall and Wolff (1999) collected these three perspectives under the label of 'capability logic' to point out that they share an orientation to steady state. Grant (1991) builds on this resource-and-capability logic to underlie Porter's industrial organisation philosophy of greater profits. The excess profits that would accrue are dependent on industry attractiveness and competitive advantage, which in turn are realised through isolating mechanisms and advantageous heterogeneity, respectively. Advantageous heterogeneity can be obtained through cost advantages or coherent differentiation of product attributes. Grant also proposes a framework for applying this resource-based approach for strategy formulation. This approach is clearly driven by the logic of setting a strategic direction, based on fruitfully exploiting existing unique resources and capabilities. He outlines a five-step procedure to implement this framework:

1. Resources need to be identified and classified. Depending on the competitive and external circumstances, opportunities need to be identified that would permit better utilisation of resources.
2. Capabilities that would use the resources as inputs need to be identified. Further, these capabilities need to be graded in terms of complexity.
3. The rent-generating potential of resources and capabilities needs to be evaluated in terms of the potential for sustaining competitive advantage as well as the appropriability of their returns. Sustainability depends on durability, non-transparency, non-transferability and non-replicability, while appropriability depends on the strength of isolating mechanisms employed.
4. Organisations must then select a strategy which best exploits the resources and capabilities, given the external opportunities.
5. Gaps, in resources and capabilities, between what is desired and what exist need to be identified and replenished or augmented through investment.

An important idea here is that evaluating the list of resources and capabilities identified in the first two steps would provide a basis for selecting the most appropriate strategy; the implementation phase is about both the exploitation of available resources and capabilities as well as the building of resources and capabilities for future use. This idea is equivalent to single-loop learning (Argyris & Schön, 1978). However, it is difficult to accurately compare the outcome of different potential resource and capability investments, given the nature of unintended consequences and unforeseen reactions that can happen. Grant does not consider whether a process of strategy selection can interact with potential strategies. Neither does he offer suggestions as to what defines an adequate process of strategy selection, or how such processes should be executed. If the different potential outcomes for different investments cannot be compared on a reliable basis, then the selection of strategy comes very close to a game of pure chance.

A reliable process that can evaluate proposed strategies and compare their potential outcomes (i.e. the equivalent of a *virtual performance*) with desired ones can help management become less passive. Instead of simply selecting the strategy with the best hypothesised outcome, strategy can now be better engineered towards desired outcomes. This is the equivalent of introducing a second loop of learning (Argyris & Schön, 1978) and this book points out how such learning can be implemented, while describing and demonstrating various tools to carry out relevant processes for strategy evaluation. However, from the point of view of RBV, virtual performance cannot become sufficiently useful until the circumstances in which resources and capabilities function are explicitly taken into account. This is just an important prerequisite; what is actually needed to generate virtual performance is the knowledge of how the dynamics of resources and capabilities are influenced by themselves as well as by their circumstances.

THE RELEVANCE OF CONTEXT

The next step to the idea that certain combinations of resources can ultimately create value is the idea that the context in which resources are deployed can also contribute to value creation. Here the context is to be understood as the 'setting' or the way in which a particular resource interacts with other resources in the organisation to create value. Even organisational capabilities may be a function of context (Collis, 1994). Simply put, the value of a given resource, at a particular time, is a function of the context it finds itself in. The metaphor of 'shifting terrain' (Rindova & Fombrun, 1999) accurately conveys three ideas. First, the context, through the nature of causal links between the resource and itself, has a continuous impact on the resource. Second, this aspect implies that context is being continuously created. Third, the context continuously influences the value of resources. Two broad questions follow from these statements: What kinds of contexts create value? How do these contexts create value?

There have been a few studies in this stream (Barney & Zajac, 1994; Helfat, 1997; Miller & Shamsie, 1996; Noda & Bower, 1996; Papadakis, Lioukas & Chambers, 1998). In particular, Miller and Shamsie (1996) undertake a longitudinal study where they look at the impact of two kinds of resources on performance in two different time periods (1936–1950 and 1951–1965). They conclude that 'whether an asset may be considered a (valuable) resource will depend as much on the context enveloping the organisation as on the properties of the asset itself'. In general, these works do provide specific examples of contexts that are involved in value creation, but they do not provide a general explanation of how contexts create value.

The managerial implication is that while managers may not be able to directly manipulate a context (particularly in the short term), neither can they ignore its impact on value-producing resources. It is therefore useful to consider a dynamic approach to answer this question, as outlined prior to this section.

THE SCEPTICAL VIEW

Foss, Knudsen and Montgomery (1995), Bromiley and Fleming (2002) as well as Amit and Schoemaker (1993) critique the propositions of the resource-based view. They point out that the characterisations of what constitute a valuable resource tend to be ex post facto (i.e. after the event rationalisations). Empirical pieces about the resource-based view typically do not explain the process through which the performance difference (usually arising from a competitive advantage) or economic rent was created in the first place, or explain the emergence of distinctive capabilities (Levinthal & Myatt, 1994). Nor is the context in which the resources will lose their 'value' specified. This makes it difficult to identify, a priori, which of the heterogeneous resources are going to generate value, and whether their heterogeneity is essential to value generation. From a philosophic point of view, Powell (2001) characterises the propositions of the resource-based view as analytic propositions. Analytic propositions, by definition, are true and difficult to verify empirically. The implication is that there need to be synthetic propositions that are empirically testable.

The contingency approach is considered inadequate (Miller, 1986, 1996) and thus, the cross-sectional approach that has been traditional to the resource-based view needs to be supplemented with the longitudinal approach (Porter, 1991). Evolutionary underpinnings may hold promise (Levinthal & Myatt, 1994; Nelson & Winter, 1982). This indirectly points to the relevance of the temporal dimension.

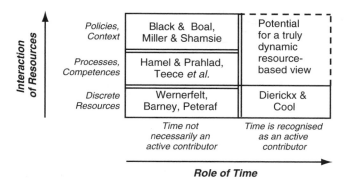

Figure 5.5. Scope for Dynamics in RVB

Priem and Butler (2001), among others, have called for the 'how' question to be answered as well as a temporal component to be incorporated as a vital step towards achieving this dynamic resource-based view. Unless the dynamic processes and mechanisms by which a firm establishes a favourable resource position are understood, the resource-based view is not only incomplete as a theory but is also unable to provide useful implications for practicing managers (Oliver, 1997). A good beginning can be made towards accommodating the temporal dimension by drawing upon the core ideas put forward by Dierickx and Cool (1989). The insight that it takes time for resources to accumulate was expressed with respect to maintaining or sustaining a privileged resource position. Figure 5.5 brings together all the perspectives on RBV expressed so far and shows the scope for a true integration of resource interaction and the role of time.

THE NATURE OF HETEROGENEITY

Essentially, such integration needs to be clear about the sources of initial heterogeneity as well as the managerial role in sustaining or even enhancing an existing heterogeneity, in order to increase existing profit margins.

Chamberlin's ideas had their impact on Penrose as well. Her seminal contribution to the resource-based view through her book *The Theory of the Growth of the Firm* (1959) contains yet another basis for the production of differentiated products. Her insight was to identify 'services' rendered from 'resources' as the actual inputs to the production process and not the 'resources' themselves. According to her, the services yielded by resources are a function of the way in which they are used – implying that the same set of resources can provide a different service or a set of services at different times to different firms. For her, the unique character of a firm derives from the heterogeneity of these available or potentially available services.

If the services that feed into the production process are open to differentiation, then it is logical to expect the final product to be differentiated as well. In other words, there could be a difference amongst the resources themselves or a difference in the way in which similar or even identical resources are managed. Penrose confirms

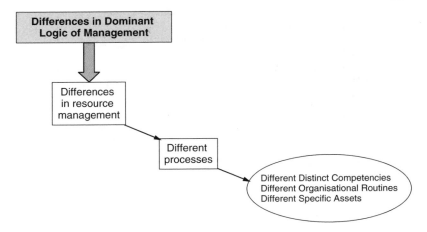

Figure 5.6. Dominant Logic as a Source of Resource Heterogeneity

that what she calls 'the range of productive services' primarily emerges from the 'interaction between two kinds of principal resources of a firm – its personnel and material resources'. This leads to questions about the origin of productive services – e.g. why are there differences in productive services and where do they come from?

An important source of heterogeneity is the influence of dominant logic[4] (Prahalad & Bettis, 1986) as a way of understanding the impact of idiosyncratic and heterogeneous traits of management on short-term and long-term performance (Figure 5.6). The conceptual foundations of dominant logic arise from diversity-driven factors such as operant conditioning and pattern recognition through positively reinforced past behaviours, the powers of paradigms to shape 'conventional wisdom' and cognitive biases. These turn out to be diverse, and are ultimately responsible for the diversity in management traits. Thus, managerial cognition, at an individual level, and organisational cognition, at a collective level, have an important role to play. Some of the ways in which cognition manifests as diverse productive services is through the activities of learning, imitation, resistance to imitation, innovation and also through the presence of a diversity of mental models.

Thus, there are essentially two kinds of heterogeneity. The first kind of heterogeneity is the one that is already there among resources while the second kind of heterogeneity lies in the logic being used by the relevant management and can show up in the way resources are managed. Although it has been traditional in RBV to specify distinguishing characteristics of such special resources that sustain the first type of heterogeneity, managers know that these characteristics are not discrete extremes, but a matter of degrees. Competition is always trying to imitate special resources; the critical issue is its speed. If these special resources are like hills that the competition has to climb, then incumbent managers seek to increase the height of the hill or make it more difficult to climb, by spending on other resources;

---

[4] Prahalad and Bettis define dominant logic as 'a mindset or a worldview or a conceptualisation of the business and the administrative tools to accomplish goals and make decisions in that business. It is stored as a shared cognitive map (or set of schemas) among the dominant coalition'.

managers competing with incumbents therefore need to transform relatively more ordinary resources to build their special resources and be keenly aware of growth opportunities. The second type of heterogeneity – i.e. the heterogeneity arising from productive services – has ultimately an influence on the first type of heterogeneity, manifesting through the process of resource interactions and resource interdependencies. Figure 5.6 summarises this idea.

Similar to Chamberlin, this line of reasoning allots a very important role to management for the generation of services; moreover, the difference in generation of services from the same resources implies that at any given point in time, disequilibrium – i.e. an unsteady state – is a more likely state of the market than steady state. Actually, managers are more familiar with this state of disequilibrium than steady state; the managerial imperative of growth is essentially a state of disequilibrium. The firm may be conceptualised as a bundle of productive resources, and the process of growth as 'a dynamic interacting process' – a series of internal or endogenous changes over time (Penrose, 1959). The building of resources that takes place is essential to facilitate growth; it is an outcome of accumulation inherent in desired expansion or intensification.

The process of accumulation through the flows of resources is more obvious when intangible resources like reputation are considered (Rindova & Fombrun, 1999); even tangible resources such as dominant designs 'emerge and crystallise'. A close study about growth reveals processes of positive and negative feedback that underlie the material and information flows amongst tangible and non-tangible resources (Noda & Collis, 2001). Even a few such feedback processes taking place simultaneously give rise to *dynamic complexity*[5] (Senge, 1990); it is extremely difficult for human beings to foresee accurately the outcomes of such complexity. The earlier sections in this chapter have brought out the lack of dynamics in RBV; this shortcoming hampers its ability to handle dynamic complexity. We therefore put forward some suggestions for managers to put into practice a more dynamic approach to resource management.

THE FIRM AS A DYNAMIC RESOURCE SYSTEM

One potential way to portray the dynamics and transformation of resources, while taking into account the process of accumulation, is to use a modelling approach. Among many potential approaches to constitute the basic structure of such a model, one approach is to use a structure of stocks and flows (Dierickx & Cool, 1989). Here stocks represent accumulations of resources as assets while flows represent the transfer of resources that take place over a time period (Sterman, 2000). A similar implicit conceptualisation of resources and productive services from resources (Penrose, 1959), as stocks and flows respectively, was made more explicit

---

[5] Senge (1990) outlines two kinds of complexity – detail complexity and dynamic complexity. Detail complexity results from the unpredictability created by the multiplicity of details – e.g. the interaction of a large number of variables, while dynamic complexity results from the unpredictability created by the trajectories of interdependent variables. Human beings find it difficult to predict the outcomes of even a very small number of interacting feedback loops.

by Mahoney and Pandian (1992). Eventually, all the processes in an organisation can be modelled as a network of stocks and flows.

The use of stocks and flows can link to performance in a rigorous manner. The current quantity at any moment of any resource stock is always equal to the sum of everything ever added to minus the sum of everything ever lost from that resource (Warren, 2002). The rate at which every resource is being filled at any moment is totally dependent upon the current levels of certain resource stocks, possibly itself. Competitive position is then a function of the levels of stocks that measure performance variables. It can be easily verified that the traditional information reported in accounting balance sheets is also based on existing levels of certain resource stocks while information reported in the income statement can be thought of as flows to or from the existing resource stocks. Earning calculations are usually ratios.

The value of the modelling approach using such a structure is to enable managers to move beyond seeing the firm as simply a collection of resources, each at its own level, at a given point in time; this constitutes a somewhat limited perspective of what a firm is. By specifying the causal links among resources, the perspective is expanded from a collection or bundle of resources to a *system of resources*. Such specification would express how the transformation of resources in the firm's activity systems (i.e. the processes) affects each other. This provides a clear ex ante link between resources, resource management and performance. Such ex ante links allow managers to design strategic initiatives with a much larger degree of freedom. Let us see how.

UTILISING THE DYNAMICS OF A SYSTEM OF RESOURCES

When a firm is specified merely as a bundle of resources and capabilities, it simply provides an indication as to what are the potential strengths and weaknesses of the firm. To get a better idea of which of the potential strengths need to be tapped and which potential weaknesses can be critical, some details of the context in which these resources and capabilities would be deployed are needed. Typically, strategists have done this by matching the existing set of resources and capabilities against prevailing opportunities and threats emanating from the environment. A qualitative judgement is then made about the nature and content of suitable strategic initiatives. This is discussed in greater detail in Chapter 6.

On the other hand if, as mentioned in the previous section, we add causal links to interconnect these resources and capabilities, then we place ourselves in a position to explore the potential behaviour of these resources under different contexts. If these causal links are specified in an appropriate quantitative manner, then the behaviour of such a model can be simulated; this generates a virtual performance for these different contexts and provides a quantitative estimate of the dynamic behaviour of the constituent resources and capabilities of the firm as well as the fate of its proposed strategic initiatives.

Further, if we add in practical policies, with the help of more causal links, for managing resources that can be implemented by management there is the added benefit of being able to understand and shape policies that are more useful in promoting the success of a given set of strategic initiatives. Below we provide a seven-step procedure to exploit the dynamics of resources and capabilities in order to select strategies in a manner that has more awareness towards their consequences:

1. Identify the resource stocks that are present and those that are needed.
2. Identify the capabilities that are present and those that are needed.
3. Identify the nature of causal links (and processes) that connect the resources and capabilities to form resources systems. Quantify these links as far as possible.
4. Identify different sets of environmental conditions which take into account the opportunities and threats prevalent.
5. Explore the performance implications of the resource systems under these different environmental conditions, given suitable strategic initiatives.
6. Design policies that can achieve the best outcomes for the available strengths, weaknesses, opportunities and threats in tune with the selected strategic initiatives and corresponding conditions.
7. Identify those resources and capabilities that need to be developed during the implementation phase.

Note that steps 1 and 2 as well as steps 5 to 7 may be iterative between themselves.

Here is an example that demonstrates the significance and utility of conceptualising resources as stocks. Consider a simplified resource system that describes a lending library. The three main resource stocks are cash, subscribers and books; we assume that this library does not have any special capabilities at this level of simplicity. Figure 5.7 shows these resources as stand-alone resources, as seen by the traditional RBV; from this the managerial imperatives to keep the system functioning are not clear – e.g. maintaining the library as a going concern. What is the impact of selling (or depleting) the number of books? What is the impact of spending cash? Is there anything that threatens the size of the subscriber base?

The picture becomes much clearer when we start integrating the causal links between the resources; Figure 5.8 offers such a view. Incidentally, with such a view one can figure out the presence of feedback loops if any, their nature and surmise their implications. This now facilitates deeper questions about strategic initiatives: should the books be sold to generate more cash or should the cash be used in buying

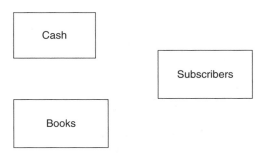

Figure 5.7. Principal Assets

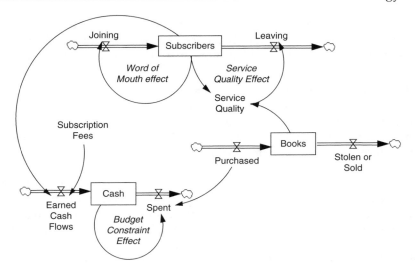

Figure 5.8. Assets with Causal Links

books? What would happen if subscribers are charged more for their membership? What would happen if service quality were to fluctuate frequently and regularly?

To answer the above-mentioned questions, one can add the impact of decisions that are made to manage the resources to the model. The nature of the initiatives chosen to be implemented will certainly depend on the preferred goals and appetite for risk on the part of management. Suitable policies to improve the attainability of the chosen strategic initiatives can then follow.

Thus, the causal links are essentially the building blocks of the dynamics of strategy as they can facilitate the transformation of a bundle of resources at a specific point in time to enable us to understand its potential dynamic pattern of behaviour. This facility to simulate the model and portray alternate versions (by implementing alternate policies or strategies) of the future of the resource system that is the firm can be recognised as the generation of virtual performance. The key point is that the generation of virtual performance is fundamental to comparing proposed strategies through their potential outcomes – it is this facility to compare strategy outcomes that converts the manager from a passive selector of strategies towards an active facilitator of better outcomes in the pre-implementation stage. The logical implication of this is that it allows for superior strategy-making – not only due to better policy design, but also due to the accompanying learning and consequent preparedness to be more flexible as the strategy is implemented with inevitable surprises from the competition and the environment.

CONCLUSION

This chapter on the resource-based view commenced with the threads of the ideas originating from Chamberlin that were eventually expressed as the resource-based view. However, his ideas were initially used in developing an alternate approach which is termed 'industrial organisation'. After reviewing the nature of the industrial organisation approach to studying firm profitability which examines the issue of firm profitability based primarily on industry level and market power-based factors, the chapter traces the development of the resource-based view in the 1980s and the 1990s. The primary distinguishing factor of this theory was its use of firm-level variables to explain the profitability of the firm; the most significant development was the enumeration of particular resource characteristics with appropriate isolating mechanisms that would guarantee sustainable competitive advantage in steady state. However, the main criticisms are also reported.

Consequently, the chapter explores the relevance of the literature on competences and brings out its similarities and complementarities to the resource-based view. The main similarity is the assumption of steady state in the development of the concept of core competence while the major contribution is the idea that 'stand-alone' resources are not as valuable without supporting competences. Next, some details are furnished about how Grant's procedure for using resources and capabilities for strategy formulation – its shortcomings vis-à-vis strategy formulation – are also pointed out. It is then proposed that these shortcomings can be addressed by taking into account the dynamics and the context of resources. This leads to an exploration of the relevance of context and the perceived need for dynamics.

A detailed look at the nature and origin of heterogeneity amongst resources provides insights into the role of context, dynamics and the associated process of accumulation in the evolution of resources through time. It hints at the nature of dynamic complexity that is characteristic of such evolution. In order to get a handle on this dynamic complexity, the concept of using stocks and flows to depict resources and capabilities is presented, with which the firm could be viewed as a system of resources. This provides a clear ex ante link between resources, resource management and performance which allows managers greater freedom to design strategic initiatives. The contrast of developing strategic initiatives the traditional way is contrasted with what can be achieved through modelling virtual performance; readers are subsequently offered a procedural framework to put this into practice along with a simple illustrative example.

We emphasize again that the generation of virtual performance is fundamental to comparing the outcomes of proposed strategies – it is this that allows the manager to become an active facilitator of better outcomes in the strategy formulation stage. The critical importance of virtual performance is explored in other chapters of the book.

REFERENCES

Amit, R.H. & Schoemaker, P.J.H. (1993) 'Strategic assets and organizational rent', *Strategic Management Journal*, **14**(1), 33–46.

Argyris, C. & Schön, D.A. (1978) *Organizational Learning: A theory of action perspective*. Addison-Wesley: Reading, MA.

Bain, J.S. (1956) *Barriers to New Competition*. Harvard University Press: Cambridge, MA.

Bain, J.S. (1959) *Industrial Organization*. John Wiley & Sons: New York.

Bain, J.S. (1972) *Essays on Price Theory and Industrial Organization*. Harvard University Press: Cambridge, MA.

Barney, J.B. (1986a) 'Organizational culture: can it be a source of sustained competitive advantage?', *Academy of Management Review*, **11**(3), 656–665.

Barney, J.B. (1986b) 'Types of competition and the theory of strategy: toward an integrative framework', *Academy of Management Review*, **11**(4), 791–800.

Barney, J.B. (1986c) 'Strategic factor markets: expectations, luck, and business strategy', *Management Science*, **32**(10), 1231–1241.

Barney, J.B. (1989) 'Asset stocks and the sustainability of competitive advantage: a comment', *Management Science*, **35**(2), 1511–1513.

Barney, J.B. (1991) 'Firm resources and sustained competitive advantage', *Journal of Management*, **17**(1), 99–120.

Barney, J.B. & Zajac, E.J. (1994) 'Competitive organizational behavior: toward an organizationally-based theory of competitive advantage', *Strategic Management Journal*, **15**(1), 5–9.

Black, J.A. & Boal, K.B. (1994) 'Strategic resources: traits, configurations and paths to sustainable competitive advantage', *Strategic Management Journal*, **15**(1), 131–148.

Bromiley, P. & Fleming, L. (2002) 'The resource based view of strategy: a behaviorist's critique'. In:Augier, M. & March J.G. (eds), *The Economics of Choice, Change, and Organizations: Essays in Memory of Richard M.Cyret*. Edward Elgar: Cheltenham, UK, pp. 319–336.

Caves, R.E. (1972) *American Industry: Structure, Conduct and Performance*. Prentice-Hall: Upper Saddle River, NJ.

Caves, R.E. (1980) 'Industrial organization, corporate strategy and structure: a survey', *Journal of Economic Literature*, **18**(1), 64–92.

Caves, R.E. & Porter, M.E. (1977) 'From entry barriers to mobility barriers: conjectural decisions and contrived deterrence to new competition', *Quarterly Journal of Economics*, **91**(2), 241–261.

Chamberlin, E. (1933) *The Theory of Monopolistic Competition*. Harvard University Press: Cambridge, MA.

Collis, D.J. (1994) 'How valuable are organizational capabilities?', *Strategic Management Journal*, **15**(Winter Special Issue), 143–152.

Dierickx, I. & Cool, K. (1989) 'Asset stock accumulation and the sustainability of competitive advantage', *Strategic Management Journal*, **35**(2), 1504–1511.

Foss, N.J., Knudsen, C. & Montgomery, C.A. (1995) 'An exploration of common ground: integrating evolutionary and strategic theories of the firm'. In: Montgomery, C.A. (ed.), *Resource-based and Evolutionary Theories of the Firm*. Kluwer: Boston, pp. 1–17.

Grant, R.M. (1991) 'The resource-based theory of competitive advantage: implications for strategy formulation', *California Management Review*, **33**(3), 114–135.

Hamel, G.P. & Prahalad, C.K. (1990) 'The core competence of the corporation', *Harvard Business Review*, **68**(3), 79–91.

Helfat, C.E. (1997) 'Know-how and asset complementarity and dynamic capability accumulation: the case of R&D', *Strategic Management Journal*, **18**(5), 339–360.

Hofer, C.W. & Schendel, D. (1978) *Strategy Formulation: Analytical Concepts*. St. Paul Minnesota West Publishing: Minnesota, MN.

Lengnick-Hall, C.A. & Wolff, J.A. (1999) 'Similarities and contradictions in the core logic of three strategy research streams', *Strategic Management Journal*, **20**(12), 1109–1132.

Levinthal, D.A. (1995) 'Strategic management and the exploration of diversity'. In: Montgomery, C.A. (ed.), *Resource-based and Evolutionary Theories of the Firm*. Kluwer: Boston, pp. 19–42.

Levinthal, D.A. & Myatt, J. (1994) 'Co-evolution of capabilities and industry: the evolution of mutual fund processing', *Strategic Management Journal*, **15**(1), 45–62.

Mahoney, J.T. & Pandian, J.R. (1992) 'The resource-based view within the conversation of strategic management', *Strategic Management Journal*, **13**(5), 363–380.

Mason, E. (1939) 'Price and production policies of large-scale enterprise', *American Economic Review*, **29**(1), 61–74.

McGahan, A.M. & Porter, M.E. (1997) 'How much does industry matter, really?', *Strategic Management Journal*, **18**(6), 15–30.

McGee, J. & Thomas, H. (1986) 'Strategic groups: theory, research and taxonomy', *Strategic Management Journal*, **7**(2), 141–160.

Miller, D. (1986) 'Configurations of strategy and structure: towards a synthesis', *Strategic Management Journal*, **7**(3), 233–249.

Miller, D. (1996) 'Configurations revisited', *Strategic Management Journal*, **17**(4), 505–512.

Miller, D. & Shamsie, J. (1996) 'The resource-based view of the firm in two environments: the Hollywood film studios from 1936 to 1965', *Academy of Management Journal*, **39**(3), 519–543.

Nalebuff, B.J. & Dixit, A.K. (1991) *Thinking Strategically: The Competitive Edge in Business Policy and Everyday Life*. WW Norton & Co.: London.

Nash, J. (1951) *Non-cooperative Games*. Annals of Mathematics, 2nd Series, Vol. 56, No. 3, pp. 405–421.

Nash, J. (1953) 'Two person cooperative games', *Econometrica*, **21**(1), 128–140.

Nelson, R.R. & Winter, S.G. (1982) *An Evolutionary Theory of Economic Change*. Harvard University Press: Cambridge, MA.

Noda, T. & Bower, J.L. (1996) 'Strategy making as iterated process of resource re-allocation', *Strategic Management Journal*, **17**(7), 159–192.

Noda, T. & Collis, D.J. (2001) 'The evolution of intraindustry firm heterogeneity: insights from a process study', *Academy of Management Journal*, **44**(4), 897–925.

Oliver, C. (1997) 'Sustainable competitive advantage: combining institutional and resource-based views', *Strategic Management Journal*, **18**(9), 697–713.

Papadakis, V.M., Lioukas, S. & Chambers, D. (1998) 'Strategic decision-making processes: the role of management and context', *Strategic Management Journal*, **19**(2), 115–147.

Penrose, E.T. (1959) *The Theory of the Growth of the Firm*. Oxford University Press: New York.

Peteraf, M.A. (1993) 'The cornerstones of competitive advantage: a resource-based view', *Strategic Management Journal*, **14**(3), 179–191.

Peteraf, M.A. & Barney, J.B. (2003) 'Unraveling the resource-based triangle', *Managerial & Decision Economics*, **24**(4), 309–323.

Porter, M.E. (1980) *Competitive Strategy: Techniques for Analyzing Industries and Competitors*. Free Press: New York.

Porter, M.E. (1981) 'The contribution of industrial organization to strategic management', *Academy of Management Review*, **6**(4), 609–620.

Porter, M.E. (1985) *Competitive Advantage: Creating and Sustaining Superior Performance*. Free Press: New York.

Porter, M.E. (1991) 'Toward a dynamic theory of strategy', *Strategic Management Journal*, **12**(Winter Special Issue), 95–117.

Powell, T.C. (2001) 'Competitive advantage: logical and philosophical considerations', *Strategic Management Journal*, **22**(9), 875–888.

Prahalad, C.K. & Bettis, R.A. (1986) 'The dominant logic: a new linkage between diversity and performance', *Strategic Management Journal*, **7**(6), 485–501.

Priem, R.L. & Butler, J.E. (2001) 'Tautology in the resource-based and the implications of externally determined resource value: further comments', *Academy of Management Review*, **26**(1), 57–66.

Rindova, V.P. & Fombrun, C.J. (1999) 'Constructing competitive advantage: the role of firm-constituent interactions', *Strategic Management Journal*, **20**(8), 691–710.

Rumelt, R.P. (1984) 'Toward a strategic theory of the firm'. In: Lamb, R. (ed.), *Competitive Strategic Management*. Prentice-Hall: Englewood Cliffs, NJ, pp. 556–570.

Rumelt, R.P. (1991) 'How much does industry matter?', *Strategic Management Journal*, **12**(3), 167–185.

Schelling, T. (1960) *The Strategy of Conflict*. Harvard University Press: Cambridge, MA.

Schmalensee, R. (1985) 'Do markets differ much?', *American Economic Review*, **75**(3), 341–351.

Selznick, P. (1957) *Leadership in Administration: A Sociological Interpretation*. Harper & Row: New York.

Senge, P. (1990) *The Fifth Discipline: The art and practice of the learning organization*. Doubleday: New York.

Sterman, J.D. (2000) *Business Dynamics: Systems Thinking and Modeling for a Complex World*. Irwin/McGraw-Hill: New York.

Teece, D.J., Pisano, G. & Shuen, A. (1997) 'Dynamic capabilities and strategic management', *Strategic Management Journal*, **18**(7), 509–533.

Warren, K.D. (2002) *Competitive Strategy Dynamics.* John Wiley & Sons: London.
Wernerfelt, B. (1984) 'A resource-based view of the firm', *Strategic Management Journal*, **5**(2), 171–180.
Wernerfelt, B. (1995) 'The resource-based view of the firm: ten years after', *Strategic Management Journal*, **16**(3), 171–174.

Chapter 6

Methods for Creating Strategic Initiatives
Robert G. Dyson

A key component of the strategic development process is the subprocess concerned with generating strategic initiatives or options. This is a part of the process where creativity has a key role to play and methods or techniques should be seen as facilitators rather than processors for automatically generating options. At the creative formulation stage it is important that criticism and evaluation are kept for a later stage in the process. Nevertheless, research (Tapinos, Dyson & Meadows, 2005) shows a strong link between the scope of formulation and the strength of the evaluation process. This is perhaps due to the almost inevitability that organisations that formulate a rich range of initiatives necessarily need a good evaluation process to help choose those initiatives that should move to implementation. Alternatively, organisations with more of a 'hunch and hope' approach more rapidly converge on a preferred option as part of the formulation process and hence often do not have a strong, critical evaluation process.

This part of the strategic development process (creating strategic initiatives, Figure 6.1) is shown with a fuzzy boundary to indicate that initiatives or options can emerge throughout the organisation. Many might develop from a top-down approach but equally important ones may be developed departmentally or through individuals bringing forward plausible new options.

In this chapter we first of all introduce a range of approaches to strategy formulation and then focus on the well-tested approach of SWOT (Strengths, Weaknesses, Opportunities and Threats) analysis and the related TOWS matrix. The relationship of SWOT/TOWS analysis to the apparently alternative approaches of resource-based planning and scenario planning is then considered and an enhanced process proposed. An application of the process at the University of Warwick is then described, which was carried out at the corporate level in the University.

METHODS FOR CREATING STRATEGIC INITIATIVES

Figure 6.2 shows a range of methods that can facilitate the creation of strategic initiatives. The resource and competency-based views play a significant role in current strategic management thinking and they are developed separately in Chapter 5.

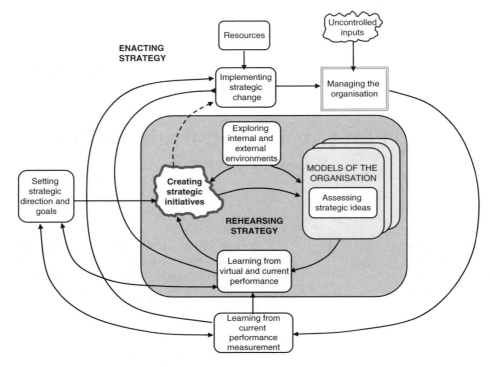

Figure 6.1. The Strategic Development Process

Figure 6.2. Methods for Creating Strategic Initiatives

In principle, they involve identifying the resources, competencies, capabilities and knowledge of the organisation and building on these to create competitive strategies. Porter's Five Forces (Porter, 1980) focuses strongly on the competitive environment of the organisation as shown in Figure 6.3.

The central force is rivalry amongst existing competitors and of course the stronger this rivalry the more difficult it is for the organisation to be profitable. Of the remaining four forces, three relate to other players and the fourth to developments

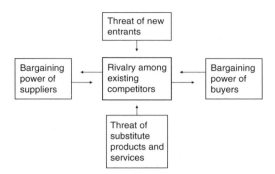

Figure 6.3. Porter's Five Forces

in products and services. The threat of new entrants is of course crucially linked to the ease of entrance to the market, and where market entry is relatively easy then over time the market is likely to become more competitive. In some markets the bargaining power of buyers may well be a significant force, and a good example of that would be the purchasing power of supermarkets, which has a tendency to drive down the price of basic supplies to them in order to increase their competitive position. In some industries however, such as – on occasion – the oil industry, it may be suppliers that are in the strongest position. For some businesses there may be a strong threat from substitute products or services. In the electronics industry there seems to be a never-ending supply of new products, whilst in recent years there has been an explosion of new services via the internet. Porter (2001) has argued that the internet eases entry to markets and therefore makes them more competitive and less profitable.

Product portfolio matrices were particularly developed to facilitate strategy formulation in businesses that have a portfolio of strategic business units (SBUs). The original matrix was the BCG matrix developed by the Boston Consulting Group (Henderson, 1970, 1973; Figure 6.4). Basically, the matrix has market share and market growth as axes and the SBUs are placed in the four quadrants of the matrix. The SBUs with high market share in a high growth market are seen as the stars and are businesses that ought to be invested in to meet the growing demand. Those in a growth market but with a low market share were questionable and investigations need to be considered to see if investment could lead to a higher market share. Businesses with high market share but in a low growth or static market are denoted as 'cash cows'. It is considered that these businesses should only receive maintenance-level investment and should be 'milked' for cash, which can then be invested in the businesses in growth markets. Finally, if any businesses fell into the low or no growth and low market share quadrant then they should be divested or closed down. These businesses are often referred to as 'dogs', as every dog has its day. More advanced versions of the BCG matrix were subsequently developed (Hax & Majluf, 1983), which were essentially refinements of the same principle. These approaches seem to have become unfashionable, perhaps due to the recent trends towards focus and outsourcing and the break-up of the large conglomerates. The

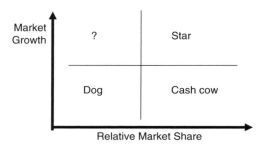

Figure 6.4. The BCG Growth Share Matrix

very concept of a balanced portfolio of business units also seems to have become unfashionable.

The PIMS studies (Profit Impact of Market Strategy; Schoeffler, Buzzell & Heany, 1974) began in the 1970s and continued throughout the rest of the 1900s. The system consisted of a database and a multiple regression model with profitability as the independent variable and a series of dependent variables such as market share, market growth, research and development intensity and degree of vertical integration. The analysis shows which of the independent variables are the strongest drivers of profitability and consistent with the BCG matrix; market share and market growth came out as two of the key drivers. Research and development intensity and vertical integration were also shown to be drivers of profitability and vertical integration became a key strategy during the 1960s and 1970s. The oil companies are perhaps the best examples of profitable vertically integrated companies. From the analysis, reports are fed back to the participating companies covering profit forecasting, strategy evaluation, if notional values of independent variables were included, and performance measurement. The ideas for creating new initiatives stemmed from a knowledge of which variables appeared to be the key drivers of profitability. Companies paid to join the system and provided data on their own companies and then received reports comparing them with similar organisations. There were a number of criticisms of the approach and these included: based solely on historical data; synergy between business units may be ignored; profitability is a short-term measure; the statistical problem of multi-colinearity between the independent variables; the controllability of independent variables and the appropriateness of comparing dissimilar businesses. One of the criticisms was that data would be needed through time in order to identify causal relationships. Unfortunately, very few of the organisations stayed with the system for a sufficiently long period of time for longitudinal analysis to be carried out. It is unresolved whether the organisations left after a few years because they did not have confidence in the system or whether they felt they had got as much from it as possible and therefore saw no point in paying to remain members.

Scenario development is considered extensively in Chapter 9. Scenarios are seen as ways of exploring the uncertainty in the external environment, and later in the chapter we show how scenarios can inform and stimulate the strategy formulation process. TQM (Total Quality Management), benchmarking and re-engineering were at one time seen as ways of strategy development. They have been criticised, however, as simply being ways of doing things smarter and therefore are relatively easy to copy. Porter has argued that strategy formulation must be about distinctiveness and sustainable competitive advantage, and re-engineering, benchmarking and TQM fall down on those criteria.

SWOT/TOWS ANALYSIS

SWOT analysis has its origins in the 1960s (Learned *et al.*, 1965). The basic idea is that organisations formulate a strategy by identifying their strengths and developing strategies building on them, identifying their weaknesses and finding ways of eliminating them or developing capability, uncovering opportunities in the environment and developing strategies to exploit them, and identifying potential threats in the environment and finding strategies to counter them.

Tesco developed **strengths** in retailing, mainly foodstuffs, but rapidly built on this strength to sell a greater variety of goods and then extended into financial services using their retail skills and strong customer base.

Jaguar, now part of the Ford Motor Company, had a considerable problem with quality in the 1980s. It is quite a difficult proposition to sell low-quality, high-priced cars. The incoming Chief Executive, John Egan, in assessing the company recognised quality as a key driver of underperformance (**weakness**) for the company and developed a strategy to improve quality. They introduced quality processes within the organisation and also were very effective at articulating the way Jaguar had improved quality externally.

When Mrs Thatcher deregulated bus travel in the UK in the 1980s, the Stagecoach Company was formed with two buses in the North East of England from which they developed what is now a global business, all from an **opportunity** identified due to deregulation. (One of the pitfalls in SWOT analysis is that opportunities in the environment, e.g. deregulation, are often confused with opportunities/options for the firm, e.g. to establish a bus company).

As a final example, and in keeping with one of the themes of the book, the University of Warwick saw the reduction of state funding to universities in the UK in the 1980s as a serious **threat** and decided to counter this by seeking to diversify their income stream. They expanded activities including the recruitment of fee-paying overseas students, the development of full-cost courses for businesses and the opening of conference centres. As a result of those and later developments, the University gained a reputation for being one of the more entrepreneurial universities, certainly in the UK.

The strengths and weaknesses are identified by doing a systematic review of the internal aspects of the organisation, known as the internal appraisal. This would involve assessing the quality of the employees and their capabilities, the strengths of brands and the competitiveness of products and services. The innovative capability would also be assessed along with customer relationships. Facilities and infrastructure would be evaluated along with their size and location and the efficiency,

	Strengths	Weaknesses
Opportunities	S O Offensive	WO Speculative (build capability)
Threats	ST Defensive	WT Desperation (build capability)

Figure 6.5. The TOWS Matrix

effectiveness and flexibility of the production processes would be considered. The financial position would also be a consideration. This internal appraisal of course implies a performance measurement system and it is interesting that it includes aspects such as innovative capability and customer relationships, which were later to become key components of the 'Balanced Scorecard' (Chapter 11). The opportunities and threats presented by the environment are assessed by an external appraisal. Again this can be carried out systematically by considering various dimensions of the environment including Regulatory, Economic, Social, Political, Environmental, Competitive and Technological (RESPECT).

In the original SWOT analysis, individual factors, e.g. strengths, were considered to see to what extent they generated new strategies. Later, Weihrich (1982) proposed the TOWS matrix (Figure 6.5) in which pairs of factors – such as strengths and opportunities – were considered together in order to generate strategies. These would be SO or offensive strategies. Similarly, one might generate WO or speculative strategies which, as they involve weaknesses, would require capability building as a prerequisite. There might also be ST or defensive strategies, and if the worst comes to the worst the organisation might even consider WT or desperation strategies, i.e. strategies to counter threats but for which there was no immediate capability. Again this class of strategies would require capability building first.

The resource and competency-based views of strategy formulation (Chapter 5) focus on the resources, competencies and capabilities (which would also include knowledge and knowledge management). This approach to systematic exploration and development of strategy is consistent with and enriches the internal appraisal of SWOT/TOWS analysis. Similarly the external focus of scenario planning, with its exploration of the political, economic, social and technological environment and of the Five Forces approach, focusing on the competitive dimension are consistent with and can enrich the external appraisal process. In particular, the incorporation of scenario development with its forward look ensures that the opportunities and threats considered are not just the present ones but also future possibilities. Crucially, however, SWOT/TOWS analysis keeps the internal and external perspectives in focus simultaneously so that a process combining SWOT/TOWS analysis with newer developments ensures a balanced perspective. The enhanced process combining methods is shown in Figure 6.6.

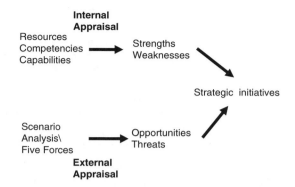

Figure 6.6. Multi-methods for Strategic Initiative Creation

STRATEGIC INITIATIVE CREATION AT THE UNIVERSITY OF WARWICK

Describing the Process of SWOT/TOWS Analysis

In the late 1990s the University of Warwick senior management team decided to have a creative session generating new initiatives for the University. This was towards the end of the term of one of the Vice-Chancellors (the Chief Executive) at a time when his successor had been appointed but not yet taken up his post. The exercise was seen as taking stock of the current situation and feeding this forward to the new Vice-Chancellor for consideration in his own leadership of strategic development. It was recognised that a new Chief Executive might well wish to suggest other forms of development but the exercise was considered to be a way of capturing the current strategic knowledge of the senior management team.

The strategic development process at that time involved producing a rolling 5-year plan, although initiatives were considered on a continuous basis, in which case they might be incorporated into the 5-year plan as a way of testing/rehearsing their impact. (The 5-year plan was principally a financial plan.) The senior management team was known as the Steering Committee and the members are listed in Figure 6.7. It should be noted that the Vice-Chancellor, Pro Vice-Chancellors and the Faculty Chairs were current or lapsed academics whilst the remaining members were professional administrators.

The author was one of the Pro Vice-Chancellors at the time and he agreed to act as the facilitator of the process. This is not common practice in the sense that there is an argument that facilitators should be totally independent of the content of the process. On the other hand, a facilitator who understands the situation may well be able to make more sense of the inputs from the participants.

The exercise (see also Dyson, 2004) began by rehearsing the strategic objectives and values of the University. The University saw itself as a research university, i.e. one in which the vast majority of academic staff were active researchers as well as teachers, and teaching was largely research-informed. The University wanted to have a high international profile and be internationally competitive, offering the full range of undergraduate, postgraduate, continuing and post-experience education.

Vice-Chancellor	Finance Officer
Pro Vice-Chancellors (3)	Estates Officer
Faculty Chairs (4)	Director of Personnel Services
Registrar	Director of Public Affairs
Deputy Registrar	President of the Student's Union
Academic Registrar	Secretary to the Committee
Administrative Secretary	

Figure 6.7. The University Steering Committee

The University wished to retain its entrepreneurial stance and to further diversify its funding base. It prided itself on having a quality physical infrastructure. For UK undergraduates the University wished to continue to develop a widening participation strategy. This was principally a local strategy and the University saw no conflict in having an international profile and working in close collaboration with the local and regional communities on this and other issues. These strategic objectives and values were consistent with the mission and strategic objectives appearing in the University's corporate plan.

The exercise incorporated the resource/competency-based view with SWOT analysis. The approach taken was to consider each factor, e.g. opportunity, in turn. The participants were seated round three sides of a square in a flat room and were asked to discuss in small groups of two or three what present and future opportunities appeared to be presented to the University from the environment (on this occasion formal scenarios were not developed). At this point it might have been possible simply to ask members to suggest opportunities, but given the presence of a number of dominant characters, not unusual in a senior management team, the facilitator asked each individual to offer one suggestion and this process was repeated until exhaustion. In all, 16 opportunities were presented. They were subsequently 'scored' by each individual on a scale of 1–5, where 1 would be an opportunity that was in fact a diversion whilst 5 would be an opportunity not to be missed (and we had better get on with doing something about it!). The top seven opportunities and their average scores are listed in Figure 6.8.

Demand for CPD (S,E)	4.1
Entrepreneurial climate (E)	4.09
Internet (T)	4.09
Brand status	4.00
Strategic alliances (P)	3.64
China (E)	3.55
Fundraising prospects (S)	3.55
(E – economic, S – social, T – technological, P – political)	

Figure 6.8. Opportunities for the University

By dropping any opportunity with an average score of less than 3, the number was in fact reduced from 16 to 14. The dimensions, e.g. economic, are shown so that it can be checked whether the factors span the range of dimensions. The highest scored opportunity was the demand for Continuing Professional Development (CPD). The University was already active in this field, both in the Warwick Business School and the Warwick Manufacturing Group, but it was felt there was scope for further development there and also development associated with the Institute of Education, the newly formed Medical School and the Law School, i.e. the more professionally orientated departments. It was felt that the economic environment was entrepreneurial, with opportunities for, for example, spin-off companies and for collaboration both with industry and the public sector. The internet was seen as an opportunity to enrich the teaching process and deliver courses to a wider audience. The brand status was seen as an opportunity, although it was in fact misclassified and should have been seen as a strength. There was a positive climate for strategic alliances including, potentially, collaborations and mergers in the UK, but also overseas. At the time there had been considerable growth in applications from China and this was seen as an opportunity to be exploited. The seventh in the list was fundraising prospects, where it was felt the climate of fundraising in the UK was improving, although it was still in its infancy compared with the USA.

Next, threats to the University were considered and the same process followed. Again the top seven appear in Figure 6.9.

After the assessment, declining government funding came out as one of the top four threats. In fact, government funding at the time was not declining and indeed was marginally increasing but there had been a decline in the amount of government funding per student over the previous 20 years, and this had strongly influenced thinking about government funding. The internet came out as a serious threat as well as an opportunity as there was a fear that perhaps virtual universities would become a dominant force and that a campus university concept might become obsolete. The other two leading threats were seen as the competition, both in the UK and overseas, from universities but also perhaps from corporate trainers, and there were concerns about the University's media profile. A serious threat was the ability to recruit sufficient high quality staff, due to what was perceived as being declining career prospects in higher education. The cumbersome decision-making was seen as a threat, although that should probably have been included as a weakness. Targeted government funding was seen as a threat as this was a time

Declining government funding (P, E)	3.45
Internet (C)	3.45
Competition (C)	3.45
Decline in media profile	3.45
Career prospects in HE (P, S)	3.36
Cumbersome decision-making (?)	3.36
Targeted government funding (P)	3.18
Planning regulations (R)	3.00

(P – political, E – economic, C – competitive, S – social, R – regulatory)

Figure 6.9. Threats to the University

Income-generating capacity	4.45
Warwick brand	4.36
Research capability	4.18
Land	4.00
Staff morale and loyalty	4.00
Student quality	4.00
Dynamism	4.00

Figure 6.10. Resources, Competencies and Capabilities

when a whole range of special initiatives were being brought out that took money away from mainstream funding and recycled it for specific projects. However, this was seen as constraining the development of the University, possibly either by not securing additional funds or by moving in directions which might not be most appropriate. The seventh highest threat was perceived to be planning regulations, as a significant proportion of the University campus was in green-belt (protected) land and the planning process for development was considerably more rigorous than on the part of the campus not in the green-belt. The issue here was that the University straddled the boundary between Coventry and Warwick District, and the Warwick District land was in green-belt. Furthermore, Coventry, a city that had suffered from declining manufacturing, saw the University as a key part of its regeneration strategy and therefore was very supportive of development, whilst Warwick District had little unemployment and although individuals in the District regularly used the University in a variety of ways, nevertheless there were pressure groups who were concerned about, for example, the impact on traffic from development and further encroachments into the green-belt.

The internal appraisal began by considering the strengths of the competencies, capabilities and resources of the University, in line with the resource and competency-based views; these are shown in Figure 6.10.

Income-generating capacity was seen as the University's leading strength with the Warwick brand as second. The University had been one of the more successful UK universities in diversifying away from the core government grant. Research capability came next and this was justified based on the University's performance in a succession of national research assessment exercises. Land was seen as a strength, as the University had been gifted initially 500 acres of land by Coventry City Council and Warwickshire County Council, and land was still available for development, albeit some of it under green-belt restrictions. Staff morale and loyalty were seen as strengths, although the staff were not actually asked for their opinions on this at the time. Student quality was seen as a strength, and again there was good evidence for this based on, for example, the achievement of entrants in national examinations. Another strength was seen as the dynamism of the University, evidenced by its continuing ability to adopt new strategic initiatives. Finally, the weaknesses of the University were addressed (Figure 6.11).

The few endowments were seen as a key weakness, perhaps mitigated by the climate in the UK for fundraising, but also due to the University's stance of seeking to earn its way. The science base was seen as a weakness, not because of the poor quality of the science departments but rather because they were seen as relatively

Few endowments	3.55
Science base	3.55
Lack of external clout	3.55
Complacency	3.18
Arrogance	3.18
Strains of expansion	3.09
Communication	3.00

Figure 6.11. Weaknesses

small compared with the competitive universities such as Oxford, Cambridge and the big London and civic universities. Lack of external clout represented concerns about the University's ability to influence national policies on higher education. Complacency and arrogance were seen as weaknesses, as were strains of expansion. And finally, communication was seen as a weakness and this embodied both internal communication and the external communication of the University's profile.

The scrutiny of the scores reveals that the highest scoring threat has a score below the top seven opportunities, and the highest scoring weakness again has a score below the top strengths. This suggests that the team were very much in an offensive mode in terms of opportunities and strengths. This was perhaps consistent with the suggestion of arrogance as a possible weakness and dynamism as a possible strength, and was borne out, to some extent, by the range and nature of the strategies generated.

The group were now encouraged to consider pairing strengths and weaknesses with opportunities and threats, as suggested by the TOWS matrix. As a result of that a range of broad strategies were suggested and these are listed in Figure 6.12. They can be placed in a TOWS matrix as shown in Figure 6.13.

Despite the strains of expansion, the opportunities/strength matches suggested the expansion path of the University should continue. It was considered that there were benefits in creating partnerships such as the recent one with Leicester University on the Medical School. It was felt that the undergraduate experience needed strengthening to support the expansion strategy. The concern about the size of science led to a view that a science strategy should be pursued building on the research strengths in science. It was also felt that there were opportunities in the environment which the strengths in social sciences could be marshalled to exploit. Development of CPD was seen as a key strategy and the human relations policy

Expansion	Continuing Professional Development
Human Resources Policy	Partnerships
Government Relations	Undergraduate Experience
Widening Participation	Science Strategy
Fundraising	Social Sciences Development

Figure 6.12. Broad Strategies

	Strengths	Weaknesses
Opportunities	Expansion, CPD, partnerships, social sciences development, widening participation, fundraising	Undergraduate experience, fundraising
Threats	Government relations, science strategy	Human resources policy, science strategy

Figure 6.13. TOWS Matrix

was felt to be an essential part of ensuring recruitment and retention of high quality staff. A campaign of government relations was seen as important, and it was agreed that the existing widening participation/access strategy should be pursued more vigorously. Finally, it was felt timely to undertake a fundraising campaign.

Although the TOWS matrix encourages consideration of pairs of factors, it is possible for a strategy to occur in more than one quadrant, as they may be driven by multiple factors, for example, fundraising was driven by the opportunity of improved fundraising prospects, by the strength of the Warwick brand and by the weakness of the existence of few endowments. Similarly, the drivers for the science strategy were the science base (weakness), research (strength) and the competition from the big science universities (threat).

The fact that different strategies can have more than a single pair of drivers means that the TOWS matrix can be recast to allow for this broadening of possibilities as shown in Figure 6.14. This enhancement does not of course aid the facilitation or the generation of strategies, but it does allow for a richer placing of strategies on the TOWS matrix and a better understanding of the coverage, with regards to the SWOTs. This phenomenon was recognised by Weihrich in the VW case. Here the strategy 'build in the USA' was driven by the opportunity of incentives to build in the USA, the internal weakness – rising costs in Germany, the external threat of the exchange rate and the VW strength in production. This puts the strategy firmly in the SWOT box at the centre of the matrix. The strategy, however, turned out to be a poor one as VW never overcame another weakness, which was its lack of experience of US labour unions of building a plant in the USA. In the end the benefits of the strategy were gained by building in Mexico, which is of course adjacent to the strong US market and might also have appeared in the SWOT box.

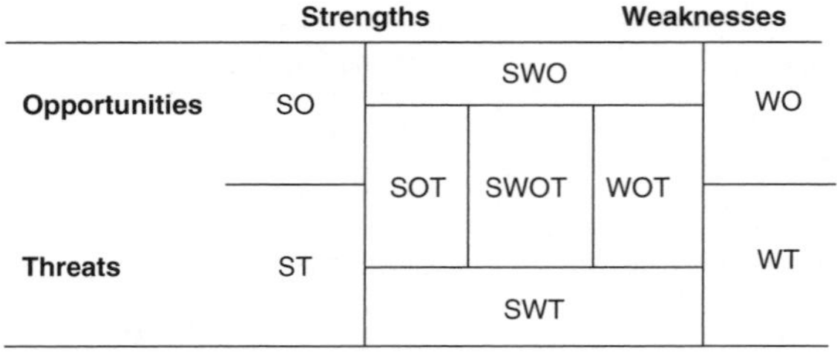

Figure 6.14. The Enhanced TOWS Matrix

Life's what Happens . . .

The analysis and the strategies generated were intended as context for the incoming Vice-Chancellor. However, to quote John Lennon, 'Life's what happens when you're busy planning something else'. Soon after the completion of the exercise the University was allocated £14 million under the Science Research Infrastructure Fund. Furthermore, the University was given 3 months in which to decide how to allocate the £14 million. The exercise thus became the context to inform a real and immediate strategic development exercise. A subgroup of the Steering Committee was set up under the chair of the senior Pro Vice-Chancellor, whose responsibilities covered research and resource allocation, and the subgroup consulted widely in the University and brought forward a series of specific strategies. Other non-research strategies were also being developed at the same time and a series of proposals were put to the University's Strategy Committee and Council. The proposals adopted and their links to the strategies generated by the TOWS exercise are shown in Figure 6.15.

The general strategy of expansion appears in several forms. It was agreed to explore the possibility of further expansion of undergraduate numbers, which might be UK/EU places requiring support from the Funding Council, or further recruitment of overseas students. A partnership had already been established for a joint Medical School with the University of Leicester and the University moved forward the agenda to acquire the Horticultural Research Institute from the government. The CPD strategy was taken forward with developments in the Institute of Health, the Warwick Medical School and the recently formed Institute for Governance and Public Management. The improving of the undergraduate experience was taken forward by a substantial extension of the Sports Centre, with a new additional sports hall, a fitness centre and an extension to the climbing wall and also the addition of a further 700 student residences on campus. The science strategy was taken forward, first of all by the relocation of Mathematics and Statistics from the Gibbett Hill satellite campus to allow physical room for the Medical School and Biological

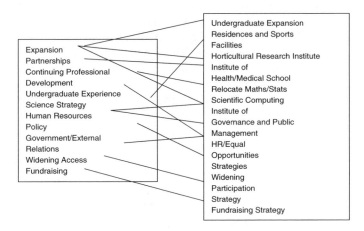

Figure 6.15. Generated Strategies vs. Adopted Strategies

Sciences to expand and also a Scientific Computing Centre was established. This focus on science bore fruit later in the years 2005/6. The University was awarded three multi-million pound research and innovation grants from the Research Councils – one in statistics, one in discrete mathematics (involving the departments of Computer Science, Mathematics and the Business School) and one in plasma physics. These were gained competitively out of a total of only 14 awarded throughout the UK. Developments in the social sciences included the establishment of an Institute of Governance and Public Management, which also potentially would raise the profile of Warwick with the government and the public sector at large. Further work was taken forward on human resources and equal opportunity strategies. The University continued its widening access policy both institutionally and through the various local partnerships for widening participation, in conjunction with Coventry University, local schools and the FE sector. On the arrival of the new Vice-Chancellor one of his priorities was to establish a fundraising strategy. Additionally the University continued its work on e-strategy, enterprise and engagement with the region, although these strategies, which were already under development, were not explicitly raised in the SWOT analysis. Another aspect of the strategy formulation process involved reviewing the key factors to see if any were not being addressed by the candidate set of strategies. One such factor was the opportunity with China, where at the time significant increases in the applications from China had been received at Warwick and indeed elsewhere. This opportunity was not picked up at the time but the following year the new Vice-Chancellor set up a China Strategy Group. This has so far led to some modest initiatives with China, and was one of the drivers of the University considering a major development in Singapore which would involve the recruitment of students from China amongst other countries. This initiative had not been taken forward at the time of writing.

MULTIPLE METHODS FOR STRATEGY CREATION

A model of the strategic initiative creation process with SWOT analysis as a central component but supported by the resource-based view, Five Forces and scenarios is shown in Figure 6.16. The strategies are generated in the context of the organisations' mission, values and strategic objectives. The SWOT analysis can be informed by a scenario development process and the systematic consideration of the organisation's resources, capabilities and competencies. In particular, the scenario development process facilitates the identification of future opportunities and threats, whilst an appraisal of the present resources, capabilities and competencies provides an assessment of current strengths and weaknesses. The pairwise consideration of SWOTs via the TOWS matrix can then stimulate the generation of strategies and there can be a check to see that no major opportunities or threats are overlooked, and that major strengths are utilised and key significant weaknesses addressed. The output of the process is a list of strategic initiatives which would still require a thorough evaluation and testing before a decision on adoption or rejection can be made.

In a more recent study the above process was used to support strategic thinking in the Warwick Business School. The process was further enhanced with the use

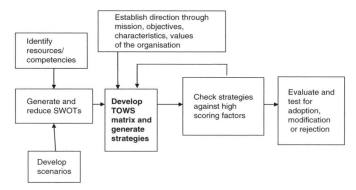

Figure 6.16. The Strategic Initiative Creation Process

of causal mapping group support using the *Group Explorer*[1] networked workstation system running alongside *Decision Explorer*[2] software to facilitate a number of stages in the process.

A series of workshops were facilitated by Alberto Franco and Frances O'Brien, two authors from other chapters in this book. The purpose of the workshops was to facilitate blue-sky thinking about the future strategy of the business school. The workshops were attended by the Dean of the School and approximately ten other staff, both academic and administrative; numbers varied across workshops although there was a core of participants who attended every workshop. The workshops were undertaken during the first half of 2006 and the output is under further consideration at the time of writing. Given the confidential nature of the output, only the process will be described here.

The initial workshop involved the development of three scenarios for the future of business schools operating in an international context. The process used to generate the scenarios is essentially the one described in Chapter 9. *Group Explorer* and *Decision Explorer* were used for the remaining stages in the process, which centred on a SWOT/TOWS analysis. *Decision Explorer* provided visual modelling and analysis capabilities (Eden, 2004; Eden, Ackermann & Cropper, 1992). The scenarios informed the identification of opportunities and threats, whilst an appraisal of current resources, capabilities and competencies informed the identification of strengths and weaknesses. Each of the SWOT categories was taken in turn and *Group Explorer* was used to facilitate the generation of factors. The networked system ensured fuller participation and anonymity, as well as higher productivity levels. *Decision Explorer* was then used for the inter-linkage of factors to form a map. Additionally each set of factors was prioritised using a voting system within *Group Explorer*. I will use the example of the opportunities to illustrate how this process worked.

---

[1] Group Explorer is a computer software product available from Phrontis Ltd (see www.phrontis.com).
[2] Decision Explorer is a computer software product available from Banxia Software Ltd (see www.banxia.com).

The workshop room was organised with tables in a horseshoe shape, facing a large screen. The participants sat around the horseshoe arrangement, each with their own computer; the computers being linked using the *Group Explorer* system, with the facilitator operating a 'master' computer located close to the screen. The process began with each participant individually inputting into their computer the opportunities that they personally could identify from the scenarios. The facilitator then organised the collection of inputs into similar groupings and once everyone had exhausted their ideas, the entire set was displayed on a screen. The software then enabled the participants (via the facilitator) to link related opportunities and thus produce a map representing the set of opportunities and their inter-relationships. A voting facility within the system was used to identify the key opportunities. This process was repeated for the threats, strengths and weaknesses.

In the final stage a TOWS analysis was undertaken. Each workshop participant was given a list of factors from a pair of categories (e.g. opportunities and strengths). A similar process was used to that described above. Each individual was invited to brainstorm their ideas for possible strategic options based on the pairing of categories, typing their own ideas into their computer. Again the software was used to link and group the collection of strategic options to produce a map showing which options were related. The set of options were then voted on using a traffic-light system, where green meant 'should go-ahead with', amber meant 'needs further reflection' and red meant 'not for further consideration'. This process was repeated for each remaining pairing of categories, i.e. opportunities and weaknesses, strengths and threats, weaknesses and threats. The output of this process was thus a rich collection of potential strategic options for further consideration, with an indication of their prioritisation.

CONCLUSIONS AND FUTURE RESEARCH DIRECTIONS

In summary, the SWOT/TOWS approach is a long-standing method that has stood the test of time, but is readily amenable to enhancement by newer methods. The approach should be seen as an ongoing injection into the strategic development process which crucially keeps a balance between the internal and external perspectives. The methods can thus stimulate strategic development. The approach adopted here included scenario development and resource and competency-based views to facilitate the creative generation of factors (SWOTs), which were then scored to allow the elimination of spurious factors. Checking for ignored factors was seen as an important addition to the process. In the University of Warwick case it can be seen that the strategies were largely of an offensive nature and the process produced a balanced range of strategic initiatives.

The enhancement of SWOT/TOWS analysis using the resource-based view, scenario planning and cognitive mapping demonstrates that there is much scope for further systematic exploration of the combination of strategy and management science tools. Strategy formulation over the years has tended to move from fad to fad, from SWOT analysis to product portfolio matrices to the resource-based view to Five Forces, with the current fad putting the others on the back burner.

Mingers (2001) and Ormerod (2001) both explore the mixing of methods to facilitate organisational intervention in general. We would advocate that combining methods is especially powerful in facilitating strategy formulation in particular and strategic development in general, where both hard and soft methods have roles to play and future developments will focus on the complementarity of methods rather than the refinement of individual methods or approaches.

REFERENCES

Dyson, R.G. (2004) 'Strategic development and SWOT analysis at the University of Warwick', *European Journal of Operational Research*, **152**(3), 631–640.

Eden, C. (2004) 'Analyzing cognitive maps to help structure issues or problems', *European Journal of Operational Research*, **159**, 673–686.

Eden, C., Ackermann, F. & Cropper, S. (1992) 'The analysis of cause maps', *The Journal of Management Studies*, 29, 309–324.

Hax, A.C. & Majluf, N.S. (1983) 'The use of the industry attractiveness–business strength matrix in strategic planning', *Interfaces*, **13**(2), 40–60.

Henderson, B.D. (1970) 'The product portfolio matrix', The Boston Consulting Group, Perspectives No. 66, Boston, MA.

Henderson, B.D. (1973) 'The experience curve reviewed, IV. The growth share matrix of the product portfolio', The Boston Consulting Group, Perspectives No. 135, Boston, MA.

Learned, E.P., Christensen, C.R., Andrews, K.E. & Guth, W.D. (1965) *Business Policy: Text and Cases*. Irwin: Homewood, IL.

Mingers, J. (2001) 'Multi-methodology – mixing and matching methods'. In: Rosenhead, J. & Mingers, J. (eds), *Rational Analysis in a Problematic World Revisited*. John Wiley & Sons: Chichester.

Ormerod, R.J. (2001) 'Mixing methods in practice'. In: Rosenhead, J. & Mingers, J. (eds), *Rational Analysis in a Problematic World Revisited*. John Wiley & Sons: Chichester.

Porter, M.E. (1980) *Competitive Strategy: Techniques for Analyzing Industries and Competitors*. Free Press: New York.

Porter, M.E. (2001) 'Strategy and the internet', *Harvard Business Review*, **79**(3), 63–78.

Schoeffler, S., Buzzell, R.D. & Heany, D.F. (1974) 'Impact of strategic planning on profit performance', *Harvard Business Review*, **Mar/Apr**, 137–145.

Tapinos, E., Dyson, R.G. & Meadows, M. (2005) 'The impact of performance measurement in strategic planning', *International Journal of Productivity and Performance Management*, **54**(5/6), 370–384.

Weihrich, H. (1982) 'The TOWS matrix: a tool for situational analysis', *Long Range Planning*, **15**(2), 54–66.

Part IV

Rehearsing Strategy

Chapter 7

System Dynamics Modelling for Strategic Development

Martin Kunc and John Morecroft

INTRODUCTION

This chapter examines the role of system dynamics modelling and simulation in corporate strategic development. The fundamentals of the approach are first illustrated with a model of growth and rivalry in a low-cost airline. This example shows how modellers go about translating a strategic business situation into a simulator. Then a larger-scale application is presented based on a modelling project for a company in fast-moving consumer goods. The purpose of the project was to evaluate a new product launch strategy in a highly competitive industry. There is a description of how the model was conceptualised with the management team and a review of simulations that were helpful in assessing the strategic initiative. The chapter concludes with insights from the modelling project and reflections on the use of the model.

Figure 7.1 shows a part of the strategic development process introduced in Chapter 1. It is the part for rehearsing strategy where modelling has a vital role to play by complementing corrective action from real-world feedback with virtual feedback to improve strategic foresight. Here selected aspects of the real world are represented to test the feasibility of strategic initiatives, both before and during implementation. Tests that reveal unsatisfactory virtual performance may suggest pre-emptive tactical adjustments to strategy implementation. Such tests may also lead to fundamental changes in strategic initiatives or even call into question the organisation's strategic goals and the strategic direction that lies behind them.

System dynamics modelling is well suited to strategic rehearsal (Morecroft, 2007; Warren, 2002). The approach is widely used in business to help people understand how strategies will play out over time, what might go wrong, and how to make changes that will improve implementation and business performance. There have been numerous applications to topics such as market growth (Forrester, 1968; Sterman, 1988), product migration strategy (Morecroft, 1984), professional staff development (Warren, 2002, Chapter 3), process improvement (Repenning & Sterman, 2002), diversification (Gary, 2005) and alliance formation (Kapmeier, 2006) to name just a few.

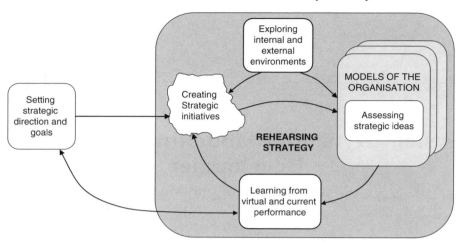

Figure 7.1. Rehearsing Strategy with Models

The modelling process engages managers in a dialogue about strategy and its likely consequences, thereby providing opportunities both for assessing strategic ideas and learning from virtual (or simulated) performance. As Senge (1990, Chapter 17) argues, the consequences of our actions in a complex system are neither immediate nor unambiguous. Models and simulators compress time and space so that it becomes possible for managers to 'experiment and to learn when the consequences of their decisions are in the future and in distant parts of the organisation'.

The typical steps in a modelling project are shown in Figure 7.2. First, managers work with the modeller(s) to articulate a problem. Together they decide the scope of the model, which parts of the business to include, which to leave out, and how the parts fit together. This activity results in a picture (or map) of the business, and leads to step 2 in which a dynamic hypothesis takes shape identifying how the parts of the business might interact to deliver the intended strategy and to determine future performance. In steps 3 and 4 (formulation and testing) the map of the business is translated into a simulator. Then finally in step 5 the simulator is used with managers to test strategy, chart the future trajectory of key performance indicators, challenge preconceptions and pet theories (by comparing simulations with people's expected outcomes) and to devise new policies that will improve performance.

Importantly, these five steps are iterative as indicated by the intricate pattern of cross connections at the centre of the figure. For example, the search for a dynamic hypothesis in step 2 may lead to a reconsideration of the problem in step 1, as the project team reviews the map of the business. Testing in step 4 may lead to changes of formulation in step 3 or even a re-thinking of the dynamic hypothesis. And so on back and forth among the steps until confidence builds that the model and simulations are providing useful insight into the strategic initiative and the implementation problems it may pose.

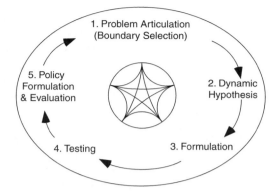

Figure 7.2. Steps in a System Dynamics Modelling Project
Source: Sterman (2000).

EASYJET AND THE RISE OF LOW-COST AIR TRAVEL IN EUROPE

A good illustration of strategic rehearsal with system dynamics modelling is provided by the entry of easyJet into European low-cost air travel in the mid-1990s. The situation is described in a case study written at the time, entitled 'easyJet's $500 million gamble' (Sull, 1999). The opening paragraph sets the scene. 'This case study details the rapid growth of easyJet which started operations in November 1995 from London's Luton airport. In two years, it was widely regarded as the model low-cost European airline and a strong competitor to flag carriers. The company has clearly identifiable operational and marketing characteristics, e.g. one type of aircraft, point-to-point short-haul travel, no in-flight meals, rapid turnaround time, very high aircraft utilisation, direct sales, cost-conscious customer segments and extensive sub-contracting. easyJet's managers identified three of its nearest low-cost competitors and the strategy of each of these airlines is detailed in the case study. But easyJet also experienced direct retaliation from large flag carriers like KLM and British Airways (Go). These challenges faced easyJet's owner, Stelios Haji-ioannou, as he signed a $500 m contract with Boeing in July 1997 to purchase 12 brand new 737s.'

easyJet – A Bright Idea, But Will it Really Work?

Imagine yourself now in Mr Haji-ioannou's role. In doing so it is important to have in mind the European airline industry as it was back in the mid-1990s when full-service air travel was the norm, delivered by large companies with decades of experience. Is it really going to be feasible for Stelios to fill those expensive new planes or is his no-frills vision just a pipe-dream? Should he sign the contract with Boeing? In his mind is a bright new business idea, a creative segmentation of the air travel market to be achieved through cost leadership. It is a great idea, but will it work? What we are suggesting is to use modelling and simulation at this early stage of strategic development, while the initiative is still under discussion, to rehearse the likely outcome. Feasibility checks of strategy are natural territory for business simulators, especially dynamic, time-dependent, problems such as rapid growth in a competitive industry. If the model generates a scenario that suggests it will be difficult or impossible to fill the planes then use the scenario to question the initiative, reconsider the initial investment in planes and modify the implementation plan.

At the time there were differences of opinion about easyJet's strategic move within the industry and even among easyJet's own management team. Some industry experts had a dismal view of easyJet's prospects (in stark contrast to the founder's optimism), dismissing the fledgling airline with statements such as 'Europe is not ready for the peanut flight'. To bring modelling and simulation into this debate we first have to visualise the dynamic tasks that face Mr Haji-ioannou and his team in creating customer awareness (how do you attract enough fliers to fill 12 planes?), and dealing with retaliation by rivals (what if British Airways or KLM engage in a price war, could they sustain such a war, what would provoke such a response?). The starting point is a map of the business, a picture created with the management team, to think about the task of attracting and retaining passengers and the factors that might drive competitor retaliation.

In this particular case the model was derived from the easyJet case study rather than direct meetings with the management team. Nevertheless, the example illustrates the principles involved and also introduces basic concepts of system dynamics modelling such as stock accumulation, feedback loops and equation formulation. The same principles were used in the more detailed fast-moving consumer goods project reported later.

Stock Accumulation

The versatile concept of stock accumulation appears in all system dynamic models (Morecroft, 2007; Sterman, 2000; Warren, 2002). Any balance sheet item in an organisation can be represented as a stock accumulation. Practical examples are finished goods inventory, capital equipment, buildings and cash – variables that wax and wane according to the firm's strategic decisions and priorities. It takes time to build up such assets or to reduce them, and that makes them important in understanding dynamics. However, not only balance sheet items accumulate in organisations. So too do employees such as factory workers, staff, engineers or designers and even intangibles like product quality, service reputation, staff morale, price or cost. All can be represented as stock accumulations.

Asset stocks accumulate their inflows and outflows in just the same way that water from a tap accumulates in a bathtub. If the inflow is greater than the outflow then the stock or level gradually rises. If the outflow is greater than the inflow then the stock or level gradually falls. If the inflow and outflow are identical then the level remains constant. This bathtub feature of assets in organisations is depicted in Figure 7.3. Here an asset stock or resource is shown as a rectangle containing a shaded area to denote a partially filled container. On the left is an inflow drawn as a valve (or tap) superimposed on an arrow. The arrow enters the stock and originates from a source, shown as a cloud or amorphous blob. A similar combination of symbols on the right represents an outflow. In this case the flow originates in the stock and ends up in a sink (another cloud or amorphous blob). The complete picture is called a 'stock and flow' network. A practical example is the number of workers

Asset stock (t) = Asset Stock (t−dt) + (Inflow−Outflow)* dt
INIT Asset Stock = 200 {an arbitrary initial value for illustration}

Figure 7.3. Asset Stock Accumulation – a Bathtub Analogy

in a factory. In this case the inflow is hiring and the outflow is layoffs. The source and sink are the pool of workers seeking employment.

The equations for a stock and flow network carry out the arithmetic of accumulation as shown in the lower half of Figure 7.3. The value of an asset stock at time t is equal to its value at the previous point in time $t-$ dt plus the difference between the inflow and the outflow over the time interval dt. Here the term 'dt' defines the length of the time step (or delta time) between the calculations performed by the simulator. Each asset stock is assigned an initial value at the start of the simulation. Asset stocks cannot be adjusted instantaneously. Change takes place only gradually through flow rates. This inertial characteristic of stocks and flows is absolutely vital to portraying dynamics.

Winning Customers in a New Segment – A Process that Involves Stock Accumulation and a Reinforcing Feedback Loop

The building blocks of system dynamics models are stock accumulations, causal links and feedback loops. Causal links show simple cause and effect relationships. Feedback loops depict closed paths of cause and effect and are of special importance because they generate dynamics. Feedback loops can be either reinforcing or balancing. Reinforcing loops are responsible for growth dynamics whereas balancing loops are responsible for goal-seeking dynamics and oscillations. By combining stock accumulations, causal links and feedback loops it is possible to create visual models of a wide variety of dynamic strategic business situations, including easyJet's $500 million gamble.

Figure 7.4 uses one stock accumulation, one reinforcing feedback loop and several causal links to show how a start-up airline attracts new passengers and communicates its new concept to the flying public. The marketing task is far-from-trivial, because when you think about it (and modelling really forces you to think hard about the practical details that underpin strategy) the company has to spread the word to millions of people if it is to fill 12 brand new 737s day after day.

Potential passengers are shown as an asset stock representing the cumulative number of fliers who have formed a favourable impression of the start-up airline. Note that these passengers have not necessarily flown with easyJet, but would if they could.[1] This rather abstract way of thinking about passengers is a convenient

---

[1] We are drawing a distinction between *wanting* a product or service and actually buying it. The distinction is important in practice because customers often go through stages of adoption. First, they become aware and interested. Then, with more time and further persuasion, they buy. The most basic feasibility check is whether the firm can generate enough interested customers to fill 12 planes.

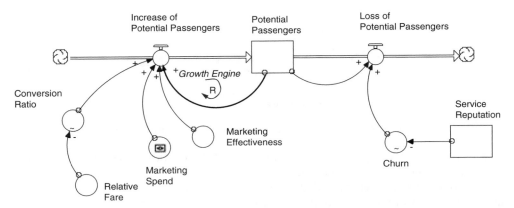

Potential Passengers(t) = Potential Passengers(t – dt) + (Increase of Potential Passengers –
Loss of Potential Passengers) * dt
INIT Potential Passengers = 5000
Increase of Potential Passengers = Potential Passengers *Conversion Ratio + Marketing
Spend*1000*Marketing Effectiveness
Conversion Ratio = GRAPH(Relative Fare)
Marketing Spend = 2500 {£thousands per year}
Marketing Effectiveness = 0.05 {Passengers wooed per £ spent}

Figure 7.4. Reinforcing Loop and Other Causal Links Driving Growth of Passengers

simplifying assumption that enables us to focus on growth of interest in low-cost
flights without the need to model the detailed operations of the company. Bear
in mind however that the scope of a model always depends on its purpose. For
example, a model to study the growth of the whole airline (rather than simply
growth of potential passengers) would include the company's internal operations
such as hiring and training of staff and investment in planes, as in Sterman's (1988)
well-known People Express management flight simulator.

The number of potential passengers starts very small (just 5000 in the model) and
grows over time. But how does growth take place? The remaining parts of the figure
show the factors that determine both the increase and loss of passengers. In practice
this information comes from the management team, coaxed out by a facilitator who
is helping the team to visualise the business.

The driver of growth is a reinforcing feedback loop shown at the centre of
Figure 7.4 and labelled 'R, Growth Engine'. In this loop potential passengers attract
new converts through positive word-of-mouth. The more potential passengers, the
greater the rate of increase of potential passengers. This causal link is drawn as a
curved arrow with a '+' sign on the arrow head to indicate a link with positive
polarity (more passengers, greater inflow). The increase of potential passengers then
accumulates in the stock of potential passengers, leading to even more potential
passengers and a greater rate of increase in potential passengers, thereby completing
the reinforcing loop. The strength of word-of-mouth is captured in a concept called
the conversion ratio, which itself depends on relative fare. As relative fare increases
the conversion rate decreases, a causal link drawn as a curved arrow with a '−' sign
on the arrow head to indicate a link with negative polarity.

These effects are captured algebraically in the equation for increase of potential passengers. The first part of the equation states that the increase of potential

passengers depends on the product of potential passengers and the conversion ratio. Intuitively, the lower easyJet's fare relative to established rivals the higher the conversion ratio and the more potent is word-of-mouth. An exceptionally low fare is a talking point among the travelling public, just as happened in real life.[2] Such a relationship would normally be sketched as a graph, based on expert opinion from the management team. In this particular case, when easyJet's fare is just 30% of rivals' fare, the conversion rate is assumed to be 2.5, meaning that each potential passenger converts 2.5 new potential passengers per year. However, at 50% of rivals' fare the conversion rate is reduced to 1.5 and at 70% it is only 0.3. Eventually, if easyJet's fare were to equal rivals' then the conversion rate would be zero because a standard fare cannot sustain word-of-mouth.

The increase of potential passengers is also influenced by marketing spend, another causal link. This link is formulated as the product of marketing spend and marketing effectiveness (shown in the second part of the equation for increase of potential passengers). Marketing spend is set at a default value of £2.5 million per year. Marketing effectiveness represents the number of new potential passengers per marketing £ spent. It is set at 0.05 passengers per £, so marketing brings 125 000 potential passengers per year (2.5 million per year × 0.05).

The loss of potential passengers depends on service reputation. The lower service reputation, the greater the churn (hence the '−' sign on the arrow head of the causal link). The greater the churn, the more the loss of passengers. Industry specialists say that service reputation depends on ease-of-booking, punctuality, safety, on-board service and quality of meals. For short-haul flights punctuality is often the dominant factor. The model does not represent all these factors explicitly but simply represents service reputation as a stock accumulation that can be initialised anywhere on a scale between 0.5 (very poor) and 1.5 (very good). If reputation is very good then fliers retain a favourable impression of the airline, so the annual loss of potential passengers is small, just 2.5% per year – an assumption made in the graph function for the churn. If reputation is poor then the loss of potential passengers per year is damagingly high, up to 100% per year. Notice there is no inflow or outflow to reputation even though it is a stock variable. The reason is that the factors driving change in reputation are outside the boundary of the model.

Retaliation by High-Cost Rivals – A Process that Involves Stock Accumulation and a Balancing Feedback Loop[3]

Figure 7.5 shows one possible way to visualise the retaliatory response of powerful European flag carriers to low-cost airlines in the early years. It is important to emphasise here the phrase *one possible way*, because there are many ways that a management team such as easyJet's might think about competitors. Part of the team model-building task is to achieve the simplest possible shared representation, drawing on the sophisticated (and sometimes conflicting) knowledge of the team

---

[2] In some cases very low fares may deter passengers due to concerns about safety. But in this particular case easyJet was flying a fleet of brand new 737s, which instilled confidence.

[3] Material in this section is taken from Morecroft, J., 1999, Visualising and Rehearsing Strategy, *Business Strategy Review*, **10**(3). pp. 21. Reproduced by permission of Blackwell Publishing.

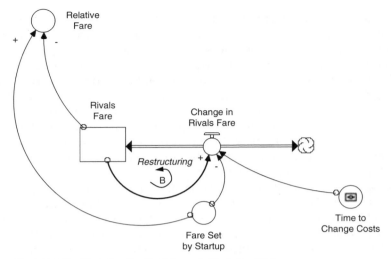

Rivals Fare(t) = Rivals Fare(t – dt) + (Change in Rivals Fare) * dt
INIT Rivals Fare = .25 {£/passenger mile}
Change in Rivals Fare = (Fare Set by Startup – Rivals Fare)/Time to Change Costs
Fare Set by Startup = .09 {£/passenger mile}
Time to Change Costs = 4 {years}
Relative Fare = Fare Set by Startup/ Rivals Fare {dimensionless}

Figure 7.5. Balancing Loop and Other Causal Links Driving Fare Reductions in High-Cost Rivals

members. A fundamental question is whether it is necessary to model competing firms in depth. Do you really need a detailed portrayal of British Airways or KLM to understand the threat such rivals might pose to the feasibility of easyJet's growth strategy?

The leader of a team-modelling project should not impose a rigid answer on this question of how much detail to include. The modeller should be sensitive to the opinions of the management team while always striving for parsimony. After all, to achieve buy-in the model must capture managers' understanding of their world in their own vocabulary. In these situations it is useful to bear in mind that experienced business leaders themselves simplify their complex world. If they did not then it would be impossible to communicate their plans. Good business modelling, like good business communication, is the art of leaving things out – focusing only on those features of reality most pertinent to the problem at hand.

Figure 7.5 shows just enough about competitors to indicate how, collectively, they could stall easyJet's growth ambitions.[4] Recall that word-of-mouth feedback relies for its contagion on the start-up's fare being much lower than rivals. But what if competing firms try to match the start-up's low price? The figure shows how such price equalisation might take place. At the heart of the formulation is a balancing loop labelled 'B, Restructuring'. Rivals' fare is shown as a stock that accumulates

---

[4] Rivals are portrayed at a high level of aggregation. The purpose is to capture in broad (but dynamically accurate) terms how rival airlines respond to price competition.

the change in rivals' fare, which in turn depends on three factors: the fare set by the start-up, rivals' fare and the time to change costs, all depicted as causal links. The use of a stock accumulation implies that it takes time and effort for the established airlines to lower their fares. They cannot reduce fares until they cut costs, and a flag carrier like BA may take years to achieve cost parity with a low-cost start-up. The process of achieving cost parity is essentially a goal-seeking process represented by the balancing loop.

To understand the operation of the balancing loop suppose, that rivals begin with an average fare of 25 pence (£0.25) per passenger mile and set themselves a goal for average fare of only nine pence (£0.09) per passenger mile – equal to the average fare set by the start-up. (Of course nowadays all airlines use revenue management systems with variable fares. But our focus is on the huge discounts originally offered by low-cost airlines that were available on most seats and enabled easyJet to grow. So a very low fixed fare for the start-up is a reasonable simplifying assumption.[5]) The magnitude of the underlying cost equalisation task is now clear – it is the 64% difference between rivals' initial fare of 25 pence (£0.25) and easyJet's fare of nine pence. Such an enormous change can only be achieved through major restructuring of the business. The change in rivals' fare is controlled by the 'restructuring' balancing loop that gradually reduces the fare to equal the fare set by the start-up. The pace of restructuring depends on the time to change costs. Normally one would expect this adjustment time to be several years, and in the model it is set at 4 years. The equations show a typical asset stock adjustment formulation. The change in fare is equal to the difference between the start-up's fare and rivals' fare divided by the time to change costs. This expression takes a negative value as long as rivals' fare exceeds the start-up's fare, thereby leading to a fare reduction. So, at the start of the simulation, the change in fare is $(0.09 - 0.25)/4$, which is a brisk reduction rate of £0.04 per passenger mile per year. This rate prevails over the first computation interval to arrive at a new and lower fare for the next computation interval, and so on as the simulation proceeds.

Overview of Feedback Loops in the easyJet Model

Figure 7.6 summarises the main feedback loops in the model, including the two loops described above and two more loops that capture route saturation and churn. The figure is a typical example of a causal loop diagram, widely used in system dynamics to highlight the main feedback loops believed responsible for dynamics. Essentially it is a word and arrow diagram that makes use of special conventions to label the polarity of causal links and feedback loops. The advantage of such a diagram is a clutter-free overview of feedback structure.

In the centre of the figure is the reinforcing growth engine from Figure 7.4. Here each of the causal links around the loop is labelled with a '+' sign to indicate positive

---

[5] Large carriers will match low seat prices regardless of cost by providing some seats at a discount. Price cuts can be implemented very quickly through on-line yield management systems that allow dynamic pricing according to load factors. But narrowly targeted discounts are an ineffective weapon for companies like BA and KLM in the competitive fight with low-cost airlines. For example, out of 150 seats there may be only 15 cheap ones. For very popular flights there are no cheap seats at all. Only cost parity can deliver competitive prices and profitability in the long term for large carriers catering to a growing population of price-conscious fliers.

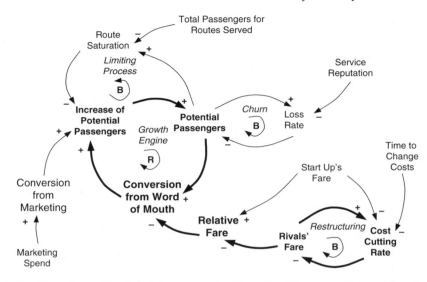

Figure 7.6. Overview of Feedback Loops for the Growth of Passenger Interest in a Low-Cost Airline

polarity. More potential passengers lead to more conversion from word-of-mouth, a greater increase of potential passengers, more potential passengers, and so on. The loop is denoted as reinforcing (R) because an imagined increase in any of its variables sets in motion a chain of cause and effect that propagates around the loop to reinforce the original increase. For this reason reinforcing loops are the drivers of growth – in this case the growth of potential passengers.

In the bottom right of the figure is the important balancing loop from Figure 7.5, involving restructuring of costs, which determines rivals' fare. There are just two concepts in the loop: rivals' fare and cost cutting rate. The loop is denoted as balancing (B) because an imagined increase in any of its variables sets in motion a chain of cause and effect that counteracts or balances the original increase. So if rivals' fare were to increase then the cost cutting rate would increase, which in turn would lead to a reduction of rivals' fare, thereby balancing the original increase. Incidentally a simple rule for determining loop polarity is to count the number of negative links around the loop. If the number is odd – 1, 3, 5, . . . – then the loop is balancing. If the number is even – 0, 2, 4, . . . – then the loop is reinforcing. In this case the number of negative links is one and the loop is balancing. The dynamic significance of the loop is that it tends to equalise rivals' fare with the start-up's fare. As a result relative fare (defined as the ratio of start-up's fare to rivals' fare) converges gradually to parity, thereby reducing the strength of word-of-mouth in the reinforcing loop.

These two loops form the core of the model and are central to the evaluation of easyJet's start-up strategy. Qualitatively, if the reinforcing loop is strong (and stimulates rapid growth) while the balancing loop is weak (and leads to very slow price equalisation) then easyJet's $500 million gamble is likely to succeed and the company will fill its planes. However, if the balancing loop is strong (and price equalisation happens quickly) then the window of opportunity for rapid growth is much reduced and easyJet's gamble may fail. This qualitative use of causal loop diagrams to interpret likely dynamics illustrates a key principle in system dynamics that 'feedback structure generates dynamic behaviour'. Simulation then provides the means to investigate dynamics carefully and rigorously.

In addition to the two loops depicted in bold there are two further loops in Figure 7.6 that capture the effects of route saturation and churn on passenger interest. These extra loops are peripheral to the immediate question of whether or not easyJet can fill 12 planes, but are important in the long run to ensure realistic limits to the growth of potential passengers in the region served by the fledgling airline. At the top of the figure is a balancing loop (labelled 'B, Limiting Process') in which route saturation eventually restricts the increase of potential passengers. Finally, in the centre-right is a balancing loop (labelled 'B, Churn') showing the effect of the start-up's service reputation on the loss rate of potential passengers.

Of course this brief model of passengers and fares is a sketch of a more complex reality. Nevertheless, it contains sufficient detail for an informative team discussion about passenger growth and price retaliation. And when simulated the model contains sufficient dynamic complexity to yield thought-provoking growth scenarios that help management to rehearse strategy.

SIMULATIONS OF GROWTH SCENARIOS[6]

The purpose of the model is to investigate easyJet's $500 million gamble to purchase 12 brand new Boeing 737s. Is it wise to order so many planes? Will it be possible to fill them? And assuming a large potential market for low-cost air travel, will easyJet be able to capture a big enough slice? A rough calculation suggests the airline needs to attract almost 1 million fliers if it is to operate 12 fully loaded aircraft.[7] That is a lot of people. What combination of word-of-mouth and marketing will attract this number of potential passengers? How long will it take? What are the risks of price retaliation by rivals? These are good questions to explore using the what-if capability of simulation.

Figures 7.7 and 7.8 show simulations of the growth of potential passengers over the period 1996 to 2000 under two different approaches to marketing spend (bold and cautious) *and* under the assumption of slow retaliation by rivals. Bold marketing spend is assumed to be five times greater than cautious spend (at £2.5 million per year versus £0.5 million per year). In both cases the horizontal straight line shows

---

[6] Material in this section is taken from Morecroft, J., 1999, Visualising and Rehearsing Strategy, *Business Strategy Review*, **10**(3). pp. 23–24. Reproduced by permission of Blackwell Publishing.

[7] Assume each aircraft carries 150 passengers and makes three round-trip flights a day. So a fully loaded plane needs 900 passengers each day ($150 \times 3 \times 2$). A fully loaded fleet of 12 planes needs 10 800 passengers per day, which is almost 4 million per year. If we make the further assumption that each potential passenger is likely to fly the available routes twice a year on round-trip flights, then the start-up airline needs to attract a pool of almost 1 million fliers to ensure commercially viable load factors. This rough calculation is typical of the sort of judgemental numerical data required to populate an algebraic model. Perfect accuracy is not essential and often not possible. The best estimates of informed people, specified to order-of-magnitude accuracy (or better) are adequate, drawing on the informal but powerful knowledge base derived from experience.

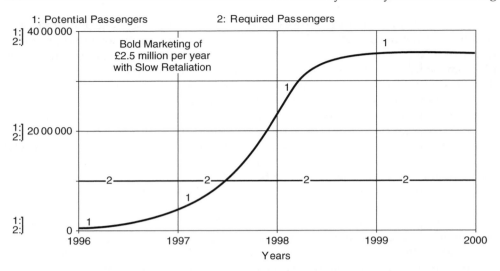

Figure 7.7. Simulation of Bold Marketing with Slow Retaliation

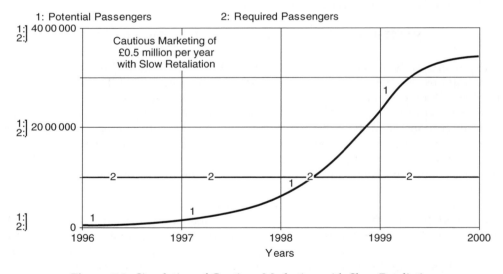

Figure 7.8. Simulation of Cautious Marketing with Slow Retaliation

the 'required' number of passengers to fill 12 planes. This line is a useful reference against which to compare the number of potential passengers. If and when potential passengers (line one) exceed required passengers (line two), the strategy is deemed feasible.

Consider first the timelines for bold marketing in Figure 7.7. The simulation begins in 1996 with a very small number of potential passengers – just 5000. The fledgling airline is virtually unknown to the flying public, despite its ambitions. In the first year of operation, bold marketing brings the airline to the attention of a growing number of fliers. By the end of 1996 there is a band of several hundred thousand enthusiastic supporters. Moreover, this band of supporters is beginning to convert more followers through positive word-of-mouth. In the interval 1997 to 1998 the number of potential passengers (line one) rises sharply as word-of-mouth continues to fuel exponential growth. By mid-1997 the number of potential passengers has reached the target of 1 million required to fill the fleet. In the remainder of the year, reinforcing growth continues. There is a huge leap of more than a million potential passengers in the last 6 months of 1997 as the powerful engine of growth continues to gather momentum. Then, in the second quarter of 1998, growth ceases abruptly as the airline's message reaches all 3.5 million fliers in the imagined catchment region it serves.

The strategically important part of the timeline is the growth phase between the start of 1996 and early 1998. Bold marketing coupled with strong word-of-mouth unleashes a powerful engine of growth which, in classic exponential fashion, begins small (and therefore invisible to rivals) and appears to snowball rapidly after some 18 months.

Consider next the timelines in Figure 7.8, which trace the build-up of potential passengers from cautious marketing. Spend is cut by four-fifths from £2.5 million a year to only £0.5 million a year. As before, the simulation starts in 1996 with only 5000 potential passengers. In the first year the airline wins few passengers – not surprising because marketing spend is much reduced. However, in the second year there is healthy growth in passengers, despite the low marketing spend. Word-of-mouth is now beginning to draw in lots of new passengers. Once the growth engine is primed it gets rolling and in the second quarter of 1998 carries the airline's passenger base beyond the target required to fill the fleet. Growth continues into 1999 until nearly all 3.5 million fliers are aware of the new low-cost service. Cautious marketing simply defers growth (by comparison with bold marketing) but does not alter the ultimate size of the passenger base. One can begin to appreciate a persuasive rationale for caution. By the year 2000 the simulated airline has saved £8 million in marketing spend (4 years at an annual saving of £2 million) yet has still spread its message to 3.5 million fliers!

Figures 7.9 and 7.10 show the same two marketing approaches (bold and cautious) under the assumption that rivals retaliate quickly. Price equalisation happens in half the time previously assumed (2 years instead of 4) and as a result both timelines for potential passengers are noticeably changed by comparison with the base case. But from the viewpoint of strategic feasibility the bold marketing timeline tells much the same story as before. At the start of 1996 the airline is almost unknown among the flying public, and by the third quarter of 1997 it has attracted enough potential passengers to fill 12 planes. Fast-acting rivals seem unable to prevent this rise of a new entrant from obscurity to commercial viability, though price equalisation measures do curtail the ultimate dissemination of the start-up airline's low-price message.

A strategically significant change is observable in the timeline for cautious marketing shown in Figure 7.10. The start-up airline is no longer able to fill its planes because it is unable to attract enough passengers. The company's rise from

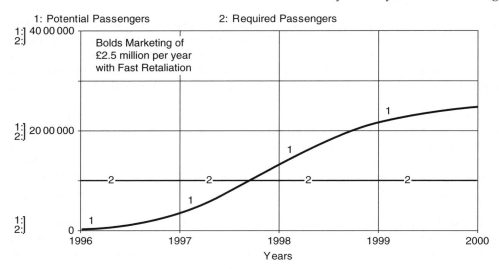

Figure 7.9. Simulation of Bold Marketing with Fast Retaliation

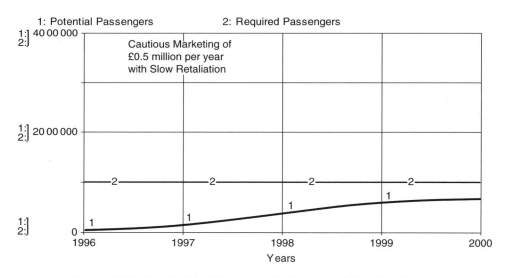

Figure 7.10. Simulation of Cautious Marketing with Fast Retaliation

obscurity to prominence never happens. Cautious marketing attracts few converts and fails to ignite word-of-mouth. By the time the low-price message has reached a few hundred thousand fliers (at the end of 1997) it is no longer distinctive. Rivals are low-price too. If this future were easyJet's its planes would be flying half-empty and it would be losing money. Fast retaliation can prove fatal in a word-of-mouth market. It is exactly this kind of 'surprise future' that simulations bring to life in order to challenge management preconceptions during the strategic development process.

A CASE STUDY IN FAST-MOVING CONSUMER GOODS

So much for our small model of passenger growth in a start-up airline. Now we turn to a much larger model that was developed with the management team of a company competing in fast-moving consumer goods, FMCG. The purpose of the project was to evaluate the launch of a new product. The study was undertaken about a year into the launch, at an early stage of market development. The new product was conceived as a premium quality replacement for a traditional product in a mature and highly competitive market sector whose profitability had been declining in recent years. For confidentiality reasons we cannot disclose the names of the actual firms and products, so we disguise the case to make it look like the UK soap market, another well-known market segment of the FMCG industry whose product innovations are familiar to most readers and quite similar to those in the real case. The disguised client firm is named 'Old English Bar Soap Company', and its main competitors are named 'Global Personal Care' and 'Supermarkets'. It is important to stress that these are fictional names, not real soap companies, and that the actual product was not soap at all, but a different category of fast-moving consumer good. Real-life market development involved a traditional product, a substitute product and a new product. In the disguised case the traditional product is bar soap, the substitute product is shower gel and the new product is liquid soap.

Market Overview

While bar soap has been the product leader in personal care since the beginning of this market, shower gels have been growing in recent years pushed by aggressive marketing campaigns and changes in lifestyle, as Figure 7.11 shows. This process has

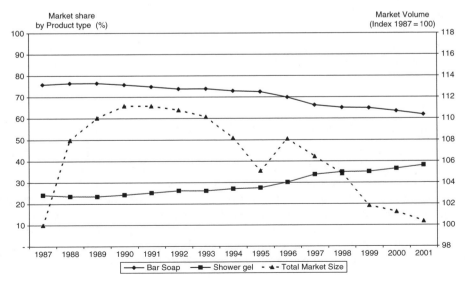

Figure 7.11. Total Market Volume and Market Share by Product in the Disguised Market (1987–2001)

been occurring in a market whose volume has been stable for many years due to high penetration of demographic segments and low population growth. Meanwhile bar soap firms have introduced variations on their traditional product in an attempt to increase sales value. These variations have been justified by consumers' willingness to buy premium soaps (instead of cheaper alternatives) as well as demographic and lifestyle changes. In spite of these developments, the general trend has been away from bar soap towards shower gels because gels offer more benefits to the user.

The two main companies are Old English Bar Soap Company with 26% market share and Global Personal Care with 31% market share. In addition there are supermarkets with 16% market share. Together these rival groupings account for most of the market in value terms. The market has always been brand-driven, with the major brands investing huge amounts of money in advertising. In recent years Old English has been offering a steady stream of new products in bar soap – its core and traditional competence – supported by high levels of advertising as it faced more competitive pressure. The company is recognised as an innovator in bar soap, but it lacks the same strength in shower gels. Global Personal Care, though a newcomer to the market, has a long tradition in fast-moving consumer goods on a global scale. Global Personal Care built its strong position in the market during the 1980s and 1990s. The company entered the soap sector for the first time in the mid-1980s when it acquired a well-known but small local bar soap brand in the UK market. Like Old English, the company has a range of products aimed at various lifestyles and consumers. But Global Personal Care is not as innovative as Old English and tends to follow rather than lead new product developments.

Supermarkets are the large supermarket chains. We decided to aggregate all their products because the big retailers follow similar competitive strategies. Traditionally supermarkets have achieved only low penetration of the market. This small presence was due to the success of branded products arising from heavy advertising and promotional support. However, a programme of systematic upgrading and innovation increased supermarkets' reputation among buyers, which yielded rewards throughout the 1990s, as market share grew steadily. Additionally, supermarkets' products are priced between 5 and 10% lower than manufacturers' brands.

The Competitive Problem and Strategic Response

New product varieties in bar soap have been driving growth in sales value in recent years, especially for Old English. However, new lifestyle trends have turned buyers to look for convenient products, helping shower gels to grow in volume at the expense of bar soaps. At the same time, the consolidation of competitors through mergers and acquisitions pushed the client company to timidly diversify into shower gels by acquiring a small firm with a strong position at the premium end of the market but outside the mass-market distribution channels. This acquisition was not the only response from Old English to increasing competition in the market.

The prospect of stagnation and declining profitability in their traditional bar soap business prompted Old English to launch an entirely new premium product, liquid soap, intended to halt the erosion of soap sales and to boost the profitability of their core business in the mature soap market. However, competitors were able to copy the product innovation sooner than expected, despite significant changes in manufacturing methods. For example, Global Personal Care launched a liquid soap product 18 months later and supermarkets followed shortly after.

A Note on the Model Development Process

The modelling team consisted of two system dynamics professionals and an internal consultant of the company. The management team consisted of senior managers from marketing, sales and manufacturing, who were the strategic decision-makers of the company. The project ran for 1 year with intermittent individual and team meetings to extract and validate the information required for the model. The model was designed to answer the following questions for the management team. How can we grow and sustain the new product in the face of stiff competition? What set of policies can help us to avoid losing revenues as happened with the old product?

MODEL CONCEPTUALISATION

The project methodology followed the five steps outlined in Figure 7.2, beginning with problem articulation and ending with policy formulation and evaluation. This methodology ensures a close interaction between the management team and modellers in order to elicit and capture managers' understanding of the strategic problem and the competitive dynamics of the industry.

The launch of liquid soap is a typical example of a strategic initiative believed to be consistent with the company's overall strategic direction and intended to satisfy its strategic goals. In this case Old English wished to maintain its traditional leadership position in soap products while at the same time remaining profitable. The modelling project was an opportunity to rehearse the thinking behind the strategy.

An initial meeting with the management team led to the stock and flow network shown in Figure 7.12. There are two conceptually separate markets. At the top of the figure is bar soap, containing established bar soap volumes for Old English on the left and competitors on the right. These volumes are represented as stock accumulations to capture the typical inertia of consumer buying habits. Volume lost to other product types is shown as outflows. Volume exchanged through competition is shown as a net flow of bar soap volume between Old English and competitors. Notice there are no inflows to the two stock accumulations, reflecting the important assumption that the market is mature. At the bottom of the figure is the new market for liquid soap in which trials of the new product lead to an accumulation of trial users who then adopt either Old English's liquid soap or competitors' liquid soap. Adoption results in an increasing number of regular users represented by two stock accumulations. Note that managers expected to attract and retain loyal customers in the new premium liquid soap market as there is no flow from regular users of Old English's liquid soap to regular users of competitors' liquid soaps.

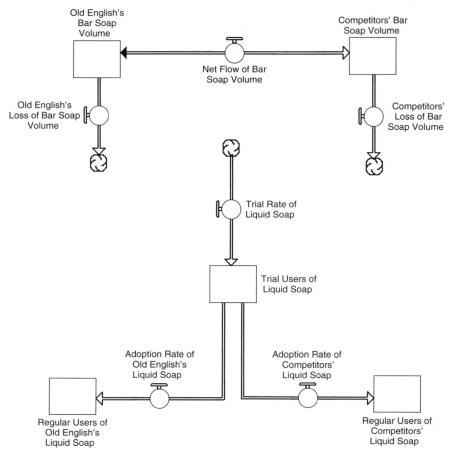

Figure 7.12. First Representation of the Management Team's View of the Market

Figure 7.12 reveals three interesting issues about the initial conceptualisation of the strategic initiative in liquid soap. First, the management team perceived the bar soap and liquid soap market segments as disconnected from each other. Second, users of bar soap were lost to 'somewhere' in the personal care market, through the outflow 'loss of bar soap volume'. In fact much of this loss was to shower gel, but since Old English's management had neither a special interest nor the capabilities to compete strongly in shower gel, the slow draining of customers to gels was not clearly recognised or at least its cumulative effect was thought to be small. This blind spot may have influenced Old English's subsequent innovation. Third, the market for the new product was believed to be a 'one-off' simple adoption process. Old English's management would convince bar soap consumers to trial the new product. These potential consumers, in the stock labelled 'Trial Users of Liquid Soap', would remain an uncertainty until they decided to adopt Old English's or a competitor's liquid soap. The strategic problem would be solved for Old English when trialling consumers became regular users of liquid soap, protected by first-mover advantage – since management believed that Old English was the only firm with the technology to produce the new product. In other words, the strategic intent was to contain competitors in the bar soap segment while the company built its leadership in the liquid soap segment. Then, liquid soap users would remain isolated from competitors' actions because of first-mover advantage.

A Refined View of the Market

After in-depth interviews with senior managers, we identified additional relevant issues that led to a modified picture of the market shown in Figure 7.13. There are

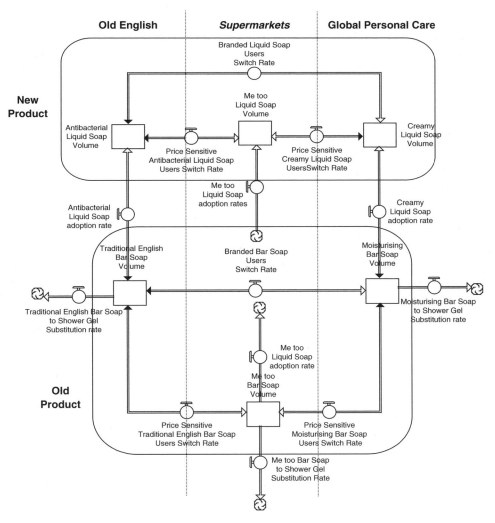

Figure 7.13. Management Team's Refined View of their Market

now three distinct competitors each with bar soap and liquid soap products. On the left is Old English with its established product 'Traditional English Bar Soap' and its new product 'Antibacterial Liquid Soap'. On the right is Global Personal Care with its established product 'Moisturising Bar Soap' and its new product 'Creamy Liquid Soap'. In the middle are supermarkets with their established product 'Me Too Bar Soap' and their new product 'Me Too Liquid Soap'.

Each of the players in the bar soap market faced a complex situation because they had to balance the attractiveness of their established products, taking account of three different forces simultaneously influencing their customers. The first force is traditional inter-firm rivalry in the bar soap market from consumer promotions and advertising, aimed at maintaining market share in bar soap. This rivalry is depicted in terms of the users switch rates between the three stocks in the bottom half of Figure 7.13 ('Traditional English Bar Soap Volume', 'Moisturising Bar Soap Volume' and 'Me Too Bar Soap Volume'). For example, the bi-flow labelled 'Branded Bar Soap Users Switch Rate' represents competition in bar soaps between Old English and Global Personal Care. Similarly, the bi-flow labelled 'Price Sensitive Traditional English Bar Soap Users Switch Rate' represents competition in bar soaps between Old English and supermarkets. The second force influencing customers is the development of the liquid soap market represented as the set of three stocks in the top half of Figure 7.13 ('Antibacterial Liquid Soap Volume', 'Me Too Liquid Soap Volume' and 'Creamy Liquid Soap Volume') and the corresponding adoption rates. The third force is the attractiveness of shower gels – a substitute product – represented as outflows from bar soap volume in Figure 7.13. For example, the outflow 'Traditional English Bar Soap to Shower Gel Substitution Rate' represents the loss of Old English bar soap volume to shower gel.

Since this is a mature market with a high level of penetration, there are no inflows to increase total volume. In other words, the development of the market is essentially a zero-sum game between brands and varieties – and in soaps this game is played against the backdrop of gradual volume loss to shower gels. While managers' expectations at Old English were to move users from bar soaps into liquid soaps (and focus groups suggested that bar soap users would indeed adopt liquid soaps) they nevertheless faced a dynamically complex problem. The company needed to transfer the users of the old established product to the new product without losing market share while improving profitability and avoiding costly price wars. Essentially they needed to simultaneously manage a growth business (liquid soap) alongside a declining business (bar soap) against strong and diverse rivals.

The next step in the modelling project was to identify the factors controlling the flows between stocks. This information was obtained from interviews with the management team and meetings with other experts from the business. Their observations were translated into diagrams and equations. There is not the space in this chapter to present all the formulations. However, the interested reader can find the complete documented model in Kunc (2005). Here we review a selection of important equation formulations describing consumers' response to competitive actions and the managerial decision-making processes responsible for these competitive actions.

Consumer Behaviour

The substitution process of bar soap for shower gel is modelled in Figure 7.13 as the outflows 'Traditional English Bar Soap to Shower Gel Substitution Rate', 'Moisturising Bar Soap to Shower Gel Substitution Rate' and 'Me Too Bar Soap to Shower Gel Substitution Rate', which can be summarised in the following equation:

Shower gel adoption rate i = Bar soap volume $i \times s$

The index i represents the different players in the market, bar soap volume i reflects bar soap monthly sales volume of a particular player (e.g. the stock 'Traditional English Bar Soap Volume' in Figure 7.13) and s is a fixed percentage per month of the volume lost to shower gels. The fixed percentage, which was defined by the management team, is a simplification of the process of change in consumers' preferences. The management team suggested that the amount of bar soap consumption substituted each month by shower gels is a fixed percentage of the remaining customers. This fixed percentage captures two shared beliefs among managers: one is that remaining bar soap consumers will gradually switch to shower gels (unless they first adopt liquid soap) and the second is that all players in bar soap are going through the same substitution process as Figure 7.13 shows.

Management also believed that the personal care market is commoditised so customers are responsive to price differences among similar products, and advertising campaigns achieve short-term volume gains rather than long-term loyalty. Price and advertising determine the net flows between consumers[8] (shown as the bi-flows 'Branded Bar Soap Users Switch Rate', 'Price Sensitive Traditional English Bar Soap Users Switch Rate' and 'Price Sensitive Moisturising Bar Soap Users Switch Rate' in the Old Product section of Figure 7.13), as summarised in the equation below:

Net flow between firms = Consumers switching due to price + Net effect of advertising

Given the existing product similarities, we considered that consumers' choice between two brands was based on the price of one brand as a reference point for comparison with the other brand – an empirical generalisation used in modelling consumer choice (Meyer & Johnson, 1995). When consumers make their decisions, the price of Old English's bar soap acts as a reference point for comparison with Global Personal Care's bar soap. Therefore, the price effect on consumers' choice was represented using the following equation:

Consumers switching due to price = f(Effective retail price i/Effective retail price j)

---

[8] The net flow between price-sensitive consumers does not include the net effect of advertising since Me Too products are not advertised.

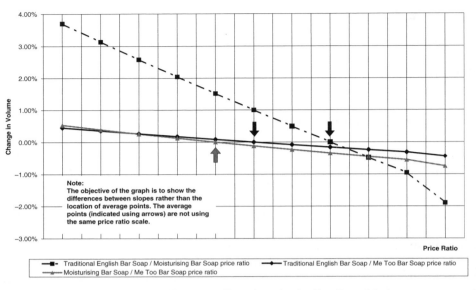

Figure 7.14. Price Response Functions in the Bar Soap Market

Effective retail price i is the suggested retail price less price discounts (where discounts are consumer promotions intended to boost short-term consumption). Despite the variety of soaps on offer, Old English's management team believed the differences between each players' soaps were small, so the model uses the average price ratio of the two brands (across all varieties) to represent the effect of price on consumers' switching rate. The price ratio affects change in volume according to the function shown in Figure 7.14. The function was calibrated using time series data for relative prices and volume.[9]

The effect of different value perceptions for competing products can be deduced from the slope of the functions shown in Figure 7.14. For example, the slope of the function for two products with similar perceived value (Old English's and Global Personal Care's bar soaps) is steeper – dashed line in Figure 7.14 – than the function for two products that customers perceive to have different value (Old English's and Global Personal Care's bar soaps compared with supermarkets' bar soaps) – light and dark solid lines. Consumers are more likely to switch between two products perceived similarly than two products perceived differently, which implies that supermarkets need to sustain bigger price differentials with respect to branded products to lure customers from branded products or to avoid losing customers.

A similar price response curve was devised for liquid soap and is shown in Figure 7.15. For comparison the equivalent price response for bar soap is shown as a dotted line.

_____

[9] Market data for calibrating the function was obtained from AC Nielsen's report of volumes and sales by distribution channel.

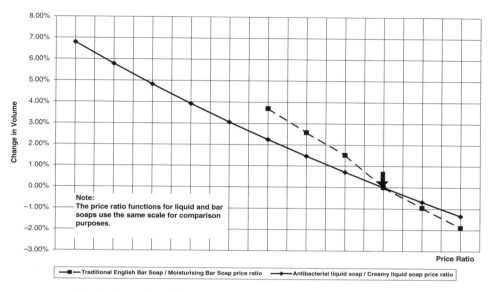

Figure 7.15. Price Response Functions for Bar and Liquid Soaps

Managerial Decision-Making Processes in Old English Bar Soap Company

The majority of the model was devoted to representing managerial decision-making processes inside the rival firms that, directly or indirectly, influence consumer behaviour. These decision-making processes include pricing, marketing, trade promotions and the management of display shelf. Manufacturing capacity management is also important as scale economies and capacity utilisation affect manufacturing cost and ultimately price. The corresponding formulations run to more than a hundred equations. They were constructed from concepts and facts gathered in many hours of meetings and sketched on a diagram occupying 12 A4 pages. Below is a brief verbal description of the formulations.

Marketing is adjusted to achieve a sales performance target. In Old English the target is past sales. So the decision-making process is as follows. When current sales volume is much less than past sales volume the company increases marketing action by offering bigger price discounts or initiating new advertising campaigns. On the other hand, when current sales volume is much greater than past sales volume the company reduces marketing action in order to improve operating cash flows. Small differences between current and past volumes tend to be ignored. The management response function is shown in Figure 7.16 and was calibrated by comparing observed volume changes with the historical behaviour of retail prices and the intensity of advertising campaigns. Interestingly, this formulation of pricing and advertising implies that Old English's managers ignore competitors' actions. They focus on their own volumes rather than benchmarking prices or volumes against Global Personal Care or supermarkets.

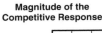

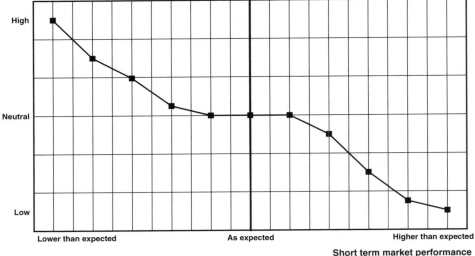

Figure 7.16. Function Determining the Strength of Competitive Response to Market Performance

Display shelf is negotiated between branded manufacturers and retailers. Share of the display shelf is a fiercely contested resource in fast-moving consumer goods, no matter how large or small the store. While big stores can offer lots of shelf space, it is easily filled by the huge proliferation of available products, thereby improving the bargaining position of retailers (Messinger & Narasimhan, 1995). The task of branded manufacturers' sales managers is to negotiate a significant share of display shelf at low cost in order to enhance daily sales and to increase the effectiveness of advertising campaigns. Conversely, retailers' management teams try to maximise the income received for allocated space by assigning the greatest share to the most profitable items. The decision-making process for changes in display shelf depends on trade margin and market share. The more market share or the greater trade margin then the larger the display shelf. This decision logic is embedded in a reinforcing feedback loop where the more shelf space, the greater sales volume, the higher market share and the more shelf space. If unchecked this reinforcing loop enables branded manufacturers to dominate the market. However, retailers can use private label products to retain some control as described later.

Manufacturing capacity is the responsibility of the manufacturing manager. The technology of liquid soap production is entirely different from bar soap and requires new equipment. So the manufacturing manager faced a strategic dilemma about how quickly to build capacity for the new product and how quickly to retire capacity for the old product. The decision-making process for the adjustment of manufacturing capacity is essentially driven by market size. The larger the expected sales volume the more capacity is needed, and vice versa. Economies of scale are important too. The greater capacity, the lower unit cost and the lower price (at a given margin), leading to more sales and eventually to more capacity. The same process also works in reverse. When sales fall, cost per unit increases due to a combination of low capacity utilisation, high fixed cost and fewer scale economies. As a result retail price increases too unless the firm reduces gross margin to maintain sales. The model captures the interplay of manufacturing cost dynamics arising from the growth of liquid soap capacity and the simultaneous decline of bar soap capacity.

Managerial Decision-Making Processes in Global Personal Care Company

The management team felt that Global Personal Care's decision-making processes were broadly similar to Old English Bar Soap Company. Therefore we modelled Global Personal Care by replicating the formulations for Old English while modifying information flows or parameters to capture important differences of managerial emphasis. For example, we assumed that Global Personal Care focuses its competitive actions on managing market share rather than sales volume. So, in Global Personal Care, promotions and advertising increase when market share falls below its historic value. Sales volume plays no significant role. Similarly, Global Personal Care's adjustment to mark-up or gross margin is formulated as a function of long-term market share instead of sales volume. We also assumed Global Personal Care offers a slightly higher trade margin than Old English in order to obtain an adequate share of shelf space despite lower market share.

Managerial Decision-Making Processes in Supermarkets

Supermarkets' pricing is much different than Old English and Global Personal Care for a number of reasons. First, supermarkets do not aspire to be market leaders. Rather, they participate in the market enough to bargain effectively with existing branded manufacturers. Second, supermarkets do not manufacture or own capacity. Instead, they buy from manufacturers that specialise in private-label products. Third, supermarkets do not promote their product through advertising. They compete on price only.

Supermarkets' pricing is intended to boost income from display shelf. The decision rule for supermarkets' pricing is influenced by trade margin received and by product sales – the two main sources of retailers' income. The income received from branded products in the form of trade margin is compared with the historical trade margin. If income from branded products falls, either as a result of a reduction in branded manufacturers' trade margin or market share, then supermarket managers reduce retail price for two reasons. First, they want to expand supermarket sales to substitute for income lost from branded manufacturers. Second, they want to force an improvement in the trade margin. However, as supermarkets expand their market share, the income from branded products will decline even more (if manufacturers of branded products do not offer higher trade margins), and supermarkets will further reduce their prices.

An extreme outcome of this interaction between manufacturers and retailers is that supermarkets will dominate the market through continuous price reductions (as has happened with Wal-Mart in some FMCG market segments). Pricing decisions that respond to income from trade margin are embedded in a reinforcing feedback loop in which price spirals downwards. Although there is a lower limit to price, it depends on the sourcing cost of supermarket products and the actual trade margin obtained from branded manufacturers. However, supermarket managers usually prefer to set a target market share that is low enough to maintain bargaining power without pushing branded manufacturers out of the market. This policy introduces an additional balancing feedback loop that halts the spiral decline in price.

That concludes the discussion of model formulations. The main assumptions and parameters were reviewed and agreed by the management team, and the model was tested and carefully calibrated. It was then ready for evaluating the new product strategy. A number of simulation experiments were conducted to understand changes in business performance and to improve the implementation of the strategic initiative in the market.

REHEARSING AND EVALUATING THE STRATEGIC INITIATIVE IN LIQUID SOAP

The first set of simulations replicate the decision-making processes followed by the management team since the launch of the product. The intention in showing this base case to the management team was to help them understand how their normal way of running the business led to the actual situation they were facing. In other words, the simulation moves them from actors in the business to spectators of their strategies, similar to playing a videotape of the performance of a football team after a match. We discussed the decision-making processes and their effects on the success of the strategic initiative.

The Base Case – Simulated Performance of the Market under Normal Operating Policies

Figure 7.17 shows the simulated sales volume for branded liquid soaps. For comparison, real time series data is also shown. Although there is not a perfect match of simulated and real trajectories, the magnitude and main trends are similar. As we will see, the simulations provide an explanation for observed behaviour and this is an important part of their value in rehearsing strategy. Old English's new product (line one) grows exceptionally fast during the first 36 months, exactly as the management team had hoped. This growth is due to two managerial actions: trialling and price reductions. The trialling effort is complemented with a large reduction in the retail price of liquid soaps that boosts the adoption rate. Meanwhile, competitors are slow to respond on price as we will see later in Figures 7.18 and 7.19.

After month 36, two factors reduce the growth rate of Old English's new antibacterial liquid soap, as shown in lines one and two in Figure 7.17. First, Old English's management stops reducing the price of the new product due to the early success

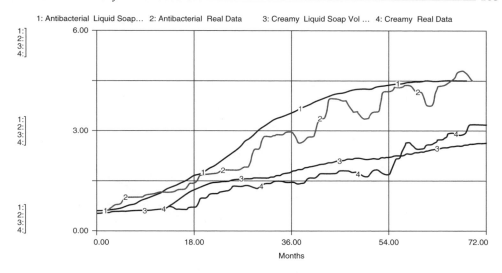

Figure 7.17. Liquid Soap: Simulated and Real Volumes

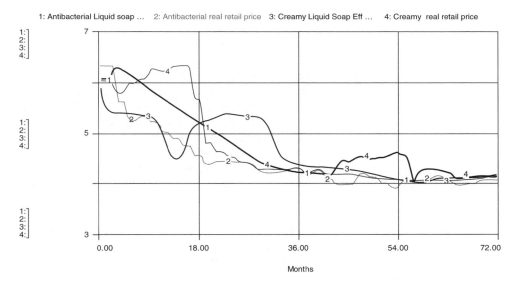

Figure 7.18. Liquid Soap: Simulated and Real Prices

of the launch. Sales volume after 3 years matches the expected market size and managers do not want to further erode the revenues from liquid soap. Second, the steady reduction in the number of bar soap users begins to slow market growth, despite the intensity of marketing actions. One lesson from the simulation is that Old English's managers might have been able to further exploit the potential of the

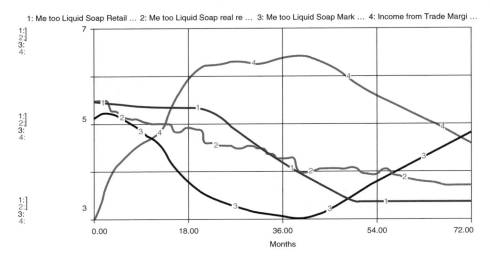

Figure 7.19. Liquid Soap: Supermarkets' Simulated and Real Prices and Simulated Income from Trade Margin

new market with more intense marketing actions at the beginning of the process. A corollary is that later marketing action is much less effective. Both these insights were useful for the company and confirm the first-mover advantage for developing the liquid soap market.

Figure 7.18 presents real and simulated retail prices in the new product market for branded products. Old English reduces price at an early stage to stimulate growth – lines one and two in Figure 7.18. Some time later, Global Personal Care also reduces liquid soap price – lines three and four in Figure 7.18, as a reaction to erosion of market share. Global Personal Care's price falls until it slightly undercuts Old English's price, in an effort to sustain market share. When Global Personal Care reduces its prices, there are two effects: one effect is to start attracting bar soap users into liquid soap, which expands the liquid soap market; the second effect is to reverse the flow of customers switching from creamy liquid soaps to antibacterial liquid soaps.

Supermarkets also reduce their prices as lines one and two (simulated and real volume) in Figure 7.19 show. Even though supermarkets are obtaining more income from trade margins (line four) due to growth in branded liquid soap sales, the retailers' desire to maintain market share (line three) is reducing supermarkets' prices. When supermarkets' market share increases, prices stabilise.

The base case simulations provide some insight into the development of the new product segment. Two particular features stand out. First, an equilibrium price for antibacterial and creamy liquid soaps is established once both firms satisfy their evolving market performance goals. Supermarkets also achieve an equilibrium price once they acquire adequate bargaining power (represented here as a market share goal). Second, Old English's volume in the new product segment reaches a plateau due to the combined effect of two factors. The first factor is the high equilibrium price that reduces the attractiveness of the new product to more price-sensitive old product users. The second factor is that Global Personal Care stops losing customers to Old English when it matches Old English's price. While supermarkets' volume grows strongly at the end of the period, influenced by the price differential with the branded products, supermarkets' market size will eventually reach a plateau, similar to the old product market, once the branded products reduce the price gap.

Memories of the Future

While the base case was important for interpreting what had happened so far, additional simulations of future time paths had much deeper impact on the management team's view of the strategic initiative. This use of the model creates 'memories of the future' (de Geus, 1997) that managers use to adjust the strategy if it appears unlikely to fulfil company objectives, or to adjust the objectives themselves. Selected simulations are presented below. We ran the model 5 years into the future using the same parameters as in the base case that assume the firm's decision-making processes continue unchanged. This business-as-usual projection led to several insights.

Firstly, the retail price of the old product (bar soap) rises in response to increased manufacturing cost – unless the company is prepared to sacrifice profitability in the highly competitive bar soap business. The increase in manufacturing cost is due to falling sales volume and fewer economies of scale in traditional bar soap production.

Secondly, future growth in sales volume of the new product (liquid soap) is limited by three factors. First, the diminishing pool of bar soap users implies that it will be increasingly difficult to sustain the conversion rate to liquid soap achieved in the previous 5 years, as the new market becomes saturated. Second, the reaction of competitors, especially supermarkets, starts to attract price-sensitive consumers of liquid soap. Third, stabilising the new product's price in the aftermath of initial successful growth establishes a price difference in favour of supermarkets' products that, in the medium-to-long-term, will erode the company's market volume.

Lack of awareness of the effect of supermarkets on the performance of the strategic initiative was a particularly important strategic misconception. To highlight this misconception we presented a comparison of three runs, as shown in Figure 7.20. First, we presented what would happen if no competitors were able to copy the liquid soap innovation: an optimistic belief in first-mover advantage that was widely shared among the management team. Sales volume of liquid soap (line one) expands swiftly in the historical period to 2004 and then settles into a pattern of sustained slow growth. Second, we showed the company's sales as if the other branded competitor were the only rival able to imitate the new product: a recognition that imitation is possible, but still an optimistic view since the branded competitor is the least disruptive rival (due to its similar cost structure and pricing policies). Sales volume of liquid soap (line two) is slightly lower than before and again seems to confirm the assumption of first-mover advantage. Finally, we showed the company's sales if both the branded competitor *and* supermarkets were able to imitate liquid soap. In this case supermarkets' capability to match the strategic initiative changed the outcome of the strategic move because they pushed price down and captured new customers from the branded products (line three).

Additional simulation experiments were run to test other ideas proposed by the management team. For example, one simulation examined the feasibility of

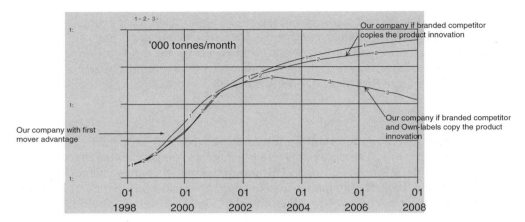

Figure 7.20. Alternative Trajectories for Sales Volume of Liquid Soap as First-Mover Advantage Fades and Additional Players are Assumed Able to Imitate the New Product

achieving a sustained growth rate of 20% per year. Another simulation investigated the pricing policy for liquid soap that would be required to move all bar soap customers to the new product in 30 months or, more ambitiously, in only 12 months. These what-ifs further enriched management team discussion of the strategic initiative.

Using the Model to Test the Strategic Initiative in Other Geographical Markets

The model was also used to test the strategic initiative in other countries such as France and Germany. The model-building process and, later on, simulations helped managers to appreciate country differences in the new product launch in terms of customers' price sensitivity factors and pricing decisions.

Concluding the Evaluation of the Strategic Initiative: Understanding the Competitive Dynamics of the Industry

The management team extracted a number of insights from the model and from simulations that clarified their understanding of competitive dynamics in the industry. This process of learning contributes to strategic development and is one of the main benefits of rehearsing strategy. In this section we present a brief explanation of competitive dynamics as revealed by the modelling project.

It is widely known that managers in the FMCG industry compete fiercely to sustain their level of participation in the market. The feedback loops in Figure 7.21 provide some insight into this phenomenon. The interaction between price and capacity is important. Sales volume drives manufacturing capacity. If manufacturing capacity rises then cost of goods sold declines due to economies of scale (and vice versa). Lower cost leads to lower price. Low price increases the value for money of the product, thereby attracting more customers and more sales volume. Once established, success breeds success around the reinforcing loop R1 (market

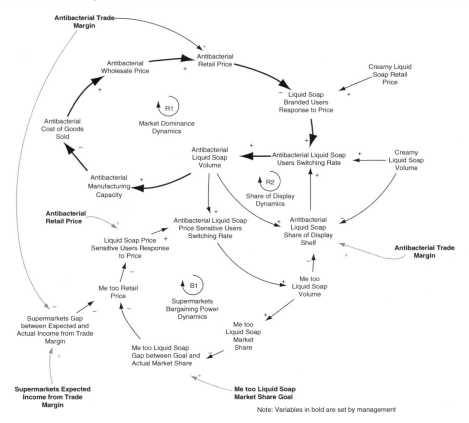

Figure 7.21. Overview of the Feedback Loops Underlying Competitive Dynamics in the FMCG Industry

dominance dynamics) leading to a gradual demise of rivals unable to compete due to their higher costs. An effective way for competitors to halt this reinforcing process is to reduce the attractiveness of the leader's products as soon as possible, either by launching similar products or by reducing prices, as occurred in liquid soap.

An additional effect is the power of retailers to control the allocation of shelf space. As mentioned, display shelf is a fiercely contested resource in the fast-moving consumer goods industry and has a major influence on the effectiveness of price promotions and advertising. Companies in the industry use trade margin to negotiate their share of display shelf with retailers. Higher sales volume and market share normally command greater share of display shelf because of the additional income for the retailer. Additional shelf space attracts more customers and higher sales volume, and these relationships form reinforcing loop R2 (share of display dynamics). However, there is more to the allocation of shelf space than sales volume alone. Retailers can use the display shelf for their own private label products and use this threat to negotiate attractive trade margins. Competitors with low market share may buy display shelf by offering a better trade margin to retailers, providing they are willing to accept a compensating reduction of gross margin in order to remain price-competitive. Private-label products enable retailers to control the strength of the two reinforcing loops R1 and R2 by exercising bargaining power through balancing loop B1 in Figure 7.21. The interaction of these three feedback loops adds significant dynamic complexity to the management of fast-moving consumer goods and to strategic initiatives such as new product launches.

REFLECTIONS ON THE USE OF SYSTEM DYNAMICS AS A TOOL FOR STRATEGIC DEVELOPMENT

System dynamics modelling and simulation have a long tradition in corporate strategic development and this chapter provides a flavour of the method by presenting two types of model. easyJet's case gives us a taste of a small but nevertheless quite insightful model – 'a back of the envelope model' – to address a dynamic challenge in a rapidly evolving market where timing to market is very important. The easyJet model condenses this core timing issue in just a few variables and feedback loops, allowing quick feasibility tests of the strategic initiative to complement managerial judgement and to challenge prevailing wisdom. This type of model rehearses the basic intuition of the entrepreneur in order to find out hidden pitfalls. It is also small enough to illustrate fundamental concepts in system dynamics such as stock accumulation and feedback loops and therefore serves a useful pedagogical purpose too.

On the other hand, the FMCG model offers a different application of system dynamics to a more complex problem that required a larger model representing not only the market but also interacting functional areas. The situation is completely different: a well-established company with a long tradition in the market struggling to survive in unknown territory. After many years of leadership, the company was facing strong competitors and a gradual erosion of its core business. Facing this dilemma, the management team needed a significant strategic innovation to shake out organisational and marketing inertia before things became worse. However, its chosen strategic innovation, which was initially very successful, took the company into uncharted waters. 'What would happen to sales and market share of the new product? How long could we maintain our leadership? We were supposed to have a first-mover advantage but growth was tailing off' were some of the comments from the management team. The model helped the management team to rehearse the launch of the new product, to investigate the effects on the established business and to anticipate the likely actions and reactions of rivals into the future. The model also provided a framework and shared understanding of competitive dynamics in the interacting markets for old and new products.

The examples show that system dynamics modelling of various forms can support the process of strategic development. There is no one perfect model of the organisation that will reveal the future outcome of strategy with certainty. Modelling is fundamentally the art and science of interpreting complexity, and there is always a choice about how much detail to include, depending on the purpose. On the one hand there are small-scale models, mere sketches of a complex reality, whose purpose is to reflect entrepreneurial intuition and rehearse the implications. On the other hand there are larger, more sophisticated models whose purpose is to facilitate strategic change by developing shared understanding of complex situations and by testing the effect of specific business policies.

REFERENCES

de Geus, A.P. (1997) *The Living Company*. Harvard Business School Press: Boston, MA.

Forrester, J.W. (1968) 'Market growth as influenced by capital investment', *Industrial Management Review*, **9**(2), 83–105.

Gary, S. (2005) 'Implementation strategy and performance outcomes in related diversification', *Strategic Management Journal*, **27**(7), 643–664.

Kapmeier, F. (2006) 'Dynamics of interorganizational learning in learning alliances', PhD Thesis, Betriebswirtschaftliches Institut, Stuttgart University.

Kunc, M. (2005) 'Dynamics of competitive industries: a micro behavioural framework', PhD Thesis, London Business School.

Messinger, P.R. & Narasimhan, C. (1995) 'Has power shifted in the grocery channel?', *Marketing Science*, **14**(2), 189–223.

Meyer, R. & Johnson, E.J. (1995) 'Empirical generalizations in the modelling of consumer choice', *Marketing Science*, **14**(3), G180–G189.

Morecroft, J.D.W. (1984) 'Strategy support models', *Strategic Management Journal*, **5**(3), 215–229.

Morecroft, J.D.W. (2007) *Strategic Modelling and Business Dynamics: A Feedback Systems Approach*. John Wiley & Sons: Chichester.

Repenning, N.P. & Sterman, J.D. (2002) 'Capability traps and self-confirming attribution errors in the dynamics of process improvement', *Administrative Science Quarterly*, **47**, 265–295.

Senge, P.M. (1990) *The Fifth Discipline: The Art and Practice of the Learning Organization*. Doubleday Currency: New York.

Sterman, J.D. (1988) *People Express Management Flight Simulator: Software and briefing materials*. Sloan School of Management-MIT: Cambridge, MA.

Sterman, J.D. (2000) *Business Dynamics: Systems Thinking and Modelling for a Complex World*. Irwin McGraw-Hill: Boston, MA.

Sull, D. (1999) 'easyJet's $500 million gamble', *European Management Journal*, **17**(1), 20–38.

Warren, K. (2002) *Competitive Strategy Dynamics*. John Wiley & Sons: Chichester.

Chapter 8

The Impact of Organisational Complexity in the Strategy Development Process

Adrián A. Caldart and Fernando S. Oliveira

INTRODUCTION

In the first chapter of this book, it was stated that there is a set of characteristics that lead towards a decision being labelled as a strategic one. One of these characteristics is the complexity and inter-relatedness of the organisational context the strategy decision-maker has to deal with. This chapter focuses on showing how the organisational complexity of the firm affects the strategy development process.

Interest in complexity and, particularly, in understanding the distinctive features that characterise complex systems has increased dramatically during the last 20 years across many disciplines. The study of complex systems focuses on understanding how parts of a system give rise to its collective behaviour, how such collective behaviour affects such parts and how systems interact with their environment. This focus on questions about parts, wholes and relationships explains the relevance of the study of complex systems in the agenda of biologists, physicists, economists, physicians, meteorologists, financial traders and organisation theorists.

Despite there not being a universal notion of what a complex system is, we can characterise them by enumerating their key properties:

- *A complex system contains many constituents interacting non-linearly*. Non-linearity occurs when some condition or some action has a varying effect on an outcome, depending on the level of the condition or the intensity of the action. One example of non-linearity is the law of decreasing returns to scale of microeconomics. Extra labour added to a fixed installed capacity will increase output at varying rates till a point where such extra labour leads output to decline as large numbers of people interfere with efficient operation in a limited space. The dynamics of a market's supply and demand show the same non-linear characteristic, leading to frequent abrupt expansions or contractions of production and drastic movements in prices of many goods.
- *The constituents of a complex system are interdependent*. We cannot optimise the performance of a complex system just by optimising the performance of its subparts and 'aggregating' them. Interdependencies create conflicting constraints

between different organisational designs. This is the reason why the development of 'best practices' only in a part of the firm frequently fails, as they don't address their impact on other parts of the firm's process.

- *A complex system possesses a structure spanning several scales.* In a firm, scales can be translated as hierarchical levels: the headquarters, the division, the business unit and the different functions within each unit, such as sales or operations and the departments within each function.

- *A complex system is capable of emerging behaviour.* A behaviour is said to be emergent, at a certain scale, if it cannot be understood when you study, separately, every constituent of this scale. No matter how well I can understand how different departments of a firm work, by reading a book, or talking to its executives, I will not be able to copy the strategy of that firm without understanding how those departments 'blend' in a unique overall strategy.

- *The combination of structure and emergence in a complex system leads to self-organisation.* Self-organisation takes place when an emergent behaviour has the effect of changing the structure or creating a new one. Through self-organisation, the behaviour of the group emerges from the collective interactions of all the individuals. Even if they follow simple rules of action, the resulting group behaviour can be surprisingly complex and remarkably effective or destructive.

Complexity theory focuses specifically on the two last properties: emergence and self-organisation.

EMERGENCE AND SELF-ORGANISATION

In responding to their own particular local contexts, the individual parts of a complex system can, despite acting in parallel without explicit inter-part coordination or communication, cause the system as a whole to display emergent patterns, orderly phenomena and properties, at the global or collective level.

Self-organisation happens when an emergent behaviour has the effect of changing the structure or creating a new one in the absence of formal authority. Self-organisation is a process in which components of a system in effect spontaneously communicate with each other and abruptly cooperate in coordinated and concerted common behaviour. The development of black markets in centrally planned economies is a clear example of how self-organisation works.

We can interpret self-organisation in an organisation as the process of political interaction and group learning from which innovation and new strategic directions for the organisation may emerge. Senior management create the context in which collaboration can happen through the development of a few simple rules and by creating vehicles that enable managers to exchange ideas and perhaps find collaborative opportunities. Examples of such vehicles are a structure promoting interdependence, systems and processes that disseminate information across units (e.g. a firm-wide intranet), the participation of managers from one business unit in the strategic review of another, high mobility of executives across divisions and opportunities for staff to meet informally.

A well-known example of self-organised behaviour with major strategic implications is the change that took place in the strategic focus of Intel from focusing on the computer DRAM memory business to becoming a microprocessors company (Burgelman, 1994). This change was not enforced vertically by senior management, but was a result of a myriad of initiatives led by middle managers of the firm who challenged and eventually changed top managers' dominant logic and 'emotional attachment' to the DRAM business.

In short we can say that the distinctive characteristic of complexity theory that differentiates it from other theories related to complex systems such as cybernetics, system dynamics, catastrophe theory or chaos theory is that it proposes an explanation of *how novelty unfolds*. That is the reason why complexity theory has received so much attention in the current business literature concerned with understanding co-evolution processes between and within firms. Such processes are certainly influenced by decisions made at the top of the firm, but are strongly shaped and, in many occasions, strongly altered by unpredictable self-organised behaviour at every organisational level.

BUSINESS FIRMS AS COMPLEX SYSTEMS

The study of firms as complex systems poses the challenge of finding an adequate methodology that enables us to represent firms as systems composed of many parts with degrees of interdependence that are not 'a given' but can be manipulated, and the ability to show emergent behaviour. Qualitative studies based on approaching firms or parts of firms as case studies provide valuable insights. However, due to the enormous number of micro interactions taking place between parts of a firm and across different levels, these insights will not be positive accounts of how firms work as complex systems but, in the best case, smart interpretations of how emergence and self-organising might take place in that firm.

During the last 10 years, strategy scholars interested in understanding the impact of complexity on the strategy development process started to rely on the use of agent-based models. In an agent-based model, individual agents autonomously make decisions based on internal rules and local information. Not being constrained by the imposition of equilibrium conditions, these models offer a degree of flexibility that permits key features of complex systems to be addressed, i.e. the representation of the firm as a reality composed of many parts interacting non-linearly, the interdependence between such parts and their ability to show emergent behaviour. Additionally, agent-based models enable the modelling of individuals that can evolve and learn in different ways. This overcomes a limitation of models developed in the tradition of the neoclassical theory of the firm that assumes all agents have identical behaviour (Arthur, 2006).

The remainder of this chapter discusses the application of agent-based modelling to organisation and strategy studies. For that purpose, first, we discuss Kauffman's *NK* model, arguably the most frequently used in recent contributions based on agent-based modelling. Next we discuss the theoretical roots that justify the application of the *NK* model to organisation studies as well as some adaptations that the model requires from its original formulation in biology. Third, we review some major contributions to the field of strategic management based on the use of this modelling technique. Fourth, we develop a set of simulation experiments based on the *NK* model in order to examine its main features and highlight its possible applications. Finally, we discuss current research challenges for scholars working with this modelling strategy and suggest promising avenues for the development of research based on agent-based modelling techniques.

AGENT-BASED MODELLING

For most of the twentieth century, biologists have assumed that 'order' was due to the effects of selection, as developed under the general label of Darwinian 'selectionist' theory. The intuitions behind this idea derived from statistical mechanics, particularly the idea of entropy. Entropy measures the amount of order in a system, with increasing disorder corresponding to increasing entropy. Left to themselves, systems are inherently disordered and unstructured. Therefore 'selective' work is necessary to achieve and maintain order. In the context of strategic management, selection is translated as competition, the force that makes firms keep 'fit' in their quest to survive and develop. Kauffman challenged this notion, suggesting that while natural selection is a prominent force in evolution, order can also emerge spontaneously due to the self-organising properties of systems. As the complexity of the system under selection increases, selection is progressively less able to alter the properties of the system. This would be the case, for instance, with a firm stalled as a consequence of excessive bureaucracy or by strong power struggles. Despite being exposed to the forces of the market, this firm remains detached from such imperatives as it is trapped in the logic of its internal processes. In these cases we can say that selection is unable to avoid the *spontaneous* order derived from the properties of the system.

This property of complex systems is clearly observed in firms, most prominently in highly diversified ones. During the 1960s many firms, notably in the USA, embarked on growth by diversification initiatives with the hope of taking advantage of opportunities for synergy with their core businesses. Extreme versions of these strategies were conglomerates such as ITT, British Oxygen Company or Litton Industries that entered into a wide range of different businesses. Although it could be argued that such diversification helped these groups to reduce the risk of their portfolios, by the early 1970s many of these highly diversified companies began to face performance problems due to their inability to manage such a degree of complexity effectively, notably at the time of allocating resources between businesses. These problems were tackled initially through the use of portfolio planning techniques such as the BCG or the McKinsey matrices, but the limitations of these techniques were soon evident due to the inability of these companies to solve their performance problems. During the 1980s, this inability of the companies to address the challenges of competition (or selection) due to their internal complexity was solved (in a distressing way) by the emergence of raiders who acquired these firms through hostile takeovers, broke them up and sold the different parts realising huge profits. While many observers considered that these restructurings were in some cases pushed too far, their massive number during the 'takeover era' (Useem, 1996) in the USA reflected to what extent the complexity of those conglomerates was enabling the firms to realise all their potential value.

Kauffman examined the relationship between selection and self-organisation and tried to find out under what conditions an adaptive evolution is optimised. This question of to what extent we want differentiation vs. integration in a firm's structure (Lawrence & Lorsch, 1967) as a way to improve performance is one of the most important ones the top manager needs to ask at the time of implementing a strategy.

Performance Landscapes

From an evolutionary viewpoint, an entity can be represented by a list or vector of features. By programming this abstraction into a computer we can build a simulation model of the process of evolution. In this kind of model, entities adapt by modifying their existing form in an attempt to enhance their performance in a payoff surface or 'performance landscape'. A performance landscape consists of a multidimensional space in which each attribute of the entity (policy decisions constituting different strategic options of a firm in a business context) is represented by a dimension of the space and a final dimension indicates the performance level of the firm. Firms typically adapt through small changes involving local search in the space of possible strategic options. In principle, such a process involves complex combinatorial optimisation. In such optimisation searches, many parts and processes must become coordinated to achieve some measure of overall success, but conflicting 'design constraints' limit the results achieved (Kauffman, 1993). For instance, major decisions on the location of production systems cannot be made without considering how these decisions might impact other activities of the firm, such as sourcing, logistics or finance.

Kauffman demonstrates that the degree of conflicting constraints affecting the evolving entity affects the topography of the performance landscape. Increasing the density of the interdependencies between policies affects the complexity of the landscape and, consequently, increases the number of possible emergent patterns of behaviour that the firm can follow. In order to model such webs of complex interdependencies, Kauffman developed the NK model.

In Kauffman's NK model performance landscapes are characterised by, essentially, two structural variables. The first variable is N, representing the number of policy decisions that characterise the firm (for instance, decisions related to marketing, operations, logistics, public relations or R&D). The second structural variable K represents the number of elements of N with which a given policy decision interacts. The higher K, the more interdependent are the parts of the firm and, therefore, the higher is the number of conflicting design constraints.

In the model, only two decisions can be made for each of the N policy variables. These decisions are represented by the values 0 and 1. Therefore, the performance landscape consists of 2^N possible policy choices, being the overall behaviour of the firm characterised by the vector $X\{X_1, X_2, \ldots, X_N\}$ where each X_i takes on the value of 0 or 1. Each X_i refers to a particular policy decision within the firm, such as advertising, product development, research on product line extensions or production planning. Following Rivkin (2000), we consider that each configuration of such decisions constitutes a strategic option that the firm can follow. In the model we assume that all policies have an equal weight on performance.

A random number, generated from a uniform distribution ranging from 0 to 1, is assigned to constitute the performance contribution of each of the policy decisions. A particular firm's overall performance is equal to the average of the performance contributions of its N policies.

Smooth and rugged performance landscapes. As stated above, interactions between policy decisions affect the topography of the performance landscape. Each attribute can take on 2^{K+1} different values, depending on the value of the attribute itself (either 1 or 0) and the value of K other attributes with which it interacts. When $K = 0$, there are no interactions between the different policy decisions. The landscape tends to assume a single-peak configuration (Figure 8.1).

In these cases, the behaviour of each actor being independent of that of others, the contribution to overall performance of each attribute is independent from others' behaviour. In this situation the mere aggregation of local improvement of performance always leads to global improvement. In other words, global maximum can be achieved merely by the aggregation of local 'best practices'. As seen in Figure 8.1, the topography of this landscape is smooth, as neighbouring points in the space have nearly the same performance value. More precisely, we can say that in these kinds

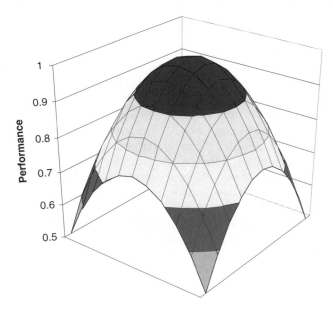

Figure 8.1. A Single-Peak Performance Landscape

of landscapes the performance values of neighbouring strategic options are highly correlated. Knowing the performance value of one point we can infer rather precisely the performance value of neighbouring points.

However, as interactions increase, the landscape becomes more rugged or multi-peaked (Figure 8.2). Multiple peaks are the direct result of interdependencies among a set of policy decisions. When $K > 0$, the contribution of a policy to overall performance is affected by the behaviour of K other policies.

For the largest possible value of K, $N-1$, each policy is affected by all the remaining ones. In these cases the performance landscape is entirely uncorrelated and the number of local performance optima is very large.

The implications of a rugged landscape are very much a function of the search behaviour of actors moving on the landscape. If they were omniscient and could readily search globally, they would be able to identify the global maxima as in smooth landscapes. However, a more realistic analysis developed within the behavioural tradition of intelligent local search (Levinthal & March, 1993; March & Simon, 1958) assumes that managers' rationality is bounded. They can identify the positive and negative gradients around and close to their current position, but are not capable of making similar judgements for more distant ones. In a rugged landscape, such incremental search procedure will lead only to the local maximum or *peak* closest to the starting point of the search process, regardless of its height relative to other peaks in the landscape. As a result of this locking in to the first available solution, a strong form of path dependence is observed and, on average, only modest performance, sometimes referred to as *competency traps*, is achieved (Levitt & March, 1988). One mechanism to overcome such 'traps' is to engage in 'long jumps', random explorations of more distant portions of the landscape. Long

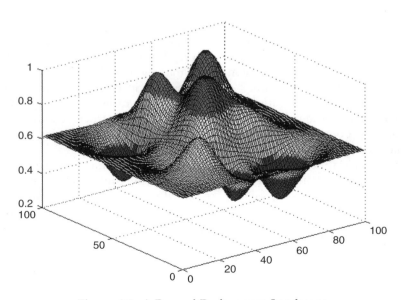

Figure 8.2. A Rugged Performance Landscape

jumps involve 'thinking outside the box', altering simultaneously many elements of N. This strategy can also be interpreted as the equivalent of a drastic strategic turnaround and prevents the company from falling into competency traps. However, such distant efforts, by not exploiting wisdom gained by past experience, are likely to result in a deterioration of performance. So, the problem of adaptation strategies in rugged landscapes can be reframed as a familiar dilemma faced by managers and organisation theorists: how to get the benefits of exploring new business models without facing the inherent risks and without losing the advantages of exploiting acquired knowledge (March, 1991).

In the following section we discuss the assumptions that underlie the application of the NK model to organisation studies. Then we will review some of the main academic contributions based on this methodology in the strategy literature.

USING THE NK MODEL IN ORGANISATION AND STRATEGY RESEARCH

As the previous discussion made apparent, the NK model allows many central concerns of students of organisational decision-making to be addressed, especially for those rooting their work on evolutionary perspectives. Behavioural evolutionism (Cyert & March, 1963; March & Simon, 1958; Nelson & Winter, 1982) conceives firms as entities that engage in problem-solving through processes of search and discovery. Unlike the classic theory of the firm, which treats firms as omniscient rational systems, behavioural evolutionism assumes that, while searching for solutions to their problems, firms adopt some form of adaptive behaviour in response to feedback about their previous performance. Their behaviour depends on the relationship between the performance they observe and the aspirations they have for that performance.

While adapting, firms consider only a limited number of decision alternatives, due to bounded rationality (Simon, 1997). Recent works that rely on optimisation/algorithm theory (Moldoveanu & Bauer, 2004; Rivkin, 2000) described strategy formulation as an intractable problem. Being managers unable to write an algorithm enabling them to find the optimal set of decisions in reasonable time, they make strategic decisions trying to *satisfy* some set of criteria rather than to optimise. Their choices depend on certain features of the organisational structure and on the locus of the search responsibility, and are heavily conditioned by the rules within which such choices occur (Cyert & March, 1963).

Brabazon and Matthews (2002) state that the concept of adaptive search developed by evolutionary theorists is meaningful only in the context of a defined search space, a means for traversing such space, and the ability to determine the quality of a proposed solution. Kauffman's NK model provided such a context and so has become the mainstream formal modelling strategy for recent work rooted in the evolutionary tradition.

Work based on the NK model has been developed and adapted by organisation theorists to model organisational problem-solving processes showing features such as bounded rationality in the consideration of decision alternatives, the existence of interdependencies between sub-units that can be manipulated by managers, decision-making based on reasoning by analogy and the existence of decision rules that bound the set of possible choices (Caldart & Ricart, 2006; Gavetti & Levinthal, 2000; Gavetti, Levinthal & Rivkin, 2005; Levinthal, 1997; McKelvey, 1999; Rivkin, 2000; Siggelkow & Rivkin, 2005).

In order to make the *NK* model suitable for research into organisations, some adaptations of the model are necessary. First, we need to address the fact that organisations are not fully decomposable systems, as implicitly assumed in the pure form of the *NK* model. Organisational problems tend to have a nearly decomposable structure (Simon, 1996). Tasks tend to cluster into subsystems, with interaction within such subsystems, on average, being stronger than interactions across subsystems. For instance, on average, we will always see more interaction within marketing than between marketing and operations. Recent contributions based on the *NK* model, such as Gavetti, Levinthal and Rivkin (2005), address this issue by defining a hierarchy of decisions and clustering decision variables into subgroups or units. Second, in social systems we cannot neglect the issue of deliberateness of behaviour. Managers may freely choose to change the firm's strategy, clearly an ability that the genotypes referred to in biology models don't have. Therefore, models may include decision rules followed by managers at the time of, for instance, deciding whether to maintain a current strategy or to modify it (Caldart & Ricart, 2006; Siggelkow & Rivkin, 2005).

MAJOR CONTRIBUTIONS TO THE STRATEGY LITERATURE BASED ON THE *NK* MODEL

Work based on the *NK* model has contributed to shed new light long-lasting debates from the strategic management literature. Next, we discuss two examples of recent and influential works from this research perspective. First we discuss Rivkin's work on the imitation of successful strategies. Then we review work that explores the relationship between cognition and experience during a firm's strategic evolution and how reasoning by analogy can nurture management's cognitive representations.

Imitating Strategies

Rivkin (2000) used agent-based simulations based on the *NK* model to show why firms find it difficult to imitate strategies from successful companies. He shows that 'complexity makes the search for an optimal strategy intractable in the technical sense of the word' (Rivkin, 2000, p. 824). Incapable of relying on algorithmic solutions, copycats need to rely on heuristics or learning to match a successful firm's strategy. However, due to complexity, firms that follow simple hill-climbing heuristics are likely to be trapped in 'local peaks', and firms that try to learn and mimic the strategy of a successful firm suffer large penalties from small errors. The importance of this model is that it explains why, despite being exposed to public scrutiny through case studies or business articles, winning strategies remain unmatched. For instance, the strategy of DELL, based on the outsourcing of manufacturing and direct sales, is widely known and understood. Something similar happens with other firms such as Microsoft, or Toyota. Yet, their business models have not been copied effectively at such scale by any competitor.

Strategy Making

Gavetti and Levinthal (2000) used an adaptation of the *NK* model to study the role and inter-relationships between search processes based on cognitive representations that are articulated in strategic plans (that they label 'forward-looking') and search processes based on the lessons learnt in previous experience ('backward-looking'). Following the notion of bounded rationality, the authors simulated cognition as a representation of the performance landscape that, being grounded on the actual landscape, has a lower dimensionality. In this way, as firms know the expected performance values associated with the value of certain attributes of the firm, they are able to identify more or less attractive sub-areas of the problem space. However, as their representation has a lower dimensionality than the real problem, they cannot foresee the most attractive peaks within each of those sub-areas, therefore suffering the risk of falling into a competency trap despite following the right strategy with respect to the attributes they understand well. This would, for instance, be the case for a car manufacturer that, despite understanding that his business needs to have a global market scope, a competitive manufacturing cost based on work on a limited number of platforms and global sourcing and high R&D budgets (success factors central to this business), fails to achieve high performance. Despite the strategy being broadly right, it fails to deliver because of what Rivkin (2000) identified as large penalties due to small errors, due to the ruggedness of the industry's performance landscape. It is interesting to note that most of the strategy 'framework' constituting the mainstream of the field, such as the SWOT analysis or Porter's Five Forces, are characterised by the same feature as Gavetti and Levinthal's model: an effort to make sense of reality based on reducing the dimensionality of the problem in order to make it understandable and manageable for decision-makers. The difference between the two approaches to modelling relies on the fact that, for instance, the Five Forces framework represents the competitive situation of the firm at a particular point in time, while *NK* models represent the *process* followed by the firm's management in its attempt to improve its strategy.

Gavetti, Levinthal and Rivkin (2005) further developed the study of the relationship between managerial cognition and strategic decision-making through the development of a highly sophisticated model of how managers reason by analogy. They show how the depth and breadth of managers' 'portfolio' of experiences can help them to make sense of novel situations and develop superior strategies reasoning by analogy. For instance, Charles Lazarus founded Toys 'R' Us in the 1950s, relying explicitly on the supermarket analogy. The basic supermarket formula, exhaustive selection, low prices and margins and high volume, has been applied by analogy across a wide range of retail categories such as consumer electronics, books or furniture.

In the following section, we present two simulation models based on the UK model that will help the reader to understand more thoroughly the logic and characteristics of the model, its advantages and limitations and their implications for strategic management and organisation.

SIMULATING THE EVOLUTION OF FIRMS USING THE *NK* MODEL

In this section we describe the experiments, settings and results of two simulations of firms' evolution based on the simplest version of the *NK* model. Our aim is to analyse the sensitivity of the model to values of the parameters *N* (the size of the organisation modelled) and *K* (the degree of interdependence between the decisions made by the company). Each of the firms has been simulated 30 different times so that we can get robust results.

The model we developed for the purposes of this chapter follows the following architecture, for any given experiment:

1. Randomly generate the decision vector $X\{X_1, X_2, ..., X_N\}$, representing a firm's strategy for a given *N*. We define as a strategy any possible combination of choices of policy decisions.
2. Evaluate the current state: generate the value of the current performance for the firm, for a given *K*. The firm's performance is equal to the average of the contributions to performance of each of the *N* policy decisions.
3. Start the game. While the maximum number of iterations is not reached:
   (a) Generate the current state's neighbour states, for a given *NK*.
   (b) Evaluate the neighbouring states, for a given *NK*.
   (c) Move to a new state if its value is higher than the current one, otherwise stay in the current state.

The algorithm used to simulate the *NK* model is represented in Figure 8.3. A step-by-step illustration of how the model works can be found in Appendix 1.

In all the experiments discussed below, firms move across the landscape according to the following algorithm. Once positioned in the performance landscape at M_0, in all cases, firms evolve following a local or 'neighbourhood' search strategy. In Kauffman's model, local search takes place when the set of business attributes is varied only incrementally. In our model, local search works as illustrated by the following example (for $N = 4$). From an initial configuration of the vector *X*, for example $\{0, 1, 1, 1\}$, with an associated performance value P_0, the firm explores a

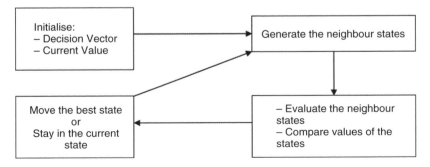

Figure 8.3. Scheme for the *NK* Algorithm

configuration adjacent to the initial one, for example $\{1, 1, 1, 1\}$, with an associated performance value P_1. If $P_1 > P_0$, the firm adopts the new form $\{1, 1, 1, 1\}P_1$ and from there explores another adjacent configuration, for example $\{1, 0, 1, 1\}$, with a performance value P_3. Otherwise, if $P_1 < P_0$, the firm does not adopt the configuration associated with P_1 and explores another configuration, for example $\{0, 0, 1, 1\}$, with an associated performance P_2. This process is repeated from M_0 through M_{30}. In this way, the company engages in local 'hill-climbing' or neighbourhood search (March & Simon, 1958) towards a peak of the performance landscape. This strategy allows firms to evolve till they reach a local peak where they stay till the end of the simulation.

In order to obtain a complete picture and understand the sensitivity of the model to changes in the parameters, we simulated firms with five different sizes, in terms of number of policy decisions ($N = 5$, 10, 15, 20, 40) and six different degrees of interdependence between such attributes or organisational complexity ($K = 0$, 1, 2, 3, 5, 10). (In all the modelled firms the restriction $K \leq N$ holds.)

Analysing the Relationship between Firm's Complexity and Performance

Figure 8.4 shows the evolution of the performance of firms of equal number of attributes ($N = 20$) and different levels of organisational interdependence or complexity ($K = 0$, 1, 2, 3, 5, 10). As the reader can see, the performance of the different kinds of firms increases at a decreasing rate of growth and eventually reaches a peak, i.e. converges to a steady state, till the end of the simulation.

The most interesting result derived from this experiment is that there is not a linear relationship between the mean performance of local optima obtained by a firm and its level of organisational complexity (or interdependence, measured by K).

Figure 8.5 represents the performance at the steady state of the experiments for the average of the 30 independent simulations for $N = 20$ and $K = 0$, 1, 2, 3, 5, 10. It shows that there is, in fact, a non-linear (quadratic) relationship between performance and complexity, implying that there is an optimal level for the complexity of an

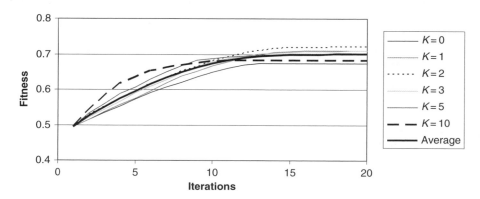

Figure 8.4. Average Performance for $N = 20$ and $K = 0$, 1, 2, 3, 5, 10

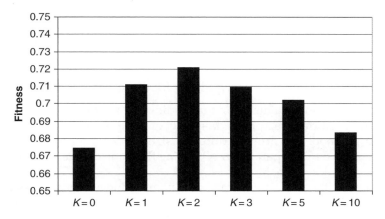

Figure 8.5. Final Average Performance for $N = 20$ and $K = 0, 1, 2, 3, 5, 10$

organisation (given its size). In this case, for a firm with size $N = 20$ the optimal level of complexity is $K = 2$.

This ability to achieve the highest mean performance at moderate levels of complexity is a property that characterises many complex systems. This led some management scholars to label this degree of complexity as 'the edge of chaos' (Brown & Eisenhardt, 1998; Pascale, 1990). The edge of chaos implies a degree of organisational complexity that is neither too low so as to lead the firm to an 'error catastrophe' (Kauffman, 1993), i.e. the inability to cope with the environmental complexity that firms face ($K = 0$ in our case) nor too high so as to lead it to the opposite extreme, a 'complexity catastrophe' (Levitt & March, 1988) – the inability of the firm to evolve beyond modest performance due to the high number of conflicting design constraints ($K = 10$ in our case). The highest levels of performance appear to be achieved for moderate levels of interdependence. This outcome confirms the idea of organisational 'ambidexterity', understood as the need to find a balance between the firm's need for order, reliability, consistency, efficiency and alignment that demands clear authority lines, bureaucratic procedures and standards, and the need for innovation, creativity and change, that demands loose links, exploration, organisational slacks and conflict. For instance, Amgen Inc., a pharmaceutical firm, manages its R&D according to these principles. On the one hand Amgen only initiates exploratory research projects under approval from top research-related senior executives with regard to budget and headcount. On the other hand the company grants 'bootleg time', equivalent to one day a week, to scientists to work on any projects they desire. In this way, scientists were able to continue working on projects they considered important, despite the fact that the company didn't find them very promising.

This simulation also shows that, despite not achieving the highest mean performance maxima, relatively complex firms tend to evolve faster in the short term. The rate of growth in performance at the beginning of the experiments is higher for $K = 10$ and $K = 5$, and lower for $K = 0$ and $K = 1$. This suggests that not only do different levels of complexity lead to different levels of performance, but also the relative performance of these different configurations vary in the short and in the long term. In other words, firms interested in short-term profits should benefit from different architectural designs than firms that give prominence to long-term results.

Analysing the Relationship between Firm's Size and Performance

The following experiment aims at understanding the relationship between the size of the firm and performance, for a certain level of organisational complexity (K). For this purpose we modelled firms of different size (understood as number of policy decisions, measured by the parameter N) having the same degree of interdependence ($K = 3$).

Figure 8.6 plots the mean performance maxima achieved by players of different size ($N = 5, 10, 15, 20, 30, 40$) with $K = 3$. The results show that performance increases with the value of N achieving a maximum mean performance, in this case, at a threshold level of $N = 15$. From then on the mean performance has no relation to size, remaining stable. These results show that the optimal level of interdependencies within a firm is contingent on its size and that firms get benefit from their ability to grow in size without increasing their complexity proportionally. This convenience of managing complex firms through a set of 'simple rules' (Eisenhardt & Sull, 2001) is consistent with accounts from successful companies such as General Electric. In 1983, the CEO Jack Welch dismantled the laborious and complex strategic planning system of GE and replaced it with a strategy playbook where businesses needed to provide simple one-page answers to five questions concerning current market dynamics, the competitors' key recent activities, the GE business response, the greatest competitive threat over the next 3 years and GE's planned response. Additionally, he mapped the complex portfolio of GE's businesses under the 'Three Circle Concept'. Under this concept, all businesses were divided into (1) core, (2) high-technology and (3) services. Only businesses that dominated their markets, i.e. being number one or number two, would be placed in one circle or another. Those outside the circles had to come up with a strategy or be divested. This initiative led to a major turnaround

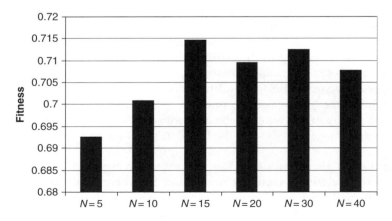

Figure 8.6. Final Average Performance for $K = 3$ and $N = 5, 10, 15, 20, 40$

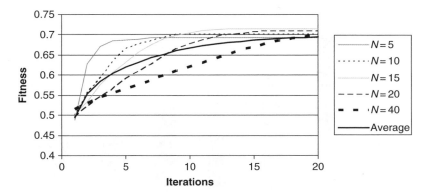

Figure 8.7. Average Performance for $K=3$ and $N=5$, 10, 15, 20, 40

of the GE portfolio, with 200 businesses being sold by 1990, while 370 new ones were acquired.

We can also analyse the dynamics of the adaptation of the different players for different values of firm size and a complexity of $K=3$. In Figure 8.7 we can see that there is a relationship between firm size and the speed of adaptation as, for example, the performance of the firm with size $N=20$ and $N=40$ grows slower than that of every other firm, but the performance of the firm with size $N=5$ was the one exhibiting faster growth. These results show that smaller firms reach a steady state faster, whereas bigger firms explore more of the state of possible strategies, as they have more possible combinations of policy decisions to explore.

A final and interesting analysis of this simulation relates to the risk associated with state space exploration. The future of a firm is not dependent upon average performance only; risk is also an important component of its valuation. The risk associated with each firm can be estimated by looking at the standard deviation of the performance achieved by each one of the 30 firms analysed for each experiment.

Figure 8.8 illustrates our results for the standard deviation in the mean local maxima achieved by firms with $K=3$ and $N=5$, 10, 15, 20, 30, 40. It shows that for constant levels of complexity the ability of the company to achieve a certain level of performance presents a lower risk as the size of the company increases. The reason for this is that the smaller the company keeping complexity constant, the shorter the length of its walk to local optima and therefore, the higher the probability of reaching peaks with a wider range of performances than firms with longer walks. Bigger firms tend to converge to very similar performance levels in the long run, whereas smaller firms converge more quickly and can end up with very different performance levels.

In conclusion, this set of experiments, based on the basic formulation of the *NK* model, clearly illustrate the ability of the model to provide valuable insights into the relationship between organisational complexity, its size and performance. Additionally, it illustrates the importance of Monte Carlo simulation as a tool to average out randomness, allowing a better analysis of the long-term relationships between the different variables.

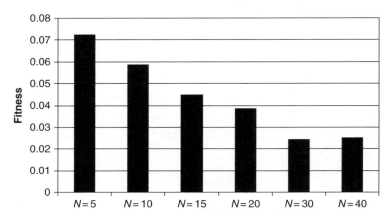

Figure 8.8. Final Standard Deviation of Performance for $K = 3$ and $N = 5, 10, 15, 20, 30, 40$

CONCLUSIONS

The purpose of this chapter was to focus our attention on complexity as it is one of the distinctive characteristics of strategic decisions. As firms are complex systems, we discussed agent-based modelling as a method that permits formal research to be done, addresses the main features of such systems, such as non-linearity, interdependencies between subsystems and emergent behaviour. We reviewed the generic architecture of the model and reviewed the theoretical roots that enable us to apply this model, with some modifications, to the realm of social science. Then, we discussed some of the most relevant and recent contributions to the strategy and organisation theory literature based on this modelling strategy. Finally, we programmed a set of simulation experiments based on the basic form of the NK model in order to show its potential as a formal research tool that permits the modelling of the impact of the complex relationships between the firm's size and complexity on its performance.

The NK model proved to provide valuable insights at the time into understanding how the relationship between firm's size and complexity affects its performance. However, despite the great progress made in NK simulation modelling applied to social studies there are still some major challenges to be addressed by scholars in their attempt to increase the relevance of this modelling framework. A major example of such a challenge is the need to address the fact that the direction of a firm's evolution and its performance are affected by the behaviour of other actors, prominently, its competitors. This *interdependent rationality* between actors constitutes a distinctive feature of strategic management in practice. Strategic initiatives from the different actors are responded to by initiatives from other actors, making strategic management essentially a *dialectic process*.

These problems can be addressed by the inclusion of an additional parameter, called C in the context of Kauffman's work, which indicates the degree of interdependence between the policy decisions of different firms, in contrast to the parameter K, discussed extensively in this chapter, which indicates the degree of interdependencies within the firm. In this way, in a market where Firm A competes with Firm B, as Firm A evolves in its performance landscape, it both changes the performance of Firm B and deforms B's performance landscape. As Firm B responds to this move from Firm A, the performance of Firm A's current strategy changes and its performance landscape deforms.

The *NKC* model has been discussed conceptually in the management literature (Levinthal & Warglien, 1999) as a model that permits the co-evolution of an ecosystem of firms to be simulated. However, the development of work applying such a model as a way to understand competitive interaction between multiple players is still in its infancy. In addition to the development of models to analyse and describe formally competitive interactions between multiple firms, there are several other debates within the strategy literature where evolutionary studies based on the *NK* model could make a valuable contribution. For instance, this model could be used to analyse the relative performances of pro-active vs. failure-induced strategic change. A variation of the model based on a hierarchy of decisions could be developed in order to understand the relationships between two different decision levels when strategies are originally developed at the lower level, in an emergent fashion.

The experiments we discussed above, plus the agent-based model research described and the emergent work based on the *NKC* model, address in a formal way all of the six essential elements of the strategy development process as discussed in Chapter 1: a sense of direction and purpose, formulation of strategic options (based on cognitive representations of the performance landscape), the (rationally bounded) evaluation of such options, addressing the impact of exogenous uncontrolled inputs (in the *NKC* model), a feedback system and strategic control. By formalising these six elements using simple computational agent-based models based on a few parameters, we can discover how these elements relate to each other and understand the principles underlying such relationships.

Finally, these models enable practicing managers to grasp very valuable intuitions on important strategic management issues such as why are successful strategies so difficult to imitate (Rivkin, 2000), why and to what extent can analogical reasoning inform strategy development in novel industries (Gavetti, Levinthal & Rivkin, 2005), why firms need to engage in periodical organisational restructurings in order to improve performance (Siggelkow & Levinthal, 2005), how different ways of managing the headquarters–business unit relationship affects performance (Caldart & Ricart, 2006) and how managers' dominant logics affect organisational strategic development processes including the development of capabilities (Gavetti, 2005).

REFERENCES

Arthur, B. (2006) 'Out-of-equilibrium economics and agent-based modelling'. In: Judd, K. & Tesfatsion, L. (eds), *Handbook of Computational Economics, Agent-Based Computational Economics*. Elsevier/North Holland: Amsterdam; 1551–1564.

Brabazon, T. & Matthews, R. (2002) 'Organizational adaptation on rugged landscapes', Working paper.

Brown, S. & Eisenhardt, K. (1998) Competing on the edge: Strategy as structured chaos. Cambridge: Harvard Business School Press.

Burgelman, R. (1994) 'Fading Memories: A process theory of Strategic Business Exit in Dynamic Environments', *Administrative Science Quarterly*, **39**(1), 24–56.

Caldart, A. & Ricart, J.E. (2006) 'An evaluation of the performance of different corporate styles in stable and turbulent environments', IESE Business School Working Paper no. 621, March.

Cyert, R. & March, J. (1963) *A Behavioural Theory of the Firm*. Prentice-Hall: New Jersey.

Eisenhardt, K. & Sull, D. (2001) Strategy as simple rules, *Harvard Business Review*, 106–116.

Gavetti, G. (2005) 'Cognition and hierarchy: rethinking the microfoundations of capabilities' development', *Organization Science*, **16**, 599–617.

Gavetti, G. & Levinthal, D. (2000) 'Looking forward and looking backward: cognitive and experiential search', *Administrative Science Quarterly*, **45**, 113–137.

Gavetti, G., Levinthal, D. & Rivkin, J. (2005) 'Strategy-making in novel and complex worlds: the power of analogy', *Strategic Management Journal*, **26**, 691–712.

Kauffman, S. (1993) *The Origins of Order*. Oxford University Press: New York.

Lawrence, P. & Lorsch, J. (1967) Organization and Environment: Managing Differentiation and Integration. Cambridge, MA: Harvard Business School Press.

Levinthal, D.A. (1997) 'Adaptation in rugged fitness landscapes', *Management Science*, **43**, 934–950.

Levinthal, D.A. & March, J.C. (1993) 'The myopia of learning', *Strategic Management Journal*, **14**, 95–112.

Levinthal, D.A. & Warglien, M. (1999) 'Landscape design: designing for local action in complex worlds', *Organization Science*, **10**, 342–357.

Levitt, B. & March, J.C. (1988) 'Organizational learning', *Annual Review of Sociology*, **14**, 319–340.

March, J.C. (1991) 'Exploration and exploitation in organizational learning', *Organization Science*, **2**(1), 71–87.

March, J. & Simon, H. (1958) *Organizations*. John Wiley & Sons: New York.

McKelvey, B. (1999) 'Avoiding complexity catastrophe in coevolutionary pockets: strategies for rugged landscapes', *Organization Science*, **10**, 294–321.

Moldoveanu, M. & Bauer, R. (2004) 'On the relationship between organizational complexity and organizational structuration', *Organization Science*, **15**, 98–118.

Nelson, R. & Winter, S. (1982) *An Evolutionary Theory of Economic Change*. Bellknap Press: Cambridge.

Pascale, R. (1990) Managing on the edge: how successful companies use conflict to stay ahead. Viking Penguin: London.

Rivkin, J. (2000) 'Imitation of complex strategies', *Management Science*, **46**, 824–844.

Siggelkow, N. & Levinthal, D.A. (2005) 'Escaping real (non-benign) competency traps: linking the dynamics of organizational structure to the dynamics of search', *Strategic Organization*, **3**, 85–115.

Siggelkow, N. & Rivkin, J. (2005) 'Speed and search: designing organizations for turbulence and complexity', *Organization Science*, **16**(2), 101–122.

Simon, H. (1996) *The Sciences of the Artificial*. The MIT Press: Cambridge, MA.

Simon, H. (1997) *Administrative Behaviour*. The Free Press: New York.

Useem, M. (1996) *Investor Capitalism: How Money Managers are Changing the Face of Corporate America*. Basic Books: New York.

APPENDIX 1. *NK* MODEL: COMPUTATION OF PERFORMANCE VALUES

1. The performance landscape is constructed (Example $N = 3$; $K = 1$)

For this purpose the performance value of every policy decision must be set taking into account the impact of its interdependencies with other policy decisions.

Performance contribution of X1 (interdependent with X2)		
X_1	X_2	Performance value
0	0	0.45
0	1	0.18
1	0	0.59
1	1	0.06

Performance contribution of X2 (interdependent with X3)		
X_2	X_3	Performance value
0	0	0.80
0	1	0.26
1	0	0.02
1	1	0.53

Performance contribution of X3 (interdependent with X1)		
X_3	X_1	Performance value
0	0	0.11
0	1	0.73
1	0	0.26
1	1	0.81

2. Different configurations of the vector are generated

Strategy M_0 (0,0,0)	
Variable	f_{wi}
X_1	0.45
X_2	0.80
X_3	0.11
Overall	**0.45**

Strategy M_1 (1,0,0)

Variable	f_{wi}
X_1	0.59
X_2	0.80
X_3	0.73
Overall	**0.71**

Perf M_1 < Perf M_0 The new strategy is adopted

Strategy M_2 (1,1,0)

Variable	f_{wi}
X_1	0.06
X_2	0.02
X_3	0.73
Overall	**0.27**

Perf M_2 < Perf M_1 No change in the strategy

Strategy M_3 (1,1,1)

Variable	f_{wi}
X_1	0.06
X_2	0.53
X_3	0.81
Overall	**0.47**

Perf M_3 < Perf M_1 No change in the strategy

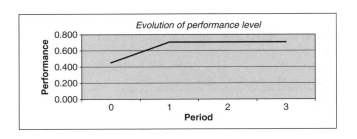

Chapter 9

Creating and Using Scenarios – Exploring Alternative Possible Futures and their Impact on Strategic Decisions

Frances O'Brien, Maureen Meadows and Martin Murtland

INTRODUCTION

This chapter is divided into five main sections. The first section provides an introduction to scenario planning by considering the following questions:

- What is a scenario?
- What are the origins of scenario planning?
- Why do people use scenario planning?
- Who uses scenario planning?

The second section of the chapter provides an explanation of how to do scenario planning, outlining and illustrating the key stages of the process. The third section of the chapter explores the relationship between scenario planning and the strategic development process. The fourth section of the chapter presents a case study describing an organisation's development and use of scenarios. The fifth and final section of the chapter reviews future directions for scenario planning.

What is a Scenario?

A scenario is a plausible image of a possible future world within which an organisation may have to operate.

A key emphasis in the above definition is the phrase 'possible future', since we don't know and cannot accurately predict what that future world will be like. Hence, a fundamental premise on which scenario planning is based is that the future is uncertain. A single scenario, giving one view of the future, takes no account of uncertainty. A set of scenarios, on the other hand, describes a number of futures, each one of which could possibly come to pass. Scenario planning is thus an approach for developing sets of scenarios.

Ducot and Lubben (1980) classify different types of scenarios according to three axes as shown in Figure 9.1:

1. The causal nature of the scenario (y-axis). At one pole are exploratory scenarios where effects are projected given an initial set of causes. At the other pole are anticipatory scenarios whose role is to offer explanations of possible causes given an initial set of effects.
2. The relationships that exist between the scenarios, reality and values (x-axis); its poles are descriptive and normative. The descriptive scenario according to Ducot and Lubben (1980) 'simply states an ordered set of possible occurrences irrespective of their desirability or undesirability'. Normative scenarios, on the other hand, are those which incorporate the values, concerns and interests of the developer or consumer of the scenarios.
3. The time dimension (z-axis). Scenarios are classified according to how they incorporate the time dimension either as trend or peripheral scenarios. Trend or time-line scenarios present unfolding events in a causally related manner to explain how events or factors in two different time periods are related. In contrast, a peripheral or cross-sectional scenario presents a description at a particular future point in time.

The three axes and their respective poles generate some 27 different possible types of scenarios. This chapter shall largely focus on descriptive and exploratory scenarios, presented both in peripheral and trend form. Chapter 2 of this book, in contrast, deals with visions of the future which can be classified as anticipatory and normative scenarios, using Ducot and Lubben's typology.

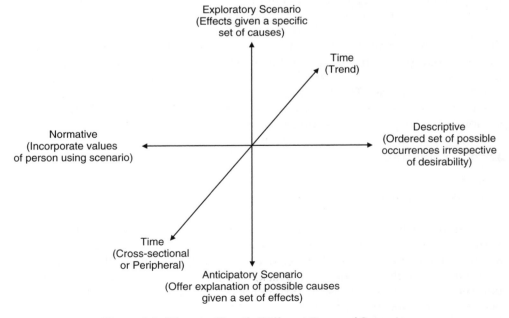

Figure 9.1. Ways to Classify Different Types of Scenarios

The development and use of any type of scenario encourages people to think about the future. Scenarios challenge people to explore the notion that the future could be different from expectations. Whilst the exact shape of the future is currently unknown, scenarios can capture the range of possible futures that may come to pass. But how should a management team plan for more than one possible future? Scenario planning approaches typically cover two phases: firstly *capturing* and *describing* future uncertainty within the scenario format, and secondly *assessing the impact* of future uncertainty and exploring what could be done about it now in the present. Scenario planning is often used in this way to help people develop organisational strategic initiatives and plans that are robust across multiple possible futures or scenarios.

Scenario planning is part of strategic development that aids creative foresight and is often used in times of accelerated change. It is a process used to create plausible stories focused on the most significant elements in an environment that challenge the various actors' perceptions and helps manage future uncertainties, test and improve decisions, learning and performance.

Some authors (see, for example, Schoemaker, 1991; Schwartz, 1991; Wack, 1985a,b) note that scenarios, rather than being predictions of the future, are a means of bounding uncertainty and understanding the dynamics of forces which together generate the future. Schwartz (1991) contrasts business forecasting and market research with scenarios, saying that the former extrapolate the trends of the present whilst the latter emphasises the possible, within the bounds of plausibility, with the aim of improving decision-making rather than producing accurate pictures of the future. However, there are authors who liken scenarios to forecasts. For example, Millett (1988) describes scenarios as conjectural forecasts and Bunn and Salo (1993) say that modern forecasting and scenarios are quite similar.

Origins of Scenario Planning

Scenarios have been used through the ages as a tool to explore the future of society and organisations. According to Bradfield *et al.* (2005), the technique was used by early philosophers like Plato and Machiavelli and visionaries like Thomas More and George Orwell. As a strategic planning tool it was used widely by the military to detail the ideal conditions for attacking an enemy or defending one's own position, e.g. von Clausewitz in the nineteenth century and Sun Tzu around 400 BC.

Scenario planning was popularised during the 1970s, when many organisations were faced with unexpected changes in their external environment. The early developments of scenario planning are usually attributed to individuals such as Herman Kahn and institutions such as the RAND Corporation and the Stanford Research Institute, in the years after the Second World War. The classic scenario planning success story is that of Shell (see Wack, 1985a,b). Through the use of scenarios, the story is told of how Shell better prepared themselves (compared with others in their industry) for the oil crisis of the early 1970s. Scenario planning helped Shell to understand that their current world, where the price of oil had for some time been below $2 a barrel, might not continue indefinitely into the future since certain players within the oil industry had the power to bring about a very different world. Foreseeing this possibility influenced Shell's planning so that when the price of oil suddenly increased fivefold, they were better prepared to cope with such an environment compared with those who had not entertained such a possibility.

Why do People Use Scenario Planning?

Scenario planning is a tool to help people think about the nature of the future and its impact on their organisation. Thus scenarios can usefully help managers to think about developments in their industry and the wider environment in times of change and uncertainty. They also provide a setting for people to develop a shared understanding of the future, which can be beneficial particularly where strong differences of opinion exist; in this way, scenarios can improve the quality of strategic thinking within an organisation. Schoemaker (1995) also believes that scenarios can be helpful if too many costly surprises have occurred in the past or if insufficient new opportunities are perceived and generated. Along similar lines, Wack (1985a) states that the purpose of scenarios is both protective, in anticipating and understanding risk, and also entrepreneurial, in discovering strategic options of which you were previously unaware.

The work of Ringland (1998), Burt and van der Heijden (2003) and Bradfield *et al.* (2005) can be combined to highlight four main uses of scenarios as shown in Table 9.1.

Scenarios also play an important role in supporting management learning. Wack (1985b) uses the phrase 'the art of reperceiving' and says the purpose of scenarios is to change and reorganise managers' microcosms, the mental models of their environment by challenging their assumptions about how it operates. d'A Hill (1994) supports this view, saying that scenario planning 'corrects inaccurate and damaging perceptions of the business environment and plays a role in building consensus among decision makers'.

Some of the many benefits of developing and using scenarios include:

- Helping individuals and groups to better understand and adjust to change.
- Helping a group to create a shared vision of the future.
- Promoting discussion about the future.
- Building consensus about the external environment.
- Improving long-term planning.
- Identifying early warning signs to enable organisations to react faster.
- Improving the assessment of potential strategic initiatives.
- Leveraging different opinions about the future.
- Gaining competitive advantage by capitalising on future changes in the market.
- Helping to create mental models of alternative futures.
- Understanding future uncertainties better.
- Helping groups to make more informed decisions.
- Providing a mentally stimulating and creative process.

Table 9.1. Four Main Uses of Scenarios

	Once only problem-solving	Ongoing surviving/thriving
Opening-up exploration	Making sense (risk assessment)	Anticipation (strategy evaluation)
Closure decisions	Developing strategy (strategy development)	Adaptive organisational learning (skills)

Coates (2000) wisely points out that 'none of the benefits of scenario planning can be realised unless the organisation has an unequivocal willingness to change and that willingness must be clear from the top down and continually reiterated and reinforced by management behaviour'.

Despite the many benefits of scenarios they do have limitations that need to be understood and avoided. Various authors have highlighted the weaknesses of scenario planning, including Burt and van der Heijden (2003) and Postma and Liebl (2005). Some of the main weaknesses are:

- Lack of linkage between the scenarios created, the actions of management and the performance of companies.
- Management disregard insight from scenarios due to their need to focus on short-term goals or issues.
- Management may still be surprised by the future despite conducting scenario planning.
- Scenario planning is a resource-intensive process.
- Scenarios are only useful if understood and acted upon by management.
- A company's culture may block insights from scenario planning or make them resistant to making the necessary changes.
- Lack of empirical studies on scenario planning that validate the technique.

Who Uses Scenario Planning?

Since the 1970s scenario planning has become a popular method for exploring future uncertainty for a wide variety of organisations and groups. For example, the approach has been applied to private sector organisations such as British Airways (Moyer, 1996), countries such as South Africa (Kahane, 1998) and public sector issues concerning, for example, the future of the UK National Health Service (Hadridge, Hodgson & Thornton, 1995). Surveys of the use of scenario planning were conducted in the 1970s and 1980s by authors such as Linneman and Klein (1979) and Malaska *et al.* (1984), demonstrating their use across a wide range of industry sectors and organisations of differing structures and sizes. Ringland's books (Ringland, 1998, 2002a,b, 2006) document some more recent uses of scenarios across both private and public sectors. Amongst her examples are (Ringland, 2002a):

- The Electrolux group, a consumer products company, whose scenario exercise led to a major strategic change in their commercial cleaning business which became more service oriented.

- Pacific Gas and Electric who used scenario planning to help challenge assumptions about the 'official future', which helped them prepare for an earthquake in California.
- An Austrian Insurance company who used scenarios to consider the competitive implications of future business environments.
- Krone, a manufacturer of telecom products, who used scenarios to help brainstorm product opportunities.

HOW TO DEVELOP AND USE SCENARIOS

A variety of methods have been developed for scenario planning. They all seek to produce multiple views of the future, by developing a set of multidimensional scenarios. They differ according to two key dimensions, the nature of the development process used to construct the scenarios and whether or not they use quantification. Schnaars (1987) differentiates between development processes that are deductive (top-down) or inductive (bottom-up). Deductive approaches to scenario development typically generate a small number (between two and four) of scenarios by selecting a subset of themes and projecting the uncertain factors into the themes in a consistent manner. Inductive approaches generate the complete set of scenarios resulting by considering all possible combinations of factor values. The complete set of scenarios is then filtered down to a more manageable number by, for example, considering only feasible combinations.

Bradfield *et al.* (2005) have classified scenario approaches into three different schools, as shown in Table 9.2. The key aspects of these three schools are as follows:

1. **Intuitive-logics models**. Covers a multitude of ways to create scenarios involving a various number of steps to derive the scenario. It appears to be the most popular due to its qualitative nature and ease of use.
2. **Probabilistic modified trend models**. Trends are modified to account for the effect of unprecedented future events. Not that widely used, which the authors believe is due to the perceived level of mathematics/statistics involved.
3. **La prospective models**. Godet (1986) states 'it is a way of thinking based on action and non-predetermination using specific methods e.g. scenarios'. Sometimes referred to as the French or European School.

Table 9.2. Different Schools of Scenario Planning

School	Main proponents
1. Intuitive Logics Models	Wack, Shell and SRI International
2. Probabilistic Modified Trend Models: trend impact analysis and cross impact analysis	Futures Group Battelle
3. La Prospective Models	Berger and Godet

The approach to scenario planning described in this chapter (O'Brien, 2004) is a qualitative, deductive approach, following the intuitive logics tradition, where the scenarios are constructed from a set of key uncertainties that shape the future of an organisation's external environment. The approach consists of the following eight stages:

Stage 1: Set the scene.
Stage 2: Generate uncertain and predetermined factors.
Stage 3: Reduce factors and specify factor ranges.
Stage 4: Choose themes and develop scenario details.
Stage 5: Check internal consistency of scenarios.
Stage 6: Present scenarios.
Stage 7: Assess impact of scenarios.
Stage 8: Develop and test strategies.

The approach is described below and illustrated with an example for the future of the UK fishing industry that was first developed in 2004. The scenarios are developed at the industry – firm level rather than the global level and could have been developed for a fishing company.

Stage 1: Set the Scene

This stage involves considering five key questions:

1. What issues/decisions should the exercise focus on?
2. Who to involve in the exercise?
3. How far ahead should people look?
4. How many scenarios to develop?
5. What have been the major causes of change?

The first question drives the exercise as it provides a focus for people's thinking. For example, a key concern may be that senior management feel they are not fully aware of the impact of changes taking place in their sector, either amongst the key players in the sector or amongst their client base.

In order to explore the issues that a scenario planning exercise should focus on, some authors suggest the use of the seven questions for the future used within Shell (taken from Ringland, 2006), as shown in Table 9.3.

A simple answer to the question 'Who should be involved in the exercise?' is 'The people who are going to use the scenarios in some way'. The key consideration however is that scenario planning is a participative process, so ideally a team of people with a range of experience from the organisation should be involved in developing the scenarios. van der Heijden *et al.* (2002) advocate the inclusion of a 'remarkable person' in the scenario team. They describe such a person as 'not part of the ongoing strategic conversation within the organisation, but . . . conversant with the industry structure, language, driving forces and key uncertainties, and ... are able to think out of the box, triggering scenario teams to surface intuitive knowledge . . . '. Consideration should also be given to the facilitation of the process, with suitably

Table 9.3. The Oracle Questions Used to Help Define the Focus of a Scenario Exercise

The vital issues (the oracle)
Would you identify what you see as the critical issues for the future? When the
conversation slows, ask: 'Suppose I had full fore-knowledge of the outcome as a genuine
clairvoyant, what else would you wish to know?'

A favourable outcome
If things went well, being optimistic but realistic, talk about what you would see as a
desirable outcome.

An unfavourable outcome
As the converse, if things went wrong, what factors would you worry about?

What cultural changes will be needed?
Looking at internal systems, how might these need to be changed to help bring about
the desired outcome?

Lessons from past successes and failures
Looking back, what would you identify as the significant events which have produced
the current situation?

Decisions that have to be faced
Looking forward, what would you see as the priority actions which should be carried
out soon?

If you were responsible
If all constraints were removed and you could direct what is done, what more would
you wish to include? (The epitaph question.)

skilled external support being sought if no appropriate internal service is available.
Guiding a team through a process which could be personally challenging and which
may last several months (van der Heijden *et al.*, 2002) requires a level of skill that
should not be underestimated.

The third question of how far into the future to look when developing scenarios
is shaped by two factors: the length of time resources are committed into the future
and the time-period during which things change in the industry. For example, a
retail organisation may use a scenario horizon of 5–10 years, whilst an oil company
would be more likely to use a further horizon, say 20–30 years.

The key issue to remember when considering how many scenarios to develop
(the fourth question) is that scenarios are developed to expand a person's thinking
about the future issues facing their organisation. To support this aim, literature commonly recommends that between two and four scenarios are developed
(Schnaars, 1987). Ringland (1998) believes that four scenarios 'encourage divergent thinking and help create a vision'. Coates (2000) states that odd numbers
with 'best, worst and most likely case draws the user to the middle, but
misses the point that alternative futures are real possibilities'. A lone scenario
should be avoided since it is deemed no better than a forecast, and more
than four is not advised due to the capacity of the human mind to juggle
multiple issues. Within these boundaries there is much scope for manoeuvre
and individual authors have their own views on how to array a set of scenario
themes.

Answering the final question, about what has caused change in the past, provides an important contextual basis for a scenario planning exercise. It is important to understand what has led an organisation or industry to where it is today, since this is a contributory factor in influencing its future direction.

A key concern for the UK fishing industry is the future of fishing fleets and employment prospects in a declining industry where fish stocks have continued to diminish over the past two decades. A set of industry-level scenarios were developed to illustrate the process; they are developed from the perspective of an organisation operating a fishing fleet in 2004, using a 10-year horizon.

Stage 2: Generate Uncertain and Predetermined Factors

The aim of the second stage is to generate a set of factors which together characterise the organisation's external environment and over which the organisation has little control. A brainstorming exercise can be used to generate a set of factors that are believed to be important to an organisation but are not under its control. Factors are written on Post-It™ notes and placed on a whiteboard, or wall. Even in a short space of time, a group can easily generate over 50 factors. The usual rules of brainstorming (e.g. no criticism of ideas) should apply to encourage a creative collection of factors to be surfaced. Once the group begins to run out of ideas, factors should be grouped into clusters in order to reduce duplication and bring the number of factors to a more manageable level. A variety of ways may be employed to reduce the number of factors. A SPECTRE (Social, Political, Economic, Competitive, Technological, Regulatory and Environmental) framework helps participants group their factors into categories; this can help them see where there may be gaps in their thinking so that they can add some more factors to give a richer picture of their external environment. Alternatively, factors can be clustered into causally related groupings which may or may not include the SPECTRE categories. Porter's Five Forces model can also be helpful in generating factors for industry-level scenarios, i.e. industry rivalry, threat of substitute products or new entrants and the power of suppliers and buyers.

For the fishing industry exercise, Table 9.4 lists the factors that were generated using a brainstorming exercise.

Stage 3: Reduce Factors and Specify Factor Ranges

The criteria for selecting the key factors that will form the skeleton of the scenarios are the two dimensions of 'level of uncertainty' about the future value of the factor, and its 'level of importance' to the organisation. Figure 9.2 illustrates this process for the fishing scenarios. Factors from the brainstorming exercise are placed on a grid based on the two dimensions described above. A process of discussion and debate is used to decide where exactly to place a factor. In Figure 9.2, the top left-hand area of the grid denotes factors which are deemed to be most uncertain in the future yet which are of key importance to the organisation. The arc drawn on the figure denotes the subjective cut-off point for deciding which factors to select for inclusion in the scenarios.

Table 9.4. Factors Generated in a Brainstorming Exercise (Repetitions Removed)

Fish-related health scares (1)	Competition (fish retailing) (12)
Attitude to healthy eating & against convenience foods (2)	Levels of non-EU fish imports (13)
	UK personal disposable income (14)
Image of fish (3)	Minimum wage (15)
Work–life balance (4)	Boat prices (16)
Household make-up (5)	Oil prices (17)
Retirement age (5a)	Fish prices (18)
Financial subsidies to fishing companies (6)	Fishing technology (19)
Fishing regulations (7)	Processing technology (20)
Europe – size & cohesiveness (8)	Pollution levels (21)
UK entry to EURO (9)	Spawning rates (22)
Exchange rates (£/EURO/$) (10)	Public awareness of conservation issues (23)
Competition (number & attitude) (11)	

Some methodologies encourage the inclusion of 'certainties' or 'predetermined factors' in scenarios whilst others focus primarily on uncertainties. A certainty is something which is reasonably predictable, for example the average age of a population in 5 years' time, whereas an uncertainty is difficult to predict, for example the dollar/euro exchange rate in 5 years' time.

A point of differentiation between approaches is the number of key factors to select. For example, the Warwick scenario methodology advises that about 12 uncertain factors (covering a range of issues) be selected along with some certain factors. The number '12' is not a hard constraint – essentially enough factors should be selected to enable a rich but manageable picture of the future environment to be created. Other methods reduce the pool of uncertainties into two key 'dimensions', each of which may cover a causally related cluster of individual uncertain factors. For example, Matthews (1976) argues that X and Y grids are a way to simplify the diverse possibilities in scenarios, i.e. into clusters of uncertainties. An example

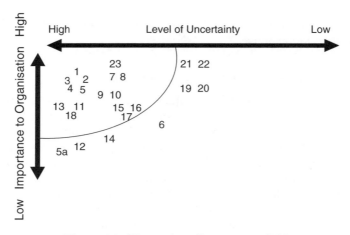

Figure 9.2. Uncertainty/Importance Grid

of this 2 × 2 approach can be seen in the Factiva case study below that plots four scenarios using content (X-axis) and technology (Y-axis).

For each factor, the range of values over which it may vary during the time horizon should now be specified. The values may be expressed either quantitatively or qualitatively; time available for researching the factors is likely to influence whether quantitative or qualitative values are ultimately used. Table 9.5 shows the reduced set of factors for the fishing exercise, along with their associated range of values which have been set subjectively by participants.

The range of values denotes the range over which participants believe a factor can plausibly and possibly vary over the time horizon that has been chosen for the exercise.

Stage 4: Choose Themes and Develop Scenario Details

As was noted earlier, Schnaars (1987) distinguishes between two types of approach that can be used to generate the scenarios – deductive (top-down) approaches which are largely qualitative in nature or inductive (bottom-up) approaches which often involve some level of quantification in the process. Deductive approaches involve setting a scenario's theme first and then projecting individual factors to be consistent with that theme. This process is then repeated for the set of scenario themes along with a check that each scenario is internally consistent. Inductive approaches, on the other hand, begin by generating the complete set of all possible combinations of factor values. This complete set is then subjected to a filtering process whereby infeasible or unlikely combinations of factor values are rejected and a smaller subset of feasible scenarios remains. A final set of scenarios may then be chosen.

Table 9.5. The Reduced Set of Factors and their Range of Values

Factor	Range of values	
Number of fish-related health scares	0	5
Attitude to healthy eating & against convenience foods	Strong	Weak
Image of fish	Innovative/fashionable	Traditional
Work–life balance	Leisure	Work
Industry technology	Radical improvement	No change
Fishing regulations	Supportive	Restrictive
Demand for fish products	Canned/frozen/fresh	
State of Europe/nature of relations	Growing	Shrinking
	Cohesive	Confrontational
UK joins EURO/exchange rates	No	Yes
	Low	High
Public awareness of conservation issues	Active	Ignorant
Level of competition	Weak	Strong
Level of non-EU fish imports	Low	High

Here we use a deductive approach. Scenario themes are generated, for example, by considering a subset of key factor values, and between two and four are selected for further development. For example, some of the most important uncertain factors arising out of stage 3 would be prime candidates for generating themes. For a particular theme, a value for each factor is selected from its range of values in order to be consistent with the chosen theme; this is done independently of other factors and their values.

This process is repeated for all chosen scenario themes, forming a scenario 'table' which lists factors and their values under each of the scenarios. Note that if any certainties or predetermined factors have been included in the set of key factors, their values will not change across scenarios. Uncertain factors typically will take different values across the set of scenarios, but there may be some scenarios for which a factor takes the same value. Table 9.6 shows the 12 uncertain factors selected for the fishing exercise; one predetermined factor was used to reflect the trend towards an ageing population. The table also shows the values that each factor will take under three different scenario themes.

The theme of the first scenario – Mad Fish – was developed from the idea that some intervention (possibly human) has harmed fish in a way that is not yet known about or understood, and that the diseased fish have in turn made the people who eat them ill. The second scenario – New Horizons – focuses on a cooperative European Union which has transferred land farming subsidies to support the fishing industry given widespread concern about the continued trend of diminishing fish stocks. The scenario explores a reframing of the fisherman's trade where the emphasis moves from catching fish to 'growing their own' fish through man-made fish farms. In the third scenario – Desert Seas – the diminishing fish stocks result in a highly competitive environment. With an absence of effective regulation caused by lack of agreement amongst European leaders, local fish catches increase, thus further diminishing fish stocks. At the same time non-EU imports flood the market. The result is even fewer fish in local seas and the impending collapse of European production.

Stage 5: Check Internal Consistency of Scenarios

In order to make sense to an audience, a scenario must be internally consistent. In other words, the story must hang together logically. To help with consistency, a cross-impact matrix can be constructed where each factor is considered pairwise with each other factor and the strength (and direction) of the relationship between them is noted in a qualitative fashion. For example, if it is believed that the factors 'health scares' and 'the image of fish' are strongly and positively related, then the cross-impact matrix would record S+ for their joint entry. The cross-impact matrix should then be used to check the internal consistency of the scenario table, with any necessary amendments made according to the relevant factor values.

It may become apparent when reviewing the cross-impact matrix that there are factors that are not related to any other factors, e.g. natural disasters. Ringland (1998) referred to these unlinked factors as wildcards, which the user may decide to discard or move into some other planning forum, e.g. disaster planning.

Table 9.6. Scenario Table for Fishing Exercise

#	Factor	Scenario 1 – Mad Fish	Scenario 2 – New Horizons	Scenario 3 – Desert Seas
1	Health scares	Major	None	None
2	Attitude to healthy eating	Strong	Convenience-driven	Weak, cost-driven
3	Image of fish	Poor	Good	Average
4	Demand for fish products	Fresh	Canned/frozen	Canned/frozen
5	Work–life balance	Leisure focus	Work focus	Work focus
6	Industry technology	No advances	New advances in farming methods	No advances
7	Fishing regulations	Tight	Subsidies for farming	Non-existent
8	Size of Europe	2004 state	2004 state	Pre-2004 members
9	UK joins EURO	No	Yes	No
10	Public awareness of conservation issues	High	Low	Low
11	Level of competition	High, non-European	High, local entrants	Low, local market collapsing
12	Level of non-EU imports	High	Low	High
Predetermined	Demographic distribution	More older, less younger	More older, less younger	More older, less younger

Other inductive methods (e.g. van der Heijden *et al.*, 2002) promote the use of influence diagrams to capture the nature of the causal relationships between individual factors. The influence diagrams are then used to help generate internally consistent scenario narratives.

Stage 6: Present Scenarios

Deciding how to present a set of scenarios is as important as generating their content. The scenario process is one where mindsets can be changed; much may therefore depend on the quality and detail of their presentation. Bunn and Salo (1993) considered scenarios credible if they were comprehensive, consistent and coherent; the tips they gave for presenting scenarios are incorporated below.

Six issues should be considered in relation to the presentation of scenarios:

1. The audience for the scenarios.
2. The purpose of the scenarios.
3. The naming of the scenarios.
4. The genre of the narratives.
5. The content of the narratives.
6. The language used for narrating the scenarios.

Just as with any presentation, the nature and size of the audience is the driving issue in deciding how to present the scenarios. For example, consider the difference between a single small internal management team compared with a larger collection of managers working across a multinational organisation. Each group may have a different set of characteristics, e.g. national and organisational culture, cognitive and learning styles of participants and time available to engage with the scenarios, which will influence how they engage with the scenarios. Likewise, it is important to clarify the purpose of the scenarios and what their presentation wishes to convey, e.g. what the future industry may look like.

The Mont Fleur scenarios (Kahane, 1998) were developed in the early 1990s to stimulate public debate about how the future of South Africa might be shaped. Four normative scenarios were developed and named after birds. Thus, Ostrich described a continuing non-representative government; Lame Duck represented a long transition to change; Icarus portrays rapid change to macro-economic populism; and Flight of the Flamingos captures a sustainable future of inclusive growth and democracy. The effective naming of vivid scenarios makes them more accessible in conversations about the future; the mere mention of the name conjures up the image of the future as captured by the scenario in the mind's eye. When used within an organisational setting, the names of the scenarios become part of the shared language that is used to talk about the future.

The genre of the scenario narratives should take account of the culture and practices of the client organisation. For example, when presenting scenarios within their organisation, the BBC World Service used the spoken word, with one scenario called 'Life in a new building' describing the possible working day and use of technology of a small selection of employees. In other situations, it may be appropriate to adopt a more unfamiliar format for presenting scenarios. Examples of different presentation formats include:

- Newspaper headlines and feature articles or web logs (blogs).
- A drama sketch involving key stakeholders.
- A letter or e-mail written at a future point in time looking back to describe past events (see, for example, 'The American military coup' described in the *Independent on Sunday* newspaper in 1993).
- TV/radio news broadcasts (typically verbally presented).

A scenario narrative should be a causally related story, which describes how the collection of key factors interacts to create a rich picture of a possible future. A narrative may be either cross-sectional in nature, i.e. set at a particular point in the future, or it may provide a timeline view explaining how the future has been arrived at from the present, for example, US President Arnold Schwarzenegger, who came to power after the change in the US constitution, said 'I'll be back' for re-election in 2019. The benefit of a cross-sectional narrative is that the future does not necessarily have to link to the past, i.e. an unforeseen discontinuity may occur. In contrast, a timeline-based narrative may appear more plausible as its evolution through time can be justified by making links with the present.

When considering the language to use, the impact of different tenses (i.e. past, present, future) on the audience should be considered. Bunn and Salo (1993) recommend using the past or present, rather than the future tense; the future conveys the notion of possibility and may not appear as convincing as a narrative written in the past tense, which conveys more certainty since something appears to have already happened. The intended audience for the scenarios should also influence the style of language used in the scenario narratives in that it should be appropriate to the cultural norms of the organisation.

Appendix 1 shows a narrative developed for one of the scenarios in the fishing exercise. The setting for the narrative is a radio interview with an entrepreneurial fisherman who has won an award for his innovative response to recent EU legislation, which has switched agricultural farm subsidies to the fishing industry. The intention of the scenario is not to suggest that an appropriate response to this scenario has to be a move into fish farming as happens in the scenario narrative, rather that a reframing of what it means to operate in this industry is indeed possible.

Stage 7: Assess Impact of Scenarios

Some scenario planning processes stop with the presentation of the scenarios. Others, however, include an appraisal of the impact of the scenarios on the organisation. For example, the Warwick method uses a SWOT analysis (Strengths, Weaknesses, Opportunities, Threats), as described in Chapter 6, to explicitly capture the perceived future opportunities and threats posed by the set of scenarios. A single analysis can be undertaken, combining the issues captured across the scenarios, or an analysis can be undertaken for each scenario.

Stage 8: Develop and Test Strategies

In order to complete the SWOT analysis, an appraisal of the current strengths and weaknesses needs to be undertaken. When the current strengths and weaknesses are combined with the future opportunities and threats, a TOWS matrix (Weihrich,

1993) of potential strategic options can be generated. Table 9.7 shows a TOWS matrix for the fishing exercise (for the fictitious fishing company). It is helpful at this stage to remember that the strengths and weaknesses are set in the present whilst the opportunities and threats are set in the future, since they are scenario-driven. Combining these timeframes within the TOWS matrix gives insight into what could be done now to address future possibilities; for example, which weaknesses should be strengthened now to counter future possible threats, or take advantage of future possible opportunities.

The robustness of each of the options generated should next be tested against each of the scenarios to support the selection of a balanced and robust portfolio. Such an exercise is by nature subjective as the group needs to decide how an option is likely to fare under each of the scenarios. Table 9.8 demonstrates, using the fishing exercise, how the robustness of options can be summarised. Clearly, a strategic option that fares well under each scenario is deemed to be robust and thus deserves serious consideration. Other options may not fare so well across the set of scenarios,

Table 9.7. TOWS Matrix Identifying Impact of Scenarios and Potential Strategies

	Strengths Skilled at catching fish Already have equipment Skilled & experienced staff Good knowledge of sea	**Weaknesses** Reliance on a single business stream High exposure to variability in many factors, e.g. weather, fish stocks, demand, prices, etc.
Opportunities Product image healthy Product easy to cook Older consumers (growing segment) like fish Subsidies for new fishing methods Common currency Expanded Europe – greater market for selling product	**SO strategies** Diversify: • Farming • JV with new European company (skill transfer) Stimulate demand: • Sponsorship • Publicity campaign	**WO strategies** Diversify: • Farming • Vertical integration, e.g. process/pack/distribute Sell up
Threats Disappearing stocks Health scares Restrictive regulations Levels of competition Exchange rates Popularity of convenience foods New entrants with new technology	**ST strategies** Diversify: JV with new entrant • Vertical integration, e.g. process/pack/distribute • Farming • Become importer Campaign for sustainable fishing	**WT strategies** Diversify: • Eco-tourism • Vertical integration, e.g. process/pack/distribute Sell up

Table 9.8. Testing the Robustness of Strategic Options

Strategy	Scenario 1	Scenario 2	Scenario 3	Robust
Diversify into farming	X	✓	X	X
Vertical integration	✓	✓	✓	✓
JV with new entrant	X	✓	X	X
Publicity campaign	✓	X	?	?
Become an importer	✓	X	✓	?
Diversify into eco-tourism	✓	?	✓	?
Sell up	✓	X	✓	?

and thus they may not appear to be 'robust'. However, there may be other reasons why it would make sense for an organisation to consider the further exploration of non-robust options – for example, to give an overall balanced portfolio or to maximise profits as robust strategies may not generate the greatest return. Once a portfolio of options has been selected, a team should resist the temptation to move immediately to action planning/implementation. Such options need to be evaluated, for example, for their feasibility. The next section points to other parts of the strategic development process which are relevant for such an evaluation activity.

Summary

This section has described the main stages of the scenario planning methodology. An example of the future of the UK fishing industry has been used to illustrate the output from some of the key steps in the process. The next section considers how scenario planning fits within the strategic development framework. The following section describes the development and use of scenarios at Factiva. It describes the scenarios developed and the process followed, including how a 2-day workshop was organised. It also highlights a number of guidelines covering practical issues for those wishing to develop their own scenario exercises.

SCENARIO PLANNING AND THE STRATEGIC DEVELOPMENT PROCESS

Scenarios represent detailed descriptions of alternative possible future worlds within which an organisation may have to operate and within which any initiatives or strategies chosen may have to succeed. Within the strategic development process, Figure 9.3 highlights the elements where scenario planning can make a contribution. In particular, the approach supports the **'exploration of the external environment'** since it is specifically designed to capture and describe possible developments in the form of scenarios or stories about what the future environment might look like. In practice, a strategic development process may begin with the development of scenarios in order to 'open up' a person's thinking about the future, to challenge their current and old ways of seeing their world and to encourage them to consider new possibilities.

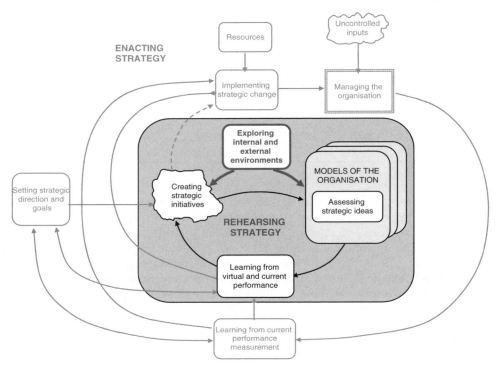

Figure 9.3. How Scenario Planning Supports the Strategic Development Process

Ideas for new, potential strategic initiatives may emerge from a scenario exercise, thus scenario planning supports **'creating strategic initiatives'**. Such new initiatives, along with existing ones, can be evaluated or tested against the set of scenarios; for example, for their robustness across a set of different possible futures. Thus scenario planning supports the **'assessment of strategic ideas'** since the scenarios provide alternative conditions against which to evaluate both new ideas and existing initiatives. Scenarios facilitate the process of **strategy rehearsal**, much in the way that a wind tunnel (van der Heijden, 2005) is used to support the design and development of an aeroplane; scenarios provide the test bed conditions against which initiatives may be tested for criteria such as durability, robustness and flexibility. If a formal model of the organisation exists, then scenarios may provide inputs in the form of exogenous variables to facilitate experimentation under different conditions. This process of taking a set of initiatives, considering their potential success or failure when projected into a number of different future scenarios and modifying the set as a result is a learning process conducted in the virtual arena, often in the minds of the participants. Hence, scenario planning supports **'learning from virtual and current performance'**. Scenario planning can also be combined with other approaches that support strategic development. For example, any robust options generated by a scenario process should be subjected to further validation and evaluation – other elements of the process and chapters of this book are relevant here, in particular decision and risk analysis (Chapter 10) can provide a way of evaluating different options against a set of criteria, whilst Chapter 12 covers the financial evaluation of strategic investments and Chapter 13 considers the issue of flexibility with its coverage of robustness analysis and real options.

Scenario planning is not only a useful framework to support a company's strategic development process, but also one that can help it to become a learning organisation. Galer and van der Heijden (1992) believed that 'underlying the planning process lies the art of "organisational conversation", the maintenance of which seems the key to productive organisational learning'. Scenario planning is an important framework to stimulate organisational conversation and the scenario planning process is a critical component of this.

Fahey and Randall (1998) also emphasised the importance of scenario learning and believed that 'scenario learning is not a simplistic, one-shot predictive process; nor is it just a sophisticated form of industry analysis. Scenario learning is a search for an understanding of how the future could change, and how an organisation could thrive by adapting to a number of particular circumstances'. To achieve this learning from scenario planning they suggest that the process should be integrated into a company's planning process. Fahey and Randall (1998) state that scenario learning occurs when an organisation:

- Uses scenarios to identify possible business opportunities.
- Tests its strategy in multiple scenarios.
- Refines its strategy based on its new understanding of what's required to succeed in a variety of possible futures.
- Monitors the results of strategy execution.
- Scans changes in the environment to determine whether future strategy change or adaptation is required.

Figure 9.4 illustrates the fit between scenario learning and a company's strategic planning process.

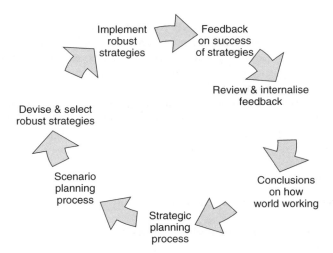

Figure 9.4. Scenario Learning Loop

CASE STUDY: SCENARIO PLANNING AT FACTIVA

This case study describes how a company operating in an industry faced with radical changes used scenario planning in 2005 as part of its strategic development process to devise and select strategies which they believed would help them succeed in the future.

The Company

Factiva (www.factiva.com) was formed in 1999 as a Dow Jones and Reuters joint venture to sell online business news and information to businesses globally. In 2006 Dow Jones bought Factiva from Reuters. Factiva provides essential business news and information together with the content delivery tools and services that enable professionals to make better decisions faster.

In 2000, Factiva invested in a next-generation platform that embraced XML and web services (then emerging technologies), which paved the way for the 2001 launch of their flagship product, Factiva.com, setting a new standard for the industry. Today, the platform enables Factiva to deliver world-class content alongside an organisation's internal data to enterprise information solutions.

By 2006, Factiva was the market leader in the online Current Awareness News and Research (CANR) market, but was a distant third when the company was formed, according to SIMBA Information (SIMBA, 2004). Factiva has more than 10 000 sources, nearly 1.8 million paying subscribers and nearly 80% of the Fortune Global 500 has an account with Factiva. The company employs 800 people world-wide and its content collection includes sources from more than 150 countries. Additionally, Factiva has been recognised with numerous awards, including the 2004 and 2006 International Business Awards for Most Innovative Company, 2005 KM World 100: Companies That Matter in Knowledge Management, 2005 Rogen Award for Business Excellence and 2005 EContent 100: Fee-based Information Service.

The Industry

Like many industries, the online CANR market is a mature industry where price competition is prevalent. The leading players in the CANR market, including Factiva, are faced by potentially powerful and disruptive new entrants, e.g. Google, Yahoo! and Microsoft (GYM) and providers of nearly-good-enough services at a much reduced price. The potentially radical changes in the market reduce the value of traditional forecasting and planning techniques. This uncertainty made the use of scenario planning more appropriate to map future strategies. Factiva needed to decide how to succeed in the future with the limited financial resources they had available.

Scenarios for the Future

Factiva used scenario planning to develop four key deliverables:

1. Scenarios – four potential future world views for the CANR market in 2010. The four scenarios were called: U2 (I Still Haven't Found What I'm Looking For); Napster; Doomsday; and Google Street Journal, see Figure 9.5.

Scenario	Summary
U2 (I Still Haven't Found What I'm Looking For)	Young people use a single wireless device. The device contains lots of different content with high personalisation and analytical features. People mix work, personal & fun. **The main focus of scenario is customers.**
Napster	Wireless is ubiquitous and interlinked, which changes the way people work. People still pay for good content but problems persist including rampant redistribution. **The main focus of scenario is legal.**
Doomsday	A search engine takes significant share of enterprise market via an ad supported business model. Some publishers change and excel in this new environment, while traditional and agile players consolidate to compete. **The main focus of scenario is competition.**
Google Street Journal	More premium content is available to 'good enough' providers. Digital natives influence enterprise purchase decisions and Google is used in the enterprise. People still struggle with information overload. **The main focus of scenario is suppliers.**

Figure 9.5. Summary of Scenarios for CANR Market in 2010

2. Leading indicators or warning indicators – to signal the emergence of each scenario.
3. Robust strategies – nine strategies Factiva felt were robust (likely to succeed) in all four scenarios. The main themes of these strategies were:
   (i) Build a ring fence around core business to defend it.
   (ii) Focus on customer intimacy to build revenues in target segments.
   (iii) Acquisitions as part of the company's growth strategy.
4. Implementation plan – how to fund and implement the robust strategies.

Two factors were found to be core to all four scenarios:

1. Content – premium content that is valued and currently paid for by users of online business information services.
2. Technology – range of technologies used to index, normalise, apply metadata, search and discover content.

Content and technology can be used to differentiate the four scenarios. Figure 9.6 plots the four scenarios using content (X-axis) and technology (Y-axis).

Figure 9.7 illustrates how, over the next 5 years, the CANR market may evolve. The content axis has three potential levels:

- Restricted content (Low) – premium content is not readily available for free on the internet and copyright protection is important.

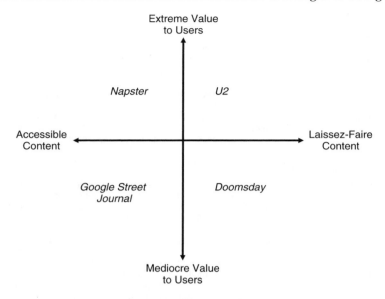

Figure 9.6. Scenario Themes
Source: Reproduced by permission of Factiva Dow Jones & Reuters Business Interactive LLC.

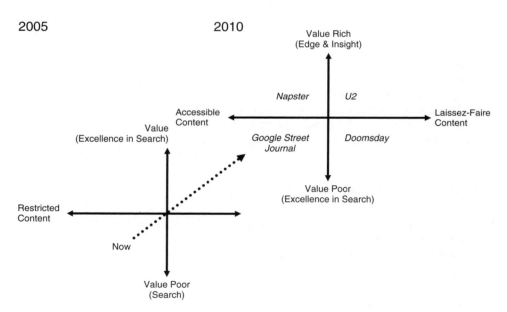

Figure 9.7. CANR Market Evolution from 2005 to 2010
Source: Reproduced by permission of Factiva Dow Jones & Reuters Business Interactive LLC.

- Accessible content (Medium) – premium content is readily available for free on the internet and copyright protection is important.
- Laissez-faire content (High) – premium content is easily available for free and copyright protection is not important.

The technology axis has three levels:

- Low value (Low) – technology only enables users to search and retrieve content, i.e. does not provide any great insight or competitive edge to users.
- Mediocre value (Medium) – technology enables users to obtain some insight from content.
- Extreme value (High) – technology enables users to obtain insight and competitive edge from content.

The 'Low' values above express the current state of content and technology in the CANR market.

It is unlikely that any single scenario will turn out to be true given the number of components it contains. It is possible that the future will be more complicated than any single scenario, with all four scenarios happening at the same time.

Figure 9.7 shows how the market may develop over the next 5 years:

- Content moves from being restricted to either being either accessible or laissez-faire.
- Technology moves from providing poor value for users to either providing mediocre or extreme value.

Practical Issues – Organising Factiva's Scenario Development Workshop

The process followed by Factiva was based on the one described earlier in this chapter and enhanced by the addition of two steps identified by Peter Schwartz, as read in Ringland (1998) (focal issue and leading indicators) and one by Martin Murtland (feedback on the performance of the scenarios) after conducting a review of scenario literature. The process thus consisted of 10 stages, as shown in Table 9.9.

Table 9.9. Stages in Factiva's Scenario Process

Stage	When carried out
1. Identify focal issue	Prior to the workshop
	***
2. Set the scene	
3. Generate factors	
4. Reduce factors	During a 2-day workshop
5. Formulate scenarios	
6. Check consistency of scenarios	
7. Present scenarios	
8. Develop and test strategies – 'Making it Happen'	
9. Identify and select leading indicators – 'Making it Happen'	
	***
10. Feedback – on the performance of scenarios	After the workshop

Stage 1 (focal issue) was identified by Factiva's Leadership Team prior to the workshop as:

What areas (strategy) should Factiva invest in to be successful in the future?

Stages 2 to 9 were completed during a 2-day scenario workshop conducted with 26 senior executives from Factiva. The executives included all members of the company's Leadership Team and CEO. Executives from various countries also represented all departments at Factiva.

Stage 10 (feedback) was gathered via an online survey completed by participants within 1 week of attending the workshop and a face-to-face interview with Factiva's CEO 6 months after the workshop. Ideally, feedback would be on the impact of the strategies implemented on the company's performance.

Martin Murtland, Factiva's Director Content Strategy & Development, championed the use of scenario planning as part of Factiva's strategic development process. To gain buy-in for the workshop, Martin conducted a dry run of the scenario process with members of Factiva's planning team. Martin's sponsors for the work were his Vice President, Simon Alterman, and Factiva's then-CEO, Clare Hart. Clare wanted to use the scenario workshop to: broaden the discussion regarding Factiva's strategy; build on work her leadership team had recently completed; and share thinking amongst Factiva's senior managers about the future.

The objective for each day of the workshop was as follows:

- Day 1 – to create scenarios for the future of the online business information market.
- Day 2 – to devise and test the robustness of potential strategies for Factiva in the future.

The agenda for each day is detailed in Table 9.10.

Figures 9.8–9.10 show the scenario workshop in progress. The workshop took place in a large room with movable furniture and plenty of working space for the groups, as can be seen in Figure 9.8. Materials such as: a workshop handbook; access to internet; online information services (Factiva.com); flipcharts; pens; markers; and Post-It™ notes were made available for groups to use throughout the exercise. Figure 9.9 shows one group discussing part of the process with some brainstormed ideas placed on the flipchart in the background. Figure 9.10 shows the deliberations of a group towards the end of the process during day 2, where the strategic ideas had been generated using the TOWS matrix.

Guidelines for Practitioners

On reading the academic literature on scenario planning there appears to be a lack of guidelines for practitioners on how to run successful scenario planning workshops. Some guidance is given in Moyer (1996), Swartz and Ogilvy (in Fahey & Randall, 1998), Ringland (1998) and O'Brien (2004). Therefore, Table 9.11 contains a list of pointers identified to help practitioners organise more effective scenario planning

Table 9.10. The Timetable for Factiva's Scenario Workshops

Day 1:

Time	Activity
8:00 AM	Breakfast
8:15 AM	Scenario Planning Workshop Context & Factiva Corporate Strategy – Clare Hart
8:35 AM	Overview of Scenario Planning
8:55 AM	Scene Setting (Existing Strategies & Trends – Product & Marketing) – Stage 1
10:00 AM	Coffee Break
10:10 AM	Generate Factors (Brainstorm, Combine, Define & Present) – Stage 2
12:20 AM	Lunch
12:50 PM	Factor Reduction (Prioritise & Define Ranges) – Stage 3
2:40 AM	Coffee Break
3:00 PM	Factor Reduction (Correlation) – Stage 3
3:25 PM	Scenario Themes & Scenario Development – Stage 4
4:35 PM	Scenario Consistency – Stage 5
5:25 PM	Scenario Creation – Stage 6
6:00 PM	**End**

Day 2:

Time	Activity
8:00 AM	Breakfast
8:30 AM	Scenario Creation – Stage 6
9:00 AM	Present Scenarios – Stage 6
10:00 AM	Strategy Robustness (SWOT) – Stage 7
11:00 AM	Coffee Break
11:10 AM	Strategy Robustness (TOWS) – Stage 7
1:00 PM	Lunch
1:30 PM	Strategy Robustness (Test) – Stage 7
3:15 PM	Leading Indicators & Sign Posts (Brainstorm & Present) – Stage 8
4:15 PM	Coffee Break
4:25 PM	Leading Indicators & Sign Posts (Making it Happen) – Stage 8
5:45 PM	Feedback & Wrap Up – Stage 9
6:00 PM	**End**

workshops. The pointers are broken into two categories, as detailed by O'Brien (2004):

1. Content – what the scenarios should focus on.
2. Process – how the scenarios exercise is organised. Contains the majority of the pointers, divided into three categories based on timing: before workshop; during workshop; and after workshop.

Figure 9.8. The Scenario Workshop
Source: Reproduced by permission of Factiva Dow Jones & Reuters Business Interactive LLC.

Figure 9.9. One of the Scenario Syndicate Groups
Source: Reproduced by permission of Factiva Dow Jones & Reuters Business Interactive LLC.

Findings of the Online Survey

All workshop participants completed an online survey within 7 days of attending the workshop. The purpose of the survey was threefold:

Figure 9.10. Presenting Part of the TOWS Strategy Generation Stage
Source: Reproduced by permission of Factiva Dow Jones & Reuters Business Interactive LLC.

1. Rate the benefits of the scenarios and the scenario planning process. These benefits (claimed benefits) were identified from frequently claimed benefits of scenarios and scenario planning within the literature.
2. Rate the usefulness associated with scenarios and the scenario planning process. Again these associations were identified from frequently claimed useful aspects of scenarios and scenario planning.
3. Detail the main strengths and weaknesses of the scenarios, i.e. open-ended questions.

The two highest rated 'claimed benefits' associated with scenario planning at Factiva were:

- Improved assessment of potential strategic initiatives; and
- A mentally stimulating process.

The two claimed benefits that were rated the least at Factiva were that the scenario planning process:

- Leveraged different opinions inside the company; and
- Helped gain competitive advantage by capitalising on future changes in the market.

Table 9.12 shows that the average usefulness of the scenario planning process by participants was 5.44 from a maximum of 7. This indicates that participants felt the scenario planning process was very useful, particularly to promote discussion and create a shared vision of the future. Participants rated least the scenarios' ability to predict the future.

Table 9.11. Summary of Pointers for Practitioners and their Associated Benefits

Content pointers, i.e. what the scenarios should focus on		
Pointer	Detail	Benefit
Firm's key issues	Focus on key issues of firm rather than as an academic exercise	Adds values, gives relevance and more useful to company and practitioner
Accuracy	Scenarios only represent the views of those who constructed them	There is no guarantee that the future is accurately predicted. The scenarios should also be taken as a collection

1. Before the workshop

Process pointers, i.e. how the scenario exercise is conducted		
Pointer	Detail	Benefit
Suitable venue	Needs necessary resources and facilities. Off-site prevents distractions and may encourage creative thinking rather than on-site. Cost may also be a factor in decision	Enables workshop organiser to focus on workshop rather than logistics
Participants' schedules	Check participants' schedules over the duration of the workshop	Enables organiser to plan what to do if participants have to leave or ensure necessary people are available
Preparation is everything	Plan what will happen when and by whom. Have a practice run including delivery	Will ensure workshop goes smoothly and increases knowledge of material
CEO & top management buy-in	Gain buy-in early from senior management and CEO	Enables them to own the process and improves buy in to findings
CEO & top management participation	If CEO participates, consider what their role is and how to use them effectively, e.g. participant or advisor. If CEO is a participant select strong-willed individuals in their team	Greater ownership of findings by decision-makers
Spread of participants	Involve people from different departments and levels of seniority	Captures the range of views and will ease the implementation of any strategy due to sense of ownership
Focal issue	Question management about their concerns to understand the key issue(s)	Ensures scenarios focus on management's deepest concerns

'Outsiders'	Involve outsiders and draw a wider internal audience into the process	Prevents group think, challenges existing assumptions but have to consider confidentiality of information
Pre-reading	Send participants reading about scenario planning and the workshop ahead of time	Helps participants understand more quickly the process and make faster progress in the time-constrained environment of the workshop
Focus	Ask participants what areas they want to spend most time on and what they want to achieve from the workshop	Adjust agenda to spend more time on areas participants will find most valuable

2. During the workshop

Agenda	Don't stick to it too rigidly	Enables ideas to be explored
Slack and buffer time	Provide sufficient 'free' time to discuss ideas and build buffer time into schedule	Enables free thought and creative thinking plus time to get back on track if things over-run or go wrong
Refreshment breaks	Provide time for coffee, lunch and comfort breaks	Plan for them as they will happen anyway. They are also a way to build buffer time
Reduce distractions	Prevent participants' distractions	Improves participants' concentration and input and helps time management
Explain process	Explain process at start and reiterate as move through it	Give participants sense of direction and purpose to understand process and its ease of use. Prevents confusion and reduces disillusionment with process at the start
Maintain enthusiasm	Plan on how to keep momentum and enthusiasm during and after workshop	Enhances value generated during and from the workshop
Workshop leaders	More than one makes it easier but need to agree each leader's role and responsibilities	Easier delivery and coordination, particularly with a larger group
Team size	Ideal is around eight. If a larger group divide into teams of no more than eight	Enables interaction inside the team and easier to coordinate

Table 9.11. Continued

Pointer	Detail	Benefit
Number of teams	Four works well, if creating four scenarios, as each team is able to work on a single scenario	Enables interaction inside the team and easier to coordinate
Company's strategy & marketplace	Articulate at start	Helps set the context and challenges faced by firm and industry, i.e. rational for scenario planning
Time management	Allow sufficient time to work through the scenario process	Gives participants time to think, contemplate and discussion ideas
Vocal participants	Use to generate ideas but do not allow them to dominate or control the process	Encourages others to participate and enables quiet people to be drawn into the discussion
Syndicate presentations	Have teams present their findings to the rest of the group	Encourages debate and shares knowledge
Participants' ideas & questions	Encourage participants' ideas but also challenge participants' thinking	Creates empathy, encourages participation, creativity and enthusiasm if conducted in a collaborative way
Reduce dead time	Ensure have next step prepared and ready to move onto it	Prevents participants being bored and seeing workshop as too long or a waste of time
Factor reduction & correlation	Explain process and importance of factor reduction and correlations	Will prevent participants seeing it as a black box and therefore have greater trust in the process and resultant scenarios
Projected values	Don't change projected levels simply because managers are unable to perceive them as fitting their view of the world	Will create scenarios that challenge rather than being too similar. The participants selected the projections in the first place. A range of possibilities are required to challenge
Realistic forecasted values	Provide access to information to enable participants to research values	Helps write challenging but realistic scenarios
Implementation of robust strategies	Leave sufficient time to do this	An area where some participants get it and gain greatest value. It also gives company something tangible to 'walk away' with
Challenge thinking	At times challenge current thinking, strategy and assumptions	Encourages participants to analyse company's strategy and move outside their comfort zone to be more creative, far-sighted and not play it safe

Access to information	Give participants access to the internet and other sources of information during the workshop	Enables participants to check information, e.g. forecasts, competitors, industry research, company information, etc. during workshop

3. After the workshop

Organise follow-up sessions	Hold follow-up sessions with a mix of new and existing participants	Maintains momentum and prevents perception by management that 'ticked the box'. Able to update scenarios and think further about their consequences
Integration with planning	Integrate scenario planning into company's corporate planning cycle	Greater acceptance of scenario planning and greater buy-in to robust strategy and everyday actions
Test question-naire	Pilot questionnaire with someone not involved in its creation but involved in the workshop	Ensures questions are clear and will obtain the desired information
Next steps	Need to consider next steps	Value created will be lost if no follow on
Communication	Devise a communication strategy to spread knowledge inside organisation	Shares knowledge and helps people understand the context of strategies and company's challenges
Feedback loop	Assess success of strategies implemented and of scenarios	Enables a company to learn and improve its strategy going forward

Table 9.12. Usefulness of Scenarios in Order of Usefulness

Question	Average
Promote discussion inside Factiva about the future?	6.24
Help Factiva create a shared vision of the future?	5.81
How useful did you find the scenario planning process?	5.71
Improve Factiva's long-term planning?	5.52
Build consensus at Factiva about the outside environment?	5.43
Usefulness to identify early warning signs to enable Factiva to react faster?	5.24
Help Factiva adjust to changes in the industry?	5.19
Help you to understand changes in Factiva's industry?	5.14
How useful will you find the scenarios generated?	5.05
Usefulness to help you predict the future of Factiva's industry?	5.05
Average	**5.44**

The most frequently quoted strengths of scenario planning by participants were: the sharing of ideas; focus on the future and strategy; building consensus and team spirit. The most frequently quoted weaknesses of scenario planning by participants were: changing of factor values; lack of time, including advance preparation time; groupthink; lack of wider participation. These weaknesses helped provide pointers to improve future workshops at Factiva.

The Outcome – After the Scenario Exercise

Faced with the possibility of all four scenarios becoming true at the same time, the question was, 'How should Factiva act?'...

Four months after the scenario workshop, Factiva reorganised to intensify efforts to build revenue in its core business and strategic initiatives (role-based applications) and optimise performance and reduce costs. Two new strategic initiatives were also launched that Martin Murtland at the time of writing leads:

1. Web content development – a rapid expansion in exploiting web and other alternative content.
2. Meta-data development – to expand use of taxonomies, ontologies and metadata.

It is possible to relate these new initiatives to the four scenarios and in particular the two axes used to differentiate the scenarios, i.e. content and technology. Factiva's reorganisation and new strategic initiatives covered six of the nine robust strategies. The other three robust strategies were covered by Factiva's existing acquisition strategy.

In an interview with Factiva's then-CEO and now Chairman, Clare Hart, 6 months after the workshop it was clear that the scenario planning process helped shape and confirm management's thinking. Clare Hart felt that scenario planning reinforced to the company the necessity of investing in metadata and web content projects. The workshop acted as a catalyst by showing the need for change. It also made it easier for Factiva to make decisions and communicate the changes inside the organisation.

> *"The value was to look at the broad issues and the main drivers in a broader spectrum for Factiva like Google Street Journal and U2 and what is likely to happen. It enabled people to get a better sense of what environment Factiva will be operating in, in the future."*
> Clare Hart, then-CEO Factiva (2005)

Clare Hart believed Factiva derived benefits from scenario planning by: the discussion about the future it promoted; the way it helped build and create a shared vision of the future; and the fact that it identified leading indicators to monitor.

A number of actionable recommendations were made and adopted by Factiva relating to the scenario planning process:

- Integrate scenario planning into Factiva's planning process.
- Wider participation of employees in the scenario planning process.
- Addition of early warning indicators to the factors regularly monitored.
- Create a learning and feedback loop by reviewing the success of existing strategies.

CURRENT ISSUES AND FUTURE DIRECTIONS IN SCENARIO PLANNING

To finish, we shall consider some possible future directions for scenario planning, or scenarios for scenarios! Three areas for further development are summarised:

1. The establishment of theory to underpin the subject field.
2. The need for more critical reflection on the teaching/learning and application of the approaches.
3. Developments to scenario planning approaches.

The Establishment of Theory to Underpin the Scenario Planning Field

Hodgkinson and Wright (2002) note that scenario planning is a 'practitioner-derived method with very little supporting evidence, other than basic anecdotal evidence, for its efficacy'. Hence there is a need for further research to explore the philosophical underpinnings and theories to support the development of scenario planning approaches, including a longitudinal study on the success of scenario planning. There is also a need to show the impact of scenario planning on a company's performance in terms of shareholder value. This will be difficult given the need to rule out other causal effects. They also note that it is typically the successful applications of scenario planning that reach publication, highlighting the need for a more reflective critical appraisal of the practice of scenario planning. On a related theme, some authors (e.g. Ringland, 2002a; Eden & Ackermann, 1998) suggest that key uncertainties in the unfolding future be monitored, however, little research has been published reporting the results of such monitoring. Likewise, neither the actual quality of the scenarios developed nor the strategies derived from them are routinely put to the test.

Critical Reflection on the Teaching/Learning and Application of the Approaches

O'Brien (2004) reports some experiences of teaching scenario planning to different participant groups. Her work highlights the similarity of experience for those meeting scenario planning for the first time, be they student or practising manager. Taking her work further, there is a need to understand better the learning process that individuals undergo whilst developing scenarios; for example, how does a participant's attitude to and knowledge of uncertainty change during the course of a scenario planning exercise? In addition, from the perspective of researchers interested in the connection between cognitive style and managerial decision-making, there have been recent calls for formal evaluation of the effectiveness of scenario-based approaches with groups of diverse composition and cognitive styles (e.g. Hodgkinson, 2004).

Developments to Scenario Planning Approaches

Throughout this chapter, a range of approaches have been identified for the development of scenarios. Undoubtedly there will be developments and improvements to the actual techniques used, either as stand-alone approaches or in some form of combined multi-methodology. One of the challenges for scenario planning posed by Millett (2003) is to explore how the intuitive and what he calls the analytical approaches can be combined into a 'progression of futuring tools'.

Millett (2003) also notes that there are a wide variety of definitions and methods for scenario planning which he claims have the potential to confuse potential clients. Another of his challenges therefore is for scenario planners to provide better clarity about the breadth of scenario approaches within the field and hence provide a better matching of methodology to client needs and organisational culture. His final challenge is to reduce the resources required to undertake a full scenario planning exercise. His suggested solution is 'for the next generation of scenario methods to eliminate, reduce or automate some of their steps to reduce the time, effort and expense, while preserving the benefits of group participation and learning' (Millett, 2003).

Many scenario planning exercises are developed from the perspective of a single organisation that is grappling with the uncertainty in its environment. The scenarios are used by the managers of the single organisation concerned to support them in deciding what strategies to adopt. An area for further research is to explore how the same scenarios might be seen from the perspectives of other stakeholders in the complex environment being addressed, and how this might be incorporated into the analysis of future actions that the organisation may consider. Interested readers might wish to review the drama theory approaches discussed in Chapter 3, and the multi-methodological exercise (combining scenario planning with two other approaches) described in Chapter 14.

We end with suggestions for research activity to support specific improvements into scenario planning processes such as the Warwick approach described here. Six areas are identified as being particularly worthy of investigation, and they fall into three categories: strategy selection; the success of selected strategies; the impact of scenario planning process on individuals and companies.

1. Strategy selection

(i) New approaches to strategy selection, that test the robustness of the strategies emerging in a more comprehensive manner, would improve the scenario planning methods such as the WBS method.

(ii) Future research could consider approaches to exploring how other stakeholders in the competitive environment might behave under the scenarios that are being developed, and how this might be factored into the organisation's selection of strategies. See, for instance, Chapter 3.

2. Success of selected strategies

(iii) There is a need for a longitudinal study into the reliability or success of scenario planning, to monitor the success of participating organisations and their adopted strategies over a longer time period (see Hodgkinson & Wright, 2002 and the comments above).

3. Impact of scenario planning process on individuals and companies

(iv) Evidence should be gathered into the impact of scenario planning on a company's performance and shareholder value, though it will be difficult to rule out other causal effects.

(v) Individuals' characteristics and their propensity to adopt the scenario planning technique, or be sceptical towards it, is worthy of further research. For instance, will practitioners with different cognitive styles (which influence our perceptions of the world) also differ in their perceptions of the usefulness of scenario planning? Moreover, if scenario planning is being undertaken as a group-based activity, will the make-up of the group (for instance in terms of cognitive styles) impact upon the performance of the group and the effectiveness of the scenario planning exercise?

APPENDIX 1. NARRATIVE FOR THE 'NEW HORIZONS' SCENARIO

Host: Welcome to Radio East Coast's Fishing Today programme on 22 September 2014. Today we catch up with Mike Salmon, the winner of this year's Fishing Fleet Foundation's award for sustained entrepreneurial regeneration.
So Mike, what's it like to be honoured by your fellow fishermen?

Mike: I'm amazed that I won the award, really. I'd never have imagined that I'd be where I am now 10 years ago. Back then, I was a traditional fisherman working with other family members, struggling to earn a decent day's wage.

Host: How did it all start?

Mike: Given the history of our industry's wars over fishing rights, I thought it pretty likely that it wouldn't be long before the seas were confirmed to be all but empty and I'd be out of a job. I don't know any other trade and was determined to stay a fisherman. After all, my family have been fishermen for 5 generations. I was in the pub one day, when we were joking around about how the Europeans would be stealing our fish till there was none left. A bloke at the bar said 'so what are you going to do about it?' 'You can't exactly plant some more fish like you do cabbages!' was the reply from a joker in the corner. This led me to think . . . 'if there are no fish in the sea, why don't we put some back – just like farmers we could replant every season'.

Host: What impact did central government have on your decision?

Mike: Well, after the Labour government won their third term in 2005, I was pretty certain that when Gordon Brown took over from Tony Blair in 2008 he would take us further into Europe. Soon after we joined the EURO, and I knew that it wouldn't be long before the whole issue of farming subsidies and the UK rebate were thrashed out. I was quite pleasantly surprised when our government negotiated subsidies for the fishing industry to replace the farming subsidies that the French had held onto for so long. I took advantage of this and set up my first cod farm in 2010. Since then we've gone from strength to strength.

Host: It was quite brave of you to go into such new territory. How confident were you of success?

Mike: I did some research at the time and realised that with the government's continued drive towards healthy eating, that fish generally had a good image amongst consumers. Also, given the trend towards working longer since the retirement age was increased to 70 recently, people have less free time and fish is a great convenience food. In the port nearest my farms, there have been a number of processors set up so I have a ready local market for my fish. They produce ready meals for the major supermarkets, and as there isn't a lot of travelling to do, we can keep prices down.

Host: Are you concerned about foreign competition?

Mike: No, not really, as I said, we've been able to set up a whole industry quite locally and this helps us keep our prices down and makes us competitive with foreign imports which by comparison seem quite pricey. One thing that I have noticed, is that the home-grown competition is increasing – basically, the other fishermen realised there's a future in fishing and they jumped on the band wagon, so if anything, local competition has become an issue, not foreign competition. We're now at a stage where the majority of European fish stocks come from fish farms farmed like mine.

Host: Thank you Mike Salmon, winner of this year's FFF entrepreneurial award, for talking to us today about how he started up in business all those years ago. Don't forget to listen in next week when we talk to Henry Haddock, spawn producer, about his latest ideas for fish farming technology. Does he really think we'll believe that whale music excites fish to spawn at a faster rate? Well that's all for today folks, now it's Laurie London with the latest weather report.

REFERENCES

Bradfield, R., Wright, G., Burt, G., Cairns, G. & van der Heijden, K. (2005) 'The origins and evolution of scenario techniques in long range business planning', *Futures*, **37**, 795–812.

Bunn, D.W. & Salo, A.A. (1993) 'Forecasting with scenarios', *European Journal of Operational Research*, **68**, 291–303.

Burt, G. & van der Heijden, K. (2003) 'First steps: towards purposeful activities in scenario thinking and future studies', *Futures*, **35**, 1011–1026.

Coates, J.F. (2000) 'Scenario planning', *Technological Forecasting and Social Change*, **65**, 115–123.

d'A Hill (1994) 'The relevance of business scenarios for Africa', *Futures*, **26**, 980–986.

Ducot, C. & Lubben, G.J. (1980) 'A typology for scenarios', *Futures*, **Feb**, 51–57.

Eden, C. & Ackermann, F. (1998) *Making Strategy – The Journey of Strategic Management*. Sage Publications: London.

Fahey, L. & Randall, R.M. (1998) *Learning from the Future: Competitive foresight scenarios*. John Wiley & Sons: Chichester.

Galer, G. & van der Heijden, K. (1992) 'The learning organization: how planners create organisational learning', *Marketing Intelligence & Planning*, **10**(6), 5–12.

Godet, M. (1986) 'Introduction to La Prospective: seven key ideas and one scenario method', *Futures*, **Apr**, 134–157.

Hadridge, P., Hodgson, T. & Thornton, S. (1995) 'Tomorrow's world', *Health Service Journal*, **5**, 18–20.

Hodgkinson, G.P. (2004) 'Towards a (pragmatic) science of strategic intervention: the case of scenario planning', AIM Working Paper Series.

Hodgkinson, G.P. & Wright, G. (2002) 'Confronting strategic inertia in a top management team: learning from failure', *Organization Studies*, **23**, 949–977.

Independent on Sunday (1993) 'The American military coup', May 16.

Kahane, A. (1998) 'Imagining South Africa's future: how scenarios helped discover common ground'. In: Fahey, L. & Randall, R.M. (eds), *Learning from the Future: Competitive Foresight Scenarios*. John Wiley & Sons: Chichester, 325–332.

Linneman, R.E. & Klein, H.E. (1979) 'The use of multiple scenarios by US industrial companies', *Long Range Planning*, **12**, 83–90.

Malaska, P., Malmivirta, M., Meristo, T. & Hansen, S.-O. (1984) 'Scenarios in Europe – who uses them and why?', *Long Range Planning*, **17**, 45–49.

Matthews, R. (1976) 'Food distribution 2010: four futures', *Progressive Grocer*, **9**, 24–32.

Millett, S.M. (1988) 'How scenarios trigger strategic thinking', *Long Range Planning*, **21**, 61–68.

Millett, S.M. (2003) 'The future of scenarios: challenges and opportunities', *Strategy and Leadership*, **31**, 16–24.

Moyer, K. (1996) 'Scenario planning at British Airways – a case study', *Long Range Planning*, **29**, 172–181.

O'Brien, F.A. (2004) 'Scenario planning: lessons for practice from teaching and learning', *European Journal of Operational Research*, **152**, 709–722.

Postma, T.J.B.M. & Liebl, F. (2005) 'How to improve scenario analysis as a strategic management tool?', *Technological Forecasting & Social Change*, **72**, 161–173.

Ringland, G. (1998) *Scenario Planning: Managing for the future*. John Wiley & Sons: Chichester.

Ringland, G. (2002a) *Scenarios in Business*. John Wiley & Sons: Chichester.

Ringland, G. (2002b) *Scenarios in Public Policy*. John Wiley & Sons: Chichester.

Ringland, G. (2006) *Scenario Planning: Managing for the future* (3rd edn). John Wiley & Sons: Chichester.

Schnaars, S.P. (1987) 'How to develop and use scenarios', *Long Range Planning*, **20**, 105–114.

Schoemaker, P. (1995) 'Scenario planning: a tool for strategic thinking', *Sloan Management Review*, **Winter**, 25–40.

Schoemaker, P.J.H. (1991) 'When and how to use scenario planning: a heuristic approach with an illustration', *Journal of Forecasting*, **10**, 549–564.

Schwartz, P. (1991) *The Art of the Long View*. Doubleday: New York.

SIMBA Information, Inc. (2004) Business and Professional Online Information Markets 2002–2006.

van der Heijden, K. (2005) *Scenarios: The art of strategic conversation*. John Wiley & Sons: Chichester.

van der Heijden, K., Bradfield, R., Burt, G., Cairns, G. & Wright, G. (2002) *The Sixth Sense: Accelerating organisational learning with scenarios*. John Wiley & Sons: Chichester.

Wack, P. (1985a) 'Scenarios, shooting the rapids', *Harvard Business Review*, **Nov/Dec**, 131–142.

Wack, P. (1985b) 'Scenarios: unchartered waters ahead', *Harvard Business Review*, **Sept/Oct**, 73–90.

Weihrich, H. (1993) 'Daimler-Benz's move towards the next century with the TOWS matrix', *European Business Review*, **95**, 4–11.

Part V

Evaluating Performance

Chapter 10

Decision and Risk Analysis for the Evaluation of Strategic Options

Gilberto Montibeller and Alberto Franco

INTRODUCTION

If an organisation has successfully engaged in the activities of negotiating strategic agendas (Chapter 4), setting strategic direction or vision and goals (Chapter 2) and creating strategic initiatives (Chapters 5 and 6), it is likely then that a number of promising strategic options will have been produced within the organisation and put forward for evaluation. Such assessment will typically involve the quantification of the perceived impacts of implementing those options. The purpose of the evaluation is to compare a number of promising strategic options against an agreed set of criteria, derived from the organisation's values and aspirations, in order to select those that have the best potential, at the time of the evaluation, to achieve the organisation's intended strategic direction, or vision (Chapter 2).

As stated in Chapter 1, this book advocates the use of models for strategic development. This chapter will therefore introduce Decision and Risk Analysis (DRA) as a formal modelling mechanism of conducting the 'assessment of strategic initiatives' element of the strategic development process model presented in Chapter 1 and reproduced below in Figure 10.1. DRA is a methodology that decomposes a decision problem into a set of smaller problems – what Keeney (1982) calls the 'divide and conquer' approach – and models the multiple (and potentially) conflicting organisational objectives and values, as well as the uncertainties, involved in the decision problem (von Winterfield & Edwards, 1986). In our case, the decision problem is one of assessing and selecting the best potential strategic options for the organisation. After each smaller problem has been dealt with separately, DRA provides a formal way for integrating the results so that a preferred course of action for the organisation can be established.

Decision and Risk Analysis has been employed extensively in practice, in organisations operating in a wide variety of fields including energy, manufacturing and services, medical, military and public policy (Corner & Kirkwood, 1991; Keefer, Kirkwood & Corner, 2004). It would be impossible to provide an extensive treatment of DRA in this chapter, and readers are invited to consult also some of the excellent textbooks on the subject (e.g. Clemen & Reilly, 2001; Goodwin & Wright, 2004). What

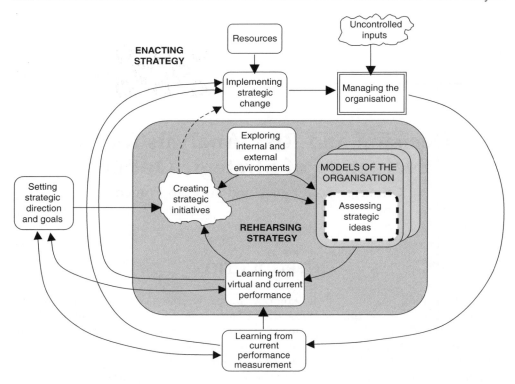

Figure 10.1. The Role of Decision and Risk Analysis Within the Strategic Development Process (highlighted by the dashed border)

we aim for in the following sections is to provide readers with a good overview that would enable them to appreciate the potential of the methods and tools of DRA when employed for strategy evaluation.

The rest of the chapter is organised as follows. The next section discusses strategy evaluation as a complex socio-technical process involving high stakes, different types of uncertainty, multiple objectives and stakeholders, and a significant amount of hard and soft data. Next, a Decision and Risk Analysis modelling framework for the evaluation of strategic options is presented, and its use is illustrated through a case study. The conclusions and implications for practice are discussed in the final section.

THE COMPLEXITY OF STRATEGY EVALUATION

The process of evaluating and selecting strategic options is not a straightforward activity. Rather, it is a complex endeavour involving *high stakes*, due to the level of financial, human and time resources needed to conduct the evaluation and to implement the chosen strategy. It also entails the collection of an overwhelming amount of *diverse and dispersed data*. There is no lack of data in modern organisations – e.g. levels of sales, customers' feedback from questionnaires, analyses of costs, different views expressed in managerial meetings, outputs from information systems. However, rather surprisingly, it is usually very hard to use all this available data systematically in a consistent way to support strategy evaluation. Besides, while some of these data are quantitative and easier to analyse, other important data for strategy evaluation are qualitative and deal with intangible issues (e.g. reputation, social responsibility, culture), which are usually difficult to elicit and evaluate.

Another key challenge presented by strategy evaluation is that it deals with *multiple and conflicting objectives*. Almost inevitably, strategy evaluation involves more than one objective to be achieved. Even commercial enterprises, which may have long-term profit as their ultimate goal, do need to take into account multiple objectives when considering alternative strategic options in a particular strategic decision (e.g. customers' satisfaction, market share, flexibility). In the public sector, the presence of multiple objectives is still more prevalent, as even the ultimate goals could be contested. In addition, if there are multiple objectives, very often they are conflicting with each other. An example could be the eternal dilemma between cost and quality when evaluating strategic options for a company's manufacturing division: the more expensive the production process, the better the product quality but the higher the final price. Similarly, when evaluating different schemes for a housing development project, a small development would perform well in meeting environmentalists' objective of preserving nature but poorly in terms of increasing housing supply and generating large profits.

But perhaps the most troublesome issue for organisations when engaging in strategy evaluation is the unavoidable presence of *uncertainty* regarding the future. Uncertainty can be distinguished as being 'aleatoric' or 'epistemic' (Hoffman & Hammonds, 1994). Aleatoric uncertainty is related to the inherent variation associated with a particular system or the environment, and is also referred to as 'variability'. For example, if a (fair) coin is tossed once, there will be only two possible outcomes: a head or a tail. However, we cannot predict which outcome we will get out of one coin toss because of the inherent variability of the coin toss. Similarly, if the probability of a small new company surviving its first 5 years is, for example, 20%, we still do not know whether such a company will indeed survive. On the other hand, epistemic uncertainty refers to a lack of complete knowledge about the problem. Thus, for example, if a company is about to launch a new innovative product into the market, it is hard to estimate whether it would be successful or not, given that the product was never released before.

We recognise, as well as others, that organisations are composed of a *multiplicity of stakeholders* with different values and aspirations, who negotiate and compete for organisational resources, and who will support those organisational objectives compatible with their own values and objectives (Eden & Ackermann, 1998). For example, if a company is evaluating different product strategies, marketing may want a customised product because they value customers' taste, and thus support solutions that increase the flexibility of assembly lines; production, on the other hand, may want a more standardised product because they value cost efficiencies, and therefore would welcome solutions that involve less adaptation of the production system.

A direct consequence of the above is that strategy evaluation is not only a technical activity but also *a social process*, where issues of problem structuring and negotiation, group dynamics and learning become critical in building up commitment for implementing the chosen strategies (Eden, 1992; Eden & Ackermann, 1998; Phillips, forthcoming).

In summary, strategy evaluation is a complex socio-technical process involving high stakes, different types of uncertainty, multiple objectives and several stakeholders, with a significant amount of hard and soft data. Decision and Risk Analysis is, in our view, a powerful way of managing the complexities of strategy evaluation. It deals with both the content and process aspects of strategy evaluation. Regarding content, it provides a clear *modelling* framework for analysing the impact of potential strategic options on multiple and conflicting objectives, as well as a potent way of representing uncertainties and consequences in the long term. In addition, it provides an audit trail to justify why a particular strategic option was recommended or chosen. With respect to process, the particular form of DRA presented in this chapter uses *group facilitation techniques* (e.g. Schein, 1998; Schwarz, 2002) to help stakeholders gain a better and shared understanding of each others' objectives and preferences, negotiate an agreed set of priorities for the organisation, and achieve a high level of commitment to the strategic options eventually chosen.

A DECISION AND RISK ANALYSIS FRAMEWORK FOR STRATEGY EVALUATION

In this section we will present a modelling framework for using Decision and Risk Analysis to support the evaluation of strategic options, using a case study to illustrate its use in practice. The DRA modelling framework is depicted in Figure 10.2. The different elements of the framework will be presented below in a linear fashion, though we recognise that strategy evaluation is a dynamic and iterative activity. Dynamic because the decision to select a particular strategic option does not necessarily come out straightforwardly after the evaluation, and may actually take some time before it is taken; iterative because the process may require several evaluation cycles, as new information is obtained and organisational priorities evolve. The DRA framework presented here is aimed at helping organisational stakeholders learn about the 'virtual performance' of potential strategies (see Chapter 1), reflect about and operationalise the values and strategic objectives of the organisation, and create robust strategic options for the strategic initiatives being tested.

Understanding the Decision Situation

The case study that we are about to present is drawn from our own experience of using DRA in practice, either in isolation or in combination with other modelling methods discussed in this book such as problem structuring methods (Chapter 4), scenario planning (Chapter 9) or SWOT/TOWS analysis (Chapter 6). Our discussion of the case below is structured around the different stages suggested by the DRA framework shown in Figure 10.2. As we mentioned before, it is important to note that in practice these stages do not have to be followed in a linear sequence. As with the other modelling approaches discussed in this book, modelling within DRA

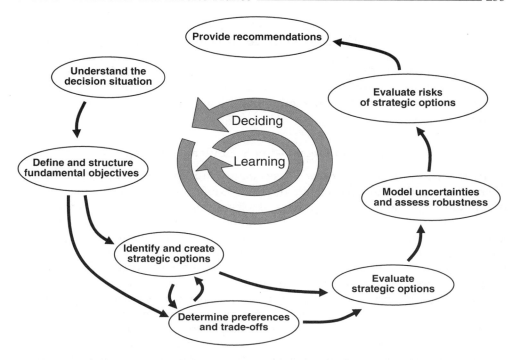

Figure 10.2. Decision and Risk Analysis Modelling Framework to Support Strategic Option Evaluation

tends to operate in a non-linear fashion, which makes it possible for the participants to cycle between the phases. Nevertheless, here we have adopted a linear approach to DRA modelling for the benefits of clarity of exposition.

We have been invited to provide decision support to a medium-size software company referred to here as SoftCo. In our first meeting, we learnt that SoftCo wanted to formally evaluate a new strategic initiative involving the development of an innovative internet search engine to compete with the leader in the market. The company had a relatively large team of software developers, and two small departments of marketing and finance. The organisation had a strong market focus, with emphasis on gaining market share.

We identified three main stakeholders (Software Development Team, Marketing and Finance Departments) and asked for a couple of representatives of each to work with us in the meetings (in this way, we could guarantee having at least one representative in every meeting and it kept the group size small).

After listening to the various descriptions of the problem by the members of the stakeholders group, we suggested that it could be considered in two independent phases:[1] firstly, the decision of which software design they would

---

[1] The two problems could be considered as a single decision, but this would add excessive complexity to the DRA models we are going to present later on.

develop; secondly, once the design is chosen, the decision of whether to hire a marketing research consultant, which could help to preview the success of the software and, also, if they should make an expensive release of the software in the market or not. The first decision was one of ranking the software designs in terms of suitability for the company. The second decision involved two binary choices: hiring or not the marketing consultant, and having an expensive or modest software release.

Defining and Structuring an Organisation's Fundamental Objectives

A crucial change that a Decision and Risk Analysis approach can bring to the process of strategy evaluation is to orientate the organisation towards a value-focused way of thinking: that the process of strategic choice should be guided by organisational *values* (Keeney, 1992). As discussed in Chapter 2, values or aspirations are those that drive the organisation's vision and strategic direction. However, organisational values are usually too broad for guiding strategy evaluation. For example, if a multi-national car company has 'provide superior service for its costumers', 'corporate image' and 'reduce costs' as its organisational values, should it close an outdated plant, laying off employees and disrupting its image in a particular country or should it update the plant's production lines and maintain production in that location? This makes it necessary to find or develop a set of *fundamental objectives* that reflect the organisational values and, at the same time, constrain the set of strategic options to be appraised (see also Keeney, 1992; and Barcus & Montibeller, 2006).

Helping organisations to define a set of fundamental objectives is one of the most important tasks of any strategy evaluation activity (whether DRA-supported or not). A fundamental objective highlights the importance of considering an issue in a strategic decision (e.g. *quality of our products*) and also indicates a direction of preference (e.g. *increase the quality of our products*). In practice, the identification and/or development of fundamental objectives is typically informed by the 'setting strategic direction and goals' element of the strategic development process, as discussed in Chapter 1.

The DRA tool to structure and characterise organisational objectives is called a *value tree*, which represents them as a hierarchy of objectives. One basic approach to develop a value tree is to start from the attributes that distinguish the strategic options and climb up, asking why these attributes matter, looking for fundamental objectives (a bottom-up approach). A second approach is to start eliciting ultimate objectives and climb down, asking how these objectives can be achieved, looking for attributes (a top-down approach). Other approaches for structuring value trees can be found in Buede (1986), Keeney (1992) and Belton and Stewart (2002).

Our first meeting with the stakeholders group showed that there was some tension between departments for the choice of a suitable software design; this had dragged on the decision for several months and that is why they asked for our help.

Marketing had been championing for the Software Design 1, as it was the most innovative one and had the potential of bringing a 20% market share of the global search engine for the company. This was strongly opposed by the Software Development team, which was concerned by the complexity involved in programming the code. The latter was supportive of Design 2, quite simple to program, and cheap, which of course pleased Finance as well. But there were concerns about the low potential market share of this design.

Marketing was also worried about the time required for the development of the software, given the fast speed in technological changes in this business and the opportunity of releasing something innovative as soon as possible.

Clearly they were using an 'alternative-focused thinking' approach, not considering in depth the organisational values involved in this decision, and thus they were entrenched in two opposing designs ('the design from Marketing versus the design from Engineering and Finance'). We asked them to forget for a while about the designs themselves and to think about which objectives were essential for this choice. After some discussion, the group agreed that four objectives were fundamental: potential market share, time for development, cost of development and programming complexity. These were represented as a value tree, as shown in Figure 10.3.

Contrary to mere performance indices, fundamental objectives must follow a set of properties that should be checked when building a value tree (Belton & Stewart, 2002; Keeney & Raiffa, 1993):

- *Value relevance.* They should consider all the essential organisational objectives involved in the decision.
- *Understandability.* They should have a clear meaning for all the members of the group involved in making the decision.
- *Operationality.* It should be possible to measure the performance of strategic options against each of the fundamental objectives.[2]
- *Non-redundancy.* They should not measure the same concern twice.
- *Preferential independence.* It should be possible to measure the performance of strategic options on one objective disregarding their performance on all other objectives.

Of the above properties the last three merit further elaboration. Problems with operationality may occur if the information, despite being fundamental, is completely

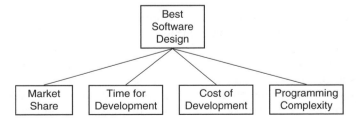

Figure 10.3. A Value Tree for the Choice of a Software Design

---

[2] This does not exclude qualitative aspects as we will discuss later on.

unavailable. For example, in one DRA application that one of us was involved in regarding the decision of buying accounts receivable by a factoring company (Ensslin, Montibeller & Lima, 2000; Montibeller, Belton & Lima, 2007), the police record of the company's owner was an important aspect to be considered according to the factoring analyst, but the information itself was unavailable – so we had to remove it from the value tree.

It is also important to make sure that the same aspect is not taken into account twice in the evaluation (the non-redundancy property), otherwise it would receive a disproportionate weight. Notice, however, that similar objectives may actually measure different concerns. For example, in the software design value tree in Figure 10.3, one could have thought that time for development and programming complexity are measuring the same issue, but while the former is concerned with the time that the software will be available for release, the latter is concerned about its technical complexity.

Preferential independence is critical for the kind of evaluation model we are going to discuss here.[3] Cases of dependence happen when the evaluation of performances on a given objective depends on the strategic option's performance on other objective(s). For example, imagine a company that is selecting a new building for its headquarters office, and is considering two aspects: the 'total floor area' (ranging from $500\,m^2$ to $1000\,m^2$) and the 'number of offices' (ranging from 30 to 80 offices). If analysed independently, a larger total area is preferred to a smaller one and also a larger number of offices is better than a smaller number. However, if the total area is only $500\,m^2$ then 30 offices are preferred to 80 offices, as otherwise they would be too small. Therefore, the preference about the number of offices depends on the total area and they cannot be considered in isolation. A practical way of dealing with preferential dependence is to redefine the objectives, usually aggregating the two dependent objectives into a single one. For instance, in the headquarters office example, the two aspects could be assessed as the average office area (m^2/office).

Notice also that statistical independence is not required between objectives, and many times two objectives are preferentially independent but statistically dependent. So while there is usually a positive correlation between cost and quality of a product (i.e. the higher the quality the higher the cost too), they may be preferentially independent: given two products with high quality, a decision-maker prefers the cheaper product than the expensive product; this preference would hold if the two products had both low quality – see Roy (1996) for a detailed discussion.

Another important concern to bear in mind when structuring a value tree concerns what actually is represented in the tree. Contrary to common sense, values and objectives are not well specified and completely defined a priori in people's minds, ready to be extracted and represented (Fischhoff, Slovic & Lichtenstein, 1988; Slovic, 1995). Nor are fundamental objectives predefined in the organisation, in reports or some other sort of formal communication. This is usually the case even if there is a clear strategic direction, or vision, for the organisation (Chapter 2). Indeed, one of the main benefits of the DRA approach is precisely helping organisational stakeholders

---

[3] There are evaluation models that can handle dependent objectives, but some of their parameters are difficult to be elicited and they are not frequently used in practice, see Keeney and Raiffa (1993) and Clemen and Reilly (2001) for details.

to reflect, understand and develop their values and fundamental objectives, which then may guide the strategy evaluation process. So we should aim to *construct* preference models that represent organisational values and objectives, which then can be employed to evaluate the performance of strategic options.

For each fundamental objective placed at the bottom level of the value tree, an associate *attribute* should be specified. This attribute is a performance index employed to measure the impact of adopting each strategic option on the organisational objective being pursued. Care should be taken in finding a suitable way of measuring the achievement of an objective, as different measurement indices may reflect different facets of the concern expressed by the objective. For example, 'unemployment rate' can be measured in different, equally valid, ways: trade unions usually support an index that generates a higher value than the one utilised by the government.

There are three types of attributes (see also Keeney, 1992; Keeney & Gregory, 2005), depending on the way they measure an objective:

- *Quantitative direct attributes* measure directly the concern expressed by the objective, are of general use and have a common interpretation. Examples may be a company's profits in euros or its market share in percentage points.
- *Quantitative indirect attributes* measure indirectly the concern expressed by the objective and are, many times, defined specifically for a particular decision. Examples may be travelling time as a proxy for the distance between home and office; or the number of stars as a proxy for the quality of a hotel. More complex indices may be used, for example the Richter scale for assessing magnitude of earthquakes, or the FTSE 100 index for measuring the value of shares traded on the London Stock Exchange.
- *Qualitative attributes* measure indirectly, using a set of qualitative levels, the concern expressed by the objective. Again they may be defined specifically for a particular decision. An example of this sort of attribute is the Beaufort wind force scale, which describes qualitatively several levels of wind strength.

We now helped the stakeholders group to define suitable attributes and define their ranges. In some cases this was quite easy: market share was going to be measured in percentage points of the whole internet search engine market and ranging from 5% to 30%; cost of development, on the other hand, was going to be measured in British pounds. Defining the range for cost of development required some research, but Finance set it between £10 million and £50 million. Time for development required some discussion about whether software specifications and planning would be included or not. At the end, all members of the stakeholders group agreed that both tasks should be included and set the limits for the attribute between 6 and 24 months.

Finding a suitable attribute for the programming complexity objective proved to be much trickier, as there was not a direct attribute easily available. One initial idea was whether time for programming could be a suitable proxy, but the software engineers went against this idea, claiming that there were soft issues that would not be covered by this index. We then decided to create a qualitative attribute with four levels, defined by the software engineers as follows: *very complex* (dedicated team of high skilled programmers, no possible use of development packages); *complex* (low use of development packages, most has to be done by skilled programmers); *standard* (basic programming and some use of standard development package, but also some parts require specialised programming); *simple* (only standard development packages are required).

Independently of its type, each attribute should follow five properties (Keeney & Gregory, 2005) to be employed in a preference model:

- *Unambiguous*. It should present a clear relationship between the impact of adopting a potential strategic option and the description of such impact.
- *Comprehensive*. It should cover the full range of possible consequences, if any potential strategic option to be considered were implemented.
- *Direct*. The attribute levels should describe as directly as possible the consequences of implementing a potential strategic option.
- *Operational*. The information required by the attribute can be obtained in practice and it is possible to make value trade-offs between objectives. That is, it is possible to analyse the compensation between weak performances on a given objective against strong performances on another objective.[4]
- *Understandable*. Consequences and value trade-offs using the attribute can be clearly understood by the stakeholder group and communicated to other stakeholders.

Usually more direct attributes are less ambiguous than indirect ones. Notice that a qualitative objective (like the quality of a hotel) can be measured either by a quantitative indirect attribute (number of stars) or by a qualitative attribute (e.g. levels describing what is high, medium or low quality for the decision analyst's client). In practice we prefer to use the former type, if we can find one suitable, as it reduces ambiguity.

A key point about comprehensiveness is that the upper and lower limits of the attribute are well specified (maximum feasible and minimum acceptable, respectively), otherwise it would distort value trade-offs. Thus in our software design case, the attribute market share should not have an upper limit superior to 30% if that is not really feasible. In the same way, its lower limit should not be inferior to 5% if this is unacceptable for the company, i.e. any design with a market share less than 5% should be ruled out.

The last property, the understandability of attributes, is critical when using DRA for supporting strategy evaluation, as it will facilitate the communication between those conducting the evaluation and reduce misunderstandings.

Once a value tree is defined and attributes specified, we can turn our focus to identification and creation of strategies, as described next.

---

[4] We will discuss value trade-offs in detail further below.

Identifying and Creating Potential Strategic Options

Among all phases of any strategy evaluation, the identification and creation of potential strategic options is certainly one of the most important. No matter how careful and sophisticated the evaluation model is, if the strategic options under consideration are weak, it will lead to a poor choice (Brown, 2005).

Producing good strategic options is not a straightforward task. Indeed, research has shown that creativity in the generation of strategies can be hindered when managers are victims of what is known as 'cognitive inertia' due to their inability to adapt their mental models in times of environmental turbulence (Barr, Stimpert & Huff, 1992; Hodgkinson, 1997; Hodgkinson & Johnson, 1994; Hodgkinson & Wright, 2002). Methods and models that enable managers to construct flexible mental models encompassing multiple frames of the future states of the environment, such as those advocated in this book – visioning (Chapter 2), problem structuring methods (Chapter 4) and scenario planning (Chapter 9) – could help managers to overcome cognitive inertia and promote creativity within a management team for the generation of good strategies and strategic options.

In this section we provide four specific ways of encouraging creativity in the identification and creation of strategic options (for more details see Keeney, 1992). First, when the organisational values and fundamental objectives for a strategic decision are explicitly listed, they can help to guide the identification of options, as they should be means to achieve the organisation's objectives. This can be done by asking the management team to imagine options that could perform really well on a single objective. For example, in locating a new power plant, an option that achieves the minimum environmental damage would be sought. This process would be repeated for each of the fundamental objectives present in the value tree. Once the list of objectives is exhausted, the same procedure can be done for two objectives at once. In the power plant location problem, options that achieve minimum environmental damage *and*, for example, minimise the distance to the main industrial customers, would be looked for.

Another way of igniting creativity is asking for ends that justify an objective. For instance, the concern about minimising the distance to main industrial customers may indicate that fulfilling their needs is an end for the company. This realisation could then help to generate other solutions for the power plant location problem such as, for example, placing small-scale generator units near the plants of its customers. Or else, a management team can be stimulated to identify means to an objective. The team could think about ways of minimising the environmental damage of the company's power plant, and again one solution would be putting small-scale generators near industrial loads.

A third way of helping to create alternatives is asking the management team to devise alternatives that would be perceived as 'good' for a given stakeholder. For example, in asking 'what would be a good power plant location for our industrial users?' the team may discover that it is one which provides reliable energy. This may lead them to think about places sheltered from the incidence of strong winds.

A fourth way is by combining options to create a new option, trying to maintain the best features of each option. For instance, in the power plant location problem, a potential option would be one that combines a reliable supply with a small environmental impact.

Although there is a natural tendency by management teams to discard options that may appear to produce some negative outcomes, it is important that any attempt at option evaluation is contained at this stage. The evaluation of strategic options should be left for the next stage of the DRA process and not intermingled with the creation of options. Once a set of such options was defined, it is then possible to create a *table of consequences*, which lists the potential impact of each strategic option on every fundamental objective, as illustrated in the software development case study below.

We started asking the group to think about software designs that could achieve the maximum performance on a given individual objective. Design 1, already suggested by Marketing, was highlighted as the one performing at the top in terms of potential market share. Design 2, supported by Finance and Engineering, was the top scorer both in terms of lower costs for development and programming complexity.

However, when considering individually the time for development, a new idea was suggested: a member of the Engineering team said that there was a faster way for developing the software, however involving more complex programming tasks and with higher costs than Design 2. We emphasised that we wanted them to avoid considering these drawbacks at this stage. The group agreed to include it as Design 3.

We used the same procedure asking for options that would impact strongly on pairs of objectives, but the group could not devise any other option. We avoided asking them about options particularly suitable for each stakeholder, as there were already tensions among them, which could be exacerbated using this procedure.

Finally we invited them to consider the combination of two designs. This has generated a positive response, and they realised it would be possible to derive a new design (Design 4) from the combination of Designs 1 and 3. At this point the group seemed to have exhausted its creativity and we decided to stop our search.

We then listed the four fundamental objectives and its attributes (between brackets) as shown in Table 10.1, and asked them to estimate the impact of adopting each software design. A quite important insight was how expensive and lengthy was the development for Design 1, and how little market share could Design 2 achieve, which caused a little bit of a shock for their respective supporters. Another insight was that there was not a dominating option, that is, one that would outperform all the others on every attribute.

Sometimes presenting the profile of strategic options (as illustrated in Table 10.2) is enough, and the management team is satisfied to make a decision or provide a recommendation based on the analysis so far. More commonly, however, there is usually a need for further evaluation. Indeed, extensive behavioural research has shown that people struggle to make consistent decisions in the presence of multiple and conflicting objectives (Goodwin & Wright, 2004). In these situations, management teams need to assess the impact of each outcome and balance the pros and cons of each strategic option. Such tasks can be aided with the use of DRA tools as presented in the next section.

Table 10.1. The Four Software Designs

Software design	Market share (% of global market share)	Time for development (months until release of beta version)	Cost of development (£)	Programming complexity
1	20	21	40 000 000	very complex
2	10	9	15 000 000	simple
3	17.5	6	30 000 000	standard
4	15	12	20 000 000	complex

Modelling Preferences and Value Trade-offs

This section presents two main DRA tools for modelling preferences in strategy evaluation: the elicitation of value functions associated with fundamental objectives and the assessment of weights for these same objectives. We start this section by describing what value functions are and how they should be elicited. Next we discuss the meaning of weights and present appropriate ways of assessing them. Finally, we present how these tools can be employed for evaluating strategic options.

Value Functions

Is one million pounds always worth the same to all? Usually not. For a cash-stripped company considering investing this amount in a new business, it could mean a lot; while for a rich multinational in the same situation, it would probably mean very little. So any attempt at evaluating strategic options must consider the relative value of performances, according to the preferences of the management team, if we are to provide meaningful recommendations.

Thus if an organisation is considering different strategic options, it is crucial that the management team express their perceived values on the impacts that the options under consideration can have, measuring the relative worthiness of each impact. The way of modelling such preferences is via a *value function*. There are two traditional methods of eliciting value functions: bisection and direct rating (Goodwin & Wright, 2004). In the *bisection method*, the management team is asked to identify mid-points of value given two anchoring levels within the range of the attribute. Bisection can be applied only for quantitative attributes. In the case of *direct rating*, the team are required to score directly some levels of the attribute. Direct rating can be employed both for quantitative and qualitative attributes. We describe both procedures in the case study below and in the form of a dialogue between us (the facilitators) and the stakeholders group. Also, we indicate our thoughts during the elicitation process within square brackets.

Once we had sensitised the group to the importance of creating value functions we started eliciting a value function for each fundamental objective. We describe the protocol for eliciting a value function for the cost of development using the *bisection* method:

Facilitators: [We first fix the upper and lower bounds of this attribute.] As you remember, the group decided that costs could run from 10 million pounds, the minimum feasible for such project, to 50 million pounds, the maximum amount the company could bear. Are those figures all right?

Group: Yes, we think so, but shouldn't we consider an ideal project with no cost at all?

Facilitators: Not really, as it isn't feasible, is it? Considering such a project would distort the analysis.

Group: Well, the lowest feasible figure is 10 million pounds, really.

Facilitators: All right, now could you please assign a 0 value [worst] to the £50 million cost and a 100 value [best] to the £10 million cost?

Group: OK.

Facilitators: [We now plot Figure 10.4a.]

Facilitators: Now what cost would be the mid-level in terms of value?

Group: Hmmm ...

Facilitators: [We change the question to a less abstract one.] Let us change the question – what would be more painful for you, increasing the cost from 10 to 25 million or from 25 to 50 million pounds?

Group: For sure from 10 to 25, as we will be moving from using our own capital towards getting a bank loan.

Facilitators: [We then decrease the first range, to try to find the equivalents point.] And what about increasing from 10 to 20 and from 20 to 50 million pounds?

Group: Well they are pretty much the same.

Facilitators: [We then plot Figure 10.4b.]

Using the same procedure for this mid-point, we found the mid-point between 20 and 50 million pounds (£25 million – Figure 10.4c) and the one between 10 and 20 million pounds (£15 million – Figure 10.4d).

Finally, a linear interpolation generated a continuous function,[5] as shown in Figure 10.4e. Notice that its shape is not linear, and if we had assumed linear preferences (i.e. that each extra pound spent would cause the same amount of pain) we would be misguiding the group.

The same procedure was employed for eliciting value functions for the quantitative attributes, as shown in Figure 10.5a–c.

The *direct rating* method was employed for assessing the value function for programming complexity, as described below:

Facilitators: [We first fix the upper and lower bounds of this attribute.] Assume that the simple programming complexity is valued at 100 (best) and the very complex one has a 0 value (worst).

Group: OK.

Facilitators: Now, what is the value of a standard programming complexity, given these two levels?

Group: We guess it is around 60 . . .

---

[5] If more precision is required, an exponential interpolation can be employed – see Clemen and Reilly (2001). In our experience a linear interpolation is easier to understand and to handle when dealing with management teams.

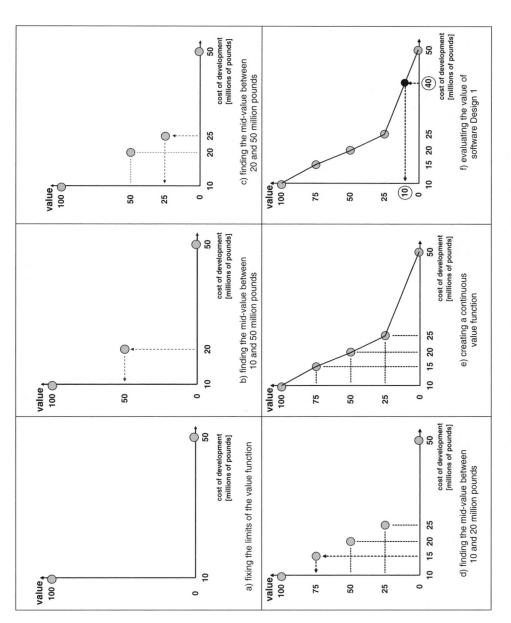

Figure 10.4 Eliciting a Value Function for Cost of Development

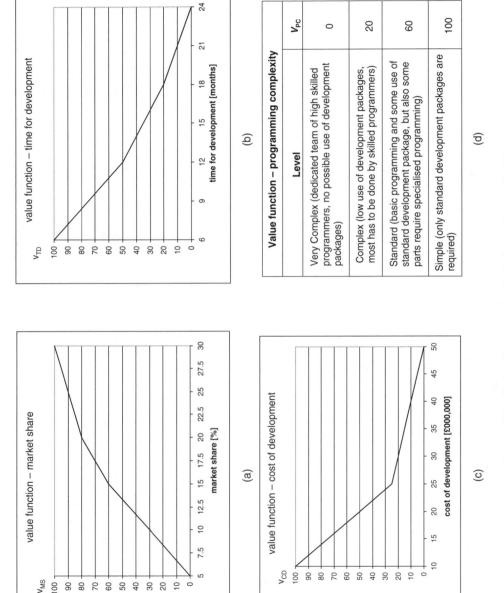

Figure 10.5 Value Functions for the Software Design Problem

Facilitators: In the same way, what is the value of a complex programming?
Group: Well, if a standard is 60 and a very complex is 0, then it should be around 20.

Figure 10.5d displays a table with these levels and scores.

In our practical experience, once managers understand the rationale for building value functions, they feel comfortable in stating their preferences in this way. However, there are some technical concerns that must be addressed throughout the process of their elicitation. The most important one is to make sure that their judgements are anchored on the worst and best levels of the attribute. Secondly, it is always a good idea to check if the judgements are consistent by comparing the difference of values between pairs of options. Thus, for example, we should ask the group if the difference in value between a simple and a standard programming complexity ($100 - 60 = 40$, see Figure 10.5d) is really about twice the difference in value between a complex and a very complex programming (from the same figure, $20 - 0 = 20$).

If there are disagreements between members of a management team about the values of some levels, these should be recorded and revisited when assessing the robustness of each strategic option, as we are going to discuss further in this chapter.

Preferences are constructed rather than discovered, so there is no such thing as value functions inside a manager's head ready to be 'extracted' (Slovic, 1995). They should be seen as facilitative tools, which may help a management team in better understanding their preferences and in supporting their decisions. Therefore the process should be guided towards learning and reflection, instead of a technocratic elicitation of preferences.

Once a value function is defined for each fundamental objective, we can use them to asses the impact of each potential strategy on the values of the organisation. This is illustrated below.

We employed the value functions for assessing the value of each software design on each fundamental objective. For example, Design 1 has a cost of programming estimated as 40 million pounds (Table 10.1). This represents 10 units of value, according to the respective value function (Figure 10.4f). Using the same rationale, we can assess the value of each software design presented in Table 10.1 using the value functions displayed in Figure 10.5.

Plotting the performances of each software design as a profile, as shown in Figure 10.6, permits a better visualisation of the pros and cons of each option and their impact on the organisation's values. When we presented this graph to the group, it was much easier to visualise that there was no dominating alternative, and that the initially favoured options, Designs 1 and 2, had some serious drawbacks, the former performing well only on market share and the latter performing relatively well on all objectives except market share.

Usually no option is found to be dominating the others when analysed via a *performance profile* display like the one presented in Figure 10.6. This is particularly common in strategic decisions, where each choice implies some tough choices and involves some potential heavy gains but also some possible drawbacks. In these

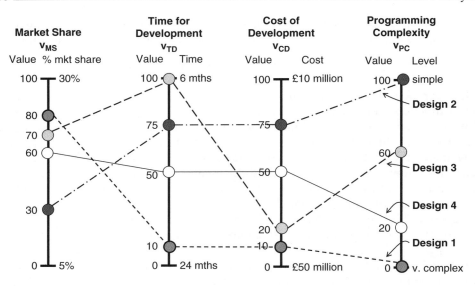

Figure 10.6. The Performance Profiles of Each Software Design

cases, members of the management team must consider the trade-offs between these pros and cons, as discussed next.

Determining Value Trade-offs

Probably nothing is more important, and more difficult, in strategic decision-making than prioritising objectives. At the end of the day, strategy-making is about priorities (Eden & Ackermann, 1998) and managers do have to decide if they are willing to accept some disadvantages of the chosen option in order to get its benefits. If a country wants more housing for its population, then it will have to carry the burden of causing some environmental impact (albeit minimised). Or it could decide to stop the construction of new houses, leaving people struggling for housing, in order to preserve its fauna and flora intact.

Unfortunately, there are many misconceptions about how objectives should be prioritised and many mistakes are made in this process (see, for details, Keeney, 2002). Perhaps the most dangerous one is to believe that weights should reflect 'importance', and thus 'important' objectives should have larger weights. An example can help in demystifying such misunderstandings. Imagine that a council is considering increasing the pedestrians' safety along a busy road and is taking into account safety and cost as fundamental objectives in this decision. A senior council member then expresses the view that pedestrians' safety is the most important objective for the council, and implies that any increase in safety is preferred to minimising cost. Would it mean that they would spend £1000 painting a zebra crossing that could save one life per year? The answer is probably yes, and therefore safety is indeed preferred to cost. Would it mean that they would build a subway under the road, requiring a complex draining system and costing £100 000, which could save two lives per year? Maybe not, as the money could be spent to save more lives elsewhere.

What is wrong with this line of reasoning is that it forgets to consider the *range* of each attribute, from its minimum to its maximum level. Trade offs have necessarily to be elicited considering those ranges. In the council example, the range of number of lives saved (from one to two lives/year) versus the range of costs for each option available for the council (from £1000 to £100 000) should be considered. Therefore any proper procedure for eliciting weights has to be anchored on the ranges of attributes.

One of the simplest methods that is based on this principle is the *swing-weights procedure*, which asks managers to value each improvement from the lowest to the highest level of each attribute (Goodwin & Wright, 2004). The software development case study below illustrates the procedure.

We now helped the group to determine their value trade-offs for the evaluation of software design options. We started presenting the ranges of the four attributes, as displayed in Figure 10.7, and proposed a hypothetical situation.

Facilitators: Imagine that you have a software design which has the worst performance on all fundamental objectives. That is, one which achieves only 5% of market share, takes 24 months to program, costs £50 million and requires a very complex level of programming. Now if you could improve the design in only one attribute, from the worst to the best level, which objective would you choose?

Group: Mmmm . . . We think it would be market share.

Facilitators: All right. So consider that this first improvement, from 5% to 30% of market share, is worth 100. [We draw an arrow on the left side of this attribute and the value of this swing (100) in Figure 10.7.]

Group: OK.

Facilitators: Now please forget about this objective 'market share'. If you had a software design that was at the lowest level on the remaining attributes (i.e. costing £50 million, taking 24 months to be developed and requiring a very complex level of programming), which one would you improve first to the best level?

Group: It could be both cost of development or time of development, but we guess we would prefer first to reduce the cost of development from 50 to 10 million pounds.

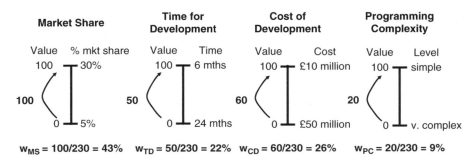

Figure 10.7. Eliciting Swing-weights for the Software Design Choice

Facilitators: All right. So if the first improvement, on market share, was worth 100, how much would value this second improvement?

Group: Around 60, we believe. [We then draw the arrow displayed in Figure 10.7, on cost of development and write the value of the swing (60) near it.]

Following the same procedure, we elicited a swing of 50 for time for development and 20 for programming complexity. These swings are the actual weights, but as we want to normalise them so they could sum up 100%, we divided each one by the total sum 230 (*w*'s in Figure 10.7).

Notice also that the swings (and weights) are dependent on the ranges of each attribute. For example, if the highest cost of development were increased from 50 to 100 million pounds, is quite likely that this would be the first attribute to be swung, getting a swing weight of 100.

The weights have a quite specific role in preference models: they are scaling constants that convert partial values into an overall value (Belton & Stewart, 2002; Roy, 1996). Therefore, in our case study, a value of 10 for Design 1 on the cost of development scale (Figure 10.4f) is worth 2.6 units of overall value, given that 26% is the weight of this objective. It is important that this meaning is clear to the management team when eliciting these parameters. Another common mistake that teams make is to believe that there are 'right' weights for fundamental objectives. We would like to emphasise that there is no such thing – weights should reflect the preferences of the management team, which are anchored on the ranges of each attribute.

Once value functions and weights are elicited, we can calculate the overall value of each strategic option as explained in the next section.

Evaluating Strategic Options

A simple model for calculating the overall value of potential strategic options is a weighted-sum *multi-attribute value function* (Belton & Stewart, 2002; Dyer & Sarin, 1979; Roy, 1996), a well-researched and widely employed evaluation tool . In this type of model, the partial value of a strategic option on every objective is multiplied by the respective weight of the objective; these weighted partial values are then summed up, as illustrated in the case study.

With the partial values v(.) of each software design (Figure 10.6) and the weight of each fundamental objective (Figure 10.7) it was possible to calculate the overall value *V*(.) for each design *a*:

$$V(a) = w_{MS}v_{MS}(a) + w_{TD}v_{TD}(a) + w_{CD}v_{TD}(a) + w_{PC}v_{PC}(a)$$

$$V(a_1) = 0.43 \times 80 + 0.22 \times 10 + 0.26 \times 10 + 0.09 \times 0 = 39.2 \approx 39$$

$$V(a_2) = 0.43 \times 30 + 0.22 \times 75 + 0.26 \times 75 + 0.09 \times 100 = 57.9 \approx 58$$

$$V(a_3) = 0.43 \times 70 + 0.22 \times 100 + 0.26 \times 20 + 0.09 \times 60 = 62.7 \approx 63$$

$$V(a_4) = 0.43 \times 60 + 0.22 \times 50 + 0.26 \times 50 + 0.09 \times 20 = 51.6 \approx 52$$

We presented these results to the group. The overall value of Design 3 was the highest one, and this reflected a growing view, within the group, that indeed it seemed to be a good choice – not only had it a good potential for market share, but it was also relatively fast to be developed. The main drawback was its cost, but clearly the company was more concerned, given the ranges of each attribute, about reaching quickly and broadly its market than in squeezing its investment budget (as shown by their swing weights, Figure 10.7).

So far we have considered multiple and conflicting objectives in relation to the evaluation of strategic options, and described how DRA modelling and tools can help in supporting such a process. We have so far, deliberately, avoided considering another important aspect of strategic decisions: uncertainties. We now focus on how to deal with them, in the next section.

Modelling Uncertainties and Assessing Robustness of Strategic Options

Chapter 9 presented scenario planning as a way to deal with environmental uncertainties during strategy-making. Typically, these uncertainties become apparent when the actual performance of potential strategies, if they were implemented, is difficult to predict. As already discussed at the beginning of this chapter, uncertainty can be aleatoric (i.e. variability) or epistemic (i.e. lack of knowledge). The latter category is particularly salient in strategy evaluation and may include, for example, uncertainties about the trade-offs managers have to make before choosing a particular strategic option, and uncertainties regarding the nature of certain events that may impact on the success of the implemented strategy. In this section, we discuss how DRA modelling and tools can be employed to elicit and understand some of these uncertainties, as well as to test the robustness of potential strategic options under these uncertainties.

Modelling Uncertainties about Value Trade-offs

The first type of uncertainty that managers have to cope with, during strategy evaluation, is about the trade-offs between fundamental objectives. We have shown how it is possible to represent those value trade-offs using weights for a multi-attribute value function. However, this is an attempt to quantify subjective values, and one could not expect precise measurements. So it is quite important to analyse the influence of changing those parameters on the final result (overall value of potential strategic options), as the case study illustrates next.

We plotted the overall value of each software design as a function of the variation of weight, for each fundamental objective, and presented these results to the group. For instance, for the cost of development objective the variation of its weight w_{CD} (from 0% to 100%) resulted in the overall value, for each software design, as displayed in Figure 10.8.

The graph shown in Figure 10.8 was plotted as follows. For Design 1, for example, two points are easily identifiable:

- When the weight for cost of development is 100%, the overall value is equal to the option's performance on the attribute, so given that its score is 10 on cost of development (see Figure 10.6), its overall value is also 10 (point ① in Figure 10.8).
- When the weight for cost of development is 26% (its weight in the evaluation model, see Figure 10.7), its overall value $V(a_1)$ is 39, as calculated before (point ② in Figure 10.8).
- As we know that the overall value of each design is a linear function (as the multi-attribute value function $V(a_1)$ is linear), we can link the points ① and ② until it reaches the vertical axis, and thus find the overall value of Design 1 for any value of w_{CD}.
- The same procedure can be employed for plotting each other design.

Figure 10.8 shows that at the present level ($w_{CD} = 26\%$), Design 3 is the preferred one, with an overall value of 63 (point ③ in Figure 10.8).

A critical requirement for any potential strategy is robustness: how strong it is in coping with different scenarios and changes in the organisational environment and also in the conditions it should operate. The analysis we just presented above can help in assessing the robustness of strategies due to uncertainties about value trade-offs. For example, looking at Figure 10.8, we can see that Design 3 is the best one if the weight for cost of development ranges from 0% to 32.2%. At this latter level, both Design 3 and Design 2 are equally valuable (point ④ in Figure 10.8), and if this weight is increased even more, then Design 2 is the more attractive one. Therefore we

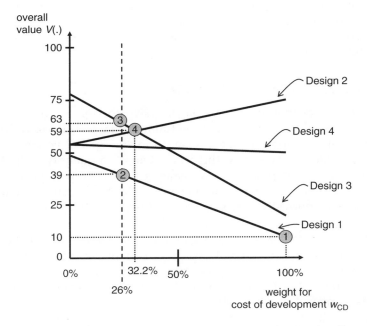

Figure 10.8. Analysing Uncertainties About Value Trade-offs

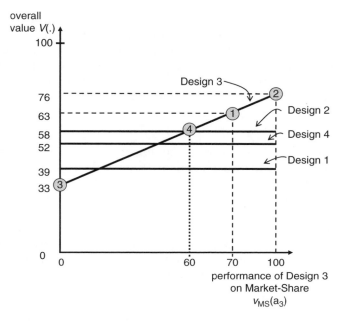

Figure 10.9. Analysing Uncertainties About Performances

see that the model is robust to low levels of uncertainty about value trade-offs (which could be increased by at least 20% of its original value without changing the best solution). The same kind of analysis can be made for every fundamental objective.

Modelling Uncertainties about Performance of Strategic Options

Any exercise of strategy evaluation requires future thinking. If a management team are considering different strategic options, then they need to imagine how these options would perform if they were implemented in practice (as illustrated in Table 10.1 for the software design case study). When there are doubts about potential performances, it is useful to carry out a formal analysis of the impact of changes in the partial performances of potential strategies. Our case study illustrates below how this can be done in practice.

The group was unsure about the performance of Design 3 in terms of market share, the most valuable objective in the decision model. We then decided to analyse what would happen if this performance changed, drawing the graph displayed in Figure 10.9. The graph shows the overall value of each software design as a function of their partial value on market share.

Notice that, in the same figure, Designs 1, 2 and 4 were kept constant [taking their values from the original evaluation, while we ranged Design 3 from its original value (point ① in Figure 10.9), then to its highest level (100, point ②) and finally to its lowest level (0 units of value, points ③) and linked the points].

The kind of analysis described above can help in assessing the robustness of a particular strategic option. For example, in Figure 10.9 we can see that Design 3 is the best one if its potential market share is above 60 units of value (points ④ in the same figure), therefore if it provides more than 15% of global market share (from Figure 10.5a). Thus the strategy can be considered robust if the chances of getting a lower level of market share are low (and not robust otherwise).

Modelling Uncertain Events

We saw that in strategic decisions we often do not know exactly the performance of our strategic options, due to the lack of knowledge or data. But there is another type of uncertainty that exerts an extremely important influence on strategic decisions. These are *uncertain events*, which managers do not have control over (for example, the performance of the stock market, a reaction of a competitor, an important change in legislation) but that will have an impact on the outcomes of the decision. DRA offers powerful tools for modelling this type of uncertainty when evaluating strategic decisions. These tools, known as influence diagrams and decision trees (see details in Clemen & Reilly, 2001), will be illustrated below with our case study.

The group considered the Design 3 robust enough and decided to go ahead and develop it. The interactive process of modelling and analysis helped to build up confidence that this design was the most suitable for the company, helping them in achieving its objectives. We now turned our focus to the second stage of the decision – the release of the software.

There were two strategic decisions to be made at this stage. The first concern was if the company should invest in an expensive release (which would cost 5 million pounds for advertisement and associated costs) or a more modest one (which would cost only 1 million pounds). Given that development costs are 30 million pounds for Design 3, the level of profit will depend on which type of release they make and also on the success of the software – these estimates are displayed in Table 10.2. The same table also shows the probability of each scenario, as assessed by the decision-makers.

Table 10.2. Consequences of the Software Release

Decision	States of nature (scenarios)	
	Major success	Minor success
Expensive release	Revenue = £50 million Costs = £35 million **Profit = £15 million** **Probability: 60%**	Revenue = £30 million Costs = £35 million **Profit = −£5 million** **Probability: 40%**
Modest release	Revenue = £40 million Costs = £31 million **Profit = £9 million** **Probability: 50%**	Revenue = £30 million Costs = £31 million **Profit = −£1 million** **Probability: 50%**

The above situation can be represented using an *influence diagram*, which is composed of three types of node: *decision nodes* to indicate that a decision has to be made; *chance event nodes* to point to an uncertain event; and *consequences nodes* to represent the consequences of decisions taken under uncertainty. In Figure 10.10, the decision node represents the type of software release; the chance node depicts the success of the software in the market; and the consequence node presents the level of profit achieved with the software release. Arrows in Figure 10.10 indicate an influence link. Thus the level of profit depends both on the option chosen and on the success of the release in the market as depicted in Figure 10.10.

An equivalent representation of this problem can be made using a *decision tree*, as displayed in Figure 10.11a. In this model, each decision is represented by a square, where branches leaving the node represent the expensive or modest release options. Each uncertainty is represented by a chance node, where branches leaving the node represent the minor or major success outcomes and attached to each branch is the probability of occurrence of the event. Thus if SoftCo. decides on an expensive release, and its product is a major success (60% probability), the estimated profit would be £15 million but a minor success (40% probability) would bring a loss of £5 million.

Given the situation described above, what strategic decision should the software company make? One way of solving this problem is using the *expected value approach* (Keeney & Raiffa, 1993) and selecting the strategy that maximises it, as we illustrate below.

In Figure 10.11b we calculated the expected value for each chance node, multiplying each level of profit by its respective probability. Therefore the expected profit for the expensive release is 7 million pounds and for the modest one is 4 million pounds. Thus, following this rule, the company should go for the expensive software release.

Influence diagrams and decision trees can also be employed to represent sequential strategic decisions, where a decision depends on previous decisions and uncertainties, as exemplified in the software development case study below.

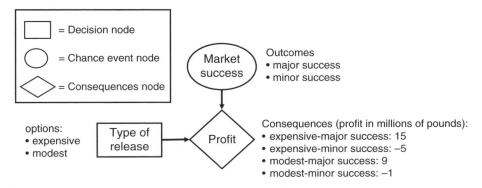

Figure 10.10. An Influence Diagram for the Software Release Decision

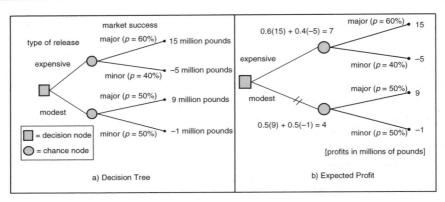

Figure 10.11. A Decision Tree and the Expected Profit for the Software Release Decision

The company was considering hiring a market research, before the software release, to assess the likeliness of success. A positive forecast about the success would increase the chances of a successful release. This problem is depicted in Figure 10.12 as a decision tree. The probability of each outcome is also shown in the same figure. It is possible to calculate the expected profit of each node, using the same procedure as described before. Following this approach, hiring the market research provides a higher expected profit (9.4 million pounds) than not hiring it (7 million pounds).

The difference between acquiring information and not acquiring it (i.e. 2.6 million pounds) is indeed the maximum amount the company should pay for acquiring information, and is known as the *expected value of sample information*. Thus decision trees can be powerful tools for estimating the value of information in strategic decisions. Also, in practice, the calculation of probabilities displayed in the branches where information is acquired is based on previous performance of the market research company in 'getting right' its forecasts, calculated using Bayes' theorem (for details see Goodwin & Wright, 2004).

Influence diagrams and decision trees should be seen as complementary in supporting strategic decision-making, as one can be derived from the other. Influence diagrams are particularly useful for structuring decision processes that involve sequential decisions and uncertainties and produce compact models. Decision trees are helpful to understand the intricacies of each strategic choice and for performing a quantitative analysis. In practice, as the probabilities attached to each outcome are usually subjectively assessed (Goodwin & Wright, 2004), appropriate elicitation procedures should be employed, since these parameters are usually prone to biases (Kahneman, Slovic & Taversky, 1982).

Also, as discussed previously, many times it is better to assess a value function that maps the financial measurement onto the organisation's values. In these cases, the only change needed in the analysis just described is to calculate the value of each outcome given its profit in a similar way as discussed for SoftCo's decision about the cost of software design. Given that in practice strategic decisions typically involve multiple objectives, a multi-attribute value function can be used to incorporate all

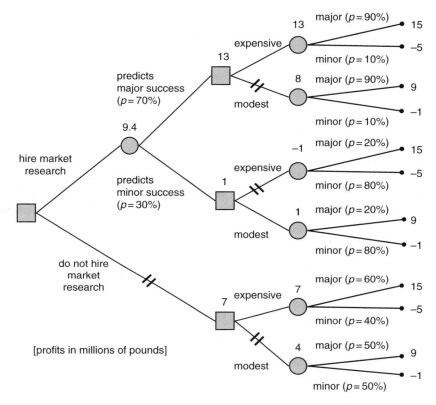

Figure 10.12. A Decision Tree for the Marketing Research Decision

the partial performances of each strategic option on a single overall value measure (as illustrated for the overall values of software designs in our case study). In both cases, either with a single or multi-attribute value function we can then calculate the expected value in the decision tree using exactly the same procedure described previously for expected profit, but using the overall value of the strategic options instead.

Different strategic options involve different levels of risk; some options can offer potentially large rewards but also incur extensive losses, while other options can provide less dramatic outcomes. Thus it is quite important to analyse the risks of strategic options, which is discussed in the next section.

Evaluating Risks of Strategic Options

If you were the manager of the company facing the strategic decision depicted in Figure 10.11a, which option would you choose: the expensive or the modest release? Some people are likely to answer that they would stick with the expensive one, while others would go for the modest option instead. Why do different people select different strategies? The reason is that these options have different levels of risk and individuals and companies exhibit different attitudes towards risk (Goodwin &

Wright, 2004): some are risk-seekers while others are risk-averse. This section present three different tools for assessing the risks of strategic options and represent the risk attitude of organisations.

Analysing Risk Profiles

A tool for assessing the risks of each strategy is the use of *risk profiles*, as presented in our case study below.

> For each strategy we plotted a risk profile, as shown in Figure 10.13, where the horizontal axis represent the levels of outcomes (profits) and the vertical axis the chance of obtaining a given level of profit. Presenting this result to our clients, they could see that the expensive option is more risky as it has a higher spread of outcomes than the modest option. Thus they can consider if they prefer the expensive strategy, which has a higher expected profit (£7 million, Figure 10.11b) but also is riskier, or the modest option, which is both less risky and has a lower expected profit (£4 million, Figure 10.11b). This choice will depend on their trade-off between return and risk.

Performing a Monte-Carlo Simulation

Figure 10.13 shows the results of a risk analysis using decision trees and the expected value approach. Alternatively, risk profiles can also be derived from running what is known as a Monte Carlo simulation (Hertz & Thomas, 1983; Vose, 2000). A Monte Carlo simulation involves using a random sample of all the possible outcomes associated with a decision to assess the risk of that decision. In the case of the software release problem, a Monte Carlo simulation of its profitability would follow three steps, as described below.

1. Generate a simulated value for profit. These values would be generated at random but within the constraints of the probabilities associated with the success of the release. For example, imagine we have a random number generator – a roulette – that produces an integer number within the range 1 to 100. The probability of a major success of an expensive release is 60%; then if the random number produced by the generator is between 1 and 60, this means a *simulated* major success. Otherwise, if the number produced by the generator is between 61 and 100, it is a *simulated* minor success of the expensive release.
2. Store this simulated profit. For instance, if the random number indicated a major success for the expensive release, store the profit of 15 million pounds (Table 10.2).
3. Cycle the previous two steps until the latest simulated profit makes little impact on the mean of the outcomes (expected value) and thus it is not worth continuing any further. This is typically reached with 1000 samples (usually known as 'iterations' or 'trials' in simulation jargon). In simulating the expensive release, we find that the expected value, calculated as the sum of each simulated profit divided by the total number of iterations, remains stable at 7 million pounds, after we reach 1000 iterations.

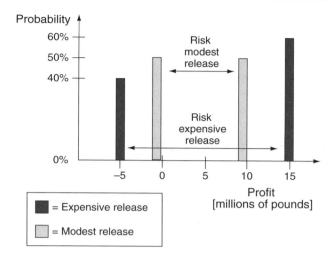

Figure 10.13. Risk Profiles for the Software Release Options

The outcome of a Monte Carlo simulation is usually summarised in the form of a cumulative distribution that shows how many outcomes of the simulation fell above each point between the minimum and maximum recorded, and in the expected value. If the profit values are generated so that they have the same probability of occurring in the simulation as in reality, then the total profit they produce will have the same probability of occurring in the simulation as in reality. This means that if a particular total is exceeded by, let us say, about 10% of the outcomes of the simulation, it has about a 10% chance of being exceeded in reality.

Figure 10.14a shows that there is a 60% chance that the total profit for the expensive release decision will exceed a value of 7 million pounds (and a 40% chance that it will be below this level of profit). Figure 10.14b shows the two risk profiles (as cumulative distributions) associated with the expensive and modest releases. As in our previous analysis, the figure shows that the expensive strategy provides a higher expected profit but also is the riskier one.

Modelling Risk Attitude

Besides this risk–return analysis, it is also possible to conduct a more sophisticated modelling of risk attitude. If the expected value rule is used as illustrated in Figure 10.11b, we are assuming a risk-neutral behaviour for the decision-maker. However, if the management team exhibits a different attitude towards risk, such an attitude can be modelled using a *utility function*, as illustrated by our case study.

> Figure 10.15 displays three utility functions for profit in the software release decision: a *risk-averse* function u_{RA} (which shows that the company is much more interested in reducing losses, measured by a large gain of utility from −£5 million to −£1 million, than seeking huge profits, as represented by the small gain of utility from £11 million to £15 million); a *risk-seeking* function u_{RS} (small gain in utility from −£5 million to −£1 million but a large gain of utility from £11 million to £15 million); or a *risk-neutral* function u_{RN} (a steady gain of utility for each amount of increase in profit).

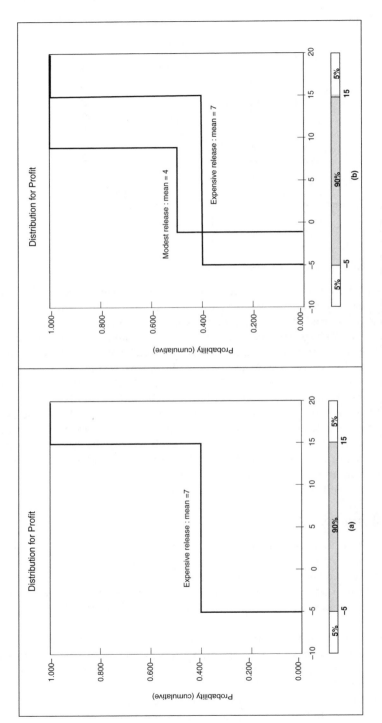

Figure 10.14. Risk Profiles Derived from Monte Carlo Analysis

These functions can be employed to assess the expected utility of each possible strategy – a major release (a_{MJ}) or a minor release (a_{MR}).

The expected utility for the major release $U(a_{MJ})$ does not depend on the shape of the utility function, as it takes the two extremes of the scale (Figure 10.11a), thus:

$$U(a_{MJ}) = 0.6u(£15 \text{ million}) + 0.4u(-£5 \text{ million}) = 0.6 \times 1 + 0.4 \times 0 = 0.6.$$

The expected utility for the minor release $U(a_{MR})$ will depend on the shape of the utility function. So if the decision-makers were risk-averse, the utility of this option is (from points ① and ② in Figure 10.15):

$$U(a_{MR}) = 0.5u_{RA}(£9 \text{ million}) + 0.5u_{RA}(-£1 \text{ million})$$
$$= 0.5 \times 0.85 + 0.5 \times 0.42 = 0.635.$$

Thus, in this case, the minor release has a higher utility than the major one, as the former is less risky .

In an equivalent way, using the risk-seeking utility function (points ③ and ④ in the same figure), the expected utility of a minor release is:

$$U(a_{MR}) = 0.5u_{RS}(£9 \text{ million}) + 0.5u_{RS}(-£1 \text{ million})$$
$$= 0.5 \times 0.36 + 0.5 \times 0.05 = 0.205.$$

Therefore the major release is preferred, as we may expect, as it is riskier.

For a risk-neutral organisation (points ⑤ and ⑥ in Figure 10.15) the expected utility of a minor release is:

$$U(a_{MR}) = 0.5u_{RN}(£9 \text{ million}) + 0.5u_{RN}(-£1 \text{ million})$$
$$= 0.5 \times 0.70 + 0.5 \times 0.20 = 0.45.$$

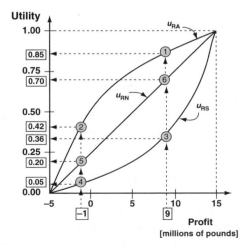

Figure 10.15. Different Utility Functions for the Software Release Decision

As we may expect, this latter result indicates that the major result should be chosen, the same as the expected profit result (Figure 10.11b), since the expected value rule assumes a neutral attitude to risk.

While a value function represents strength of preferences, as we have seen before, a utility function models not only strength of preferences but also risk attitude. The use of utility functions in practice, however, may impose a heavy elicitation burden on management teams, as they require hypothetical questions involving lotteries (Goodwin & Wright, 2004). Many times, again in practice, it is possible to use a value function as a proxy of a utility function (von Winterfield & Edwards, 1986) or some standard shape utility functions that do not require detailed elicitation (Clemen & Reilly, 2001), as illustrated in our case study.

Extending the idea of utility, it is possible to build a multi-attribute utility function (see, for details, Keeney & Raiffa, 1993) with a partial utility function associated with each attribute, but again this requires some stringent properties (in particular preferential independence) and can increase the complexity of the model. As discussed at the beginning of this chapter, strategic decision-making and evaluation are in themselves complex socio-technical tasks that require significant interaction with members of management teams. Thus it is important to ensure that any evaluation model provides an appropriate balance between complexity and rigour (Edwards, von Winterfeldt & Moody, 1988). As Phillips (1984) argues, evaluation models should be only 'requisite'. That is, one that provides sufficient insights to a management team for addressing a decision-making situation.

Once risks are assessed, the management team is in a position to either make a choice or provide a set of recommendations to other stakeholder groups.

Providing Recommendations

The final stage of a DRA evaluation process is choosing the strategic options that provide more value to the organisation, given the level of acceptable risk that it wants to bear. Notice that it is meaningless to speak in terms of an 'optimal solution' in this context, as every strategic option will have strengths and weaknesses and its choice will depend on the organisation's fundamental objectives, as well as the trade-offs made between these objectives.

DRA does not intend to provide an 'objective', technocratic, solution detached from the organisation strategic direction. On the contrary, it attempts to model the subjective aspects involved in any strategic decision, making them explicit and clear, thus enhancing the possibility of negotiation and agreement for the way ahead. Thus the results from the model should be seen as means to achieve the organisational strategies, using a coherent and systematic way of analysing complex decisions.

CONCLUSIONS

This chapter was concerned with the process of strategic options evaluation and has presented Decision and Risk Analysis as a modelling framework to conduct such a process. The aim of the DRA approach is to help a management team arrive at a robust choice. To achieve this, DRA takes into account the organisation's values and objectives, it makes use of value trade-offs to compare potential strategic options, and it analyses uncertainties and the robustness of options in a systematic and transparent way.

It is important to note, however, that due to the unpredictability of the future, even a sound DRA evaluation process can produce recommendations that may lead to poor outcomes when implemented, and vice versa. The only thing we can be sure of is that a DRA process will increase our chances of 'getting it right the first time round' (Russo & Schoemaker, 2002). DRA allows managers to learn from the 'virtual performance' (see Chapter 1) of potential strategic options by developing and using value and risk models. Such models force managers to be explicit about the organisation's preferences and values so that the rationale for making their choices is clear and agreed upon.

We have mentioned that a good DRA process for strategic option evaluation must be facilitated so that issues of group dynamics, cognitive biases and negotiation are adequately managed during the evaluation. Two types of 'facilitations' should be avoided: a strong-handed facilitator, who tries to impose his view and tries to add up content upon the group and the model; and a weak facilitator, that leaves the group to its own destiny. The best facilitation style is the one that manages properly group dynamics but avoids interfering with model content, while making sure that the technical properties of the model are followed (Phillips & Phillips, 1993).

Finally, as we emphasised previously, the DRA process that we described in this chapter is mainly recursive and interactive. As shown in Figure 10.2, following a forward direction (anti-clockwise) of phases moves the group towards deciding, from the divergence of the problem structuring to the convergence of selecting potential strategies. On the other hand, the backward direction (clockwise) is needed when the group is learning; the facilitator should be keen in going back to initial stages and changing the decision models, as the group revises their preferences and values, identifies new potential strategies and understands better their environment.

REFERENCES

Barcus, A. & Montibeller, G.(2006) 'Supporting the allocation of software development in distributed teams with Multi-Criteria Decision Analysis', *Omega – The International Journal of Management Science* (forthcoming-doi: 10.1016/j.omega.2006.04.013).

Barr, P.S., Stimpert, J.L. & Huff, A.S. (1992) 'Cognitive change, strategic action and organizational renewal', *Strategic Management Journal*, **13**, 15–36.

Belton, V. & Stewart, T. (2002) *Multiple Criteria Decision Analysis*. Kluwer: Norwell, MA.

Brown, R. (2005) *Rational Choice and Judgment – Decision Analysis for the Decider*. Wiley: Hoboken, NJ.

Buede, D.M. (1986) 'Structuring value attributes', *Interfaces*, **16**, 52–62.

Clemen, R. & Reilly, T. (2001) *Making Hard Decision with Decision Tools*. Duxbury: Pacific Grove, CA.

Corner, J.L. & Kirkwood, C.W. (1991) 'Decision and risk analysis applications in the operations research literature, 1970–1989', *Operations Research*, **39**, 206–219.

Dyer, J.S. & Sarin, R.K. (1979) 'Measurable multi-attribute value functions', *Operations Research*, **27**, 810–822.

Eden, C. (1992) 'Strategy development as a social process', *The Journal of Management Studies*, **29**, 799–811.

Eden, C. & Ackermann, F. (1998) *Strategy Making: The journey of strategic planning*. Sage: London.

Edwards, W., von Winterfeldt, D. & Moody, D.L. (1988) 'Simplicity in decision and risk analysis'. In: Bell, D.E., Raiffa, H. & Tversky, A. (eds), *Decision Making: Descriptive, normative and prescriptive interactions*. Cambridge University Press: Cambridge.

Ensslin, L., Montibeller, G. & Lima, M.V.A. (2000) 'Constructing and implementing a DSS to help evaluate perceived risk of accounts receivable'. In: Haimes, Y.Y. & Steuer, R.E. (eds), *Research and Practice in Multi-Criteria Decision Making*. Springer: Berlin.

Fischhoff, B., Slovic, P. & Lichtenstein, S. (1988) 'Knowing what you want: measuring labile values'. In: Bell, D.E., Raiffa, H. & Tversky, A. (eds), *Decision Making: Descriptive, normative and prescriptive interactions*. Cambridge University Press: Cambridge.

Goodwin, P. & Wright, G. (2004) *Decision Analysis for Management Judgement*. John Wiley & Sons: Chichester.

Hertz, D.B. & Thomas, H. (1983) *Risk Analysis and its Applications*. John Wiley & Sons: New York.

Hodgkinson, G.P. (1997) 'Cognitive inertia in a turbulent market: the case of UK residential estate agents'. *Journal of Management Studies*, **34**, 921–945.

Hodgkinson, G.P. & Johnson, G. (1994) 'Exploring the mental models of competitive strategists: the case for a processual approach'. *Journal of Management Studies*, **31**, 397–416.

Hodgkinson, G.P. & Wright, G. (2002) 'Confronting strategic inertia in a top management team: learning from failure'. *Organization Studies*, **23**, 949–977.

Hoffman, F.O. & Hammonds, J.S. (1994) 'Propagation of uncertainty in risk assessments: the need to distinguish between uncertainty due to lack of knowledge and uncertainty due to variability'. *Risk Analysis*, **14**, 707–712.

Kahneman, D., Slovic, P. & Tversky, A. (eds) (1982) *Judgement under Uncertainty: Heuristics and biases*. Cambridge University Press: Cambridge.

Keefer, D.L., Kirkwood, C.W. & Corner, J.L. (2004) 'Perspective on decision analysis applications, 1990–2001'. *Decision Analysis*, **1**, 5–24.

Keeney, R.L. (1982) 'Decision and risk analysis: an overview'. *Operations Research*, **30**, 803–838.

Keeney, R.L. (1992) *Value-Focused Thinking: A path to creative decision-making*. Harvard University Press: Cambridge, MA.

Keeney, R.L. (2002) 'Common mistakes in making value trade-offs'. *Operations Research*, **50**, 935–945.

Keeney, R.L. & Gregory, R.S. (2005) 'Selecting attributes to measure the achievement of objectives'. *Operations Research*, **53**, 1–11.

Keeney, R.L. & Raiffa, H. (1993) *Decisions with Multiple Objectives: Preferences and value trade-offs*. Cambridge University Press: Cambridge.

Montibeller, G., Belton, V. & Lima, M.V.A. (2007) 'Supporting factoring transactions in Brazil using Reasoning Maps: a language-based DSS for evaluating accounts receivable', *Decision Support Systems*, **42**, 2085–2092.

Phillips, L. (1984) 'A theory of requisite decision models', *Acta Psychologica*, **56**, 29–48.

Phillips, L. (forthcoming) 'Decision conferencing'. In: Edwards, W. (ed.), *Advances in Decision and Risk Analysis*. Cambridge University Press: New York.

Phillips, L. & Phillips, M. (1993) 'Facilitated work groups: theory and practice', *Journal of Operational Research Society*, **44**, 533–549.

Roy, B. (1996) *Multi-criteria Methodology for Decision Aiding*. Kluwer: Dordrecht.

Russo, J.E. & Schoemaker, P.J.H. (2002) *Winning Decisions: Getting it right first time*. Currency Doubleday: New York.

Schein, E.H. (1998) *Process Consultation Revisited: Building the helping relationship*. Addison-Wesley: New York.

Schwarz, R. (2002) *The Skilled Facilitator: A comprehensive resource for consultants, facilitators, managers, trainers, and coaches*. Jossey-Bass: San Francisco, CA.

Slovic, P. (1995) 'The construction of preference', *American Psychologist*, **50**, 364–371.

von Winterfield, D. & Edwards, W. (1986) *Decision Analysis and Behavioral Research*. Cambridge University Press: Cambridge.

Vose, D. (2000) *Risk Analysis*, 2nd edn. John Wiley & Sons: Chichester.

Chapter 11

Performance Measurement

Efstathios Tapinos and Robert G. Dyson

INTRODUCTION

This chapter presents the concept of performance measurement, highlighting its role within the strategic development process. Performance measurement in the strategic development process model (Chapter 1) has a multitask role. It is connected with 'managing the organisation', since it monitors and controls the implementation of the strategies. It is also connected with 'setting the strategic direction and goals', which shows the importance of the alignment between performance measurement and organisational direction. Simultaneously it is linked with 'rehearsing strategy' and 'implementing strategic change', demonstrating that performance measurement provides feedback to various stages of the strategic decision-making process. In this chapter, we explore performance measurement providing an overview of the concept. Moreover, we present case studies to illustrate the implications of performance measurement within real organisations.

Performance measurement has been at the centre of attention for a long time, even if integrated and pluralistic frameworks and models have been developed only recently, particularly after the highly influential article of Eccles (1991) *'Performance measurement manifesto'*. Performance measurement is viewed as part of the control system in the organisation. However, recent research in the field shows that performance measurement systems can be transformed to performance management systems. This chapter is structured in five sections. The first section summarises the basic concepts regarding performance measurement. The second section discusses the most important performance measurement models and frameworks, and presents in detail the Balanced Scorecard, the most popular framework. The third section discusses performance measurement in the public sector and non-profit organisations. The fourth section presents two recent studies: the first one presents the performance measurement system in the University of Warwick and the second one discusses the development of the performance measurement system in the Coventry Partnership. The last section of this chapter discusses the future directions of the performance measurement-related research.

PERFORMANCE MEASUREMENT – BASIC CONCEPTS

Performance measurement is considered to be one of the topics that attracts a lot of attention, both in the academic and practitioner world. Neely (2002) observed that performance measurement is a diverse subject because researchers from very diverse backgrounds are involved in its study: from accounting and operations management to psychology, sociology and economics. It is believed that the underlying principle behind the popularity of performance measurement is that 'what gets measured gets done'. Greiling (2005) extends this principle, suggesting a great range of further implications. Mapping those implications as a diagram, we created Figure 11.1. This figure shows that the measurement and assessment of organisational performance influences both the decision-making process and the people involved in strategic decision-making and strategy implementation. The impact of performance measurement is multidimensional, covering all levels of the organisational hierarchy. As can be seen in Figure 11.1, performance measurement is related to the improvement initiatives within the organisation, which usually take place at the operational/functional level. It also affects decision-making at the strategic level, providing useful information which might influence the outsourcing strategy of the organisation. At the corporate level, it has vital linkages with the sustainability of the organisation and its ability to learn and develop.

The pluralistic nature of performance measurement makes its study very complicated and multi-prismatic. To highlight the complexity of the performance measurement concept, Lebas and Euske (2005) suggested nine propositions that attempt to cover the broadness of the concept.

Proposition 1: *performance can only be expressed as a set of parameters and indicators, that are complementary and sometimes contradictory, that describes the process through which the various types of outcome and results are achieved.*

Proposition 2: *understanding performance relies on the identification of a causal model that describes how actions today can influence results in the future.*

Proposition 3: *performance, because it is a social construct, is a concept with no objective description. Each person defines it in her or his own way.*

Proposition 4: *performance does not have the same meaning if the evaluator is inside or outside the organisation.*

Proposition 5: *performance is always connected or attached to a domain of responsibility.*

Proposition 6: *performance exists only if outcome and results can be described or measured so that they can be communicated for someone to decide to do something within the shared model of causal relationships.*

Proposition 7: *the relevance of the causal model needs to be continuously validated both within and without the organisation.*

Proposition 8: *performance indicators or measures should not be confused with what they only partially describe.*

Proposition 9: *performance is a relative concept requiring judgement and interpretation. Performance is effecting a superior process or result relative to the referent.*

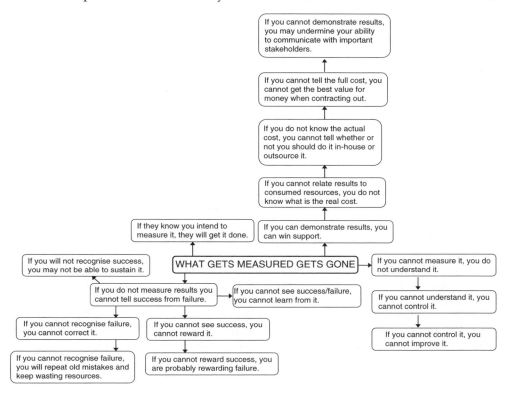

Figure 11.1. What Gets Measured Gets Done

Lebas and Euske's propositions highlight different points of view for performance measurement. Studying performance measurement and particularly trying to design and implement a performance measurement system is a challenging process. Some of the propositions emphasise the difficulties of identifying meaningful performance indicators and measures, while others highlight the inter-relationships and interdependencies of performance measurement with the other elements of the organisation, and particularly the strategic development processes. In essence, Lebas and Euske's propositions point out the fact that organisational performance and success depend on personal and social interpretations and perceptions; therefore, measuring them is not a standardised process that can be applied by all organisations.

There is a lot of confusion on the differences between performance measurement, performance measures and performance measurement systems. Neely *et al.* (1995) explain that performance measurement can be defined '*as the process of quantifying efficiency and effectiveness of action*', a performance measure is '*a metric used to quantify the efficiency and/or effectiveness of action*' while a performance measurement system is '*a set of metrics used to quantify both the efficiency and effectiveness of actions*'. The integration of performance measurement within the strategic development process is reflected in more recent approaches to define the concept; for example, Gates (1999) suggests that the evolution of performance measurement is the 'strategic performance measurement system', which is defined as '[the set of processes which] *translate business strategies into deliverable results. Strategic performance measurement systems combine financial, strategic and operating business measures to gauge how well a company meets its targets'*.

To gain a broad view of the concept of performance measurement it is worth examining the evolution of the concept over time. One of the most comprehensive reviews of the performance measures, which are mostly used at the corporate level, is provided by Wilcox and Bourne (2003), who suggest that the evolution of performance measurement at the corporate level can be divided into three different periods:

(i) 1850–1925: the development of cost and management accounting.
(ii) 1974–1992: the development of the multidimensional performance measurement frameworks.
(iii) 1992–2000: the development of strategy maps and cause and effect diagrams.

The first period was dominated by the return on investment (ROI). In the second period there was a shift to the paradigm of value (Ampuero, Goranson & Scott, 1997), with greater emphasis initially on earnings per share (EPS) and price/equity multiples, and later on return on equity (ROE), return on net assets (RONA) and cash flow. The third period is characterised by the development of more sophisticated approaches like the economic value added (EVA), earnings before interest, taxation, depreciation and amortisation (EBITDA), total shareholder equity (TSR) and the broader (beyond financial measures) more integrative frameworks like the balanced scorecard. (This broader perspective was recognised much earlier however in the field of operational research and more specifically multi-criteria decision-making; see, for example, Chapter 10.)

The importance of performance measurement within the strategic development process was emphasised by earlier literature from the field of strategic planning. Dyson and Foster (1983) suggest that one of the 13 elements of an 'effective strategic planning process' is the 'depth of evaluation', highlighting the need to develop pluralistic measures combining financial and non-financial measures in order to obtain holistic assessment of the organisational activities and performance achievements. Neely, Bourne and Adams (2003) concentrate their description of performance measurement's evolution by referring to the efforts made after the 1980s, distinguishing three generations of systems developed for measuring organisational performance. The first generation focused on the development of the 'balanced measurement systems' following the criticism of traditional (accounting-based) performance measurement systems by Kaplan and Norton. The Balanced Scorecard (Kaplan & Norton, 1992, 1996, 2001) is the most characteristic framework developed. The second generation integrated the previous models by *'mapping the flows and transformations'* (Neely, Bourne & Adams, 2003). Pike and Ross (2001) suggest that in this generation of performance measurements the emphasis is placed on the transformations rather than the individual stock measures. The most characteristic example of this generation of performance measurements is the strategy map (Kaplan & Norton, 2001). Another noticeable suggested methodology is the 'success and risk maps' (Neely *et al.*, 2000). The third generation of performance measurement focuses on organisations' efforts to seek greater clarity by linking financial to non-financial indicators, emphasising the linkages between *'intangible dimensions of organisational performance and the cash flow consequences of these'* (Neely, Bourne & Adams, 2003). The greatest change in the evolution of performance measurement took place with the integration of non-financial measurements into the existing systems, which were accounting-based. The integration of the performance measurement concept has been attributed to the shortcomings of the traditional accounting-based measures as summarised by Yeniyurt (2003), who argued that:

(i) They are inadequate for strategic decisions (Kaplan & Norton, 1992).
(ii) They are historical and backward-looking (Ittner & Larcker, 1998).
(iii) They lack predictive ability to explain future performance (Ittner & Larcker, 1998).
(iv) They provide too little information on root causes (Ittner & Larcker, 1998).
(v) They do not link the non-financial metrics to financial metrics (Kaplan & Norton, 1992).
(vi) They report functional, not cross-functional processes (Ittner & Larcker, 1998).
(vii) They do not consider intangible assets (Bukowitz & Petrash, 1997).
(viii) They do not measure the value created (Lehn & Makhija, 1996).
(ix) There are too many measures; new ones are needed that have broader content, being able to describe more with less numbers (Frigo & Krumwiede, 1999).
(x) Traditional metrics do not aggregate from an operational level to a strategic level (Frigo & Krumwiede, 1999).

IMPLEMENTATION OF PERFORMANCE MEASUREMENT

It is commonly admitted that there is no 'magic' toolbox, which would ensure the successful design and implementation of a performance measurement system; however, it is important to follow a series of stages to ensure the alignment of the performance measurement system with the organisational strategy and direction. The first stage should be concentrated on designing the performance measurement system; at this stage the managers involved should define which are their expectations and goals from the utilisation of this system. Then the organisational direction and strategy should be translated into performance measures and specific targets may be selected. The second stage consists of developing the performance measurement practices, by identifying suitable approaches to collecting the information that is needed, analysing it in such a way that it is meaningful at the various decision-making and control levels and presenting it in the most effective way. At this stage, the implications of the performance measurement system for the whole organisation have to be considered and the performance measures should be cascaded to all levels of the hierarchy. The third stage should consist of putting the performance measurement system in place. An additional stage for implementing a performance measurement system should be the review of the effectiveness of the actual system itself and its update if necessary.

Neely *et al.* (2000) summarise the works of Globerson (1985), Keegan, Eiler and Jones (1989) and Maskell (1989) in order to suggest a list of rules and guidelines for the development of performance measurement systems:

   (i) Performance criteria must be chosen from the company's objectives.
  (ii) Performance criteria must make possible the comparison of organisations that are in the same business.
 (iii) The purpose of each performance criterion must be clear.
  (iv) Data collection and methods of calculating the performance criteria must be clearly defined.
   (v) Ratio-based performance criteria are preferred to absolute numbers.
  (vi) Performance criteria should be under the control of the evaluated organisational unit.
 (vii) Performance criteria should be selected through discussions with the people involved (customers, employees, managers).
(viii) Objective performance criteria are preferable to subjective ones.

McCunn (1998) found that 70% of performance measurement initiatives fail. It is therefore very important to explore the reasons determining the success or failure of performance measurement initiatives. Bourne *et al.* (2002), referring to the work of Meekings (1995), Kaplan and Norton (1996), Bierbusse and Siesfeld (1997), McCunn (1998), Hacker and Brotherton (1998) and Schneiderman (1999), summarise them using Pettigrew, Whipp and Rosenfield's (1989) model of *'context, content and process'*.

Contextual issues: (i) a highly developed information system is needed, (ii) time and expense are required and (iii) the lack of leadership and resistance to change.

Processual issues: (i) lack of vision and strategy, (ii) strategy being linked to resource allocation, (iii) lack of negotiation in goal setting, which is driven by stakeholder requirements and (iv) striving for perfection undermined success.

Content issues: (i) strategy being inadequately linked to departmental, team and individual goals, (ii) the large number of measures adopted, (iii) poor definition of the metrics utilised and (iv) ineffective quantification of results in areas that are more qualitative in their nature.

In addition, de Waal and Coumet (2006) summarised 34 studies referring to the reasons why the design and implementation of performance measurement is unsuccessful. They have identified 31 different problems, which were further surveyed with a number of industry experts. The 10 most commonly met problems were:

   (i) Lack of leadership commitment.
  (ii) Lack of performance measurement culture.
 (iii) The performance measurement system has a low priority or its use is abandoned after the change of management.
  (iv) Management puts low priority on the performance measurement system implementation.
   (v) The organisation does not see (enough) benefit from the performance measurement system.
  (vi) Resistance from organisational members.
 (vii) Lack of a clear and understandable strategy.

(viii) Organisational members are not adopting the right management style.
  (ix) Too much focus on the results of the performance measurement system implementation, while the change process is ignored.
  (x) Lack of cause and effect relations or over-complexity due to too many casual relations.

As can be observed, the majority of the most common pitfalls reported by de Waal and Coumet (2006) are contextual and content issues rather than processual. This shows that the design and implementation of performance measurement is not only an issue of designing the right processes and having the right management systems in place, but a greater effort and change is required. The development of the performance measurement culture depends on the maturity of the organisation and people involved (Tapinos, 2005) and therefore time, resources and commitment are essential elements for the successful implementation of a performance measurement system.

STRATEGY DEVELOPMENT AND PERFORMANCE MEASUREMENT

To understand the role of performance measurement within the strategic development process it is worth referring to the Strategic Development Process (SDP) model presented and analysed in the first chapter. Figure 11.2 shows which elements of the SDP model are related to performance measurement. In essence, this model suggests that performance measurement has a twofold role: (i) monitoring and control and (ii) enhancing organisational learning. At the setting of the strategic goals, expected standards of performance are defined. This process is the first stage for designing the performance measurement system. Based on these standards, organisational activities and performance achievements are evaluated in order to assess their alignment with the strategic direction. Simultaneously, the output of the performance measurement system is used within strategy rehearsal and for the review of the strategic direction.

The fact that results of performance measurement are fed into strategic decision-making, particularly for setting the strategic goals and consequently for setting the strategic direction, shows that double-loop learning can potentially be achieved (Tapinos, 2005). Based on Argyris and Schon's (1978) definition of learning, it is understood that single-loop learning is achieved if the output of performance measurement is only used to evaluate the achievement of the organisational goals, and to correct the strategies which have produced the undesired results. However, as the SDP model suggests, performance measurement's feedback is directly linked with the setting of the strategic direction. This means that performance measurement can potentially lead to setting and/or revising the strategic direction, which ensures that the source of producing the strategies to be implemented is enhanced with the information collected by performance measurement. This is double-loop learning because corrective action is taken with regard to the process (direction setting), which influences the development of strategy. Figure 11.3 shows graphically the

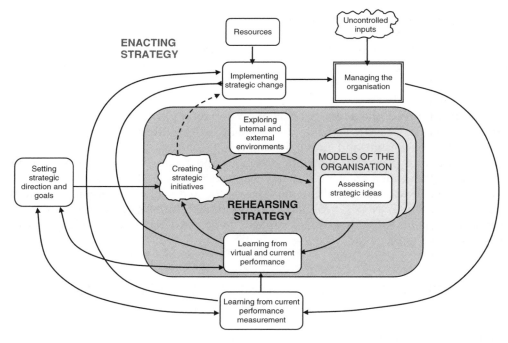

Figure 11.2. Strategic Development Process

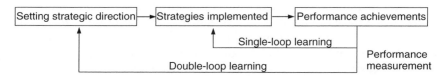

Figure 11.3. Performance Measurement and Learning
Source: Adapted from Argyris and Schon (1978).

difference between single- and double-loop learning with regard to performance measurement.

BASIC FRAMEWORKS OF PERFORMANCE MEASUREMENT

Following the increasing interest in performance measurement for the industrialists and the academics, a great variety of models and frameworks have been developed to enhance the approach and process undertaken for the evaluation of organisational performance achievements. To classify these models we can divide them into two categories: (i) self-assessment frameworks and (ii) business performance measurement models.

Self-assessment frameworks are models that can be used by organisations to assess their activities and performance against particular standards. The two most widely acknowledged self-assessment frameworks are: Malcolm Baldridge National Quality Award (MBNQA) and the Business Excellence Model (BEM). The MBNQA is a seven-point framework (Figure 11.4), which has been established by the National Institute of Standards and Technology in the USA. The seven points are (NIST, 2006): (i) leadership, (ii) strategic planning, (iii) market and customer focus, (iv) measurement analysis and knowledge management, (v) human resources focus, (vi) process management and (vii) results. The BEM is published by the European Foundation for Quality Management (EFQM) and it is considered the European approach for self-assessment, promoting innovation and learning (EFQM, 2006). BEM consists of nine criteria (Figure 11.5) divided into 'enablers': (i) leadership, (ii) policy and strategy, (iii) people, (iv) partnerships and resources, (v) processes and 'results', (vi) customer results, (vii) people results, (viii) society results and (ix) key performance results. Both models suggest specific characteristics that organisations should exhibit for each of the proposed dimensions in order to benchmark themselves against excellence. It is interesting to note that both models emphasise the importance for organisations of assessing their performance holistically and not only through financial results. It is also worth mentioning that the EFQM model distinguishes between enablers and results showing the cause and effect relationship and interdependence between all levels of the organisational hierarchy, to improve the organisational performance.

Business performance measurement models are an approach to managing the measurement of the performance achievements. A great variety of models and frameworks have been proposed in the last two decades. The greatest majority of these models highlight the need to integrate financial and non-financial performance measures and at the same time emphasise the need to link strategy and performance measurement. Bititci *et al.* (2000) summarised the most important ones:

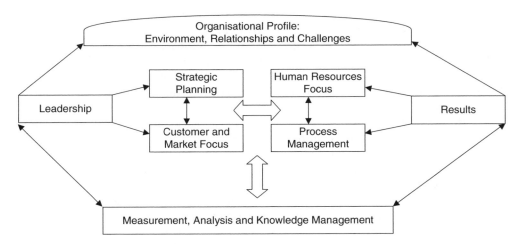

Figure 11.4. Malcolm Baldridge National Quality Award
Source: NIST (2006); http://www.quality.nist.gov/PDF_files/2006_ Business_Criteria.pdf.

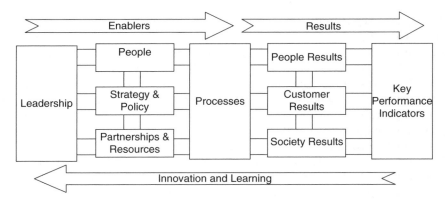

Figure 11.5. EFQM Excellence Model
Source: EFQM (2006). Copyright © 1999–2003 EFQM

- Strategic Measurement Analysis and Reporting Technique (SMART) (Cross & Lynch, 1989).
- Performance measurement for world class manufacturing (Maskell, 1989).
- Performance measurement questionnaire (Dixon, Nanni & Vollmann, 1990).
- Balanced Scorecard (Kaplan & Norton, 1992).
- Cambridge performance design process (Neely *et al.*, 1995).
- Performance criteria system (Globerson, 1985).
- Skandia's navigator (Edvinsson & Marlone, 1999).
- Integrated performance measurement systems reference model (Bititci & Carrie, 1998).
- Performance prism (Neely, Bourne & Adams, 2003).

It is important to note that the majority of the integrated performance measurement frameworks highlight the need to create an alignment between strategy and performance measurement. Furthermore, all these models propose pluralistic views of performance evaluation. The Balanced Scorecard emphasises the necessity to achieve a balance between financial and non-financial measures, while models like the performance prism extend the broadness of measures by proposing a stakeholder approach to performance measurement. The Balanced Scorecard is the most widely implemented performance measurement model, which is why it is presented analytically in the following section.

Another role for performance measurement is in benchmarking. This is particularly valuable where a set of units, e.g. bank branches, restaurants or schools, is to be managed and the aim is to identify the best performers and raise the performance of the other units to that level. The units are characterised by having multiple inputs and outputs and the technique of data envelopment analysis (DEA) has been developed which provides an aggregate performance measure allowing the identification of best performing units and peers for the under-performing units. The method was developed by Charnes, Cooper and Rhodes (1978) and some of the practical issues encountered in applying the method appear in Dyson *et al.* (2001).

THE BALANCED SCORECARD

The Balanced Scorecard's usage in organisations is estimated to range between 35% and 60% depending on the survey sample. Silk (1998) found that approximately 60% of Fortune 1000 companies are engaged in the implementation of the BSC. Lower usage percentages (35%) have been observed in global surveys (Tapinos, Dyson & Meadows, 2005). The basic principle of this model is putting equal (balanced) emphasis on financial and non-financial measures (Kaplan & Norton, 1992). The first edition of the Balanced Scorecard suggested that there are four main perspectives – financial, internal, customer and innovation (which later became learning and growth) – and measurements should be based on these. The graph representation of the balanced scorecard is shown in Figure 11.6.

According to the creators of the Balanced Scorecard (Kaplan & Norton, 1992), these four perspectives should be directly linked to the 'vision and strategy' of the organisation. The financial perspective should examine *'if we succeed, how will we look to our shareholders?'*, the internal perspective should consider *'to satisfy customers and shareholders, at which processes must we excel?'*, the learning and growth perspective should address *'how can our organisation continue to learn and improve?'* and the customer perspective should investigate *'how do we create value for our customers?'*. Figure 11.7 shows an example of some metrics for each element of the balanced scorecard.

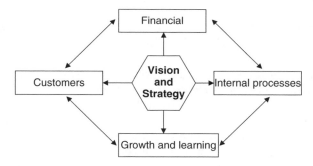

Figure 11.6. The Balanced Scorecard
Source: Kaplan and Norton (1996).

Financial	Customer	Internal Process	Learning & Growth
• Return on investment (ROI)	• Number of customer complaints	• Delivery on time	• Number of patents filed
		• Technology optimisation	
• Revenue growth	• Market share		• Training budget

Figure 11.7. Example of Balanced Scorecard Measures

The implementation of the balanced scorecard varies for each organisation according to its characteristics and strategy. In practice, the majority of the organisations have designed balanced scorecards that are not identical to the original model. For example, Chow, Haddad and Williamson (1997) contrast the Balanced Scorecard in five organisations from different industries showing that balanced approaches for performance measurement can be developed based on the individual needs of each company. For example, one of their case studies was an electronics company whose scorecard included measures on finance, internal processes, innovation, customers and employees, while a commercial bank's included shareholders, customers, employees and community.

The growth of social responsibility initiatives in the last decade has influenced the design of the scorecards, and it is quite common for one of the key elements to be the impact on society or community. A characteristic example is the 'steering wheel', Tesco's version of the Balanced Scorecard. Tesco's scorecard (Tesco, 2006) identifies five key dimensions in their performance: finance, customer, operations, people and community, see Figure 11.8. At the centre of the scorecard is the statement of direction: 'Every little helps', which according to their annual report is the driving force for Tesco's growth and success.

The concept of the Balanced Scorecard is continuously being updated. Lawrie and Cobbold (2004) distinguish three generations of scorecards. The first generation is based on the early work of Kaplan and Norton (1992), when the organisations start introducing non-financial performance measurements. This generation of balanced scorecards was about 'putting vision and strategy at the centre of the performance measurement' (Kaplan & Norton, 1992). The criticisms and the challenges of the Balanced Scorecard's design and its implementation in particular, Butler, Letza and Neale (1997), Ahn (2001), Irwin (2002) and Radnor and Lovell (2003), led to the development of the second generation of scorecards. Lawrie and Cobbold (2004) found that the innovations of the second generation were to suggest that the relationship between each of the four perspectives, the strategic objectives of the organisation and the performance measurements, should be mapped; furthermore, the mapping of this relationship was enhanced by identifying causality between the elements of the model produced. This development in the Balanced Scorecard led the original inventors of the concept to suggest that it developed 'from an improved measurement system, (to) a management system [...] with a strategic orientation'. The third generation of scorecards has incorporated 'destination statements'; these define the targets of 'where the organisation should be' in a specified time frame, for example considering the financial perspective the destination statement would be the ROI to increase by 15% within the next 3 years. The review of the evolution of the Balanced Scorecard does not imply that all the organisations implementing this management technique are developing scorecards of the third generation.

The second and third generations of the Balanced Scorecard are an integration of the performance measurement concept. Initially, the Balanced Scorecard was developed as a tool to operationalise strategy (vision/mission) through the measurement of the performance. However, the use of strategy maps, and particularly destination statements, integrates the use of performance measurement into performance management. Mapping the inter-relationships and the dynamics between key performance measurements is an approach to managing the organisation through the

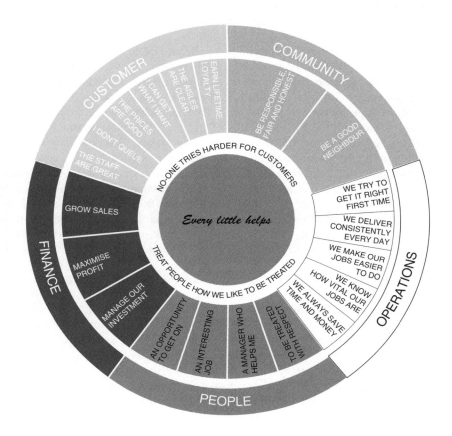

Figure 11.8. Tesco's Steering Wheel
Source: Reproduced by permission of Tesco's Annual Report (2006). Steering Wheel from Page 8.

prism of performance achievements. To a large extent, the development of strategy maps is part of 'rehearsing strategy' from the SDP model (see Figure 11.2 and Chapter 1). Strategy maps are models that depict the impact of each performance measure on the others within the overall vision and strategy of the organisation. There are a lot of similarities between strategy maps and the applications of system dynamics and multi-criteria decision analysis (MCDA) models to performance measurement (Belton & Stewart, 2002; Santos, Belton & Howick, 2002).

The integration of performance measurement into performance management shows the importance of the performance measurement concept and emphasises the need to consider it as an integral part of strategic decision-making, as highlighted by the strategic development process model, in the first chapter of this book. Furthermore, the integration of balanced scorecards and strategy maps reinforces the linkage between 'learning from current performance measurement' and 'learning from virtual and current performance measurement'.

PERFORMANCE MEASUREMENT IN THE PUBLIC SECTOR AND NON-PROFIT ORGANISATIONS

Performance measurement is classified by Behn (1995) as one of the 'Big Questions' in modern public management.[1] Both public sector and non-profit organisations have recognised the importance of performance measurement and have been engaged with its implementation. Brignall and Modell (2000) explain that its utilisation has increased in the last two decades, particularly in advanced economies, which under the umbrella of 'new public management' has tried to improve the *'efficiency and effectiveness, so as to reduce their demands on taxpayers, while maintaining the volume and quality of services supplied to the public'*. Gianakis (2002) observed that performance measurement systems in the public sector are systems that *'represent efforts to bring private-sector incentive systems and market mechanisms to the management of public sector'*. Smith (1993) highlights that some earlier attempts to address the issue of performance measurement within the UK public sector was the 'Comparative Statistics' initiative; in 1982 the Audit Commission was created to maximise the efficiency and effectiveness of local government.

Public sector and non-profit organisations have a distinct difference to private companies in that their primary goal is not financial output. This alters the meaning of success for these organisations and consequently the measurement of their performance achievements. Brooks (2002) contrasts for-profit organisations with public sector ones, to observe that governments' goals are neither one-dimensional (profit) nor particularly well defined. In parallel, Forbes (1998) highlights that *'even the prospect of developing surrogate quantitative measures of organisational performance is often difficult because nonprofit organisations frequently have goals that are amorphous and offer services that are intangible'*. Furthermore, according to Kanter and Summers (1987) there is distinct difference in the values of non-profit organisations, which have a rather 'societal' character. Smith (1993) concluded that performance measures for the public domain must be *'genuine indicators of some aspect of outcome'*. Wang (2002) suggests that the ultimate performance measures in the public sector are: administrative accountability, managerial and operational efficiency and effectiveness, service quality and citizen trust. However, measuring the ultimate goals of the public sector is a challenging process. Smith (1993) notes that in both public sector and non-profit organisations it is difficult to gain consensus among the various stakeholders as to what are the actual output and objectives. This results in a greater difficulty of measuring and interpreting such output.

Greiling (2005) explains that the utilisation of performance measurement in the public sector exceeds the limits of monitoring and control, contributing to: (i) the modernisation of public budgeting, (ii) the effectiveness of obligatory or voluntary reporting, (iii) the improvement of contract management, (iv) the development of a reliable basis for inter-administrative comparisons/benchmarking, (v) the enhancement of the internal diagnosis system and (vi) the support of strategic

---

[1] The other 'Big Questions' are: motivate people to work for public purposes and break the cycle of micro-management (Behn, 1995).

decision-making. Similarly Bruijn (2002), contrasting the positive and negative effects of performance measurement in the public sector, found that it: (i) brings transparency, (ii) is an incentive for output and (iii) is an elegant way of shaping accountability, while at the same time performance measurement: (i) prompts concentrating on satisfying specific quantitative targets, (ii) adds to internal bureaucracy, (iii) blocks innovation and (iv) blocks ambition.

Julnes and Holzer (2001) highlight that even if there exists a growing number of publications that discuss the value of performance measurement in the public sector (Wholey, 1999), their use is not universal in all public sector organisations. Gianakis (2002) argues that the main constraints in the successful implementation of performance measurements in the public sector are that:

(i) Political jurisdictions manifest unique elements that limit the generalisability of administrative systems and the comparability of measures.
(ii) Public sector accounting systems make it difficult to assign costs to programmes.
(iii) It is difficult to integrate performance measurement and budgeting processes to focus on issues of comprehensiveness and fairness of the measurement system.
(iv) There is a reluctance of legislative bodies to focus on substantive policy issues in the formal budget process.

To facilitate performance measurement in the public sector and non-profit organisations a number of normative approaches and models have been developed. Micheli and Kennerley (2005) reviewed those attempts and found that frameworks developed for for-profit companies cannot capture the peculiarities of public and non-profit organisations. The same authors identified a range of models developed for public sector and non-profit organisations (see, for example, Boland & Fowler, 2000; Brignal & Modell, 2000; Kushner & Poole, 1996; Osborne et al., 1995). There is a third category which consists of those who modified established performance measurement models to make them adapt to the needs of public sector and non-profit organisations. Kaplan (2001) proposed a specialised version of the Balanced Scorecard. There is a growing number of public sector and non-profit organisations, which have been engaged, with the implementation of the Balanced Scorecard (see, for example, Gooijer, 2000).

Reviewing the existing theoretical propositions and empirical investigations regarding performance measurement in the public and non-profit sector, it is apparent that, since there is no universally applicable performance measurement system, each organisation should be very careful with the design and implementation of its performance measurement system. It is very important that the system in place will be based on what really matters for each organisation and would provide a clear picture to its stakeholders. It is also important that the performance measurement system is not an imitation of a popular framework, but a well-considered management tool, which will monitor and control the alignment of the activities and performance achievements with the overall strategy and direction. At the same time, it will be a system that will collect, analyse, interpret and feed the appropriate information to the appropriate decision-making level.

STRATEGIC DEVELOPMENT AND PERFORMANCE MEASUREMENT AT THE UNIVERSITY OF WARWICK[2]

Higher education in the UK, and particularly the academic institutes, has been the focus of research for the last 20 years. The changes in the funding system in the mid-1980s (Reform Act 1988), combined with the internationalisation of the competition between the universities, has made their study very significant in the academic world. Universities as institutions were functioning in a stable environment in the UK, with a very clear purpose of existence and well-defined activities. The inclusion of the polytechnics as universities, in parallel with the decrease in government funding per student, have created an increasing competition between them (Johnes & Cave, 1994). Etzokwitz (1988) suggests that the universities today are undergoing a 'second revolution'; the first one was when research was added to teaching, as an academic function (Jencks & Riesman, 1968). This second revolution concerns the incorporation of 'economic and social development in their mission'. The implementation of new practices of management and governance (Clark, 1998) has made them interesting case studies from a management and business point of view (Galloway, 1992; Pettigrew, Ferlie & McKee, 1992). The changes in the environment have created the need for more effective planning in the universities. For example, Grigg (1994) suggests that in order to survive in the 1990s, the universities were forced to review their mission and the overall frame of strategies for their implementation.

We investigated performance measurement and particularly its role within the strategic development process in the University of Warwick. This study was conducted based on the principles of in-depth case study (Yin, 1993) and documented material was combined with semi-structured interviews. In order to achieve broader coverage, we examined the practices at both the corporate and departmental levels. At the corporate level a number of senior academic officers, including the Deputy Vice-Chancellor and one of the Pro Vice-Chancellors, were interviewed. At the departmental level we studied three departments: Department of Physics, Warwick Business School (WBS) and a non-academic department, Hospitality Services. At each department the interviews included members of faculty and staff from levels of the hierarchy.

Strategy Development at the University of Warwick

The development of strategy in the University of Warwick takes place at various levels, as in most organisations of similar size. The overall organisational direction is set at the corporate level by the senior management. According to the data collected in the interviews, the Strategy Committee, which is a joint committee of some members of the Senate and some of the Council[3] to advise on strategic issues of the

---

[2] This case study has been published in Tapinos, Dyson and Meadows (2005).
[3] Council is the executive governing body, responsible for the finance and estate of the University. Senate is the supreme academic authority, responsible for the academic activities of the University (Warwick, 2006).

Our mission is:

- To build an institution widely recognised, at a regional, national and international level, as a world leader in research and teaching.
- To conduct research across all academic departments which makes a significant contribution to the extension of human knowledge and understanding.
- Through our teaching and research programmes to equip our graduates with the necessary education and skills to make a significant contribution to the economy and to society as a whole.
- To recruit students and staff with outstanding potential and to provide the best support and facilities to foster teaching, learning and research of the highest quality.
- To serve our local and regional communities through the provision of excellent and innovative teaching, research, training, cultural, enterprise and employment opportunities.
- To exploit opportunities for collaboration and partnership with other HEIs, educational institutions and commercial partners.
- To strengthen and diversify our activities in the fields of industrial and business liaison, innovation, exploitation and entrepreneurialism, thereby supporting economic growth and regeneration.
- To continue our tradition of making a high quality and challenging University education available to those who are capable of benefiting from it.

Figure 11.9. University of Warwick's Mission Statement (Warwick, 2005)

University, develops the strategy of the University. The Strategy Committee meets twice or three times each term, when its members discuss and develop long- and shorter-term strategies. The strategy development in the University of Warwick is driven by its direction, which emphasises excellence in research and teaching. See Figure 11.9.

The University's strategy is communicated formally and informally to the Heads of the Departments, who have the responsibility to design the strategy for their departments in alignment with the University's direction. Each department has a different approach to the development of the strategy, which depends on the level of its autonomy. For example, the Business School is one of the more autonomous departments in the University and its strategic decision-making is not financially dependent on the University's planning. On the other hand, the Physics Department is less autonomous and most of the decisions made have to be approved by an appropriate committee at the corporate level of the University. This phenomenon creates different structures within each department and different processes in the decision-making. In particular, the Business School has to feed the information collected by performance measurement at the appropriate level of decision-making internally, while the Physics Department has to supply the information to the corporate of the University. This means that the departments with greater autonomy have to develop the strategic initiatives that will implement the strategy themselves. The departments with less autonomy select their strategies through a wider consultation and approval with the centre of the University. Each department has a number of different committees, which develop and implement its strategy. The communication and implementation of the strategy is realised by formal and informal practices.

Performance Measurement at the University of Warwick

At the corporate level, the University of Warwick evaluates its performance based on three key dimensions: academic excellence, teaching excellence and finance. An extensive number of performance measures are collected regarding these three key dimensions, and all the academic related ones are published in the 'Academic database'. The 'Academic database' is a booklet containing measures of academic-related figures such as student numbers, student drop-out rates and first class degrees awarded per department. It should be highlighted that even if no specific model or theoretical framework has been followed for the development of the performance measurement system in the University of Warwick, its set of measures is quite balanced across the three key dimensions. Nevertheless, the interviews conducted, especially with the senior academic officers, suggested that the financial measures and particularly income generation had a stronger influence in the decision-making than the other two.

Performance measurement in WBS concentrates on the assessment of the academic achievements, the financial performance and the department's corporate image. The performance measurement system is an integrated part of the department's operations since it is predefined, based on specific documented procedures. The corporate image of WBS is measured by its appearance in the media and its position in the league tables, whose criteria are carefully taken into consideration. Its financial performance is evaluated by the surplus in its income – expenses equation. Therefore, its income-generation activities are measured. On the academic front, the student numbers are carefully monitored in terms of applications, number of accepted students and the entry level. The performance in teaching is monitored with quantitative measures, such as the students' feedback, and with qualitative measures by the external examiners scheme. Regarding research, performance measurement is associated with the appraisal system. Each staff member goes through an annual review of the number of books written, conferences attended and published articles in refereed journals. The academic performance is also evaluated with the external exercises by the Higher Education Funding Council for England (HEFCE). These are the Teaching Quality Assessment (TQA) (now replaced by quality audits) and the Research Assessment Exercise (RAE). The fact that the RAE influences the governmental funding of the University is one of the reasons for setting very specific targets with respect to research achievements; for example, each staff member knows exactly how many publications he or she should produce within a given time frame.

The performance measurement system in the Physics Department is based on a limited number of assessments. The main focus is the measurement of the income-generation activities and the academic achievements. The income-generation activities are measured by the number of applications made for grants and the number of successful ones. Concerning the academic achievements, the student numbers and entry levels are constantly measured and taken into consideration. Teaching is evaluated by the measurement of students' complaints and the qualitative comments of the external examiners. Research is assessed by the publications produced and the conferences attended. In the Physics Department, the only target set in terms of the expected performance is the number of applications for grants made. It should also be highlighted that the performance is measured through informal practices, which take place irregularly. The appraisal system is not part of the performance measurement system.

Hospitality Services operates as a business unit, and at the time that this research took place it was in the process of implementing a balanced scorecard across the whole department. Four 'key results areas' have been defined, for each area the 'actions/tasks' necessary to be undertaken have to be determined and for each action/task a list of appropriate 'measures of performance' has been set. Furthermore, their balanced scorecard identifies the 'competencies, development/training' required, providing the deadlines for their achievement and the person responsible for the monitoring of their realisation. It is worth mentioning the four 'key results areas', which are: (1) finance, (2) customer satisfaction, (3) staff (human resources) and (4) continuous improvement. At the time that the interviews were conducted, the balanced scorecard was used only at the corporate level and they were trying to cascade it down so that each division of Hospitality Services has its own balanced scorecard for its own operations. The departmental scorecard is used to define the 'goals/targets/objectives' for each employee, with the 'actions required' and the corresponding 'measures of success'.

Overall the performance measurement system in the University of Warwick consists of a central system that fulfils the requirements for data by the centre of the University, which is fed by the performance measurement system of each department. There is not a standard performance measurement system that is used by each department. The performance measurement system of each department is shaped by the needs of its strategic decision-making, which are related to its level of autonomy and purpose.

Performance Measurement within the Strategic Development Process at the University of Warwick

The performance measurement system of the University is engaged with both financial and non-financial assessments. Its financial measures are recorded extensively in its annual review. Nevertheless, the interviews with the members of the top management teams revealed that even if financial measures influence the strategic planning of the University, its perceived success is not measured by these figures. It is primarily the academic standing that constitutes the University's feeling of being successful. In the non-financial measurements, the measurement of the academic achievements can be seen as an assessment of the institution's quality.

One of the criticisms of the existing system, as determined by the interviews conducted, is that the assessment of the quality of the academic performance is driven by the financial implications and benefits related to it. A number of academics also expressed their doubts as to whether academic quality should be measured with the indicators set by the RAE. This is reinforced by the staff's perception (not shared by the top management team members) that the appraisal–reward system is linked to indicators coming from the Research Assessment Exercise (RAE). The problem of assessing the quality of research is not new to the academic world. Oliver (1993) discusses the difficulties of developing an 'appropriate' measurement, explaining that the volume of research output does not mean quality, whereas the use of more sophisticated approaches, such as citation indices, has limitations with regard to time constraints.

Analysis of the employees' perceptions and interpretations of the University's direction led to the understanding that the performance measurement system has been the means for communicating the University's strategy. The staff members have clearly stated that their interpretation of the University's main strategy comes from the measurement of their performance. The emphasis placed on setting specific targets for the research outcomes, either in terms of publications or grants applied/approved, has been appreciated as an indication that the University is 'research-led', as far as the academic departments are concerned. Similarly, in the non-academic department, the fact that there is an emphasis on monitoring the financial surpluses has been interpreted that the University has a very clear direction with regard to the non-academic activities. Wang (2002) found that the performance measurement's outcome is used mainly for external communication to the stakeholders of an organisation. However, this case research has shown that performance measurement is a means of communicating internally the organisational direction and strategy. Furthermore, this case study found that performance measurement improves the organisational learning within the organisation either by disseminating its strategy or by providing vital information to facilitate the strategic development process.

One of the most important observations made, in this case study, is that there exists significant variation in the perceptions and interpretation of the University's direction. The fact that the employees' perceptions of the University's 'direction' are not always accurate, or in agreement with perceptions of the senior management, is an additional support for the importance of the design and development stages for the performance measurement systems.

Implications

The investigation of performance measurement within the strategic development process in the University of Warwick has found that it has a multi-prismatic role. Performance measurement is the key activity for the monitoring and control of the organisational performance achievements. However, its utilisation not only contributes to the monitoring and control, as it enhances organisational learning and at the same time is a means for communicating strategy. This creates a clear implication for the utilisation of performance measurement systems: the managers involved in their design and development should take into consideration that the system in place should not only evaluate the performance achievements but also provide the right type of information at the appropriate level of decision-making. Furthermore, managers should consider whether their performance measurement system communicates the right messages to the internal and external stakeholders.

PERFORMANCE MEASUREMENT IN PARTNERSHIPS

If performance measurement in individual organisations is a challenge then an added complexity occurs in partnerships, and this is discussed by focusing on a particular partnership, the Coventry Partnership. The Partnership is a public/private/voluntary/community partnership charged with developing and implementing a community plan for Coventry, which aims to improve the quality of life for the disadvantaged communities and neighbourhoods (priority neighbourhoods) of Coventry (UK).

The Coventry Partnership is a statutory Local Strategic Partnership and has government funding (neighbourhood renewal funding – NRF) to further its aims. The Partnership was formally established to succeed the Coventry City Forum, a similar body, but the new body had community representation, which was lacking in the Forum. The Partnership Board spent some 2 years developing a community plan in a highly consultative way. The plan involved identifying priorities for improving the quality of life, and Theme Groups covering for example health and wellbeing, community safety, the environment, learning and training, and equalities and communities, were set up. The Theme Groups initiated a series of projects aimed at addressing the priorities of the plan, many of which received NR funding. The general approach was to formulate pilot projects, which plausibly would address the priorities and evaluate them. If the projects were successful they would either receive further NR funding or be adopted by one or more of the partners (a process known as mainstreaming). The initial purpose of the Partnership was to some extent compromised by the government wishing the Partnership to pursue their national (floor) targets, which did not necessarily coincide with the priorities, and later the local authority (Coventry City) signed a local area agreement (LAA) with the government, which gave access to further funding and included governmental targets. This focus towards service delivery in the statutory sector and governmental targets, and away from local priorities, caused some difficulties, and in particular risked disengaging some of the non-statutory partners (e.g. the private sector companies, universities and voluntary organisations).

The Partnership has a performance management system, managed by the Progress, Impact and Evaluation (PIE) group of the Partnership, whose core requirements are:

- To monitor overall performance and review delivery of specific projects.
- To manage a process of performance improvement.
- To manage a process of improving partnership working.

For specific projects, performance management initially considered the plausibility of the projects in addressing community plan priorities. An NRF team in the City Council then had the task of monitoring the delivery of the projects and ensuring accountability for the expenditure. For projects funded by the LAA a parallel monitoring system was necessary. Some of the projects were evaluated further for their impact by the Community Research and Evaluation Service (CRES). Overall performance was monitored by a range of performance indicators available on the CoventryStatistics website, and perceptions of the quality of life in priority neighbourhoods were assessed by an annual household survey.

For performance improvement the PIE group ran a series of workshops which considered progress against targets and reassessed the priorities of the plan. This led to an improvement plan and in 2006 a revised community plan was produced. With regard to partnership working, two specific issues were identified: the extent to which partners own plans were influenced by the community plan priorities and the general involvement of the private sector, particularly below board level.

A particular requirement of government was for a trajectory of targets on the performance indicators (PIs) and for the Partnership to be judged against progress against the trajectories. A typical example would relate to litter and the priority of securing 'cleaner and more attractive neighbourhoods'. A typical trajectory would be as shown in Figure 11.10.

Projects to address the issue would involve city services, schools, Business in the Community and community groups. The performance against the targets was wholly within local control and therefore judging the performance of the Partnership in meeting the targets was appropriate. However, for other areas this was not necessarily the case. For example, in the employment field a priority was 'higher employment in disadvantaged neighbourhoods' and the trajectory is shown in Figure 11.11.

The Partnership was able to sponsor projects on advisory services for the long-term unemployed, personal development and on inward investment. All these and other measures would support the reduction in the level of the PI. However, outside the control of the Partnership Peugeot decided to close its car assembly plant on the outskirts of Coventry and this has a negative impact for which the Partnership can hardly be held accountable. A more complex case occurs in learning and training, where a priority is 'improved educational attainment for children, especially those

Performance Measure	Units	2004/5	2005/6	2006/7	2007/8
Fewer areas with high levels of litter	% sites surveyed below standard	37	32	28	25

Figure 11.10. A Trajectory for an Environment Performance Indicator

Performance Measure	Units	2004/5	2005/6	2006/7	2007/8
Fewer households with no-one in paid work	% households	22	20	18	17

Figure 11.11. A Trajectory for an Employment Performance Indicator

Performance Measure	Units	2004/5	2005/6	2006/7	2007/8
Number of schools in priority neighbourhoods with over 50% of pupils achieving level 5 at key stage 3	# schools	2	3	4	5

Figure 11.12. A Trajectory for a Learning and Training Performance Indicator

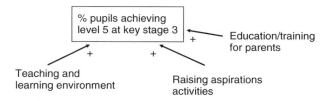

Figure 11.13. Support for Educational Attainment

in disadvantaged neighbourhoods'. The trajectory on one of the PIs is given in Figure 11.12.

Here the Partnership has sponsored a range of activities, including working with schools to raise attainment and aspirations, improving the teaching and learning environment and working with parents. This support is shown in Figure 11.13.

The positive signs on the arrows indicate improvement in the PI due to the activities. However, the disadvantaged neighbourhoods have a moving population with people aspiring to move out and being replaced by families in disadvantaged circumstances, such as teenage mothers and families with limited competency in English. The dynamic of the situation is shown in Figure 11.14.

The diagram shows that some Partnership activities can indeed lead to improved educational attainment, but others might in fact decrease attainment through their

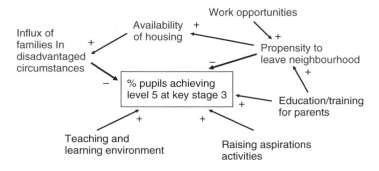

Figure 11.14. Dynamics of Moving Population

impact on the population in the neighbourhood. The setting of trajectories, assessing progress and holding the Partnership accountable can thus be problematic and the system would require modelling to arrive at appropriate measures, although even then there would be considerable uncertainty surrounding them.

Performance measurement and management is not straightforward in individual organisations. In partnerships there is added complexity due to such factors as the scope of responsibility and accountability of the partnership, the alignment of partnership plans and priorities with those of individual partners, and where they are in the public sector, the alignment of local and national priorities.

FUTURE DIRECTIONS FOR PERFORMANCE MEASUREMENT

The field of performance measurement is an interdisciplinary field and there are developments on all fronts of the organisational spectrum. There is a growing body of literature that is working towards the identification of performance measurement practices, which would capture most effectively specific organisational activities that are vitally important for the organisations and at the same time are difficult to be evaluated. For example, there is a need to develop robust approaches to measure intangible assets and particularly to develop performance indicators for intellectual capital, innovation, knowledge and learning (see, for example, Marr, Gray & Schiuma, 2004).

Another very interesting and simultaneously very important future direction for performance measurement is the development of performance measurement systems that are predictive rather than reactive. For example, Wilcox and Bourne (2003) suggest that it is essential to identify performance measurements that will detect a problem before it occurs and provide the appropriate feedback to minimise its effects.

The launch of the SDP model (Chapter 1) calls for new research in the field of performance measurement. The SDP model places 'rehearsing strategy' at the core of strategy development. 'Rehearsing strategy' is linked with performance measurement through the 'learning from current and virtual performance measurement'. This link requires further theoretical and empirical investigation to establish how performance measurement can influence the rehearsing of strategy. In parallel, it should be investigated how the measurement of the organisational performance is going to be influenced by the rehearsing of the strategy. Perhaps, the latter is going to indicate crucial performance measures and this potentially will enhance the ability of the performance measurement system, to predict future performance outcomes and achievements.

Currently there is a significant research activity on enhancing the current understanding for organisation-wide performance measurement systems. It has been understood that the majority of the existing performance measures or performance indicators are rather operational or functional and do not provide adequate information for strategic decision-making. Therefore researchers try to enhance the linkages between performance measurement and the strategic development process, because as Melnyk, Stewart and Swink (2004) pointed out *strategy without metrics is useless, metrics without strategy is meaningless*.

REFERENCES

Ahn, H. (2001) 'Applying the balanced scorecard concept: an experience report', *Long Range Planning*, **34**(4), 441–452.

Ampuero, M., Goranson, J. & Scott, J. (1997) 'Solving the measurement puzzle: how EVA and the balanced scorecard fit together', *Perspectives on Business Innovation Journal*, Center for Business Innovation, Issue 2.

Argyris, C. & Schon, D. (1978) *Organizational Learning: A Theory of Action Perspective*. Addison-Wesley: New York.

Behn, R.A. (1995) 'The Big Questions of public management', *Public Administration Review*, **55**(4), 313–324.

Belton, V. & Stewart, T.J. (2002) *Multiple Criteria Decision Analysis: An Integrated Approach*. Kluwer Academic: Dordrecht.

Bierbusse, P. & Siesfeld, T. (1997) 'Measures that matter', *Journal of Strategic Performance Measurement*, **1**(2), 6–11.

Bititci, U.S. & Carrie, A.S. (1998) *Strategic Management of the Manufacturing Value Chain*. Kluwer Academic: Dordrecht.

Bititci, U., Turner, T. & Begemann, C. (2000) 'Dynamics of performance measurement systems', *International Journal of Operations and Production Management*, **20**(6), 692–704.

Boland, T. & Fowler, A. (2000) 'A systems perspective of performance measurement in public sector organisations', *The International Journal of Public Sector Management*, **13**(5), 417–429.

Bourne, M., Neely, A.D., Platts, K. & Mills, J. (2002) 'The success and failure of performance measurement initiatives: perceptions of participating managers', *International Journal of Operations and Production Management*, **22**(11), 1288–1310.

Brignall, S. & Modell, S. (2000) 'An institutional perspective on performance measurement and management in the "new public sector"', *Management Accounting Research*, **11**, 281–306.

Brooks, A. (2002) 'Can nonprofit management help answer public management's "Big Questions"', *Public Administration Review*, **62**(3), 259–267.

Bruijn, H. (2002) 'Performance measurement in the public sector, strategies to cope with the risks of performance measurement', *International Journal of Public Sector Management*, **15**(7), 578–590.

Bukowitz, W.R. & Petrash, G.P. (1997) 'Visualizing, measuring and managing knowledge', *Research-Technology Management*, **40**(4), 441–456.

Butler, A., Letza, S.R. & Neale, B. (1997) 'Linking the balanced scorecard to strategy', *Long Range Planning*, **30**(2), 242–253.

Charnes, A., Cooper, W.W. & Rhodes, E. (1978) 'Measuring the efficiency of decision making units', *European Journal of Operational Research*, **2**, 429–444.

Chow, C.W., Haddad, K.M. & Williamson, J.E. (1997) 'Applying the balanced scorecard to small companies', *Management Accounting*, **79**(2), 21–27.

Clark, B.R. (1998) *Creating Entrepreneurial Universities. Organizational Pathways of Transformation, Issues in Higher Education*. IAU Press/Pergamon: New York.

Cross, K.F. & Lynch, R.L. (1989) 'The SMART way to define and sustain success', *National Productivity Review*, **9**(1), 23–33.

de Waal, A. & Coumet, H. (2006) 'Lessons learned from the balanced scorecard', Performance Measurement Association Conference, London, UK.

Dixon, J.R., Nanni, A.J. & Vollmann, T.E. (1990) *The New Performance Challenge – Measuring Operations for World-Class Competition*. Dow Jones-Irwin: Chicago.

Dyson, R.G., Allen, R., Camanho, A.S., Podinvoski, V.V., Sarrico, C.S. *et al.* (2001) 'Pitfalls and protocols in DEA', *European Journal of Operational Research*, **132**, 245–259.

Dyson, R.G. & Foster, M.J. (1983) 'Making planning more effective', *Long Range Planning*, **16**(6), 68–73.

Eccles, R.G. (1991) 'The performance measurement manifesto', *Harvard Business Review*, **Jan/Feb**, 131–137.

EFQM (2006) 'European Foundation for Quality Management', [online] www.efqm.org (accessed 19/7/2006).

Edvinsson, L. & Malone, M.S. (1999) *Intellectual Capital: The Proven Way to Establish Your Company's Real Value By Measuring Its Hidden Values*. HarperBusiness: New York.

Etzokwitz, H. (1988) 'The norms of entrepreneurial science: cognitive effects of the new university–industry linkages', *Research Policy*, **27**, 823–833.

Forbes, D.P. (1998) 'Measuring the unmeasurable: empirical studies of nonprofit organization effectiveness from 1977 to 1997', *Non-profit and Voluntary Sector Quarterly*, **27**(2), 183–202.

Frigo, M.L. & Krumwiede, K. (1999) 'Balanced scorecard: a rising trend in strategic performance management', *Journal of Strategic Performance Measurement*, pp. 42–48.

Galloway, T.D. (1992) 'Threatened schools, imperiled practice: a case for collaboration', *Journal of American Planning Association*, **58**(2), 229–240.

Gates, S. (1999) 'Aligning strategic performance measures and results', The Conference Board.

Gianakis, G. (2002) 'The promise of public sector performance measurement: anodyne or placebo', *Public Administration Quarterly*, **26**(1/2), 35–59.

Globerson, S. (1985) 'Issues in developing a performance criteria system for an organization', *International Journal of Production Research*, **23**(4), 639–646.

Gooijer, J. (2000) 'Designing a knowledge management performance framework', *Journal of Knowledge Management*, **4**(4), 303–314.

Greiling, D. (2005) 'Performance measurement in the public sector: the German experience', *International Journal of Productivity and Performance Management*, **54**(7), 551–567.

Grigg, T. (1994) 'Adopting an entrepreneurial approach in universities', *Journal of Engineering and Technology Management*, **11**(3/4), 273–298.

Hacker, M.E. & Brotherton, P.A. (1998) 'Designing and installing effective performance measurement systems', *IIIE Solutions*, **30**(8), 18–23.

Irwin, D. (2002) 'Strategy mapping in the public sector', *Long Range Planning*, **35**(6), 637–647.

Ittner, C.D. & Larker, D.F. (1998) 'Are non-financial measures leading indicators of financial performance? An analysis of customer satisfaction', *Journal of Accounting Research*, **36**(1), 1–46.

Jencks, C. & Riesman, D. (1968) *The Academic Revolution*. Doubleday: New York.

Johnes, G. & Cave, M. (1994) 'The development of competition among higher education institutions'. In: Bartlett, W., Le Grand, J. & Propper, C. (eds), *Quasi-Markets in the Welfare State*. Sage: Thousand Oaks, CA.

Julnes, P. & Holzer, M. (2001) 'Promoting utilization of performance measures in public organizations: an empirical study of factors affecting adoption and implementation', *Public Administration Review*, **61**(6), 693–708.

Kanter, R.S. & Summers, D.V. (1987) 'Doing well while doing good: dilemmas of performance measurement in nonprofit organization and the need for a multiple-constituency approach'. In: Powell, W.W. (ed.), *The Nonprofit Sector: A Research Handbook*. Yale University Press: New Haven, CT.

Kaplan, R.S. (2001) 'Strategic performance measurement and management in nonprofit organizations', *Nonprofit Management & Leadership*, **11**(3), 354–371.

Kaplan, R.S. & Norton, P.D. (1992) 'The balanced scorecard – measures that drive performance', *Harvard Business Review*, **Jan/Feb**, 71–79.

Kaplan, R.S. & Norton, P.D. (1996) *The Balanced Scorecard: Translating strategy into action*. Harvard Business School Press: Boston.

Kaplan, R.S. & Norton, P.D. (2001) *The Strategy-Focused Organization: How Balanced Scorecard Companies Thrive in the New Business Environment*. Harvard Business School Press: Boston.

Keegan, D.P., Eiler, R.G. & Jones, C.R. (1989) 'Are your performance measures obsolete?', *Management Accounting*, **June**, 45–50.

Kushner, R.J. & Poole, P.P. (1996) 'Exploring structure–effectiveness relationships in nonprofit arts organizations', *Nonprofit Management and Leadership*, **7**(2), 119–136.

Lawrie, G. & Cobbold, I. (2004) 'Third-generation balanced scorecard: evolution of an effective strategic control tool', *International Journal of Productivity and Performance Management*, **53**(7), 611–627.

Lebas, M. & Euske, K. (2005) 'A conceptual and operational delineation of performance'. In: Neely, A. (ed.), *Business Performance Measurement: Theory and Practice*. Cambridge University Press: Cambridge.

Lehn, K. & Makhija, A.K. (1996) 'EVA and MVA: as performance measures and signals for strategic change', *Strategy and Leadership*, **24**(3), 24–31.

Marr, B., Gray, D. & Schiuma, G. (2004) 'Measuring intellectual capital – what, why, and how?'. In: Bourne, M. (ed.), *Handbook of Performance Measurement*. Gee: London.

Maskell, B. (1989) 'Performance measures of world class manufacturing', *Management Accounting*, **4**, 32–33.

McCunn, P. (1998) 'The balanced scorecard: the eleventh commandment', *Management Accounting*, **Dec**, 34–36.

Meekings, A. (1995) 'Unlocking the potential of performance measurement: a guide to practical implementation', *Public Money & Management*, **Oct/Dec**, 1–8.

Melnyk, S.A., Stewart, D.M. & Swink, M. (2004) 'Metrics and performance measurement in operations management: dealing with the metrics maze', *Journal of Operations Management*, **22**(3), 209.

Micheli, P. & Kennerley, M. (2005) 'Performance measurement frameworks in public and private sector', *Production Planning & Control*, **16**(2), 125–134.

Neely, A. (ed.) (2002) *Business Performance Measurement: Theory and Practice*. Cambridge University Press: Cambridge.

Neely, A.D., Mills, J.F., Gregory, M.J. & Platts, K.W. (1995) 'Performance measurement system design – a literature review and research agenda', *International Journal of Operations and Production Management*, **15**(4), 80–116.

Neely, A.D., Mills, J.F., Platts, K.W. & Huw, R. (2000) 'Performance measurement system design: developing and testing a process-based approach', *International Journal of Operations and Production Management*, **20**(10), 1119–1128.

Neely, A., Bourne, M. & Adams, C. (2003) 'Better budgeting or beyond budgeting?', *Measuring Business Excellence*, **7**(3), 22–28.

NIST (2006) 'Malcolm Baldridge National Quality Award criteria', [online] www.quality.nist.gov (accessed 19/7/2006).

Oliver, N. (1993) 'Quality, costs and changing strategies of control in universities in the UK', *Journal of Educational Administration*, **31**(1), 41–47.

Osborne, S.P., Bovaird, T., Martin, S., Tricker, M. & Waterston, P. (1995) 'Performance measurement and accountability in complex public programmes', *Financial Accountability & Management*, **11**(1), 19–34.

Pettigrew, A., Whipp, R. & Rosenfield, R. (1989) 'Competitiveness and the management of strategic change processes'. In: Francis, A. & Tharakan, P.K.M. (eds), *The Competitiveness of European Industry: Country Policies and Company Strategies*. Routledge: London.

Pettigrew, A., Ferlie, E. & McKee, L. (1992) *Shaping Strategic Change*. Sage: Thousand Oaks, CA.

Pike, S. & Ross, G. (2001) 'Measuring and decision support in the knowledge society', The 4th World Congress on Intellectual Capital, Hamilton.

Radnor, Z. & Lovell, B. (2003) 'Defining, justifying and implementing the balanced scorecard in the National Health Service', *International Journal of Medical Marketing*, **3**(2), 174–188.

Santos, S., Belton, V. & Howick, S. (2002) 'Adding value to performance measurement by using system dynamics and multicriteria analysis', *International Journal of Operations and Production Management*, **22**(11), 1246–1272.

Schneiderman, A. (1999) 'Why balanced scorecards fail', *Journal of Strategic Performance Measurement*, Special Edition, pp. 6–11.

Silk, S. (1998) 'Automating the balanced scorecard', *Management Accounting*, **11**(17), 38–44.

Smith, P. (1993) 'Outcome-related performance indicators and organizational control in the public sector', *British Management Journal*, **4**(2), 135–151.

Tapinos, E. (2005) 'Strategic development process: examining the relationship between organizational direction and performance measurement', PhD thesis, Warwick Business School, University of Warwick, UK.

Tapinos, E., Dyson, R.G. & Meadows, M. (2005) 'The impact of performance measurement in strategic/corporate planning', *International Journal of Productivity and Performance Management*, **54**(5/6), 370–384.

Tesco (2006) 'Annual Report 2006', [online] www.tesco.com.

Wang, X. (2002) 'Assessing performance measurement impact: a study of U.S. local governments', *Public Performance & Management Review*, **26**(1), 26–43.

Warwick (2005) 'Mission statement and corporate plan for the period 2003 and 2006', [online] http://www2.warwick.ac.uk/insite/info/gov/corporateplan/ (accessed 13/07/2006).

Warwick (2006) 'Governance. Committee Structure. University of Warwick', [online] http://www2.warwick.ac.uk/insite/info/gov/atoz/structure (accessed 13/07/2006).

Wholey, J. (1999) 'Performance-based management', *Public Productivity & Management Review*, **22**(3), 280–299.

Wilcox, M. & Bourne, M. (2003) 'Predictive performance', *Management Decision*, **41**(8), 806–816.

Yeniyurt, S. (2003) 'A literature review and integrative performance measurement framework for multinational companies', *Marketing Intelligence & Planning*, **21**(3), 134–142.

Yin, R. (1993) *Applications of Case Study Research*, Applied Social Research Methods Series, Vol. 34. Sage: Thousand Oaks, CA.

Chapter 12

A Financial Perspective on Strategic Investments

Robert H. Berry

INTRODUCTION

The relationship between finance specialists and strategists has not always been comfortable. At times financial and strategic perspectives have been seen as contradictory and competitive. On other occasions they have been seen as complementary, with finance offering one among several perspectives on a strategic decision and proving capable of providing valuable concepts and techniques. On still other occasions finance has claimed the territory of strategic decision-making as its own; in an organisation that operates on shareholder value management principles, finance claims to rule!

This chapter is written in the belief that the finance and strategic perspectives are complementary. This belief is based around three ideas: shareholders are only one among several groups of stakeholders; measurement problems are not always best dealt with by expressing everything in money terms; the assumptions underpinning modern finance do not always adequately represent the environment in which strategic decisions are made.

A strategic decision shapes an organisation to face the future. It typically involves a difficult-to-reverse, current commitment of resources with consequences spreading out through time. Irreversibility is often associated with the acquisition of capital assets, perhaps land, buildings or equipment, though assets can be intangible. This chapter therefore emphasises the financial evaluation of an asset acquisition. This process is known in the finance literature as capital investment appraisal or capital budgeting.

Before beginning the discussion of the process of capital budgeting it is important to note that a project which is to be evaluated must already have been identified and, to some extent at least, described. Financial evaluation presupposes, for example, the prior identification of a market to be supplied, a product to be delivered, a machine capable of producing the product and a planned quantity of product to be produced. The financial evaluation may lead to the re-evaluation of any or all of these prior statements, but something must be there before the financial evaluation can start. Finance evaluates alternative projects and guides a choice between them. It should not appear too early in the strategy development process. Project identification is a creative process and creativity is not best served by an insistence that every idea should face a 'value for money' test as soon as it is articulated.

MONEY MEASUREMENT

The finance perspective on an investment decision involves expressing the elements of a decision in money terms. The key questions relate to when cash flows out of an organisation and when it flows in to an organisation. It is important to realise that cash flow and profit are not the same thing. A simple example makes this point clear. If a unit of product is sold in the current period then its price features in a profit calculation whether or not it is a sale for cash or a sale on credit. If it is a credit sale, there is no cash inflow in the current period. The cash inflow occurs when the customer pays, whenever that might be. Given the widespread reporting of profit figures and the apparent concern with profits by analysts and pundits it is reasonable to ask why finance concentrates on cash flow rather than profit. Firstly, an organisation pays its bills and pays interest and dividends in cash not profit. Secondly, accounting profit is too easy to manipulate and misrepresent. In the aftermath of Enron and Worldcom the shortcomings of reported profits are perhaps more obvious today than ever before (Benston & Hartgraves, 2002). Finally, accountants use profit to provide a measure of performance over an arbitrary slice of the life of an organisation or project, and allocations of costs and revenues between time periods can be quite arbitrary. In strategic decision-making and investment appraisal the concern is with performance over the entire economic life of the project, and therefore such allocations are unnecessary.

Unfortunately, a concentration on cash flow does not mean that profit can be ignored. There are two reasons for this: companies are required to produce annual reports based on accounting profit and use of this concept is therefore widespread; tax, which is a cash flow, is generally calculated on the basis of a variant of accounting profit. Table 12.1 is designed to show the computation of a project's net cash flow. It also shows the inter-relationship of profit, tax and cash flow.

The project in question involves the immediate purchase of an asset for cash. Row O of the table shows the cost of the asset, £5000, as a cash outflow, or negative cash flow, appearing in column 0. Operation of the asset in question will generate the pattern of turnover shown in Row A of the table. Turnover is sales revenue whether sales are for cash or on credit. Although sales occur throughout a year, they have been aggregated at each year end. So, for example, the £16 500 of sales made between point in time 0 and point in time 1 are shown as occurring 1 year from now, in column 1. As can be seen, it is anticipated that the project will generate sales in each of 5 years. Row B of the table shows the pattern of cost of goods sold that the project will involve. In manufacturing companies cost of goods sold consists of materials, labour and overhead (manufacturing costs that cannot be directly linked to particular products). Row C shows the difference between turnover and cost of goods sold, or gross profit as it is known. Row D identifies further expenses which must be deducted to calculate profit for the period. These normally include

Table 12.1. Cash Flow Analysis

Item/period	0	1	2	3	4	5	6
A Turnover		20 000	30 000	45 000	40 000	35 000	
B Cost of Goods Sold		−11 000	−16 500	−24 750	−22 000	−19 250	
C Gross Profit		**9000**	**13 500**	**20 250**	**18 000**	**15 750**	
D Expenses		−2000	−3000	−5000	−4500	−3000	
E Operating Profit		**7000**	**10 500**	**15 250**	**13 500**	**12 750**	
F Depreciation		1000	1000	1000	1000	1000	
G Capital Allowances		−1250	−1250	−1250	−1250		
H Taxable Profit		**6750**	**10 250**	**15 000**	**13 250**	**13 750**	
I Tax Paid			−2228	−3383	−4950	−4373	−4538
E Operating Profit		7000	10 500	15 250	13 500	12 750	
F Depreciation		1000	1000	1000	1000	1000	
J Change in Inventory	−4500	−3000	−2000			6000	3500
K Change in Debtors		−1400	−1100	−1300	−400	2200	2000
L Changes in Creditors	500	300				−600	−200
M Operating Cash Flow	**−4000**	**3900**	**8400**	**14 950**	**14 100**	**21 350**	**5300**
M Operating Cash Flow	−4000	−800	4500	11 100	13 800	24 000	5000
N Change in Stock of Cash	−1000					1000	
O Investment	−5000						
I Tax Paid		0	−2228	−3383	−4950	−4373	−4538
P Free Cash Flow	**−14 000**	**3100**	**10 673**	**22 668**	**22 950**	**41 978**	**5763**

marketing, distribution and administrative expenses. Deducting expenses from gross profit produces the operating profit series in Row E.

At this point in this chapter it is assumed that the project under consideration is financed entirely by equity – the company undertaking it can't raise debt finance for it. Were there any relevant debt finance the interest paid would be subtracted from operating profit as part of the process of calculating the tax bill, since interest is typically a tax-deductible expense. The issue of project financing will be dealt with later in this chapter.

The next section of Table 12.1 is used to calculate the additional taxes the company undertaking this project will pay. Row F identifies the amount of depreciation that has already been charged during the calculation of profit. Depreciation deducts the cost of the asset over its useful life as part of the profit calculation. It reflects the fact that the machine is being 'used up' in the production process. Depreciation is already present in cost of goods sold in Table 12.1. The pattern of depreciation which has been deducted from profit has been chosen by the company undertaking the project. If the tax authorities treated this, company-determined, depreciation charge as a tax-deductible expense then they would have ceded to the company the right to determine the pattern of its tax payments. Generally tax authorities don't allow companies this freedom, and require depreciation to be added back to profits before the calculation of the tax bill as is shown in Row F. To compensate, the tax authorities specify a standardised pattern (or patterns) of depreciation which companies can use in the calculation of taxable profit. These standardised patterns vary from country to country. In the UK depreciation acceptable for tax calculation purposes is known as capital allowances. The pattern of allowances can vary with the type of asset acquired and the size of the company undertaking the investment. In Table 12.1, Row G shows capital allowances calculated at 25% of the cost of the asset per year. (This pattern of allowances does not reflect any specific national context.) Row H shows the resulting taxable profit.

To calculate the flow of cash to the tax authorities it is necessary to know the tax rate to be applied and the timing of the tax payment. Again these features of the tax system vary from country to country. Table 12.1 assumes a tax rate of 33% and assumes the tax is actually paid 1 year after the end of the year in which profit is earned. This issue of timing of tax payments is often overlooked in discussions of investment appraisal techniques and can be important.

Now that operating profit has been used to generate the tax element of cash flow it ceases to be relevant to the process of investment appraisal. It can therefore be transformed into operating cash flow. The first step in this transformation involves adding back depreciation to operating profit. As has been indicated, depreciation does not involve cash outflows. The second stage involves stripping the effects of credit sales and credit purchases out of the profit figures. Any increase in credit sales outstanding (known as debtors or receivables) has to be deducted from profit and any decrease added back to profit. Similarly, any increase in credit purchases outstanding (known as creditors or payables) has to be added back to profit and any decrease deducted from profit. It is also necessary to recognise that some materials that were used in making the products sold during a period may not have been bought during that period but may have come from inventory. Therefore, increases in inventory must be deducted from profit and decreases in inventory must be added back to profit. The transformation of operating profit into operating cash flow can be summarised in the following equation:

$$\text{Operating cash flow} = \text{Operating profit} + \text{Depreciation} - \Delta\text{Debtors} - \Delta\text{Inventory} + \Delta\text{Creditors}$$

It should be pointed out that these changes in debtors, inventory and creditors in large part are reversed over the life of a project. The early years of a project may see a build-up of inventory, say, but inventory can be decreased when the project comes to an end. Of course, spoilage may mean that not all investment in inventory can be recovered just as bad debts mean that not all debtors can eventually be turned into cash. Rows E, F, J, K, L and M, in columns 1 to 5, show the build-up of operating cash flow.

The final section of Table 12.1 transforms operating cash flow into what is called free cash flow, the measure of project consequences that finance specialists are interested in. The cost of acquiring the asset and tax are deducted from operating cash flow. One further deduction, which often causes confusion, is also made. Distinguish carefully between cash flow and a stock of cash. (Opening stock of cash plus cash inflow less cash outflow equals closing stock of cash.) A new project often requires the establishment of a stock at cash. This will support transactions, support the seizing of unanticipated opportunities, and protect against unanticipated problems.

Thus some cash has to be taken out of circulation and held in support of the project. This build-up of a stock of cash must be deducted from operating cash flow and any reduction in the stock of cash must be added to operating cash flow. This is shown in Row N. Row P contains the free cash flow series generated by the project being analysed.

It is important to note that free cash flow is defined to be gross of payments to suppliers of finance. Dividend payments have not been deducted. Interest payments would not have been deducted even if the assumption of 100% equity finance had not been made. Obviously, financing costs need to be taken into account when evaluating a project, but these costs are not dealt with as deductions from cash flow. This point will be returned to later in this chapter.

It is also worth noting that the lag in tax payments means that the cash flow consequences of the project can extend beyond the economic operating life of the assets. The lag also introduces the possibility of a negative cash flow as the final element in the cash flow series generated by a project, although other factors, e.g. clean-up operations after open cast mining, can generate the same phenomenon. This has implications for the calculation of some of the summary measures of cash flow series discussed later in the chapter.

So far the discussion has emphasised the distinction between cash flow and profit and the role of the taxation system. There are four other issues to be dealt with before the process of identifying and measuring the cash flow consequences of the decision to undertake a project is complete. The first is simple; consequences follow decisions, so expenditures prior to a decision are not relevant to the cash flow calculation. The classic example is expenditure on market research undertaken prior to the decision to undertake a project finally being taken. These expenditures are a sunk cost, which will not be changed whether the decision is made to undertake the project in question or abandon the idea. In the oft repeated phrase, 'Sunk costs are irrelevant'.

A second issue to be considered is how widely the boundary of the project should be drawn for the purpose of calculating cash flows. The cash flow consequences of a project are best thought of as the difference between two cash flow series, the cash flow the organisation will experience if the project is undertaken and the cash flow the organisation will experience if the project is not undertaken. If, for example, the project involves sale of a product which will compete with another element in the organisation's product mix, then any drop in sales of competing products should be taken into account when calculating the incremental cash flow due to the project. The aim is to capture all cash flow consequences of the project. This issue is discussed further when project interdependencies are considered later in the chapter.

Some cash flow consequences are difficult to identify because they are cash flows that are foregone. These can slip past unnoticed. Suppose that the project under consideration requires warehouse space and that the organisation owns a warehouse which has spare capacity. It is tempting to think of this spare capacity as a free good, but this may not be the case. If there is a rental market for warehouse space then reserving the spare space for the project is equivalent to doing without a cash flow from rental payments. The project cash flow should reflect this loss. Even if there is no current alternative use for the warehouse space, reserving it for the project now means that it won't be available to satisfy any need which arises in the future. If a project makes use of already owned resources it should be charged with the cash flow forgone because they cannot be put to their next best possible use. (This is the economists' concept of opportunity cost.)

The final issue which must be dealt with here is that of inflation. Should cash flows be measured in real terms with inflation stripped out, or in nominal terms with inflation built in? It is possible to carry out a sensible investment appraisal process in either real or nominal terms, but it is most easily done in nominal terms. So, cash flows should be based on prices which will rule in the future not on current prices. Care should be taken not to simplistically assume that all cash flow elements will inflate at the same rate. It is generally unreasonable to assume that product prices, raw material prices and labour costs will all inflate at the same rate.

SUMMARY MEASURES FOR CASH FLOWS

Capital investment appraisal involves examination of the cash flow series generated by a project with the aim of determining whether the project is acceptable or unacceptable, or better or worse than a competing project. A number of ways of summarising cash flow series are available, which may help this examination. They include the payback period, the accounting rate of return, the net present value and the internal rate of return. Evidence on patterns of use of these summary measures can be found in, for example, Graham and Harvey (2001).

In what follows C_0 will represent the cash flow at the beginning of the life of the capital project (usually a negative initial investment) and C_i the cash flow in each following year i. As in Table 12.1, it is assumed that C_i occurs at the end of year i. The cash stream representing a project is thus:

$$C_0, C_1, \ldots, C_i, \ldots, C_n$$

where n is the life of the project in years. Textbooks usually assume that cash flows C_1 to C_n will be positive but this may not always be true and C_n in particular may be negative if the end of the project involves a large tax payment or some kind of clean-up operation (e.g. levelling and restoring the site after open cast mining). To demonstrate the mechanics of summary calculations the data set in Table 12.2 will be used.

Net Present Value

Care was taken when discussing the measurement of cash flow in identifying when a cash flow will occur. The reason is that cash received earlier is more valuable

Table 12.2. Project Cash Flows

Year	0 C_0	1 C_1	2 C_2	3 C_3	4 C_4	5 C_5	6 C_6	7 C_7
Cash flow	−10 000	985	3739	8840	9682	17 096	7485	−622

than cash received later, since it can be invested to earn interest. If money can be lent at 10%, £1 today will be worth £1.10 next year, assuming no inflation. The link between value today (present value) and value next year (future value) is:

$$\text{Present value} \times (1 + r) = \text{Future value}$$

Here r is the interest rate, an opportunity cost of holding cash. The link between value today and value in N years is equally simple:

$$\text{Present value} \times (1 + r)^N = \text{Future value}$$

The act of calculating a future value from a present value and an interest rate is known as compounding. Discounting reverses this process to express future cash flows as present value equivalents:

$$\text{Present value} = \text{Future value}/(1 + r)^N$$

Compounding and discounting allow cash flows that occur at different points in time to be expressed as values at a common point in time. This makes it easier to compare different cash flow series.

Net Present Value (NPV) is a cash flow-based summary measure produced by a discounting exercise. All the cash flows generated during a project's economic life are discounted back to their present values. These present values are then aggregated. The sum is net of the initial investment, which is of course already in present value terms, hence the term net present value. The general formula for NPV is:

$$\text{NPV} = C_0 + C_1/(1 + r) + C_2/(1 + r)^2 + \cdots + C_n/(1 + r)^n$$

If the interest rate is 10% then the NPV of the cash flow data used earlier in Table 12.2 is:

$$\text{NPV} = -10\,000 + 985/1.1 + 3739/(1.1)^2 + 8840/(1.1)^3 + \cdots - 622/(1.1)^7 = 21\,761$$

The decision rule for NPV is to accept any project with a positive NPV and reject all others. A positive NPV means that the project is yielding higher returns than can be obtained by simply lending at the rate of return r. This interpretation suggests that r is a minimum acceptable rate of return to suppliers of capital.

The rate of return r is usually known as the discount rate. Since it has been argued earlier that cash flow series should be in nominal rather than real terms, the discount rate should also include an allowance for inflation. A typical value for r in percentage terms might thus be made up as follows:

$$r\% = \text{Real rate of interest} + \text{Inflation rate}$$

$$= 1 + 3$$

$$= 4\% \text{ say}$$

This addition of real and nominal components is in fact oversimplifying things, but in an acceptable fashion if the inflation rate is low. $(1+r) = (1+i)(1+\text{inf})$, where i is the real rate of interest and inf is the rate of inflation, would be more appropriate. (In fact, r is usually taken to have three components, a real rate of interest, a component equal to the expected level of inflation and a component to allow for the riskiness of the project. Risk will be dealt with later in the chapter.)

NPV is much favoured by mainstream finance textbooks (Brealey, Myers & Allen, 2006). It is cash flow-based, takes all cash flows into account, takes into account the time value of money and, given an appropriate choice of discount rate, takes into account the required rate of return on the part of suppliers of capital. An NPV function is available in Excel. Care should be taken when using this since it assumes that the first cash flow occurs at time period 1 not time period 0. In capital budgeting terms it is best used to calculate the present value of future cash flows. The initial investment value can then be deducted.

Net Terminal Value

A similar measure to NPV, which assesses the value of a project at its termination, is the Net Terminal Value (NTV). Using the previous notation:

$$\text{NTV} = C_0(1+r)^n + C_1(1+r)^{n-l} + \cdots + C_i(1+r)^{n-i} + \cdots + C_n$$

Since $\text{NTV} = \text{NPV}(1+r)^n$, a decision rule to accept any project with a positive NTV would lead to the same decision as an evaluation using NPV.

Internal Rate of Return

The Internal Rate of Return (IRR) is defined as the rate of return that yields a zero NPV in a discounted cash flow calculation. It is the value of r such that:

$$C_0 + C_1/(1+r) + \cdots + C_i/(1+r)^i + \cdots + C_n/(1+r)^n = 0$$

Spreadsheets such as Excel include built-in formulae to allow the calculation of IRR. However, since iterative procedures are involved, care needs to be taken to ensure that the result is sensible. The attraction of IRR is that it yields a rate of return measure that can be interpreted as the highest rate of interest at which the company could afford to finance the project. Hence a decision rule for IRR involves a target rate of interest to be exceeded by the IRR if the project is to be accepted.

IRR is widely used in practice and is often thought to be equivalent to NPV. However, if a project's NPV is not a smoothly declining function of the discount rate, NPV and IRR can generate conflicting recommendations. Conflicts can also arise when comparing two projects. Finally, while a project always has a unique NPV it may not have a unique IRR. Each time there is a sign change in a cash flow series a further solution to the IRR equation comes into existence. While not all of these may make economic sense, some confusion can arise. For the cash stream in Table 12.2 the corresponding IRR is 48.8%.

Despite potential problems, IRR remains popular with practitioners. This may be because it reflects corporate objectives such as growth, or because it is a familiar measure that managers feel they understand, or simply because it is a rate of return rather than a lump sum (Dorfman, 1981).

Fixed Interest Equivalent Rate of Return (FIE)

The popularity of IRR has led to several reformulations designed to remove perceived problems with the measure while retaining its essential characteristics. FIE is one example. In the calculation of IRR it is assumed that any surplus funds generated by the project can be reinvested at a rate of return equal to the IRR. For a project yielding a high return this may be an optimistic assumption, and as a result IRR may be unrealistically high. A more realistic assumption may be that surplus funds can be reinvested and capital raised at the discount rate appropriate to an NPV calculation.

This alternative measure of performance can be obtained in the following way. Calculate the NTV of the investment as if cash flows are borrowed if negative, and invested if positive, using the discount rate that would be used in an NPV calculation. Using the data in Table 12.2 gives a value of £42 407. Then calculate the repayment that would have to be made if funds for the project were borrowed at the discount rate that would be used in an NPV calculation. Again using the data in Table 12.2 gives a value of £20 109. Now find the interest rate that would have to be earned on the borrowed funds to generate the repayment plus the NTV of the investment. For the data in Table 12.2 the FIE is 29.7%.

The Excel function MIRR offers a generalised version of this calculation in that the borrowing and reinvestment rates in the NTV calculation and the rate at which funds can be borrowed do not have to be the same.

FIE is thus a rate of return measure taking account of the time value of money. In general it will give a lower value than IRR. The measure does not receive widespread coverage in the finance literature. It has been presented here because of its common-sense interpretation and widespread availability through the Excel spreadsheet.

Payback Period

The simplest summary measure in common use is the payback period. This is the number of years before the project's initial investment is paid back by the project's later cash flows. For the cash flow stream in Table 12.2 the payback period is 3 years. This is calculated by cumulating project cash flows that occur after the initial investment, until the sum exceeds the initial investment.

The decision rule involves comparing the calculated payback period with some predetermined target period. If the calculated figure is less than the target then the project should be accepted.

There are a number of obvious inadequacies with the payback period as a measure of performance. Firstly, it does not use all the available information, ignoring as it does the cash flows after the payback period. Secondly, it ignores the issue of time value of money for cash flows within the payback period. (The discounted payback rule is a variant designed to remedy this shortcoming.) Finally, there is no indication of how to set the target payback period. Despite these factors, the payback period has its defenders, and surveys indicate that it is in common use in combination with other summary measures. This may be because it is a crude measure of liquidity, and hence useful to firms unwilling to use outside sources of finance. It may also be a reflection of management's perception of the quality of available cash flow data or of the costs of data collection. Finally, there is always the possibility that it is a simple approach to dealing with risk by managers who see cash flows arising further in the future as having greater risk.

Accounting Rates of Return (ARR)

This summary measure, alone among those considered in this paper, is based on accounting profit rather than cash flow. There are innumerable variants of the measure differing only in the way in which the accounting numbers involved are defined. Essentially, the measure is a ratio. The numerator is the average profits of the project after depreciation and taxes, while the denominator is the average book value of the investment. The decision rule is based on some predetermined target value. If the calculated ARR is greater than the target value then the project should be accepted.

Once again this summary measure suffers from a number of problems; arbitrary target value and arbitrary definition of accounting numbers being the major ones. Finance texts treat this measure with little respect.

RISK AND FINANCIAL EVALUATION

When discussing payback period the suggestion was made that managers might ignore cash flows occurring in the more or less distant future because they were seen as too risky to take into account. With that exception, so far in this chapter the idea that future cash flow figures are estimates with probability distributions has been ignored. This omission will now be remedied. Essentially cash flow figures which until now have been implicitly viewed as certain values should be viewed as expected values. There is thus a potentially difficult forecasting task underpinning each one. Here is another gap in the finance approach to investment evaluation. These forecasts are largely taken as given. Who produces them and how they have been produced are questions largely ignored in the finance literature. Furthermore, techniques proposed in the finance literature for exploring risk are largely drawn from the operational research literature.

In the rest of this chapter a distinction is made between a risky situation and an uncertain situation. In a risky situation there is enough information to allow probability distributions to be developed. In an uncertain situation probability distributions are not available. (Certainty is of course a case of degenerate probability distributions; one possible outcome and hence a probability of 1.)

Exploring Risky Cash Flows

Risk analysis as a way of supporting the capital budgeting decision has a long history, being first proposed by Hertz (1964). This approach explicitly recognises risk by assigning probability distributions to factors affecting the various components that are aggregated to make up project cash flow. So, for example, sales revenue in a given year might be represented by the equation

$$\text{Sales revenue} = \text{Sales} \times \text{Price}$$

Here both sales and price would be assigned probability distributions. This would of course result in sales revenue having a probability distribution. The same approach would be applied to the various cost elements, tax flows and changes in working capital generated by a project. Hence cash flow in each time period would appear with a probability distribution. A simulation model in the capital budgeting context may need to recognise both dependencies between variable values at the same point in time and through time. For example, if an investment project involves the establishment of several sales outlets for a product it is unlikely that sales from each outlet will be independent of sales from all other outlets. Nor is it likely that the volume of sales of a product in one period is independent of sales of the product in the preceding period. Recognising and modelling dependencies is far from simple, but the availability of built-in facilities in various computer packages has eased the implementation process. The Excel package and the add-ins Crystal Ball and @Risk are useful tools in this context. Several modern management science texts provide Excel-based treatments of simulation, for example Winston and Albright (2001).

The obvious use that can be made of simulation models is to try out alternative project configurations and operating policies to see how cash flow distributions are affected. The problem of deciding which configuration and policy changes are worthwhile can be solved by extending the simulation activity to produce distributions of the summary statistics discussed earlier. Decision rules can be reformulated in terms of the expected values of summary statistics and perhaps extended to take into account the probability of falling below minimum acceptable levels. Where summary statistics involve a discounting procedure, a common approach is to discount at a risk-free rate to generate the distribution of the summary statistic.

The risk analysis process presents few computational problems given the availability of modern-day computer facilities. On many occasions a spreadsheet environment, with or without an additional simulation package, may suffice. However, the ease with which the mechanics of a simulation exercise can be carried out brings its own dangers. GIGO, or garbage in garbage out, can be a major problem. The basic probability distributions which are combined to give the distributions of cash flows and summary statistics must be specified. Someone must state not only what volume of sales is to be expected in say 3 years' time, but also what probability distribution the volume of sales will follow. An Excel add-in such as @Risk allows the selection of a wide variety of probability distributions, but it is questionable whether there is enough information about the future behaviour of many of the variables involved in a capital budgeting decision to allow a reasoned choice. Experience suggests that specification of best case, worst case and most likely value of a variable is as much as is likely to be available in many circumstances. Therefore, despite the range of distributions which can be specified it is probably unwise to select anything other than a simple triangular distribution in many circumstances.

Despite the inherent problems, a simulation model designed to support a capital budgeting decision is likely to add value in many ways. Its construction will require analysts and managers involved in a project to be explicit about their assumptions. This can encourage discussion and hence increased understanding. Furthermore, experimentation with the model can identify which assumptions are critical and which less so. Experience with the model may also prove a valuable training aid for managers who will be charged with implementing the project.

It is important that when building a simulation model attention should be given to the potential sources of risk as well as to the representation of risk in probability distributions. Data on past sales is likely to present an imperfect guide to future variability. The system which generated that history of sales data comprised the company without the project under consideration, its suppliers, customers and competitors. A major investment project is designed to provoke a response from at least one of these groups; possibly the intention is to change customer behaviour and take a larger share of a target market. However, other system elements may well also respond. Contemporary business policy teaching places considerable emphasis on competitive reaction and project design needs to pay considerable attention to this (Porter, 1980). Implicit in the assertion that a project has a positive NPV is a claim that some aspect of the project is unique to the company and can be protected. If, for example, a project involves the development of a new product, then there must be some barrier preventing competing firms from entering the same market. As soon as competition becomes effective potentially both product price and sales volume will be depressed. Positive NPVs are created in the period before competition becomes effective. If there are no proprietary components in a project specification, nor any entry barriers keeping the competition out, then the project is not going to have a positive NPV. If the cash flow figures and discount rates suggest otherwise then they are wrong. In all probability cash flow distributions and discount rates have not reflected the risk of competitive action.

Risk-Adjusted Discount Rates (RADR) and Certainty Equivalents

Rather than leave the evaluation of risk outside the discounting process, as described in the previous section – where concern with risk enters the analysis after distributions of summary measures have been obtained – it is much more common to discount future cash flows using a risk-adjusted discount rate. The approach is straightforward. The expected value of a future cash flow distribution is discounted using a discount rate that includes an allowance for the riskiness of the future cash flow. A discount rate can now be thought of as being built up from three components:

$$k\% = \text{Real rate of interest} + \text{Expected inflation rate} + \text{Premium for risk}$$

The size of the risk premium can be determined in a variety of different ways. For the moment, it will be assumed that the decision-maker is an owner-manager, and the risk premium is subjectively determined and reflects the individual's evaluation of the seriousness of the degree of risk present.

Using the risk-adjusted discount rate approach the present value of a risky future cash flow X, occurring one period hence, is given by:

$$PV(X) = EV(X)/(1+k)$$

Here EV is the expected value operator and k is the risk-adjusted discount rate.

An alternative to calculating a risk-adjusted discount rate is to find a certain cash amount which the owner-manager views as no more and no less acceptable than the risky cash flow X. This certain cash amount is known as a certainty equivalent. Using the certainty equivalent approach the present value of a risky cash flow X occurring one period hence is given by:

$$PV(X) = CE(X)/(1+i)$$

Here CE is the certainty equivalent operator and i is the risk-free rate.

If the same individual produces both a risk-adjusted discount rate and a certainty equivalent cash flow in a consistent fashion then it must be true that:

$$PV(X) = EV(X)/(1+k) = CE(X)/(1+i)$$

Sometimes it is useful to view $CE(X)$ as $\alpha EV(X)$, where $0 < \alpha < 1$ is normally the case for a risk-averse individual. At other times conceptualising $CE(X)$ as $[EV(X) - RP]$, where RP is a risk premium, normally positive for a risk-averse individual, may be appropriate.

The RADR and certainty equivalent approaches are underpinned by a careful identification of future cash flow distributions, perhaps developed using the simulation approach discussed earlier. An NPV produced from these approaches will typically be lower than that produced by a simulation-based NPV distribution given that the decision-maker whose risk attitudes are being captured by either α or RP is risk-averse.

The inter-relationship of CE and RADR processes can be illustrated analytically by assuming that the future cash flow X under consideration is normally distributed with mean μ and variance σ^2, and that the owner-manager's utility can be represented by (Berry & Dyson, 1980, 1984):

$$U(X) = 1 - \exp(-aX)$$

This form of utility function exhibits constant risk aversion if $a > 0$. As has been said, $CE(X)$ is defined as a certain cash amount $CE(X)$ that is equally as acceptable as the risky cash amount X. In other words, the certain cash amount's utility is equal to the expected utility of the risky cash amount. Expected utility is

$$EV\{U(X)\} = \int \{1 - \exp(-aX)\}.1/(\sigma.\sqrt{2\pi}).\exp\{-(X-\mu)^2/(2\sigma^2)\}.dX$$

$$= 1 - \exp(-a\mu + \frac{1}{2}a^2\sigma^2)$$

Since $U\{CE(X)\} = EV\{U(X)\}$, then by definition $CE(X) = U^{-1}EV\{U(X)\}$. Since $U(X) = 1 - \exp(-aX)$, then

$$U^{-1}(X) = -1/a.\log(1 - X), \text{ for any } X$$

and

$$CE(X) = -1/a.\log\{1 - [1 - \exp(-a\mu + \frac{1}{2}a^2\sigma^2)]\}$$

$$= \mu - \frac{1}{2}a\sigma^2$$

If the cash flow X occurs 1 year ahead, then as has been said, either $CE(X)$ can be discounted at a risk-free rate i, or $EV(X) = \mu$ can be discounted at a risk-adjusted rate k. Therefore

$$CE(X)/(1 + i) = \mu/(1 + k)$$

and

$$1 + k = \mu(1 + i)/CE(X) = \mu(1 + i)/(\mu - \frac{1}{2}a\sigma^2)$$

For a positive value of the utility function parameter a, which implies risk aversion, then for this cash flow the risk-adjusted discount rate k will exceed the risk-free rate i.

The Management Viewpoint

The utility function approach to capturing attitudes to risk presents a number of practical difficulties. As with the simulation approach, it requires the formulation of probability density functions, but additionally it requires the formulation of a utility function. This raises a number of questions; in particular, whose utility function is it? The choice-making individual has been described so far as an owner-manager. This description sidesteps the problem of conflict of interest inherent in large-scale organisations, which are typically characterised by a separation of ownership and control. Managers and owners are therefore better seen as separate groups with potentially different interests. One view is that shareholders are the legitimate owners of the company and that managers are employed as agents. To the extent that contractual arrangements, incentive structures, and capital and product market pressures are effective, managers will act in the interests of shareholders and the issue then is how to take the utility of shareholders into account. However, there are other stakeholder groups in an organisation who can be thought of as having a longer-term commitment to the organisation than shareholders – who can liquidate their involvement by the simple act of selling a share. On this view, managers can reasonably be thought of as having to reflect a wider range of considerations than simply shareholder well-being. In these circumstances the utility functions of managers might be thought of as the appropriate basis for risk evaluation.

The utility function approach, conceptually at least, is applicable to the owner-managed organisation. It might also have applicability to the managers of large organisations. However, while the identification of an owner-manager's utility function might be difficult, it appears feasible. Capturing the utility function of a management team runs into greater problems. Consensus may be difficult to come by!

The risk-adjusted discount rate and certainty equivalent formulae presented in the previous subsection have been shown to be functions of σ^2, the variance of the cash flow distribution. This emphasis on a total risk measure is not a characteristic of shareholders, as will now be shown.

The Shareholders' Viewpoint

It might be thought that if there are possible difficulties in getting consensus among the members of a management team, the difficulties in getting consensus among shareholders will be impossible. For example, according to its 2004 Annual Report and Accounts, Boots plc had 106 762 shareholders as at 31 March 2004. Even if only those with the largest shareholdings are considered significant, 122 shareholders each held over 1 million shares. What are managers supposed to do, survey all shareholders each time there is a major capital budgeting decision to be made? The response of the finance specialist to this problem is to consider what exactly a company can do for its shareholders. Shareholders can maximise utility if the company maximises the purchasing power it makes available to them. The company can achieve this if the share price is maximised. Shareholders can trade shares in the capital market to generate a preferred pattern of cash flow and hence can maximise consumption. A company operating in the interests of its shareholders should therefore maximise its share price (Haley & Schall, 1979).

To understand how this idea of operating in the interests of shareholders might work, assume that the future is characterised by one of several possible states of nature and that a project under consideration generates a different cash flow, one period in the future, for each state of nature. Risk in the project's cash flow therefore stems from a lack of knowledge about which state of nature will occur (Bossaerts & Ødergaard, 2001). Suppose that among the various securities traded in the capital market are a set of digital options, one for each state of nature. The jth digital option will pay its owner £1 if the jth state of nature occurs, but £0 if any other state of nature occurs. Suppose the jth digital option has a current price in the capital market of p_j. Whatever pattern of cash flow the project under consideration generates, a shareholder can duplicate it by buying and selling digital options. The net cash outflow involved in doing so will be $\sum n_j p_j$, where n_j is simply the number of units of the jth digital option traded by a shareholder. If the jth option is bought then $n_j < 0$, while if the jth digital option is sold then $n_j > 0$. The question the management of a company must ask is very simple; can shareholders acquire the future cash flows promised by the project being considered more cheaply by transacting in the market than by the company undertaking the project on their behalf? The key comparison is between the cost of creating a future cash flow pattern by buying and selling securities in the market or by undertaking an investment in land, buildings, plant and equipment, etc. If capital market transactions are cheaper then the capital budgeting proposal cannot be a shareholder wealth-maximising, and hence utility-maximising, decision.

In a very real sense the preceding paragraph encapsulates the finance perspective on decision-making. To act in the interests of shareholders, don't do anything for them that they can do more cheaply themselves!

The mechanics of the process described can, of course, cause problems. Digital options, as described, are hard to find. Nevertheless, the basic idea can be implemented in a variety of ways. The most common approach is to look at the capital market to discover the risk-adjusted discount rate that shareholders would apply to a project. An early approach to this task is Gordon's Growth Model. The basic insight is that the market price of a share is the discounted stream of future dividends. If the problem of forecasting a stream of future dividends is sidestepped by the assumptions that next period's dividend per share is D_1 and that dividends will grow at $g\%$ per annum thereafter, then the current share price P_0 is given by:

$$P_0 = D_1/(k - g)$$

Here, k is the shareholders' required rate of return. Rearranging this equation gives:

$$k = (D_1/P_0) + g$$

The capital budgeting task therefore requires managers to find a quoted company in the same line of business as the project they are considering, calculate the required rate of return using Gordon's Growth Model, and discount project cash flows using that discount rate. If the NPV for the project is positive, then the project generates a higher rate of return than shareholders require for that pattern of cash flows.

While Gordon's Growth Model is still useful under some circumstances, there are more widely used models that attempt to capture shareholders' required rates of return. The most widely used appears to be the Capital Asset Pricing Model or CAPM (Perold, 2004). This stems from a realisation that the risk to which owners of a share are exposed has two components, diversifiable and undiversifiable risk. Undiversifiable risk reflects the economy-wide factors that impinge on all companies. Diversifiable risk stems from factors that are company-specific. In a well-functioning market shareholders will only be compensated for holding undiversifiable risk. This is measured by the beta of a share, which is defined as

$$\text{Beta} = \text{Covariance}(R_j, R_M)/\text{Variance}(R_M)$$

Here R_j is the return on the jth security and R_M is the return on the market portfolio. The expected or required rate of return (in a well-functioning market these two rates coincide) is given by

$$EV(R_j) = i + \beta_j[EV(R_M) - i]$$

Here i is the risk-free rate in the economy. The required rate of return from an investment in a security is equal to the risk-free rate plus an allowance for the riskiness of the security. The allowance for risk is the product of the premium a well-diversified portfolio earns above the risk-free rate and the riskiness of the security relative to that of the market. Beta risk is not the total risk measure that concerns managers. The reason shareholders and managers view risk differently is that shareholders are viewed as having a well-diversified portfolio of investments while managers are less well diversified. A substantial proportion of their cash flow comes from the human capital they have invested in the organisation for which they work.

CAPM supports both a risk-adjusted discount rate and a certainty equivalent approach to discounting. If the decision is whether or not to acquire for C_0 an asset that generates a one-period-ahead cash flow C_1, then on a CAPM basis the NPV in certainty equivalent form is (Berry & Dyson, 1980):

$$\text{NPV} = -C_0 + \frac{\text{EV}(C_1) - \frac{\text{Cov}(C_1 R_M)[\text{EV}(R_M) - i]}{\text{Var}(R_M)}}{1 + i}$$

and a consistently defined risk-adjusted discount rate is given by:

$$1 + k = \frac{(1 + i)}{1 - \left\{ \left[\frac{\text{Cov}(C_1 R_M)}{\text{EV}(C_1)} \right] \frac{[\text{EV}(R_M) - i]}{\text{Var}(R_M)} \right\}}$$

While seldom used in practice, these formulations serve to indicate some little understood implications of CAPM. Firstly, it is possible that the numerator in the expression for $(1 + k)$ can be greater than 1, indicating that a risk-adjusted discount rate can in some circumstances be negative. The expression for $(1 + k)$ also indicates the importance of the cash flow summary statistic $\text{Cov}(C_1 R_M)/\text{EV}(C_1)$. Any two cash flows with this measure in common justify the same discount rate. It does not matter if the cash flow has a positive or negative expected value. The key issue is the ratio of the expected value of the cash flow to the covariance of the cash flow with the return on the market portfolio.

The emphasis on creating value for shareholders is central to the finance perspective on project evaluation, or indeed on any decision-making or control process going on in a company. Value is interpreted very specifically in terms of the price that would hold if a project's cash flow stream could be traded separately in the capital market. The shareholder perspective is therefore underpinned by a view of capital markets as always producing prices that appropriately reflect cash flows streams' characteristics. The capital market is viewed as being efficient, that is to say prices quickly and accurately reflect all relevant information. To the extent that capital markets are efficient, then pricing models such as CAPM capture meaningful information about shareholders' required rates of return. However, inefficiency in the sense of slow adjustment to the impact of new information, or persistent misinterpretation of information, or lack of access to information, will make market prices uninformative as far as shareholders' required rates of return are concerned. Managing for shareholder value then becomes much more of an art than the science that finance texts suggest it can be. Shareholder value-maximising managers must act in what they believe are the best interests of shareholders without access to the information about shareholder preferences which well-functioning capital markets can generate. Finance theory and financial models such as CAPM are, under these circumstances, perhaps better thought of as suggestive rather than prescriptive.

CAPM: A Practical Approach

As has been said, the formulae presented in the previous subsection are not in widespread use. It is more usual to make use of CAPM in the form

$$\text{EV}(R_j) = i + \beta_j[\text{EV}(R_M) - i]$$

Here $\text{EV}(R_j)$ is the required rate of return for a security of a given risk and can serve directly as a required rate of return, k, on a project. The first step in calculating a suitable discount rate for a project is to find an existing quoted company in the same line of business as the project. The beta of a share in this quoted company can be found using regression analysis. Typically, 60 monthly observations are used in a regression of return on the share against return on the market portfolio. The slope coefficient in this regression is an estimate of beta. Often regressions are estimated for the shares of several similar companies and the resulting betas are averaged. Company beta estimates are widely published in many economies. In the UK, the London Business School's quarterly *Risk Measurement Service* is a popular source. Therefore, regression analysis is normally an outsourced element of the capital budgeting process. The beta estimate, together with estimates for the market risk premium and the risk-free rate, allow calculation of a rate of return required by shareholders for an investment in that type of business. This can serve as the project discount rate.

The choice of proxies for the risk-free rate and for the market risk premium varies between practitioners. The risk-free rate is typically based on the return offered by an investment in securities issued by government, but some prefer to use the rate offered by a short-term security, while others prefer the rate offered by a longer-term security. There is even more debate about the size of the market risk premium. The debate is, of course, over what it will be. Many practitioners argue that historic averages overestimate the likely future market risk premium (Ogier, Rugman & Spicer, 2004).

Alternatives to CAPM

As has been said, the use of CAPM as an approach to estimating the rate of return a shareholder would require from a project is widespread. However, the validity of this approach is increasingly subject to academic challenge and alternative models of the determination of the rate of return required by shareholders are available (Fama & French, 2004). A recurring theme in the finance literature has been the discovery of empirical evidence which contradicts CAPM. At the present time the contrary empirical evidence produced by Fama and French is most widely cited. Their basic conclusion is that beta does not explain the spread of rates of return observed in the market, and that a combination of company size and the ratio of a company's book to market value does better at this task.

Less is heard these days of the Arbitrage Pricing Model (APM) (Ross, 1976). While theoretically convincing, its lack of empirical content has prevented widespread adoption of this model. Put simply, this model asserts that there can be more types of non-diversifiable risk than the single type, market-related risk, used in the CAPM. However, the theory underpinning the APM does not specify either the number of sources of non-diversifiable risk or their names. Empirical studies are therefore typically based around a researcher's prior view of important risk factors, or on a factor analysis exercise.

FINANCING A PROJECT

So far the assumption has been made that project financing will come from shareholders, either from cash retained in the firm or from a new equity issue. There is, however, another possible source of finance, the bond market. Companies can borrow. Because interest on company borrowing is tax-deductible, the potential cheapness of debt financing should be considered when evaluating a project. The key question is how much additional debt financing a project will make possible. This will depend on the stability of the project's cash flows and the marketability of the assets involved in the project if, for whatever reason, the project has to be abandoned.

A simple model of the impact of debt financing on the value of a project, the Adjusted Present Value (APV) model, is

$$V_L = V_U + TD$$

Here V_U is the value the project will have to shareholders if it is 100% equity financed, and V_L is the value the project will have if the debt financing it makes available is used. D is the market value of the debt raised and T is the corporate tax rate. The steps to be taken in the adjusted present value approach are straightforward, value the project as if it were to be 100% equity financed and add an amount to reflect the tax deductibility of interest payments. V_U is calculated as discussed in earlier sections of this chapter, by discounting free cash flow at the shareholders' required rate of return (Luehrman, 1997).

An equivalent approach, the Weighted Average Cost of Capital (WACC) model, also discounts free cash flow but reflects the tax deductibility of interest in a revised discount rate. The WACC discount rate is

$$\text{WACC} = k_E \frac{E}{V_L} + k_D (1 - T) \frac{D}{V_L}$$

Here E is the market value of equity and D is the market value of debt. By definition, $V_L = E + D$. k_E is the shareholders' required rate of return given the presence of debt in the capital structure of the project, and k_D is the required rate of return to suppliers of debt finance. As before, T is the corporate tax rate (Ross, Westerfield & Jaffe, 2005).

In the APV approach free cash flow is discounted at the shareholders' required rate of return on the assumption that there is no debt in the capital structure of the project. If this rate is designated r, then k_E used in the WACC formula will be greater than r. A simple argument to support this claim is that interest on debt is a fixed charge against a project's cash flow. The residual cash flow going to equity thus becomes more risky and shareholders ask for a higher rate of return to compensate for this higher risk. It is important to distinguish between the two related measures, the shareholders' required rate of return when the project is 100% equity financed (the ungeared cost of equity) and the shareholders' required rate of return when there is debt in the project's capital structure (the geared cost of equity).

When discussing the practical application of CAPM in capital budgeting it was pointed out that an estimate of a project's beta could be obtained by discovering the beta of a company, or companies, in the same line of business. The presence of a tax benefit to debt complicates this process. It is unlikely that the companies chosen as being in the same line of business as the project under consideration will be 100% equity financed. Therefore, the rate of return required by their shareholders will reflect not just the riskiness of the line of business but also the risk generated by debt financing. The beta calculated from a regression of returns on a share against returns on the market portfolio will therefore be a geared beta. As it stands, this is of little use. For the APV approach the ungeared cost of equity that can be derived from an ungeared beta is required. For the WACC calculation a geared cost of equity is required, but the cost of equity must reflect the gearing chosen for the project not the gearing of the comparator company or companies. The beta that results from the regression analysis needs to be ungeared to produce the cost of equity required for the APV calculation. To produce a shareholders' required rate of return for the WACC calculation it must be ungeared and then regeared to reflect the project's capital structure.

The relationship between geared and ungeared betas is

$$\beta_E = \beta_U + (1 - T)(\beta_U - \beta_D)\frac{D}{E}$$

Here β_E is the geared equity beta, β_U is the ungeared equity beta and β_D is the debt beta (debt too can be risky). T, E and D are the corporate tax rate and the market values of equity and debt. This formula allows an ungeared beta to be calculated from a geared beta and the debt to equity ratio that reflects that gearing. The formula is often simplified by the assumption that debt is riskless, i.e. $\beta_D = 0$. Once an ungeared beta has been calculated, an ungeared required rate of return to equity can be calculated for use in an APV calculation. Also, the ungeared beta can be regeared to a level consistent with a desired capital structure and a geared required rate of return to equity produced for use in a WACC calculation (Ross, Westerfield & Jaffe, 2005).

The basic APV model, with which the WACC model is generally consistent, has an alarming implication; project value increases until the project is 100% debt financed! Since the APV model is also a model of the value of a company with debt in its capital structure, the model suggests that most companies should adopt – or have adopted – very high levels of debt. Since high levels of debt are relatively uncommon, something must be wrong with the model. There are two obvious shortcomings. Firstly, personal taxes may act to reduce the benefit of corporate tax deductibility that shareholders gain. Secondly, financial distress becomes more likely as borrowing levels rise, thus offsetting any tax benefit to debt once debt reaches a certain level. Therefore, the APV and WACC models overstate the tax benefit to debt. If it is thought that there is effectively no tax benefit to debt, then the arguments presented in this section can be ignored. Betas do not have to be ungeared, there is no benefit due to tax deductibility of interest and shareholders' required rate of return is unaffected by a project's financing mix. The size of the tax benefit to debt is widely debated (Ogier, Rugman & Spicer, 2004).

REAL OPTIONS

There is a curious contradiction between the idea of managers as strategic thinkers innovating and redesigning an organisation to face the future and the idea of managers implicit in the capital budgeting process described in this chapter. The issue is not the question of whether or not managers operate in the interests of shareholders. Agents can innovate on behalf of their principals just as easily as they can innovate on their own behalf. Rather, the issue is whether managers innovate and respond to changed circumstances or not.

The capital budgeting procedures discussed so far are based around expected cash flows where expectations are formed when a project is conceived. But why has this project come into being? Perhaps past expectations have not been met and a response is required, or because future expectations are unsatisfactory and pre-emptive action needs to be taken. Given that managers are innovating and responding in creating the idea of a project, why does project evaluation not acknowledge their ability to intervene if a project goes off the rails? The expected cash flows are an average of the consequences of future opportunities and threats, but faced with an opportunity innovative managers will seize it, and faced with a threat innovating managers will at very least minimise adverse consequences.

The NPV calculations discussed so far are best thought of as giving the value of the project if managers will have no freedom of action once a project has been initiated. If there is some freedom of action, if managers have the right but not the obligation to intervene during the course of a project, then an NPV calculation underestimates the value of the project. The added value that can be created by managerial intervention needs to be taken into account.

A 'right but not an obligation' is the definition of an option. Financial options are traded securities giving rights but not obligations. A call option is a right to buy a specified underlying asset and a put option is a right to sell a specified underlying asset. An option contract also specifies the period of time over which, or the point in time at which, the option (right to do something) can be exercised. If an option is American then exercise is allowed on or before a particular date. If an option is European then exercise is allowed only on a particular date. Exercise of an option is generally not free since an exercise price has to be paid for the underlying asset. A call option will not of course be exercised unless the value of the underlying asset exceeds the exercise price, while a put option will not be exercised if the price of the underlying asset does not exceed the exercise price.

The Black–Scholes model calculates the value of a European call option on an underlying asset whose price follows geometric Brownian motion. Suffice to say this is an acceptable model for the price path of a quoted share through time. The Black–Scholes value of a European option to buy a share is a function of five parameters, the current price of the share, the remaining life of the option, the exercise price of the option, the risk-free rate of interest and the volatility of the underlying asset. Volatility is the annualised standard deviation of the continuously compounded rate of return the asset earns.

The basic idea in real options analysis is that managerial flexibility can be thought of as the possession of options and these options can be valued in the same way that financial options can be valued. Thus the options to expand a project, or to contract a project, or to abandon a project are candidates for valuation. Project deferral can also be thought of as an option; it is rarely the case that a project must be begun now or forfeited. Projects as they are originally conceived may contain options, but they can also be redesigned to create them. A machine can be designed to use one type of raw material or several. Thus machine design can create the option to switch between raw material types and thus offer protection against future material shortages and price rises (Amram & Kulatilaka, 1999).

The real option approach to investment appraisal recognises that commitment to a project is not a once-and-for-all decision. A project is viewed as a sequence of decision points at which options appear, and are either exercised or left to expire unexercised. The option approach therefore has similarities to Rosenhead's use of the concept of robustness (Rosenhead, Elton & Gupta, 1972). Rosenhead's advocacy of making robust decisions translates into a recommendation to keep options open. There is, however, a major difference. Rosenhead analyses an uncertain world where insufficient knowledge is available to allow forecasts of probability distributions. Option theory works in a risky world where good knowledge of probability distributions is available. As a consequence of this distinction, Rosenhead makes no attempt to place a money value on robustness whereas the real options approach aims to calculate values which can be added to a project's basic NPV. (The issue of flexibility, robustness and real options is the subject of Chapter 13.)

There is a case for arguing that the real options approach is over-ambitious (Triantis, 2005). While the Black–Scholes model is unlikely to be the valuation model of choice in a real options application, a similar set of inputs to that required by the Black–Scholes model is likely to be required. While numbers are often produced to support a real options application, the GIGO problem referred to earlier in this chapter may be relevant here also. The Black–Scholes prices for options to buy or sell shares can be compared to the prices at which shares actually trade and the appropriateness of the Black–Scholes model for the task of pricing options on shares therefore tested. Very few real option applications allow a similar testing of the validity of the pricing mechanism being used. The calculation produces a numerical output, but what interpretation can be placed on the number? If the shareholder value maximisation perspective is at the heart of the financial evaluation, then the option value should replicate the price at which the option would trade in a well-functioning capital market. In other words, the option value should be the price of a 100% equity financed firm which has only one asset, the option in question. Whether or not a calculated real option price approximates to a market base price is more often than not an open question.

There is a growing sense among some academics and practitioners that the valuation aspect of the real options approach needs to be played down. Creation and recognition of options should be pursued, but the calculated values need to be treated with some caution.

PROJECT INTERDEPENDENCIES

The financial evaluation process requires the identification of a project's incremental cash flow. It is generally likely that acceptance of a project will have an impact on a company's existing activities and the cash flow consequences of this impact need to be identified as part of the project's incremental cash flow. This can be difficult. For example, if a new warehouse is added to an existing production and distribution system, the sources of supply to various markets are likely to change. The change in product flows will change the costs of transportation and these may be difficult to estimate without a computer model of the entire distribution system.

Acceptance of a project may also have implications for the cash flows of other projects being considered. The simplest example of this type of interdependency is the case of two mutually exclusive projects. In these circumstances either the NPV of the difference in cash flow between the two projects must be calculated, or the NPVs of both projects must be calculated and compared. Mutually exclusive projects can be thought of as the most extreme example of projects competing for the use of scarce resources. Skilled manpower may be in short supply, forcing a choice between projects or at very least a reduction in the number of positive NPV projects which can be simultaneously accepted. In these circumstances the NPVs of different combinations of projects must be examined to see which combination makes best use of the scarce resource. With a small number of projects, combinations can be relatively easily generated and evaluated. However, as the number of individual projects increases, or additional constraints appear, then use of a standard optimisation approach such as mixed integer programming may become necessary. In the single constraint case a shortcut method might be to rank each project according to NPV per unit of scarce resource used and to accept projects according to their ranking on this measure. While this is a simple approach, because of the indivisibility of projects it does not guarantee an optimal use of the scarce resource. When there are multiple resource constraints, simple ranking methods are inappropriate.

Capital Rationing

Capital rationing, a limit on the amount of capital available for investment, is often thought to be a constraint on the set of investment projects that can be undertaken. As with manpower rationing the implication for project selection is that simple accept/reject decisions cannot be made on individual project proposals. A simple ranking process, or the use of a mathematical programming approach, are again possible extensions to the project selection process. The use of linear programming for capital rationing was proposed by Wiengartner (1963), and an early application in a practical situation is due to Chambers (1967). These mathematical programming models are typically multi-time period models with constraints applying in each year. Integer programming is of course preferable with indivisible projects. A solution to a linear or integer programming model identifies the set of projects that maximises the NPV or NTV subject to the various constraints imposed. There are of course alternatives to mathematical programming approaches; simulation of project combinations selected using simple heuristics and a genetic algorithm, are two among many possibilities.

It is often argued that capital rationing constraints are illusory in the sense that capital for good projects is always available through the financial markets. Certainly there is usually no reason why capital constraints should be hard in the sense that they cannot be violated under any circumstances. Mathematical programming models need not be rejected on this basis, however, and can be an effective tool for exploring the consequences of different levels of availability of capital. Capital rationing can also serve as an implicit recognition that there is in fact another constraint, such as a shortage of skilled project managers, at work.

Taxation-Induced Interdependencies

Despite the recognition of potential interdependencies between projects and the existing activities of the companies undertaking them, the standard financial evaluation approach still emphasises analysis of individual projects. A project is seen as good or bad no matter what other projects might also be under consideration. The issue of interactions is coped with by broadening the definition of a project so that all economically dependent opportunities are bundled into a single project.

However, the workings of national tax systems can render this approach invalid. Two common elements of national tax systems will be discussed here, capital allowances (also discussed earlier in this chapter) and multiple tax rates. In earlier sections of this chapter it was assumed that there was a single corporate tax rate. In fact, many countries vary the rate of corporate tax according to the level of profit a company earns. For example in the UK, for the financial year 2006 companies with profits less than £300 000 pay tax at the small companies rate of 19%. Companies with profits in excess of £1 500 000 pay tax at the full rate of 30%. Companies with profits in between these two limits pay tax at the full rate reduced by what is called marginal relief. Again in the UK for the financial year 2006 capital allowances on plant and machinery are available at a rate of 25% per annum on a reducing balance basis. However, for certain classes of environmentally beneficial technology 100% of the cost of the asset can be deducted from profit for tax purposes in the year the asset is acquired.

In any country the system of capital allowances and corporate tax rates is liable to be changed periodically, becoming an additional source of variability in cash flow projections. For example in the UK, prior to April 1984, all capital investment in plant or machinery, as opposed to investment in environmentally beneficial technology, attracted the 100% initial allowance.

The simplest way to demonstrate the complications introduced by the tax system is to imagine a company which next year expects a profit of £1.2 million. On the assumption that tax rates will be unchanged next year, the company expects to be paying tax at less than the 30% rate. Suppose the company can undertake two investment projects, each of which will add £250 000 to next year's taxable profit. An evaluation of either project will reasonably use a rate less than 30% to calculate the after-tax profit and hence cash flow. However, if both projects are positive NPV projects, and both are undertaken, then aggregate profit next year will be £1.7 million and £200 000 of profit will be taxed at the higher rate of 30%. The relevant tax rate which a company will face cannot be determined until a decision has been made as to which projects to undertake. But, to calculate each project's after-tax cash flow the tax rate must be known! The problem is that the tax system has created an interaction between projects.

Berry and Dyson (1979, 1997) showed that the capital allowance system is also a possible cause of interdependencies between proposed projects, and between ongoing activities and proposed projects. These possibilities are illustrated in the following simplified example. Consider a firm with cash flows from ongoing activities, and with two projects, A and B, under consideration. These cash streams are shown in Panel 1 of Table 12.3. It is assumed that tax is paid on cash flow rather than profit, that cash flow is taxed at a rate of 30% and that there is no lag in tax payment. A 100% initial capital allowance is also assumed to be a feature of the tax system (to make the interaction effect more obvious). If capital allowances cannot be fully set against profit as soon as they become available, then any remainder is carried forward until it can be used to reduce the tax bill on future profit. It must be emphasised at this point that the presence of tax-induced interdependencies is a real-world phenomenon, not one artificially created by these simplifying assumptions.

If projects A and B are evaluated independently, using a discount rate of 10%, then NPV(A) is £75.5 and NPV(B) is −£2.9. This evaluation takes tax into account but treats each project as a separate entity, separate from other projects but also from the firm considering undertaking it. These calculations are not shown in Table 12.3, but can easily be duplicated by setting the cash flows from ongoing activities to zero in Panels 3 and 4 and by allocating all of A's capital allowances to period 1 and all of B's capital allowances to period 2. Discounting of the resulting after-tax cash flows utilises the 10% rate. Using the normal decision rule project A should be accepted and project B rejected.

Panel 2 of Table 12.3 shows the NPV of the firm over the 2-year time horizon if neither project A nor project B is accepted. Panel 3 shows what happens when project A is added to the firm. The capital allowances from project A shield the time period 0 cash flow from ongoing activities from tax. The remaining £60 of capital allowances are carried forward and used to reduce the tax bill in period 1. Since part of the reduction in the tax bill occurs earlier than if the project is considered in isolation, the incremental NPV created by project A, £76, given by NPV(ongoing activities + A) less NPV(ongoing activities), is higher than for project A when it is considered in isolation. Panel 4 shows a similar analysis for project B. Its capital allowances shield cash flow from ongoing activities from tax in periods 0 and 1. The remaining capital allowances reduce tax in period 2. The incremental NPV of project B is however still negative at −£1.36. The possibility of tax-induced interactions between a project and the company's cash flows from ongoing activities should now be clear. The projects' capital allowances can be used to reduce tax bills on profits earned elsewhere in the company.

Panel 5 looks at the situation if both projects A and B are accepted. The key point to note is that allowances generated by project B can be used to reduce the tax bill created by the period 1 cash flow of project A. As a result, the tax benefits of the capital allowances generated by project B are taken earlier than if project A is not accepted. Because of the time value of money, the reduction in the tax bill becomes more valuable the earlier it occurs. The incremental NPV of project B can now be re-estimated. It is the difference between NPV(ongoing activities plus A plus B) less NPV(ongoing activities plus A). This is £0.83. Project B, which has a negative

Table 12.3. The Impact of Project Interdependencies

Panel 1 – Basic Data			
Tax rate	0.3		
Discount rate	0.1		
	0	1	2
Ongoing activities	20	20	20
Project A	−80	210	0
Project B	−150	0	190

Panel 2 – Ongoing Activities			
	0	1	2
Ongoing activities	20	20	20
Tax	−6	−6	−6
After-tax cash flow	14	14	14
NPV	38.29752		

Panel 3 – Ongoing Activities plus Project A			
	0	1	2
Ongoing activities	20	20	20
Project A	−80	210	0
Capital allowances	20	60	
Taxable cash flow	−80	170	20
Tax		−51	−6
After-tax cash flow	−60	179	14
NPV	114.2975		
Incremental NPV	76		

Panel 4 – Ongoing Activities plus Project B			
	0	1	2
Ongoing activities	20	20	20
Project B	−150	0	190
Capital allowances	20	20	110
Taxable cash flow	−150	0	100
Tax		0	−30
After-tax cash flow	−130	20	180
NPV	36.94215		
Incremental NPV	−1.35537		

Panel 5 – Ongoing Activities plus Projects A and B			
	0	1	2
Ongoing activities	20	20	20
Projects A and B	−230	210	190
Capital allowances	20	210	
Taxable cash flow	−230	20	210
Tax		−6	−63
After-tax cash flow	−210	224	147
NPV	115.124		

Incremental NPV of B = 0.826446.

NPV when considered on its own, creates value when taken on in combination with project A. Both projects A and B should be accepted!

This analysis clearly demonstrates the interdependencies between proposed projects and between projects and ongoing activities that the workings of the tax system can bring about. Consideration should therefore be given during financial appraisal of projects to the possibility of project combinations as well as individual projects. There is of course a problem. If there are N projects then 2^{N-1} combinations must be generated and evaluated. Berry and Dyson (1979, 1997) show how various aspects of the UK tax system can be incorporated into a mathematical programming model for project selection. Combination generation, evaluation and selection of the best combination are dealt with by the mathematical programming model. Berry and Smith (1993) show that a genetic algorithm is also capable of selecting an optimal combination of projects.

Correlations

When future cash flows are risky, correlations between projects' cash flows are apparently another source of project interactions. It is conceivable that two risky cash flow streams can combine to produce a riskless cash flow stream for the project combination. Perhaps surprisingly, from the perspective of shareholder value maximisation this may be irrelevant. A well-diversified shareholder is concerned only with non-diversifiable risk, which within the CAPM framework is represented by beta. The reduction in total risk possibly generated by combining projects is irrelevant to them. However, correlations between cash flows can be important if a project appraisal is being carried out in a stakeholder value framework. The reduction of risk is beneficial to managers and employees because it represents a reduced risk of corporate failure. As was said earlier, managers and employees are concerned with total risk not simply that part which cannot be diversified away. Of course, this view will also be shared by a shareholder who is unable to hold a well-diversified portfolio.

FINANCIAL APPRAISAL AND STRATEGIC EVALUATION

The financial appraisal of a strategic initiative from a shareholder perspective involves representing the initiative as a cash flow stream and then computing the summary measure NPV. The riskiness of the future cash flows can be understood with the help of risk analysis, and scenario planning. These cash flows are then transformed into their anticipated impact on the company's share price through risk-adjusted discounting, using say the capital asset pricing model and real option theory.

The shareholder value approach would suggest that appropriate financial appraisal is sufficient, and the sole criterion of acceptance of a strategic initiative should be the enhancement of shareholder value. This position can be criticised on three grounds, however. Firstly, even if it is accepted that the shareholders are the only relevant group of stakeholders, it may not be sensible to attempt to capture all aspects of a strategic initiative in a financial appraisal. Some factors may be unquantifiable, others difficult to quantify, and even when quantified not easily translated into cash flows. The shareholder value approach does not argue that significant features of a project which cannot be expressed in cash terms should be ignored. Rather, it asks that their market value consequences should be considered in whatever way is best. Secondly, a potential problem with the finance perspective is the possibility that the capital market exhibits inefficiency. In this case, proxies for shareholder value must replace the share price in the decision-making process. Finally, a multiple stakeholder perspective would inevitably bring concerns other than stock market value implications into consideration. The widely made assertion that a company run in the interests of its shareholders will automatically be run in the interests of all stakeholder groups is unproven at best. Either because multiple stakeholder groups are being taken into consideration, or because translation of all significant dimensions of a project into cash flows is considered undesirable or infeasible, a strategic initiative needs to be evaluated against a set of multiple objectives.

A long-standing approach is via gap analysis. This involves specifying a desired future position for a company as a consequence of its objectives, and comparing the likely position of the company if no new strategic development takes place – the base case. The task is then to identify actions which will remove any gaps between targets and base case. Of course, the investigation of strategic possibilities may lead to revision of targets rather than the immediate identification of courses of action. This rational planning approach has much in common with the share-holder value maximisation approach. They differ only in the sense that multiple objectives are the norm in gap analysis. While there are questions about the effectiveness of this approach, and about whether it is ever more than a post hoc way of rationalising what has been done, it informs much of modern performance measurement literature. The balanced scorecard approach to performance measurement, for example, typically uses four classes of objectives/measures corresponding to a financial perspective, a customer perspective, an internal business perspective and an innovation and learning perspective.

To evaluate strategic initiatives, gap analysis needs to be extended in two directions. Firstly, the impact of any new initiative on the measures must be evaluated and displayed. Secondly, risk or uncertainty, whichever seems the most appropriate characterisation of the company's circumstances, needs to be taken into account. If the situation can be reasonably characterised as risky then the concepts of risk-adjusted discount rates and certainty equivalents are available for use. If the situation is uncertain then scenario planning and robustness analysis are at hand. A robust strategy is one which is predicted to close the gaps under as many scenarios as possible.

CONCLUSION

This chapter has provided an overview of financial investment appraisal. A variety of approaches which can contribute to the process have been discussed, and the sources of difference between them emphasised. One question remains to be answered: how best to put the component parts of an appraisal together in practice?

Current financial orthodoxy combines a stochastic simulation to generate cash flow distributions, the use of CAPM-generated risk-adjusted discount rates, and a supplementary real options analysis. The danger with this approach is the possibility that it encourages spurious precision in estimates. Managers and analysts may force uncertainty into a risk framework simply to allow the evaluation process to operate. While largely ignored in finance practice, scenarios and robustness analysis may well be a more appropriate approach in many circumstances. Nor should the underlying economic rationale of an investment project be ignored. Before any simulation model, or discounting, or option evaluation takes place, a simple question should be asked, 'If we can undertake this project, then why can't, indeed why hasn't, the competition?' If there is no good answer to that question, then the project is unlikely to be worth undertaking.

Perhaps this point is best made by recounting the story of a heavily disguised consultancy project. Throughout the developed world local government bodies collect domestic refuse and dispose of it. One such local authority in one region of one country noticed that the price for waste paper suitable for recycling at local paper mills was high. A project proposal was developed which involved asking households to keep waste paper separate from other domestic refuse, and purchasing vehicles to be used to collect the waste paper and deliver it to local paper mills. A sophisticated simulation model was developed to ensure that operating procedures would keep transportation costs, etc. to a minimum. Considerable thought was given to the risk that volumes of waste paper would vary. Even more thought was given to the choice of an appropriate risk-adjusted discount rate. In the event local authority staff concluded they had a positive NPV project, but asked a consultant to check the financial logic and details of the computation. The computation was never checked. Simple questions were asked instead. How much waste paper do the local mills need? How many local authorities of similar size are close to the paper mills? The problem with the analysis rapidly became clear. No account had been taken of the possibility that competition to supply waste paper from other local authorities might appear, and there was in fact no reason to believe it would not appear very quickly indeed. Faced with an increased supply of waste paper local mills would drop their prices and local authority revenue would decline.

Hopefully the message is clear. If there is no reason why a project cannot be quickly duplicated by the competition then the project is not a positive NPV project. Only when there are barriers that can delay or prevent competitive action is there a possibility that the project has a positive NPV. The financial perspective on strategy is perhaps best thought of as a reflection in cash flow terms, where possible, of the answers to some very basic questions. In that sense finance and strategy are mutually supportive, not competitive.

REFERENCES

Amram, M. & Kulatilaka, N. (1999) *Real Options: Managing Strategic Investments in an Uncertain World*. HBS Press.

Benston, G. & Hartgraves, A.L. (2002) 'Enron: what happened and what we can learn from it', *Journal of Accounting and Public Policy*, **21**, 105–127.

Berry, R.H. & Dyson, R.G. (1979) 'A mathematical programming approach to taxation induced interdependencies in investment appraisal', *Journal of Business Finance and Accounting*, **6**, 425–442.

Berry, R.H. & Dyson, R.G. (1980) 'On the negative risk premium for risk adjusted discount rates', *Journal of Business Finance and Accounting*, **7**, 427–436.

Berry, R.H. & Dyson, R.G. (1984) 'On the negative risk premium for risk adjusted discount rates: reply and extension', *Journal of Business Finance and Accounting*, **11**, 257–268.

Berry, R.H. & Dyson, R.G. (1997) 'Tax induced project interactions'. In: Lapsey, I. & Wilson, R. (eds), *Explorations in Financial Control*. ITB Press.

Berry, R.H. & Smith, G. (1993) 'Using a genetic algorithm to investigate taxation induced interactions in capital budgeting'. In: Albrecht, R.F., Reeves, C.R. & Steele, N.C. (eds), *Artificial Neural Nets and Genetic Algorithms*. Springer-Verlag: Berlin.

Bossaerts, P.L. & Ødegaard, B.A. (2001) *Lectures on Corporate Finance*. World Scientific: Singapore.

Brealey, R.A., Myers, S.C. & Allen, F. (2006) *Principles of Corporate Finance*, 7th edn. McGraw-Hill Irwin: New York.

Chambers, D.J. (1967) 'Programming the allocation of funds subject to restrictions on reported results', *Operational Research Quarterly*, **18**, 407–432.

Dorfman, R. (1981) 'The meaning of internal rates of return', *Journal of Finance*, **36**, 1011–1021.

Fama, E.F. & French, K.R. (2004) 'The capital asset pricing model: theory and evidence', *Journal of Economic Perspectives*, **18**, 25–46.

Graham, J.R. & Harvey, C.R. (2001) 'The theory and practice of corporate finance: evidence from the field', *Journal of Financial Economics*, **60**, 187–243.

Haley, C.W. & Schall, L.D. (1979) *The Theory of Financial Decisions*. McGraw-Hill: New York.

Hertz, D.B. (1964) 'Risk analysis in capital investment', *Harvard Business Review*, **42**, 95–106.

Luehrman, T.A. (1997) 'Using APV: a better tool for valuing operations', *Harvard Business Review*, **75**, 145–154.

Ogier, T., Rugman, J. & Spicer, L. (2004) *The Real Cost of Capital*. FT Prentice-Hall: New Jersey.

Perold, A.F. (2004) 'The capital asset pricing model', *Journal of Economic Perspectives*, **18**, 3–24.

Porter, M.E. (1980) *Competitive Strategy*. The Free Press: New York.

Rosenhead, J., Elton, M. & Gupta, S.K. (1972) 'Robustness and optimality as criteria for strategic decisions', *Operational Research Quarterly*, **23**, 413–429.

Ross, S.A. (1976) 'The arbitrage theory of capital asset pricing', *Journal of Economic Theory*, **Dec**, 343–362.

Ross, S.A., Westerfield, R.W. & Jaffe, J.F. (2005) *Corporate Finance*. McGraw-Hill: New York.

Triantis, A. (2005) 'Realizing the potential of real options: does theory meet practice?', *Journal of Applied Corporate Finance*, **17**, 8–16.

Weingartner, H.M. (1963) *Mathematical Programming and the Analysis of Capital Budgeting Problems*. Prentice-Hall: New Jersey.

Winston, W.L. & Albright, S.C. (2001) *Practical Management Science*, 2nd edn. Duxbury. Location?

Chapter 13

Flexibility, Robustness and Real Options

Robert G. Dyson and Fernando S. Oliveira

INTRODUCTION

The importance of *flexibility* in the strategic development process goes back to the formative days of strategic planning. One of its earliest manifestations was in the guise of *contingency planning*. For example, Argenti (1974) in his book *Systematic Corporate Planning* defines a contingency plan as 'a component of a corporate plan designed as a response to an event E that is thought to be highly improbable (but possible) but of such importance that it must be allowed for in the plan'. Such plans are often in place in the event of say fire, computer system failure, bird flu or terrorist attack, but more generally contingency plans can be associated with any flexibility in the planning process aimed at dealing with the uncertainties of the future. This flexibility can often be captured in the form of a *decision tree*, as discussed in Chapter 10.

Gupta and Rosenhead (1968) and Rosenhead (2001) formalised a version of flexibility and *robustness* as key aspects of the strategic development process and this approach is discussed in the following section. More recently the concept of *real options* has been developed as a method of introducing flexibility into strategic decision-making. In option theory a call option is the ability to pay a small sum of money now which allows a share to be bought (or not) at some specified time in the future at a predetermined price. Option theory involves evaluating the price of the option. In real options the focus is on a real asset or strategic initiative (or option) rather than a share and the analysis involves valuing flexibility in strategic decision-making. Real options are treated in later sections of the chapter.

In this chapter we compare the use of robustness analysis, decision trees and the real options approach as different ways of representing flexibility in strategic decision-making: we analyse the advantages and disadvantages of the methods and we identify possible complementarities in these approaches. Finally, we apply the methods to an example in the electricity industry.

ROBUSTNESS ANALYSIS AND FLEXIBILITY

Rosenhead (2001, p. 188) defines robustness analysis as a particular perspective on embedding flexibility in the planning process in situations where 'an individual, group or organization need to make commitments now under conditions of uncertainty, and where these decisions will be followed at intervals by other commitments'. With a robustness perspective the focus will be on the alternative immediate commitments that can be made, which will be compared in terms of the range of possible future commitments with which they appear to be compatible. The approach is to analyse which initial commitments will keep open the greatest number of desirable future end states given that the uncertainty of the future is defined by a discrete set of possible futures (or scenarios in our terms). The approach is illustrated in Figure 13.1.

At node 1 in Figure 13.1 there is a choice of three decisions/strategic initiatives which may or may not be mutually exclusive. At a second stage there are further choices at nodes 2, 3 and 4, and at a third stage there are choices at nodes 5–9. The choices at the third stage lead to end states 10–20. In an uncertain world the value of the end states will vary. In the example, the uncertainty is assumed to be captured by two scenarios and each end state is either desirable or undesirable under a particular scenario. (The method can of course be extended to further scenarios and additional values for the end states rather than just desirable and

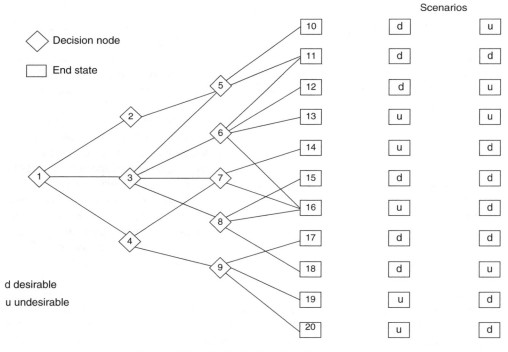

Figure 13.1. A Multi-stage Decision Process

undesirable.) For illustration, the choice (1,2) may be to launch a new product, (1,3) may be to enter a new market, whilst (1,4) may be to diversify through an acquisition. As the future unfolds further choices become available at the second and third stages. Under the first scenario, say a sustained global boom, further expansionary strategies will be considered. Under the second scenario, say a move to more local production due to the risk and high cost of global travel, a different set of alternatives will emerge. The end states might represent a particular product (or market) configuration.

The immediate commitment involves the first stage decisions (1,2), (1,3) and (1,4). Robustness analysis involves determining which initial choices keep the greatest number of desirable end states in play. In the example, if we plot the pathways from (1,2) we can see that end states 10 and 11 are possible. For (1,3), 10–16 and 18 are possible whilst for (1,4), 14, 16, 17, 19 and 20 are possible. The robustness of a first-stage decision given a particular scenario is defined by equation (13.1):

$$\text{Robustness} = \frac{\text{Number of desirable end states reachable}}{\text{Total number of desirable end states}} \qquad (13.1)$$

Under the first scenario there are six desirable end states and decision (1,2) can lead to two of them, i.e. 11 and 12, and thus has a robustness score of 2/6, i.e. 1/3. (1,3) can lead to five desirable end states and has a score of 5/6 and so on for each first-stage decision under each scenario. The robustness matrix is as shown in Table 13.1. If we assume that either scenario is plausible then decision (1,3) appears attractive as it keeps the greatest number of options (end states) open in scenario 1 and is relatively robust under scenario 2. However, it does not give access to end state 17, which may be highly desirable under either scenario. However, Rosenhead does not propose that the robustness scores are followed slavishly, but rather that the analysis should 'initiate a process of reflection and research, aimed at clarifying participants' understanding of the nature of the predicament that confronts them'.

In terms of the strategic development process model (Chapter 1, Figure 1.7), the robustness approach highlights the importance of building flexibility into the strategy creation process, only taking decisions when they are necessary (i.e. not taking possible future decisions until the future has begun to unfold), and in general of keeping your options open as long as possible. In robustness analysis flexibility is regarded as the ability to delay a commitment, i.e. you delay the final state to

Table 13.1. Robustness Matrix

Decision	Scenario	
	1	2
(1,2)	2/6	1/7
(1,3)	5/6	4/7
(1,4)	1/6	5/7

which you are going to commit your firm by the end of the planning horizon by keeping your options open.

REAL OPTIONS, VALUATION AND FLEXIBILITY

Real options is another tool devised to introduce flexibility as a major concept in strategic planning and project valuation. In one of the first academic papers on this topic McDonald and Siegle (1986) studied the optimal time of investment in an irreversible project, taking into account that the firm has the possibility of delaying the project. (They showed that the correct calculation of the timing to invest in a project should take into consideration the comparison of the value of investing today with the value of investing at all possible times in the future.) Moreover, Pindyck (1991) also emphasises the importance of flexibility and its value in strategic planning. He showed that the possibility of delaying an investment, giving the firm an opportunity to wait for new information before taking the final decision to commit to the project (this is similar to the statisticians' concept of expected value of perfect information), and the presence of uncertainty and irreversibility (in certain decisions), increase the value of flexibility (as a firm can decide to change the course of a project after receiving more information about the stochastic variables influencing the value of the project). Dixit (1992) has also shown that the flexibility inherent in a given project has a positive value: this is supported by his observation that firms invest in projects with a return rate three to four times the cost of capital, i.e. firms only invest if the price rises well above the long-run average cost (on the other hand, firms with operating losses stay in business for a long time). This shows that the flexibility inherent in the option to enter or leave a market may significantly increase the rate of return provided by an investment.

As another example of the use of options to increase flexibility we have the work of Abel and Eberly (1996), who analysed the use of real options to model investment problems under the existence of reversibility (i.e. in cases in which there is an increased flexibility). They presented costless-reversible and irreversible investment as the opposite ends of a wide spectrum that includes costly reversible investment (although a firm may resell the assets acquired during the investment, the resale prices may be below replacement costs). Following Bertola and Caballero (1994), they showed that under uncertainty, and in the presence of costly reversibility, there is a range of inaction under which the company will not invest: leading to the interesting insight that consideration of flexibility can actually lead to inaction, in certain circumstances.

The main conclusion from all these analyses is that flexibility increases the value of the firm. In this case, the value of the firm which, following Trigeorgis (1998a), we call strategic net present value (NPV) equals the sum of the static NPV (without taking into consideration the existence of options) and the value of the options.

Moreover, in the real options approach flexibility is regarded as the ability to delay, change or abandon a commitment due to the reception of new information that changes the way the firm perceives the problem. The recommitment will happen during the planning process. The firm commits itself sequentially, step-by-step as the future unfolds, assuming that it always chooses the best possible options.

Types of Real Options

Overall the literature has developed the following main types of real options, which are aimed at increasing the flexibility and value associated with different types of strategic decisions within a firm and these should be considered in the strategy creation process. Following Trigeorgis (1998b, p. 2), we have at least the following options:

(a) Option to invest in the future (at cost I). The firm holds an option to buy valuable land or resources (which turn out to have a value V). In this case, I represents the exercise price of the real option. The value of the option to invest would be equal to $\max(V - I, 0)$, resembling the value of a financial call option.

(b) Option to abandon. If the market conditions get worse than expected, management has the option to abandon indefinitely the project then valued V, receiving the resale value (A) of the assets owned. In this case the value of the option is equal to $\max(A - V, 0)$, resembling the value of a financial put option.

(c) Time-to-build option. The investment is divided into different stages, creating the option to abandon the project if the new information is unfavourable to future developments. This represents a compound option in which, at each stage s, the firm compares the required investment (I_s) with the value of the subsequent stages (V_s). The value of the option, at any given stage, will be $\max(I_s - V_s, 0)$, resembling a financial put option.

(d) Option to expand. If market conditions are more favourable than expected the firm may expand or secure more resources. In the case of the option to expand, if the current value of the project is V, after expansion it would equal V_e and the required investment is I_e. The value of the option to expand would then be $\max(V_e - V - I_e, 0)$, resembling a financial call option.

(e) Option to shut down. If the market conditions are worse than expected the firm may temporarily shut down, restarting when the market recovers. Let V_d represent the value of the project after shutting down. Then the value of this option would be equal to $\max(V_d - V, 0)$, resembling a financial put option.

(f) Option to restart. If market conditions improve the firm may restart production. In this case the firm aims to receive the production revenue V by paying the variable costs of production I_v. The value of this option is equal to $\max(V - I_v, 0)$, resembling a financial call option.

(g) Option to switch. If the prices or demand change, management may have the option to change the input (or output) mix. For example, an electricity generation firm owning several generation technologies (for example, combined cycle gas turbines and pumped storage) may use one plant or the other at different times depending on the time of the day. At night, when prices are lower it shuts down the natural gas turbine and uses electricity to pump up the water to the pumped storage reservoir. During the day, at the average demand hours it runs the natural gas turbine and does not run the pumped storage plant. At the peak times of price (or if there is a fast increase in price) it runs both the natural gas turbine and the pumped storage turbine. This example shows that in the management of a simple portfolio of electricity generation plants there are several interacting options, such as shut down and restart, and that these options lead to a change in the mix of fuel input used to generate electricity.

(h) Growth options. An early investment may be seen as the start of a chain of inter-related projects giving access to future growth opportunities – multiple interacting options. As we will illustrate in a later example, a firm may make an initial decision to enter a market as a way to open the door to other investments and opportunities.

In order to tackle realistic problems, the real options community has also analysed the issue of adapting the basic theoretical framework to solve real problems. For example: Cortazar, Schwartz and Salinas (1998) presented an application of real options to the valuation of environmental investments. Bollen (1999) developed an option valuation framework that explicitly incorporated a product life cycle. Huchzermeier and Loch (2001) applied real options theory to evaluate flexibility in R&D projects. Smith and McCardle (1999) applied real options to the analysis of project development in the gas and oil industry.

Risk-Neutral Valuation

There are several different methods to compute the value of an option, based on partial differential equations (this is the method used in the Black–Scholes formula; Black & Scholes, 1973), based on dynamic programming (this is the base of the binomial model we will follow in this presentation) or based on simulation (this method follows the Monte Carlo approach in which the same simulation is repeated over and over again and the option value is the average in all the runs of the model).

The risk-neutral approach developed by Cox, Ross and Rubinstein (1979) is central to all these methods. This approach is based on the observation that in a perfectly rational world there are no arbitrage opportunities.[1] In this case, the authors observed that it is possible to build a portfolio (combining the option and the underlying asset on which the option is written) that earns a risk-free rate of return. In this case, the value of this portfolio, and of the option, is independent of the preferences for risk.

As an example illustrating the existence of a riskless portfolio, consider an option to sell a combined cycle gas turbine (CCGT) for a price I, which can be exercised 1 year from now. This CCGT will have a value V_1, 1 year from now, which will depend on the expected spark spread (i.e. the difference between the electricity price and the fuel price).

In order to build a risk-free portfolio, if the firm owns a CCGT plant, it buys a put option (to sell this plant 1 year from now), and writes a call option (giving a

---

[1] We say that there are arbitrage opportunities if it is possible to make an instantaneous profit with no risk. For example, assume that the exchange rate between the US dollar and the British pound is 1 GBP = 1.88079 USD and the exchange rate between the US dollar and the euro is 1 EUR = 1.281 USD. Then, if there are no arbitrage opportunities the exchange rate between the British pound and the euro will be 1 GBP = 1.46822 EUR. Otherwise, a trader can make a profit without risk just by buying and selling currencies.

Table 13.2 An Example Illustrating the Formation of a Risk-less Hedge

Value of the:	$V_1 < I$	$V_1 \geq I$
CCGT plant	V_1	V_1
Put option	$I - V_1$	0
Call option	0	$-(V_1 - I)$
Portfolio	I	I

buyer the right to buy the plant 1 year from now).[2] The value of this portfolio, 1 year from now, is described in Table 13.2.

Therefore, this analysis shows that this portfolio has no risk; it's value is always equal to I. *Consequently, in order to evaluate such an option we use as discount factor the risk-free interest rate, r.* Furthermore, the present value of the portfolio is equal to the cost of buying it today as, otherwise, there would be arbitrage opportunities, as represented in equation (13.1) (in which P is the cost of buying a put option, C is the value received by the call option and V_0 represents the current value of the CCGT plant).

$$P - C + V_0 = \frac{I}{(1+r)} \tag{13.2}$$

There are other ways of using real options to reduce risk. For example, electricity generation firms tend not only to own part of the generation assets (instead of owning their totality) but also to sell long-term contracts on the value of the generation of a given plant, during a given period. This type of contract can be modelled using real options, in order to compute the value of the extra flexibility that the firm benefits from. Moreover, this extra flexibility carries no risk, as we shall see.

In this case, we assume that a firm writes a call option on a given generation asset (selling to another firm the right to buy that asset at a price I), which is combined with an investment in such an asset in order to produce a risk-free portfolio. (This is an important analysis as it shows how a firm can use real options to invest with no risk.)

Assume that the firm writes a call option on a CCGT plant (with value C), to be exercised in a year, with an exercise price I, and that the current value of the CCGT plant is V_0. Moreover, assume that the CCGT's value, 1 year from now (V_1), can only assume two possible values: high (V_H) and low (V_L). How much should the firm charge for the call option? What percentage of the CCGT's capital should the firm buy?

---

[2] These options can be traded over the counter in which the firm finds a buyer and a seller interested in the contract. For example, any company interested in developing a similar portfolio would assume the buyer or seller role. By exchanging these option contracts the two firms would be able to remove risk from their investment, as shown next. In this case, these contracts are tailored for the specific use planned. One important limitation of this analysis is that in practice it is difficult to find an option contract that completely hedges risk. The theory of real options assumes that the market is complete and that it is always possible to find all the assets required to build a risk-free portfolio.

Table 13.3. Value of a Portfolio with a CCGT and a Written Call Option

Value of the:	High value	Low value	Range
CCGT	V_H	V_L	$V_H - V_L$
Call option, with exercise price I	$V_H - I$	0	$V_H - I$
$V_1 - C$	I	V_L	$I - V_L$

The value of the portfolio composed of the written call option and the ownership of a plant is described in Table 13.3. From the analysis we can see that this portfolio is **not** risk-free as, in general, V_L can be different from I.

In order to compute the risk-free portfolio we need to compute the *hedge ratio (h)*:

$$h = \frac{V_H - I}{V_H - V_L} \tag{13.3}$$

Then, in order to compute the risk-free portfolio we buy the h part of the capital of a CCGT plant, see Table 13.4. By rearranging equation (13.3) it is easy to show that $I - (1 - h)V_H = hV_L$ and, therefore, we have a risk-free portfolio.

We are now able to answer the first question: how much to charge for the call option? As the value of the portfolio is risk-free, then to buy an h part of the CCGT plant and to write a call on the value of a CCGT plant has a current value (in the absence of arbitrage opportunities) equal to the present value of the portfolio, computed using a risk-free interest rate r, represented in equation (13.4).

$$hV_0 - C = \frac{hV_L}{1 + r} \tag{13.4}$$

Therefore, we can conclude that, when we have a complete market, all the cash flows should be discounted at the risk-free interest rate, as this represents the correct valuation from the perspective of a risk-neutral agent.

The Value of Risk

A second question we need to answer is: how do we price risk? In the development of a strategic project, management aims to achieve a rate of return as high as possible, by assuming a given level of risk. Therefore, inherent to any strategic move there is a level of risk and a sequence of cash flows that need to be priced, in order to decide if the project should be pursued or not.

Table 13.4. A Risk-Free Portfolio with a CCGT and a Written Call Option

Value of the:	High value	Low value	Range
CCGT	hV_H	hV_L	$h(V_H - V_L)$
Call option, with exercise price I	$V_H - I$	0	$V_H - I$
$V_1 - C$	$I - (1 - h)V_H$	hV_L	0

Traditionally, the value of a project would be computed using the weighted average cost of capital (e.g. Brealey & Myers, 1991, Chapters 2 and 3). This cost of capital would reflect the risk of the project (or of the firm as a whole). This discount rate (the weighted average cost of capital) could then be used within a decision tree (as presented in Chapter 10) to discount the cash flows and compute the value of the project. However, the problem with this discount rate is that it is *subjective*, dependent on the specificities of the firm, and it does not respect the principle of non-arbitrage.

The real options theory answers this question by respecting the non-arbitrage principle and using risk-neutral valuation. A very interesting discussion on the use of decision trees to model real options can be found in Smith and Nau (1995), Brandão, Dyer and Hahn (2005) and Smith (2005).

From our analysis in the previous section we know that all the cash flows should be discounted using the risk-free rate of return. Therefore, in order to understand how the 'market' values risk (and to compute the value of a project), real options theory uses two possible methods:

(a) It builds a portfolio of assets whose cash flows replicate the ones of the project the firm is developing. Then the value of the project is equal to the value of the replicating portfolio.
(b) It computes the probabilities (called 'risk-neutral') associated with the transitions between states such that the present value of the discounted cash flows equals the current value of the replicating portfolio. These risk-neutral probabilities are used to compute the value of the project, replacing the *subjective probabilities* used in the decision trees (as presented in Chapter 10).

(a) The replicating portfolio method

The firm needs to compute the value V of a strategic project whose value is assumed to follow a geometric Brownian motion (see Hull, 1993, section 9.6 for a detailed explanation on modelling geometric Brownian motion with binomial lattices). In order to compute the value of this project we choose a traded stock with current price S and a risk-free security (that pays an interest rate r). Given the volatility and rate of return of this stock, it is known that at any given time the stock price will move up to Su or down to Sd (where u is greater than 1 and $d = \dfrac{1}{u}$).

In order to replicate the cash flow of the project we need to determine how much to invest in the stock (B_1) and in the bond (B_0). Equations (13.5) and (13.6) represent the value of the portfolio when the value of the stock goes up or down, respectively.

$$B_0 (1+r) + B_1 Su \qquad (13.5)$$

$$B_0 (1+r) + B_1 Sd \qquad (13.6)$$

As we know the value of the project in the two states up (V_h) and down (V_l) of the replicating portfolio, then the quantities we need to invest in the stock (B_1) and bond

(B_0) can now be determined by solving the system of equations (13.7), in which B_0 and B_1 are the variables:

$$B_0 (1 + r) + B_1 Su = V_h \tag{13.7}$$
$$B_0 (1 + r) + B_1 Sd = V_1$$

Finally, using the no-arbitrage argument, the current price of the replicating portfolio is equal to the value of the project, as presented in equation (13.8):

$$V = B_1 S + B_0 \tag{13.8}$$

(b) The risk-neutral probabilities method

At each stochastic node in the decision tree we replace the *subjective probabilities* of transition between states by the risk-neutral probabilities. Given the value V of the replicating portfolio, computed at any node of the tree, we can solve equation (13.9) in order to find p (the risk-neutral probability of moving up). These probabilities will be the same in each node of the tree (for as long as the process generating the cash flows is stable) and therefore, we do not need to compute the replicating portfolio for each node.

$$B_1 S + B_0 = \frac{p V_h + (1 - p) V_1}{1 + r} \tag{13.9}$$

By replacing equations (13.7) in equation (13.9) and solving in order to find p we get the formula to compute the risk-neutral probabilities at any node, represented by equation (13.10), when we only have one source of uncertainty.

$$p = \frac{1 + r - d}{u - d} \tag{13.10}$$

COMPARING ROBUSTNESS ANALYSIS, DECISION TREES AND REAL OPTIONS

So far we have described how robustness analysis, decision trees and real options theory can be used to incorporate flexibility into the decision process. We can now compare these approaches, identifying the merits of each one of them (see Table 13.5).

The main advantage of robustness analysis is its simplicity and the very low level of information required in order to introduce flexibility into the problem. Another of its strengths is to assume that all the forecasts are wrong and therefore the classification of the possible states is prone to error. (This is the main idea behind robustness as, if the classifications can be wrong, the firm should leave accessible as many desirable states as possible so that at the end of the planning period some of them are still reachable.) Hence, the robustness concept goes beyond the maximum expected value criterion to analyse the benefits of a given decision. A decision is good if it has a good possibility of leading the firm to a desirable (satisfactory expected value) state, independently of the expected value associated with the initial

Table 13.5. Comparing the Robustness Analysis and the Real Options Approach

Criterion	Robustness analysis	Decision trees	Real options
Flexibility	– It is realised by leaving as many open options as possible.	– Decisions are made step-by-step. – As the decision process proceeds a firm is able to change the plan of actions. – Every plan of actions is conditional on the future realisations associated with the stochastic variables.	– Decisions are made step-by-step. – As the decision process proceeds a firm is able to change the plan of actions. – Every plan of actions is conditional on the future realisations associated with the stochastic variables.
Uncertainty	– There is no uncertainty regarding the intermediate states reached for a given set of decisions. – There is uncertainty regarding the value of each one of the states after these are reached.	– There is uncertainty regarding the states reached by a given sequence of actions. – Uncertainty is *subjective.*	– There is uncertainty regarding the states reached by a given sequence of actions. – Uncertainty is *objective* and determined by the market.
Information required	– Easy to obtain. – Qualitative. – Subjective.	– Difficult to obtain. – Quantitative. – Subjective.	– Difficult to obtain. – Quantitative. – Objective.
Risk profile	– Not analysed.	– Risk is subjective. – Firms maximise the expected utility.	– The risk is priced by the market. – Firms are risk-neutral.
Valuation	– Only through the desirability or otherwise of the end states.	– Central topic. – Valuation is subjective and it is dependent on the perceptions of the firm developing the project.	– Central topic. – Valuation is objective and it is determined by the market.

decision. Most importantly, this analysis serves as a very good tool to chart some of the possible future states of the world after a few interacting decisions, enabling a qualitative discussion of the strategic moves available to the firm.

The main disadvantages of using robustness analysis arise from the sources of its strength, i.e. the low information required and the qualitative nature of the analysis. It is designed for a discussion about the firm's strategy at a given point in time and uncertainty is only incorporated through end state scenarios (although the analysis can be reviewed at each stage of the process).

Another weakness of this method is the lack of quantitative awareness as it is not able to answer the following question: which decision should the company take in the last stage of the decision process when no state is desirable or there is more than one desirable state. For these reasons, robustness analysis by itself is not able to provide all the information required by the decision-maker when developing a strategy. However, it is designed to contribute to the strategic development process by making flexibility a focus of the discussion.

The main advantage of the decision tree and real options approaches is the introduction of flexibility into decision-making by computing conditional strategies. That is, in the strategic development process the strategies designed by the firm are already conditioned on the set of possible paths of the environment. In this case, a firm is not certain that it is able to achieve a given state (even though it assumes that it can compute the value of that state) and, therefore, in order to introduce flexibility into its strategy a firm computes policies that are conditional on the future development of the world. Moreover, the decision trees and real options approaches attempt to compute the value of each option that the firm has available, and in this way are able to compute the value of flexibility (i.e. the increase in the firm's value due to the options available at any given time). Most importantly, the decision trees and real options theory provide a framework to think about flexibility. By using these approaches firms can look for possible options within a given strategic decision, states in which the course of action can be changed and, in this way, the value of the firm increased. Additionally, the real options approach has a very important advantage over traditional decision trees: the use of risk-neutral valuation, which values the project taking into account its market value by computing risk-neutral probabilities and the replicating portfolio.

The main disadvantages of real options are its reliance on quantitative data and on the existence of a portfolio capable of replicating the cash flows associated with a given strategic decision, which can be very difficult to compute. The main disadvantages of the decision trees are the quantitative approach, as these data can be hard to obtain, and the dependence on the subjective perceptions of the firm.

Overall, robustness analysis on the one hand, and decision trees and the real options theory on the other hand, look at flexibility in very different, and complementary, ways. Whereas robustness analysis sees flexibility as the possibility of choosing amongst the highest number of possible desirable states (after a sequence of strategic decisions), real options theory (and decision trees analysis) sees flexibility as the possibility of changing the course of action at each step of the way. In a sense we could argue that whereas the robustness approach only focuses on the long-term performance of the firm, real options theory and decision trees are able to connect short-term decisions to long-term performance.

For all these reasons, there is a major advantage of robustness analysis (when compared with decision trees and real options) that makes it an important tool for the strategic development process. The robustness approach commits the firm to a set of strategic decisions that leads to a full set of desirable states (without committing the firm to any of them), so in a sense it keeps flexibility by avoiding pursuing a given set of decisions. On the other hand, real options theory (and decision trees) can advise the undertaking of a given project just because there is a possible sequence of actions that are highly profitable (with a certain probability). Therefore, the firm commits itself to a given set of conditionally optimal strategic decisions. *As a consequence, the optimal policy computed by using real options (or decision trees)* **may not be robust**, *as it may be over-reliant on one desirable state.*

Next, we exemplify the use of the robustness analysis, decision trees and the real options approaches, using an example from the electricity market.

AN EXAMPLE FROM THE ELECTRICITY MARKET

The aim of this exercise is to exemplify the use of robustness analysis and the real option approach in the context of the electricity market, illustrating the advantages and limitations of the methods.

We analyse the case of a firm that is planning to enter the UK electricity market. The firm is considering buying existing plant (a CCGT or a coal plant) or investing in new plant (a CCGT or a coal plant). The market entry is highly risky, as there are two main sources of uncertainty: electricity prices (that are dependent on the other firms' behaviour, on regulation and on demand) and fuel prices in general.

After analysing the current market the firm concludes that the cost of investing in a 1 GW CCGT plant is about £380 (million) and in a 1 GW coal plant is £200 (million). It also concludes that the cost of buying existing or building new capacity is the same. For this reason, and to speed up the process, the firm is considering buying a CCGT or a coal plant, in a first stage. Then, after 2 years of experience in the market, they would invest in new capacity (again in a 1 GW CCCT or coal plant). The planning horizon for this project is 10 years.

The main source of uncertainty is the long-term electricity price. The firm believes that this price is mainly dependent on regulatory action and investment. As the government is due to publish (within 2 years) an important document defining its policy for the electricity sector during the next 20 years, the firm expects to have a much better idea of this price after the government publishes this document.

Another important source of uncertainty is the fuel cost and, more specifically, the gas price. This price is a function of the internal supplies from the North Sea (that are expected to decrease) and of the access to importations from mainland Europe. Another important source of uncertainty is the access to the supplies from Russia and from Arabic countries, which influence the long-term gas prices in the world. The firm believes that within 10 years these main uncertainties will also be reduced as the connections to Europe and Russia will be better.

The current risk-free interest rate (r) is 5% and the weighted average cost of capital (k), for this firm, is 15%. The two sources of uncertainty are modelled using a binomial tree (high, low) for both electricity and gas prices. The firm believes that the probability of having high gas prices in the future is about 70% and high electricity prices have a probability of 40%. By combining these uncertainties the company analyses several different combinations of acquisitions, investment and uncertainties, computing the expected cash flow for each one of them.

Let us first analyse this problem using a decision tree, see Figure 13.2. In the decision tree solid squares represent decision nodes, while solid circles represent stochastic nodes. All the monetary values are in £ million and probabilities in percent.

The decision tree starts with a decision point in which the firm decides between investing in a CCGT plant, in a coal plant or delay (and possibly abandon) the investment. The first stochastic node represents the uncertainty regarding electricity prices (the firm believes that prices will be high with a 40% probability and that they are not dependent on its investment strategy). In the third stage, the firm decides between investing in a CCGT plant, in a coal plant or no investment at all. In the final stage the uncertainty regarding the gas prices is realised. The firm believes that prices will be high with a 70% probability and that they are independent from its investment strategy. The payoffs associated with each strategy are the present value of the payoffs during the project, using a discount rate of 15%.

In the first decision node the firm can buy a CCGT or a coal plant, or it may delay or abandon the option. The optimal decision (signalled with True) is to delay the project until the uncertainty related to the government document is resolved. The expected value of the project, after the government publishes the document, is £76 million, see Figure 13.3. The value of the delay or abandon decision is computed using the formula $\max(0, (0.6*0 + 0.4*208)/1.05^2)$ in which zero represents the value of the decision to abandon and $(0.6*0 + 0.4*208)/1.05^2$ represents the value of delaying the project for 2 years. In the delay option the firm receives the expected value of the optimal action when electricity prices are low (which is to abandon the project) and when the electricity prices are high (which is to buy and invest in a coal plant, with a present value of £208 million).

In this case the value of the option to delay the project is equal to £40 million, which is equal to the difference between £76 and £36 million (the value of the project if the firm decides to buy a coal plant).

It should finally be noticed that in the second stage there is an option to abandon the investment project (although keeping the plant already bought). This option has no value if the electricity prices are high, but it can have a substantial value when prices are low, by reducing losses. This option has a value of £70 million if the firm buys a CCGT plant and a value of £61 million if the firm buys a coal plant.

We can now analyse the project using real options. As shown by Brandão, Dyer and Hahn (2005), these real options can be modelled as decision trees in which all the cash flows are discounted at the risk-free interest rate and the probabilities used at the stochastic nodes are risk-neutral. In this case, the project is valued as if it would be traded in the market.

As presented, in order to proceed with the risk-neutral valuation we first need to identify a portfolio of traded assets capable of replicating the project cash flows at each one of the possible states. Then we can compute the risk-neutral probabilities (which replace the subjective probabilities of the company) and discount all the cash flows at the risk-free interest rate. In order to build this portfolio we use a risk-free

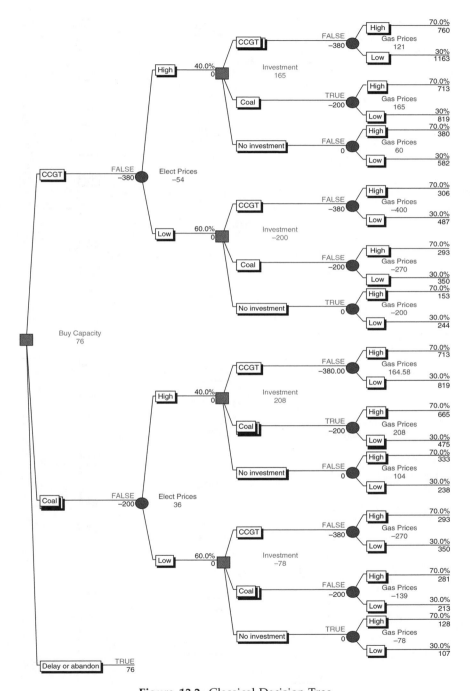

Figure 13.2. Classical Decision Tree

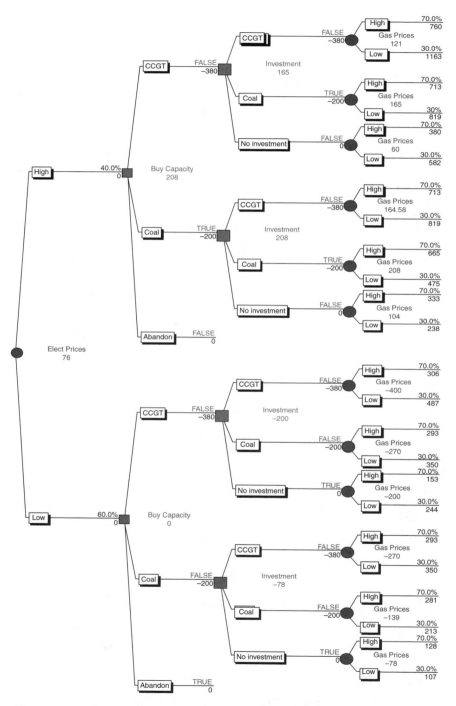

Figure 13.3. The Decision to Delay or Abandon in the Classical Decision Tree

security that provides an interest rate of 5% a year, and British Energy (BE)'s stock price. (It should be noted that BE's stock price and our investment are negatively correlated, as BE owns mainly nuclear plants, but for as long as this correlation is strong this asset can be used to compute the value of the project.)

The current value of BE's stock price is 730 pence. In order to model its evolution in the next 10 years (our planning horizon) we use a two-step (the first step for the first 2 years and the second step for the last 8 years) binomial tree that assumes that BE's stock prices follow a geometric Brownian motion (as suggested earlier).

As the sources of uncertainty are different (and electricity prices are more important) the firm expects that in the case of high electricity prices the value of BE will increase by 50% within 2 years, and that in the case of high gas prices the value of BE will increase by about three times in the last 8 years of the project (at a rate of about 15% a year). The binary tree in Figure 13.4 models the evolution of BE's stock price. This model differs slightly from the classical geometrical Brownian motion as we consider that uncertainty changes over time (as we know that we have two different sources of uncertainty), and therefore, instead of using a binomial lattice we use a binomial tree.

In this case, the computation of the risk-neutral probabilities needs to be done step-by-step, from the last nodes to the first node. Moreover, we need to compute two different risk-neutral probabilities, one for each of the stages (2 years and 10 years). (If we were using the replicating portfolio approach we would need to compute a different portfolio for each stochastic node in the decision tree.)

We are now in a position to compute the risk-neutral probabilities by using formula (13.9) (note that we *cannot* use formula (13.10), as the process followed by BE's model is *not* a classical geometric Brownian motion). The risk-neutral probabilities for the first 2 years are computed by the formula $730 = \dfrac{1095p + 487\,(1-p)}{(1+0.05)^2} \Leftrightarrow p =$ 0.523. In the case of the last 8 years the risk-neutral probabilities can be computed

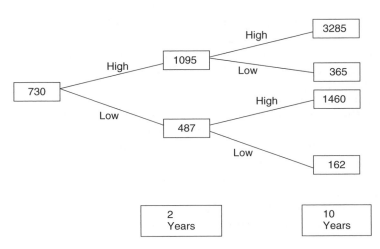

Figure 13.4. Binary Tree to Model the Evolution of BE's Stock Price as a Function of Gas Prices (in pence)

either by analysing the upper or the lower branches. If using the upper branches we get $1095 = \dfrac{3285p + 365\,(1-p)}{(1+0.05)^8} \Leftrightarrow p = 0.429$ and if using the lower branches we would get the same value, $487 = \dfrac{1460p + 162\,(1-p)}{(1+0.05)^8} \Leftrightarrow p = 0.429$.

This represents a first important output of this analysis. We can analyse how the firm's subjective probabilities compare with the market-based probabilities. Regarding the evolution of gas prices it seems that the firm is conservative. Whereas the firm expects gas prices to go up with a 70% probability, the market-based probability is only 42.9%. Regarding the electricity price again the firm is conservative as it attributes a probability of 40% to high prices, whereas the market-based probability is 52.3%.

We can now replace the subjective probabilities by the risk-neutral probabilities and recalculate the value of the project using the cash flows discounted by using the risk-free interest rate. These calculations are represented in the real options tree in Figure 13.5.

The first new result to notice is that to delay is not the optimal decision any longer. The value of the delay or abandon decision is calculated by the formula max(0, (0.477*226 + 0.523*1557)/1.05²), in which zero represents the value of the decision to abandon and £836 (million) = (0.477*226 + 0.523*1557)/1.05² represents the value of delaying the project for 2 years, see Figure 13.6. However, this time the best policy is to invest, therefore the delay option has no value.

The optimal policy is to buy a CCGT plant, and 2 years from now, if the electricity prices are high, we will invest in another CCGT plant (with an overall net present value of £1557 million), if the electricity prices are low we invest in a coal plant (with an overall net present value of £226 million). Therefore, the value of this project is £914 million, which is the weighted average of these two investments. Finally, the option to abandon the investment project has no value under risk-neutral valuation.

Under robustness analysis the initial decisions and second-stage decisions are similar to the previous approaches but the uncertainty is captured through scenarios at the end state. The robustness structuring of the problem is shown in Figure 13.7. This follows the approach of the earlier example but (following Rosenhead, 2001, p. 196) the end states under the scenarios are taken to have four possible outcomes: desirable, acceptable, undesirable and catastrophic. Scenario 1 relates to the situation of a high cost of gas coupled with high electricity prices. Under this scenario investing in two CCGTs is acceptable but two coal-fired generators is more desirable due to the lower cost base. Not investing at all would be a poor choice. Scenario 2 assumes a high cost of gas due to shortages but a low electricity price due to a range of alternative methods of generation including perhaps coal, nuclear and sustainable sources. Under this scenario a decision to have invested in two CCGTs would have been catastrophic. Scenario 3 assumes a low cost of gas and high electricity prices and here investing in CCGTs would have been the best option, with not investing being unacceptable. Scenario 4 assumes low gas and electricity prices and here a single CCGT might have been the most desirable strategy.

The robustness analysis of the situation involves constructing a robustness matrix but can also include a debility (unhealthy) matrix to allow for the poor choices

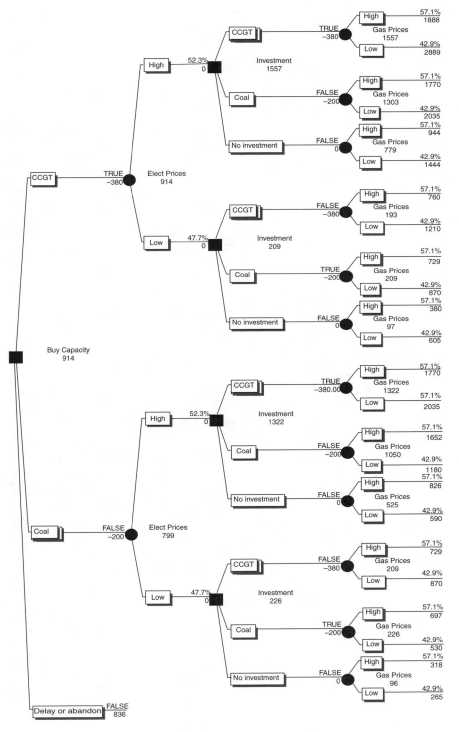

Figure 13.5. The Real Options Tree

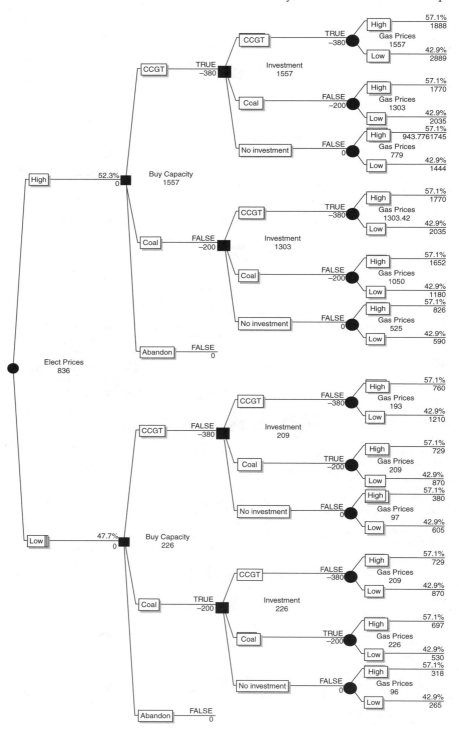

Figure 13.6. The Decision to Delay or Abandon in the Real Options Tree

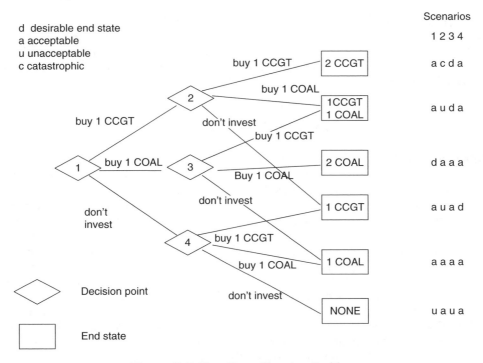

d desirable end state
a acceptable
u unacceptable
c catastrophic

Figure 13.7. Two-Stage Planning Problem

Table 13.6. Option Evaluation

Robustness Matrix (end states d and a) Scenario				Debility Matrix (end states u and c) Scenario			
Decision	1	2	3	4	1	2	3	4
(1,2)	3/5	0	3/5	3/6	0	2/2	0	–
(1,3)	3/5	2/4	3/5	3/6	0	1/2	0	–
(1,4)	2/5	2/4	2/5	3/6	1/1	1/2	1/1	–

as shown in Table 13.6. In the robustness matrix we can calculate that there are a total of five good end states (four acceptable and one desirable) under scenario 1. Three of these are accessible from decision (1, 2), three from decision (1, 3) and two from decision (1, 4). We can similarly compute the other elements of the matrix. The debility matrix focuses on the poor choices (undesirable and catastrophic) and there is only one of these under scenario 1, three under scenario 2, one under scenario 3 and none under scenario 4. Decision (1, 2) leads to the greatest number of poor strategies in scenario 2.

From the robustness matrix we can see that (1, 3) dominates the other two decisions, keeping the greatest number of options open. It also dominates the other two in the debility matrix, given that here low scores are preferred. Robustness analysis would point us in that direction therefore. Option (1, 2) perhaps leads to the most desirable outcome under the most favourable circumstances, but performs poorly under scenario 2. This is the option preferred by the real options approach and this perhaps suggests that robustness analysis might lead to safer choices but not to the extent of doing nothing.

CONCLUSIONS AND FUTURE RESEARCH DIRECTIONS

Robustness analysis and real options (using decision trees) can be used to model flexibility and uncertainty in strategic development. They treat flexibility differently. Robustness maintains strategic flexibility by leaving as many options open as possible, whereas the real options theory aims to introduce uncertainty into strategic development by introducing decision points (during the execution of a strategy) that can change the decision path.

Uncertainty represents the main reason why firms need to be flexible when developing strategic plans. The robustness approach models uncertainty by postulating that as the value of any strategic plan leads to an uncertain payoff a firm should keep as many options as possible open so that it can change its commitment to any given plan at any time. The decision trees approach to model uncertainty is to introduce stochastic nodes in which *nature* influences the value of the project, by using subjective probabilities to model the likelihood of certain events. The real options theory uses this same approach introducing the market valuation – through the computation of risk-neutral (objective) probabilities.

Overall, we have shown that these methods of modelling flexibility in strategic decision-making are complementary. The decision trees approach is subjective, requires a large data set and represents the perceptions of the firm. The real options model aims to develop market-based models of strategic flexibility. As shown in the example, if the firm's and the market's perceptions are very different then these two methods may lead to different decisions. The robustness analysis is subjective as well; it is a qualitative approach, and has the main advantage of not committing the firm to an uncertain strategic path. As shown in the electricity markets example, the robustness approach can lead to investment strategies that disregard the most profitable strategy (as it may lead to a less flexible strategic decision path) in order to keep the strategic plan with the highest number of attractive alternative plans, leading to a different strategy from the one that would be chosen by using real options.

The future direction of research in the topic of flexibility needs to be driven by both theoretical and practical concerns. We think that the robustness approach can be developed further by considering interacting decision-makers and by introducing risk aversion into the decision-maker's problem. Moreover, the incorporation of models of learning, by which firms can iteratively change the interactions between the different decisions, can be important.

In the real options approach some examples that explicitly model the interactions between decision-makers have already been analysed. For example, Smit and Ankun (1993) modelled corporate investment in a duopolistic industry showing that under competition there is a lower tendency to postpone projects. Grenadier (1996) has also modelled the interaction in a duopoly (in the real estate industry), under the assumption of perfect rationality. Kulatilaka and Perotti (1998) have also studied the interaction between two companies as a one-shot first-entrance game (a model of strategic growth options in a duopoly), strongly emphasising the value of the initial investment as the acquisition of opportunities relative to competitors (they view strategic investment in conditions of uncertainty as a commitment to a more aggressive future strategy). However, only small examples have been analysed and, so far, there is no theory developed for the analysis of oligopolistic and complex industries. Another important issue is the modelling of interactions between the different strategic decisions considered and being implemented by a firm.

REFERENCES

Abel, A.B. & Eberly, J.C. (1996) 'Optimal investment with costly reversibility', *The Review of Economic Studies*, **63**(4), 581–593.

Argenti, J. (1974) *Systematic Corporate Planning*. Nelson: England.

Bertola, G. & Caballero, R. (1994) 'Irreversibility and aggregate investment', *Review of Economic Studies*, **61**, 223–246.

Black, F. & Scholes, M. (1973) 'The pricing of options and corporate liabilities', *Journal of Political Economy*, **81**(3), 637–654.

Bollen, N.P.B. (1999) 'Real options and product life cycles', *Management Science*, **45**(5), 670–684.

Brandão, L.E., Dyer, J.S. & Hahn, W.J. (2005) 'Using binomial trees to solve real-option valuation problems', *Decision Analysis*, **2**(2), 69–88.

Brealey, R.A. & Myers, S.C. (1991) *Principles of Corporate Finance*, 4th edn. McGraw-Hill: New York.

Cortazar, G., Schwartz, E.S. & Salinas, M. (1998) 'Evaluating environmental investments: a real options approach', *Management Science*, **44**(8), 1059–1070.

Cox, J., Ross, S. & Rubinstein, M. (1979) 'Option pricing: a simplified approach', *Journal of Financial Economics*, **7**(Sept), 229–263.

Dixit, A. (1992) 'Investment and hysteresis', *The Journal of Economic Perspectives*, **6**(1), 107–132.

Grenadier, S.R. (1996) 'The strategic exercise of options: development cascades and over-building in real estate markets', *Journal of Finance*, **51**(5), 1653–1679.

Gupta, S.K. & Rosenhead, J. (1968) 'Robustness in sequential investment decisions', *Management Science*, **15**, 18–29.

Huchzermeier, A. & Loch, C.H. (2001) 'Project management under risk: using the real options approach to evaluate flexibility in R&D', *Management Science*, **47**(1), 85–101.

Hull, J. (1993) *Options, Futures, and Other Derivative Securities*, 2nd edn. Prentice-Hall: New Jersey.

Kulatilaka, N. & Perotti, E.C. (1998) 'Strategic growth options', *Management Science*, **44**(8), 1021–1031.

McDonald, R. & Siegel, D. (1986) 'The value of waiting to invest', *Quarterly Journal of Economics*, **101**(4), 707–728.

Pindyck, R. (1991) 'Irreversibility, uncertainty, and investment', *Journal of Economic Literature*, **29**(3), 1110–1148.

Rosenhead, J. (2001) 'Robustness analysis: keeping your options open'. In: Rosenhead, J. & Mingers, J. (eds), *Rational Analysis for a Problematic World Revisited*. John Wiley & Sons: Chichester.

Smit, H.T.J. & Ankun, L.A. (1993) 'A real options and game-theoretic approach to corporate investment strategy under competition', *Financial Management*, **Autumn**, 241–250.

Smith, J.E. (2005) 'Alternative approaches for solving real-options problems', [Comment on Brandão *et al.*, 2005], *Decision Analysis*, **2**(2), 89–102.

Smith, J.E. & McCardle, K.F. (1999) 'Options in the real world: lessons learned in evaluating oil and gas investments', *Operations Research*, **47**(1), 1–15.

Smith, J.E. & Nau, R.F. (1995) 'Valuing risky projects: option pricing theory and decision analysis', *Management Science*, **41**(5), 795–816.

Trigeorgis, L. (1998a) *Real Options, Managerial Flexibility and Strategy in Resource Allocation*, 3rd edn. MIT Press: Boston.

Trigeorgis, L. (1998b) 'Real options and interactions with financial flexibility', *Financial Management*, **22**(3), 202–224.

Part VI

Combining Approaches to Support Strategic Development

Chapter 14

Gone Fishing: A Case Study

Jim Bryant, Maureen Meadows, John Morecroft and Frances O'Brien

INTRODUCTION

Overview of the Chapter

In this chapter we describe how we made use of a particular combination of modelling frameworks in a single case study. Our intention, from a teaching perspective, was to demonstrate to students on a specialist Masters programme at Warwick Business School how the insights generated by the three selected frameworks complemented each other, and also to show what aspects of a case situation were emphasised by each of these frameworks. Within a wider context, we were seeking to answer research questions regarding the bespoke composition of what are generally referred to as multi-methodology (Mingers & Gill, 1997) interventions: that is, we were attempting to better understand how a variety of formal modelling perspectives might best be used together to support the strategic development process.

Our designed application should obviously be of interest to management educators, since it is of quite a general nature: while we chose to use a local, topical situation as the subject of our study here, the approach that we describe could as easily be replicated with many other case situations; nor is it limited to the particular modelling frameworks that we happened to select. However, our intention in this chapter is much broader. It is our view that the strategic development process as a whole can often be strengthened more by the use of a portfolio of the approaches that have been described in this book than by the use of just one isolated technique or framework. We return to a discussion of this point towards the end of the chapter.

The chapter begins by providing a short theoretical context in which to locate our work with more than one framework. We then move on to describe the taught programme in which we made use of the approaches, and explain how we used them to offer our students some alternative ways of viewing a complex, uncertain, conflictual situation. The student responses are included. Finally, some conclusions and reflections are presented, and a way forward discussed.

Multi-methodology

Guidance for combining approaches in strategic development is not easy to find. Often, for instance, the inclusion of approaches is determined more by the exigencies

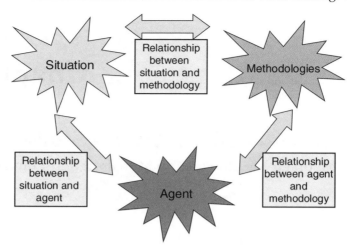

Figure 14.1. Three Key Aspects of Multi-methodology Design

of the moment, by the capabilities and competencies immediately to hand, and by the prejudices or ignorance of all concerned, than by any more sophisticated considerations. Mingers (in Rosenhead & Mingers, 2001, Chapter 13) has valuably identified three key aspects that need to be considered in multi-methodology design: these are summarised in Figure 14.1.

Here a three-way relationship is seen between the *situation* in which strategic change is occurring, the change *agent* who is seeking to use a structured approach to model what is going on and to stimulate change, and the particular *methodology* that this agent may bring to bear on this occasion. In turn, the three relationships between these elements give rise to a number of questions that create the design of the rehearsal of strategy. Some of the key questions that arise under each heading are shown in Figure 14.2.

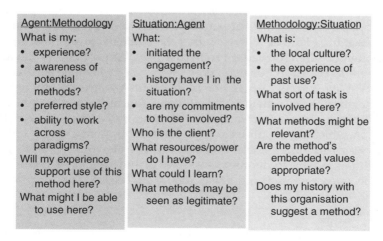

Figure 14.2. Key Questions Concerning Multi-methodology Design

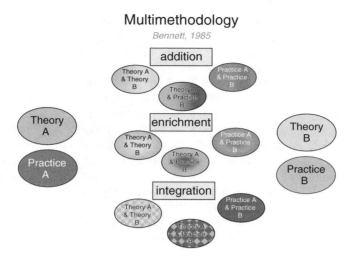

Figure 14.3. Three Approaches to Multimethodolgy

A cursory review of these questions easily reveals the sort of contingencies that may shape a particular application. The agent–methodology relationship principally concerns the preferences and capability of the agent and the perceived appropriateness of drawing upon different elements in his/her repertoire. The situation–agent axis focuses upon the process that the agent may construct for his/her 'client system': that is upon the manner in which a rehearsal process is used within the organisation. The situation–methodology pairing concerns the relevance of particular approaches for a situation: so, for instance, drama theory is especially well suited to conflictual situations.

When several approaches are used together their integration may be achieved in various ways. Bennett (1985) pointed out (see Figure 14.3) that there were at least three distinguishable ways of using approaches together: addition, enrichment and integration. In *addition*, a situation is typically first addressed by one framework and then subsequently (or simultaneously) by another. The payoff comes from contrasting the results of these independent framings. In *enrichment*, one approach takes the dominant role and provides a structure for the whole process: other approaches are drawn upon as felt necessary to supplement the outcomes of this main framework. In *integration*, as in addition, there is greater parity between the importances of the approaches included: however, this time the frameworks are used in tandem, with a designed interface between the elements of analysis.

Motivation for the Research

The authors, from four different institutions, share a common research interest in the use of frameworks, methods and structured approaches to support strategic development, while having particular expertise in three different areas – drama theory, system dynamics and scenario planning. Each of these has been the subject of an earlier chapter in this book. The teaching 'experiment' described here was a valuable opportunity to examine the links between our core interests, and the ways in which the three approaches might be complementary. Our common 'world view' was that such methods and models can help people to think strategically about the future, in situations exhibiting high levels of conflict, complexity and uncertainty.

The authors believe that a range of 'hard' and 'soft' models and processes can be viewed as supporting strategic development. For instance, a 'hard' model (such as a system dynamics model that includes objective operating constraints in a competitive industry) can represent a complex context in which strategy must be enacted, while 'soft' models (such as drama theory-based representations of a complex set of stakeholder perspectives on a contested issue) can act as facilitative devices for a strategic conversation between interested parties. The agenda for teaching and research described here was to take three different models that are used to support strategic development and to explore both the relationships between the models and the reactions of students (as modellers and as 'consumers of models') to their application in a single problem situation which contained elements of conflict, complexity and uncertainty.

In terms of our earlier discussion of multi-methodology, we were clearly being opportunistic and pragmatic in making use of approaches with which we were especially familiar (agent–methodology relationship). However, as we did so, we felt that the complementary insights that would be generated would have particular value in the case situation in which we had chosen to immerse the students (methodology–situation axis). We had no deep prior acquaintance with the subject of the case study (agent–situation matching) and so were able to approach it with open minds. In Bennett's terms we were here using an additive model, though there were some elements of integration present when we ran the experiment for the second time, as will be described below.

THE CASE STUDY

The Experimental Context

The MSc in Management Science and Operational Research at Warwick Business School, University of Warwick is a 1-year, full-time course of around 55 students. The majority of the students come to the MSc immediately after their undergraduate degrees with little work experience; around half of the group are overseas students (from outside the EU). Their first degree disciplines represent a diverse range of backgrounds, but all have strong quantitative skills. The teaching described below took place on a final-term, elective module entitled 'Strategic Operational Research', which typically attracts around 25 students. The students have already completed a set of core modules, including statistics, operational research techniques (such as optimisation), computing and information systems, and an introductory management module.

The module in Strategic OR has a long history from its inception in the early 1980s when it was known as 'Analytical Aids to Strategic Planning', to its current format where it is delivered, under different titles and teaching formats, to three different groups of students. The first variant, 'Operational Research for Strategic Planning', is taken by the largest group of students who are final-year undergraduates, from a variety of nationalities and backgrounds, including mathematics, statistics and business-related degrees. The second variant, 'Strategic Development: Methods and Models', is taken by predominantly practising managers from a range of Warwick's Executive MBA programmes. The final variant, 'Strategic OR', is taken by the smallest group of students studying for a specialist Masters degree in Management Science and Operational Research.

The syllabus of the Strategic OR module is supported by the framework for an effective process of strategic development (presented later as Figure 14.13, or refer to Chapter 1 for a fuller discussion), which is used to introduce and organise the module. Subsequently, a range of methods and models are introduced. The core elements of the module have traditionally been scenario planning, and a form of corporate modelling (recently system dynamics). Other elements have included some or all of: drama theory, visioning, risk analysis, gaming, balanced scorecard and other structured approaches to strategy support.

First Iteration: Spring 2005

In 2005, the module was to be delivered during January and February in three 'blocks'; each block consisted of two consecutive days (a day representing 6 hours of teaching time, 9 am to 12 noon, and 2 pm to 5 pm). There was to be a gap of 3 weeks between the blocks. Given their common research interests outlined earlier, the authors decided to introduce a new element to the module, which was an integrative exercise labelled 'Fishing for Strategy'. Alongside the conventional delivery of introductions to scenario planning and system dynamics, a series of three 'new' sessions was designed as follows:

- During Block 1, a half-day was to be devoted to an exercise based on the 'Fish Banks' gaming simulator (a system dynamics-based model described further below).
- During Block 2, a half-day exercise in drama theory, entitled 'Going Fishing', was to be undertaken.
- Finally, during Block 3, the students were to undertake a half-day exercise on scenario planning for the fishing industry, followed by a half-day of reflection on the work undertaken and other discussion to 'wrap-up' the module.

As previously stated, one aim of this new integrative exercise was to explore linkages between our areas of expertise by applying three modelling approaches to a common problem area. The fishing industry was identified as a suitable application area for a number of reasons. First, public and expert concerns about falling fish populations were a 'hot topic' in the popular press at the time the exercise was being prepared, and so the students were likely to have a general awareness of the issue without specific expert knowledge. Second, the 'Fish Banks' gaming simulator (a system dynamics model) had already been developed and was well understood by one of us (JM). Third, the problem area appeared to exhibit the characteristics of complexity, uncertainty and conflict that made it suitable for the application of other modelling approaches such as drama theory and scenario planning.

Second Iteration: Spring 2006

The exercise was repeated with a new student group in Spring 2006, and with due consideration to some of the areas for potential improvement that emerged on the first iteration. In particular, the following changes were made. Slightly more time was allowed for the exercise; this was allocated to the drama theory 'block', with the aim of increasing the students' understanding of the activities involved in building drama theory models (and hence highlighting the role of the model builder, alongside the role of the 'consumer' of models). In addition, the ordering of the first two elements of the exercise was reversed; i.e. the students experienced the drama theory element of the exercise in the first 'block' of the module, before experiencing the system dynamics element in the second 'block' a few weeks later.

A number of changes were also made to the third element of the exercise, scenario planning. In the first iteration, scenarios were built with a named company in mind (Flatfish). In the second iteration, it was decided to make greater use of the output of the drama theory exercise, by asking the students to work towards strategies for the five stakeholder groups that they had adopted in the drama theory session. To this end, scenarios were built at an industry level, rather than at the company level. This is discussed further below.

Each of the three modelling approaches is now described in turn.

The 'Fish Banks' Gaming Simulator

'Fish Banks Ltd' is a gaming simulator based on a system dynamics model of the fishing industry. The simulator is used to support a group role-playing exercise and was originally devised by Meadows, Fiddaman and Shannon (2001) to teach principles for sustainable management of renewable resources. Participants are organised into teams, representing the management of up to six rival fishing companies. The aim for each team is to maximise its own asset value by the end of the game in competition with rivals. The game is run over a number of rounds. In each round teams can make a set of decisions including whether to buy or sell ships, and whether to position ships in the deep sea, shallow sea or in harbour. Teams make their decisions in the light of strategic objectives they agree at the start of the game and based on information they receive about the consequences of previous decisions, e.g. the quantity of fish caught in the last round, and the profitability of the business at the end of that round. Before playing the game the students had already attended a number of lectures on system dynamics, and were therefore aware of the principles behind a model such as Fish Banks, in general if not in specific terms.

In this exercise a commercial fishery is viewed as a competitive industry comprising natural fish stocks and multiple rival firms, each operating one or more ships. The firms are interconnected because they share a regional population of fish. Sometimes the interconnection and mutual dependence is very strong and generates surprisingly complex dynamics. The essence of the managerial problem for participants (and for fishing fleet operators in the real world) is to achieve profitable growth while maintaining the right balance between the natural renewable resource, fish, and the man-made resource, ships. However, over-investment and the 'tragedy of the commons' (Gordon, 1954; Moxnes, 1998) characterise the typical and dismal dynamics of this industry and firms' dynamic behaviour. Individual firms, seeking to maximise their wealth and share of the catch, find themselves engaged in a race to grow until, unexpectedly, the natural resource collapses. The usual and catastrophic outcome is an ocean without fish and, at the same time, large idle fishing fleets. However, this outcome is not pre-ordained since fish regenerate and fish stocks can, in principle, be sustained indefinitely.

Different teams typically adopt different strategies, some pro-actively and aggressively expanding their fleets and others adopting a much more cautious approach to investment (Kunc & Morecroft, 2006). It is a huge challenge for any firm (and management team) to survive in such dynamically complex conditions, where performance is so critically dependent on an appropriate balance of ships and fish. Here the regeneration rate of fish is a non-linear function of an imperfectly known fish stock and the catch depends on diverse motives and actions of rivals as they build and deploy their fleets.

The game is played under the following conditions that ensure a level playing field for all teams:

- The business concept of rival fishing firms is quite simple as well as their strategic choices: they can expand or not expand the fishing fleet, allocate the fleet between two fishing areas (the deep sea or coastal waters) or stay in the harbour, and trade ships with other teams.
- Each team (firm) starts with the same number of ships and the same amount of cash.
- All players receive the same briefing about the modelled fishing industry including the size range of the initial fish population and the effect of fish stocks on fish regeneration and the catch per ship.
- The productivity of all ships is identical.
- The price of fish is fixed and is the same for all teams, so the income of rival fishing firms is determined entirely by fleet size and the allocation of the fleet between the deep sea, coastal waters and the harbour.
- At each decision period all teams have access to the same information about the state of the fishery including their own catch (but *not* rivals' catches and *not* the fish population), their own fleet size, total industry fleet size and the allocation of the fleet between the deep sea, coastal waters and the harbour.
- There are three uncertainties which are similar for all teams: the fish population size, the real catch rate per ship and competitors' intentions/strategies.
- Only the game administrators know the true size of the fish population and the total catch per period.

A diagram of the model underlying Fish Banks is shown in Figure 14.4 using the stock and flow symbols introduced in Chapter 7. The fish population is shown on the left of the figure. There are two stock accumulations 'Fish Population Coastal' and 'Fish Population Deep Sea' representing two independent fish populations. Each fish population increases through regeneration, which is a non-linear function of fish density (defined as the ratio of fish population to maximum natural fishery size). Each fish population decreases through a harvest rate proportional to the allocated fleet size. When the harvest rate exceeds the regeneration rate the fish population falls and vice versa, so the sustainability of the fishery depends on

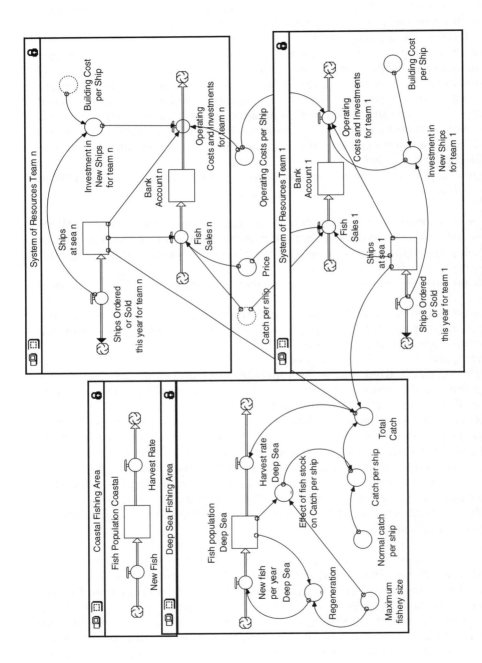

Figure 14.4. Simplified Stock and Flow Diagram of Fish Banks Ltd

Source: Kunc, M.H. & Morecroft, J.D.W., Competitive Dynamics and Gaming Simulation Lessons from a Fishing Industry Simulator, *Journal of the Operational Research Society*, advance online publication, 26 July 2006 [DOI: 10.1057/palgrave.jors.2602246]. Reproduced with permission of Palgrave Macmillan.

players collectively maintaining an appropriate balance between harvesting and regeneration. The exact size of the two fish populations and the regeneration rate is deliberately not revealed to the teams at any point in the game since this information is not known with certainty in the real world. Participants know only the size range of the initial populations, which is 2000–4000 fish for the deep sea and 1000–2000 fish in the coastal area (these nominal values can easily be rescaled into say thousands of tonnes to fit a realistic fishery).

The assets and operations of rival fishing companies are shown on the right of Figure 14.4, where team 1 is depicted at the bottom and team *n* at the top. Each company manages two main stock accumulations: ships at sea and a bank account. For visual simplicity only the total number of ships at sea is shown, even though the fleet can be located in the coastal area, deep sea or harbour. Teams' decisions on ships ordered or sold are represented as a flow rate that increases the fleet size when new ships are ordered or decreases the fleet size when ships are sold. The bank account accumulates fish sales minus operating costs and investments. The value of fish sales is equal to the number of ships at sea multiplied by the catch per ship and price. The catch per ship is the same for all teams and depends non-linearly on the fish population. When fish are scarce the catch per ship is low, but then increases quickly to reach a stable plateau as fish become more plentiful.

The game provides a powerful illustration of the long-term dynamics of the fish population, and the perils of over-fishing. Figure 14.5 shows the typical game behaviour in terms of fish, catch and ships, scaled on an index from 0 to 8 for easy comparison. The chart shows how difficult it is for players to comprehend

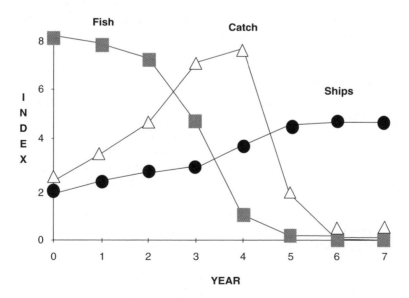

Figure 14.5. Typical Game Behaviour

Source: Reproduced by permission of Dennis Meadows, from debriefing materials of the educational simulation, Fishbanks Ltd. The same may be obtained from http://www.sustainer.org/ tools_resources/games.html/

that over-investment is taking place and to foresee its consequences. The catch rises to a peak index value of almost 8 in year 5, even as the fish population declines precipitously. This steady rise in the catch encourages further investment in ships because it is profitable to do so. Since teams do not know the fish population for certain they tend to ignore it in their ordering decisions and focus instead on the tangible catch. Only when the catch itself begins to decline in year 6 is the incentive to buy more ships eliminated. But by then there are far too many ships operating in the fishery and the fish population is so low that regeneration cannot possibly keep pace with the catch, even though the catch itself is dwindling towards zero. The game illustrates vividly that over-depletion of the fish population can be difficult – or impossible – to rectify, at least in the short to medium term.

The Fish Banks exercise was run in a single lecture theatre by one instructor and an assistant. The class of 25 students was divided into six groups of similar size who all received a standard 20-minute briefing about the objectives of the game and the main characteristics of the simulated fishery. Teams were then allowed a further 20 minutes to agree a strategy for their fishing company and write it down in a couple of paragraphs for later use. The game play then commenced. There were six or seven rounds of decision-making lasting between 10 and 15 minutes each. At the end of the game the results were compiled and shown to the class. Finally, there was a debriefing. Students briefly presented and defended their teams' strategies and performance. The instructor reviewed the feedback structure of the game and led a discussion of the lessons for sustainable management of fisheries (and renewable resources more generally). The entire exercise (briefing, game play and debriefing) lasted about 3 hours. A prize (champagne or chocolates) was awarded to the winning team with the highest asset value (cash plus salvage value of ships) at the end of the game. In both iterations of the exercise the teams generated trajectories for ships, catch and fish very similar to Figure 14.5.

'Going Fishing' – Drama Theory

'Going Fishing' was an immersive drama – the nature of these structured role-plays is described in Chapter 3 – that was designed to expose the 'political' aspects of fisheries management. Whereas the Fish Banks simulator focused upon the interactions (specifically the competition for marine catch) between fishing companies, 'Going Fishing' was designed within broader boundaries and captured the relationships between the key stakeholder groups that were shaping the future of the worldwide fishing industry.

The construction of the drama involved a number of stages. These broadly followed the process of confrontation management shown earlier in Figure 3.5 of Chapter 3. From preliminary reading around the topic, it was apparent that this was a domain in which there were highly polarised views: strident warnings against over-fishing were moderated by papers on the economic management of natural resources and contested by other lobby groups. A preliminary 'long list' of stakeholders was created (Figure 14.6).

It was clear that there were a number of major 'bones of contention' that concerned and divided stakeholders. These included (with the major concerned stakeholders):

Fishermen – Indigenous
Fishermen – British
Fishermen – European
Fishermen's Leaders
Pirates
Cod and haddock fishermen
National Federation. Of Fishermen's Orgs
Ex-fishermen
Retailers – traditional
Retailers – green
Fish Processors
Fish Distributors
Fish Consumers [inc. products, fryers, restaurants, etc.] – North traditional
Fish Consumers [inc. products, fryers, restaurants, etc.] – North green
Fish Consumers-South
Foods that are alternatives to fish
Governments – South with fish interests
Governments – North with fish interests
Secretaries of State for Environment
M.S.C. (Marine Stewardship Council)
Environmentalists
Legal Regulators (e.g. EU)
Prince of Wales
Law/Regulatory Enforcers (e.g. navies, coastguards)
Media
Centre for Fisheries, Environment and Aquaculture Science
Government Researchers/Statisticians
I.C.E.S. (International Council for the Exploration of the Sea)
Department of Health (e.g. public health, nutritionists)
Vegetarians
Future Generations
Dolphins and other unintended casualties of fishing
Leisure interests (e.g. tourists)
Marine and coastal users
Suppliers to the fishing industry (e.g. boatyards/builders, bait, nets, crates, fuel/lubricants)
Suppliers to the fish processing (e.g. freezers, packaging)
By-products of the fish industry (e.g. glues etc.)
Communities dependent on fishing
Politicians (e.g. local MPs) concerned about economic impact of fishing

Figure 14.6. 'Long List' of Stakeholders for Going Fishing

Character	Options (written as bipolar choices: '...' denotes 'rather than')
'Responsible' fishermen	decommission ships (including partially)... maintain fleet discredit... accept scientific hypotheses become pirates... stay law-abiding
'Pirates' [i.e. unregulated fishermen]	catch fish wherever they can... become 'respectable' leave the fishing industry
'Green' advocates	press for 'green' labelling... [NOT] disrupt fishing industry
'Indigenous' people	press their governments for protection mobilise anti-Western sentiments
Global fish industry	establish and respect 'green' labelling... indiscriminate buying of 'grey' fish present fish as a luxury product... mass production develop fish farming
International Regulators	limit fishing police fishing restrictions
Fish industry value net	diversify... stay with fishers raise prices for niche market... [NOT]
National Governments	subsidise fishing industry... [NOT] encourage fishermen to decommission... [NOT]

Figure 14.7. Options Initially Available to Major Stakeholders in 'Going Fishing'

- 'Ethical' fish products: Retailers, Consumers (North), Processors.
- Who gets the fish?: Regulators, Fishermen, Pirates.
- Size of fish catch: Environmentalists, MSC, Scientists (Fishermen).
- Affordable nutrition: Consumers (South), Fishermen (South), Fishermen (North).

To create a manageable role-play in which participants' positions would be challenged, yet where their interests and concerns would not be too diverse, a subset of just eight representative stakeholder groups was selected from the original list, and for each of them the principal choices available to them at the commencement of the drama were set down. These are as shown in Figure 14.7.

These opportunities and the assumed values and aspirations of the characters would pose drama-theoretic dilemmas for each party. Some of these are summarised below:

'Responsible' fishermen
Co-operation and trust dilemmas (others (e.g. pirates) are tempted to renege on agreements to keep within quotas so why should the 'responsible' fishermen not do so either?)

'Pirates'
Persuasion dilemma (the mood may swing behind regulation; then how can they encourage anyone to permit even limited unregulated fishing?)

'Green' advocates
Trust dilemma (how can they get the food industry to commit irreversibly to 'green' labelling?)

'Indigenous' people
Persuasion dilemma (they have no really potent threat available to them)

Global fish industry
Co-operation dilemma (fishermen suspect that the food industry will move into less unpredictable fish farming instead of 'fish hunting')

International regulators
Threat dilemma (not entirely happy about imposing draconian regulations as implementation may be an intractable problem)

Fish industry value net
Co-operation dilemma (convincing fishermen that they won't exploit a shrinking customer base)

National governments
Positioning dilemma (while they would ideally prefer self-regulation and a sustainable fishing industry, this is unrealistic and the electorate in any case needs time to be won round . . .)

These dilemmas would provide the dynamics of the role-play exercise. This was achieved by the writing of briefing documents for each character that would state their initial position and fallback actions in the arenas that concerned them, as well as their initial perceptions of the other stakeholders. In the drama itself it would then be up to the characters to interact with others (in a totally free-form manner) to press for their own ends, and to try to reach agreements with or to dominate others. These exchanges would have emotionally to be handled in such a way that, for example, incredible promises (e.g. to cement a deal) might be believed.

In the event, because of the numbers attending on the day, our student participants were organised into just five teams for the exercise. Each team was a character in the drama – 'traditional' fishermen, unrestricted fishermen ('Freedom of the Oceans' – abbreviated to FOTO – or 'the pirates'), the food industry, the Green lobby and European governments. Once they had assimilated their briefing materials (this is an important stage in which groups resolve any internal differences and establish their interaction strategy with others), they were required to work with other characters to produce a joint response to a posited call for a world fisheries policy. Each team had its own syndicate room close to the other teams and could choose its own 'modus operandi': for instance, face-to-face meetings were allowed, as were e-mail communications between the syndicate rooms. At the end of the drama the students came together, first in role, then out of it to discuss the outcome that they had produced.

Below we summarise the outcome of the exercise (the students' reflections are given later). On the first 'run', the sequence of interactions was broadly as follows:

- The 'Food Industry' group suggested a meeting with representatives of all groups, to decide an agenda for discussion.
- The 'Government' group asked all groups to submit views.
- 'Food Industry' said it would support 'Government' in its regulatory role provided it gets (financial?) support in return.
- 'FOTO' (the unregulated fishermen or 'pirates') affirmed its objectives to 'supply fish to the population' and rejected the evidence for over-fishing.
- 'Traditional Fishers' asked 'Government' to defend it from indiscriminate fishing by 'FOTO'.
- 'Greens' asked 'Food Industry' to co-operate in 'green labelling'; also sought 'Government' controls on 'FOTO' and to ban imported fish; wanted to create public awareness of issues.
- 'Food Industry' was concerned about rising fish prices.
- 'Traditional Fishers' sought reduction in scale of (FOTO?) fishing.
- 'Food Industry' indicated to 'Government' its willingness to invest in fish farming, but requested its help in reducing public fears of the health dangers of farmed fish.
- 'Government' tried to draw all views together and took on responsibility for producing the final statement of intent.

We ran a very similar role-play with a second student cohort and the outcome was rather different. Whereas in the first 'run' the 'Government' group had taken a strong leadership role, and the unregulated fishermen were effectively ostracised, in the second 'run' a more conciliatory result was achieved, though with dubious ethical implications (e.g. the covert purchase of 'pirated' fish by the food industry) and significant concessions by the 'Government' over subsidies and fishing rights. The fact that the outcomes were so different is not a deficiency: it simply demonstrates that the groups were able to manage their confrontations and the dilemmas that we gave them in innovatively distinct ways.

'Flatfish' – Scenario Planning

Earlier in the module, the students had been introduced to a structured scenario planning method which is well established at Warwick Business School (the method is described in Chapter 9). The students had already applied the method to the development of scenarios and strategies for a range of organisations in a diverse set of industries, and presented their work to each other. For the purposes of this exercise, they were then introduced to a company called Flat-fish (http://www.flatfish-ltd.co.uk/, accessed 25 May 2006) based in Grimsby (a town on the east coast of England), and asked to create scenarios for the external environment (the fishing industry, etc.) that the firm might have to face in the future.

The class agreed upon a shortlist of key factors to drive two scenarios. Due to time constraints, detailed work on scenario narratives was done in two parallel groups. Creative formats were chosen in order to engage the rest of the class in the presentations that followed. The first scenario, entitled 'Sushi Galore', focused on issues of technological change (such as fish farming and genetic modification) in a context of powerful multinational corporations such as Tesco, the UK-based supermarket. However, these issues were presented in the format of a children's story: 'Once upon a time, a sardine and a haddock gave birth to a genetically modified fish called a saddock in a Tesco fish farm . . . '

The second scenario was entitled 'The Naked Fish', a reference to one of many popular cookery programmes on UK television at the time of the exercise. Continuing this theme, elements of the scenario – such as the list of key factors – were presented as a list of ingredients and cooking instructions. For instance, 'Pre-heat your oven to very low production costs. Take a pinch of legislation, add a cup of bargaining power . . . '

In the second iteration, a different approach was adopted to the scenario planning element of the exercise, involving large-group and small-group work. First, the class were asked to work together to generate a set of scenarios for the fishing industry, following the early steps of the method outlined in Chapter 9. When the scenarios had been drafted, the students were asked to work in the five stakeholder groups that they had adopted for the drama theory element of the exercise, and to use a TOWS matrix (Weihrich, 1993) to generate strategies for their stakeholder groups.

A summary of the three scenarios generated by the students is given in Table 14.1; four of the key factors are chosen to give a flavour of each scenario.

Table 14.1. Summary of Three Scenarios Generated

Key factors	Scenario 1 – 'Fishtanks'	Scenario 2 – 'Oysters Galore'	Scenario 3 – 'Iceberg UK'
Fishing technology	Strong growth in fish farming	Intensive fishing methods	'Smarter' fishing methods
Disposable income	Low (high unemployment)	High	Medium
Fish consumption	Low; there are health-related concerns about a new and unknown fish disease (from fish farms?)	High; there are high levels of health awareness, and fish is perceived to be an important part of a healthy diet	Medium
European unity	The EU is steady in size, and stable politically; fishing regulations are tightening	The EU is steady in size, and stable politically; fishing regulations are relatively loose	The EU is growing and unstable; fishing regulations are tight

REFLECTIONS AND THE WAY FORWARD

Reflections from the Students (first iteration)

When all three of the above elements had been completed, the students were asked to reflect upon and compare the three approaches to modelling that they had experienced. Their comments identified some strengths and weaknesses of each of the three approaches.

'Fish Banks' (system dynamics) made them very aware of giving full consideration to competitors and their actions; it was an enjoyable exercise that provided some quantification of a complex situation; however, it also simplified the complexity, e.g. the teams did not feel the impact of regulation during the exercise.

'Going Fishing' (drama theory) brought out the importance of negotiation, communication and misunderstandings; it captured the range of stakeholder views; yet, within limited timescales, the students were not always confident that they were playing the allocated roles with accuracy or full conviction.

'Flatfish' (scenario planning) gave them a 'feel' for the range of possible alternative futures, and for the benefits of challenging conventional thinking; however, some students had found it difficult to decide which scenarios to focus on, and were (uncomfortably) aware that full consideration had not been given to *all* possible futures.

Our Reflections on the Content of the Exercise (first iteration)

Combining the three approaches allowed a more rounded treatment of a complex issue than is usually possible, and highlighted the range of uncertainties that players in the industry in question may have to deal with. For instance, drama theory drew attention to political uncertainties, system dynamics was particularly powerful at illuminating systemic uncertainties (such as the surprising collapse of fish stocks and the reasons for over-fishing in a competitive industry), and scenario planning allowed participants to explore a range of external uncertainties for the organisation concerned.

The exercise appeared to increase awareness and broaden the vision of the students. However, it is harder to say whether a direct contribution to forward strategy was achieved on the first 'run', although time constraints meant that the participants spent less time on exploring the consequences of their modelling for the strategic plans that the firm might already have in place.

The exercise brought together three different 'levels' of modelling: drama theory was undertaken at an 'industry' level with its interacting stakeholders of national governments, regulators, fishermen, pirates, consumers and the food industry; system dynamics was undertaken at a 'regional fishery' level with its population of fish and rival fishing fleets; and scenario planning at the 'firm' level with its key external uncertainties. The three levels were usefully complementary, but this feature was not fully exploited within the boundaries of this short exercise.

We, and the students, believe that the sequence in which they undertook the three exercises was important in shaping their behaviour. For example, because the 'Fish Banks' exercise (which came first) had highlighted the dangers of over-fishing, the 'Green' group (environmentalists) probably found it easier to build an alliance during the drama theory exercise – and environmental concerns were also selected as an important dimension of the scenario planning activity in the final block of the exercise.

Our Reflections on the Educational Experience (first iteration)

The exercise encouraged a deeper, critical and comparative appraisal of the methodologies than would otherwise have been achieved during the module. The time allocated to reflection on the final day of the module encouraged a personal integration of conceptual frameworks on the part of the students.

We have already commented that the time constraints compromised the learning achieved on this occasion. For instance, during 'Fish Banks' and 'Going Fishing', the students were simply 'consumers' of models, i.e. they were not expected to acquire the modelling skills to build system dynamics and drama theory models, but were presented with existing models. Using existing models enhanced their strategic appreciation, but did not build their analytical and modelling skills. This is a point that we attempted to address in the second iteration of the exercise.

Figure 14.8 summarises some of the points emerging from the above discussion.

Reflections from the Students (second iteration)

Once again, at the end of the exercise, the students were asked to reflect upon and compare the three approaches to modelling. The main points, both positive and negative, can be summarised as follows.

'Going Fishing' (drama theory) once again emphasised the importance of negotiation, and allowed the students to explore stakeholder interests and to build understanding and empathy for other participants by immersing themselves in the problem situation. However, some of the students commented that they felt relatively uninformed in the roles that they were asked to play; others noted that the exercise did not necessarily have a clearly defined conclusion, and that any attempt to bring it to one felt unrealistic. Drama theory did appear to some to be a time-consuming and resource-intensive approach.

'Fish Banks' (system dynamics) helped the students to begin to put a structure on the complex issues that they were faced with; they began to think in terms of

	Uncertainties explored	'Level' of modelling undertaken	Issues highlighted by the exercises set
System dynamics	Systemic	Regional Fishery	Competitors and their actions, over-fishing
Drama theory	Political	Industry	Negotiation, communication, misunderstandings
Scenario planning	External	Firm	Wide range of possible futures, benefits of challenging conventional thinking

Figure 14.8. Comparing the Three Methods Used

the interactions of factors, feedback loops and causality, and felt that this method brought them closest to 'a true reflection of the system' and to a clearly defined conclusion. However, they noted that no consideration was given to the views of stakeholders – as they had already experienced drama theory, the issue of multiple perspectives was perhaps at the front of their minds.

Scenario planning was felt to be an approach that recognises the difficulty of measuring uncertainty, and that can help to produce recommendations and highlight contingencies. For some of the students, the lack of quantification in the scenario planning method that they were following was an area of concern (as they are students on an MSc in Management Science and Operational Research, the students typically have strong academic backgrounds in quantitative subjects, and are very familiar with the use of quantitative methods such as optimisation and statistical analysis).

Our reflections on the Content of the Exercise (second iteration)

The second iteration of the exercise was more obviously successful at achieving a contribution to forward strategy. TOWS matrices were successfully used to generate ideas for strategic options for each of the stakeholder groups, and some of the groups also had time to assess the robustness of their possible strategies under the scenarios that the whole group had generated.

The sequence in which the students undertook the three elements of the exercise was again believed to be important in shaping their behaviour. For example, because the drama theory exercise (which came first in the second iteration) had increased the students' understanding of (and empathy for) a range of stakeholder positions and concerns, it is likely that the range of factors generated in the scenario planning exercise represented a relatively rich list, highlighting trends and issues of concern to a broad set of interested parties.

Once again, the exercise as a whole encompassed modelling at three different 'levels'. As in the first iteration, system dynamics was undertaken at a 'regional fishery' level and drama theory at an 'industry' level (with groups representing a range of key stakeholders in the industry). In the second iteration, scenario planning spanned the 'industry' and 'organisation' level, as scenarios were developed by the entire student group for the fishing industry as a whole, but strategic options were generated and evaluated by five groups representing the five key stakeholders from the drama theory exercise. The authors believe that, as in the first iteration, the three levels were usefully complementary. Further work is needed to understand and exploit this complementarity to a greater extent; however, Figures 14.9 and 14.10 summarise our reflections on the work undertaken thus far.

Figure 14.9 identifies some of the strengths of each of the three approaches adopted. In our experience, these strengths complement one another, as illustrated in Figure 14.10.

We return to Mingers (2001), as summarised in Figures 14.1 and 14.2, to structure our remarks.

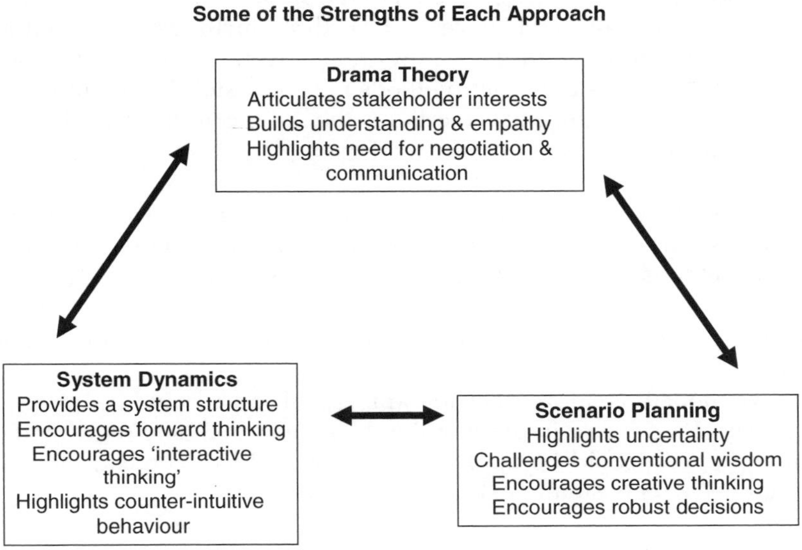

Some of the Strengths of Each Approach

Drama Theory
Articulates stakeholder interests
Builds understanding & empathy
Highlights need for negotiation &
communication

System Dynamics
Provides a system structure
Encourages forward thinking
Encourages 'interactive
thinking'
Highlights counter-intuitive
behaviour

Scenario Planning
Highlights uncertainty
Challenges conventional wisdom
Encourages creative thinking
Encourages robust decisions

Figure 14.9. Some of the Strengths of Each Approach

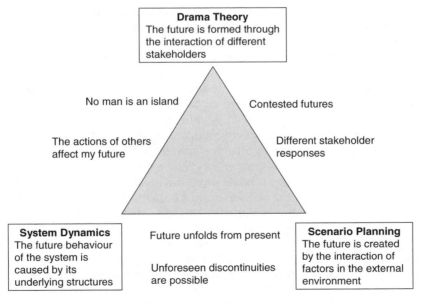

Drama Theory
The future is formed through
the interaction of different
stakeholders

No man is an island   Contested futures

The actions of others   Different stakeholder
affect my future   responses

System Dynamics   Future unfolds from present   **Scenario Planning**
The future behaviour   The future is created
of the system is   by the interaction of
caused by its   Unforeseen discontinuities   factors in the external
underlying structures   are possible   environment

Figure 14.10. Complementarity between Approaches

- Agent–methodology: we used the methods we are most familiar with – other methods and agents may bring benefits to the situation explored.
- Situation–methodology: we believe that all three methods were well suited to the problem situation (Figure 14.9 shows this), given its complexity, conflict and range of uncertainties – but other methods may also suit the situation.
- Agent–situation: we were not experts on the fishing industry; other situations could be addressed by us with these methods.

The authors would call for further experiments and case studies in multi-methodology, along the lines of the exercise described here. The comments above suggest that new agents, new methods and new situations may all bring further insights, e.g.

- The same exercise could be run by other facilitators at other institutions (new agents).
- Alternative modelling approaches for strategy rehearsal could be introduced into the exercise, alongside or in place of the three described here (new methods).
- A similar exercise could be applied to a new problem context, other than the fishing industry (new situations).

Our Reflections on the Educational Experience (second iteration)

The authors believe that, in the second iteration as in the first, the exercise encouraged a deeper, critical and comparative appraisal of the methodologies than would otherwise have been achieved during the module. The time allocated to reflection on the final day of the module once again encouraged a personal integration of conceptual frameworks on the part of the students, and remains an essential element of the exercise.

However, time constraints continued to compromise the learning achieved on the second iteration of the exercise. During the system dynamics exercise, the students were again simply 'consumers' of the model, i.e. they were not expected to acquire the modelling skills to build a system dynamics model of a fishery. That would require a complete course dedicated to system dynamics. Instead, they were taught enough about reinforcing and balancing loops to appreciate the feedback structure underlying 'Fish Banks' and other business simulators. Similarly, during the second iteration of the exercise, the students were given a greater insight into the concepts required to build drama theory models. It is unrealistic to suppose that, in a single course, students will master the skills to build for themselves such a range of models. However, they can and do develop practical insight into the value of complementary methods and that was our principal intention. Moreover, MSc students who attend the Strategic OR module have the option to take additional specialist elective courses to develop specific modelling and problem-structuring skills.

Finally, we return to Bennett's (1985) suggestion (discussed earlier) that there are at least three ways of using approaches together: addition, enrichment and integration. The first 'run' of the exercise was largely an *additive* exercise (see Figure 14.11); the problem situation was addressed by three methodologies, with critical reflection (e.g. contrasting the three independent framings) really only taking place – at least explicitly – at the end of the exercise. The second 'run' contained some element of

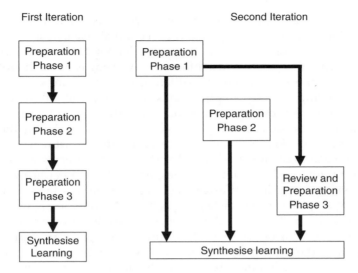

Figure 14.11. Overview of the First Two Iterations

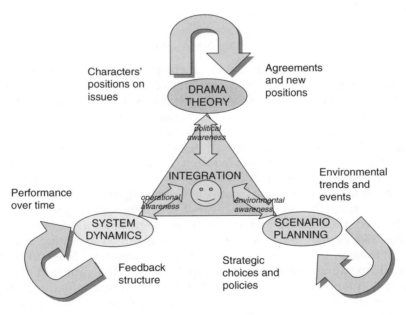

Figure 14.12. Plan for the Third Iteration

enrichment, as the drama theory exercise (which came first on this occasion) was used to provide a structure for part of the scenario planning activity (i.e. generating strategies for the stakeholder groups).

A future 'run' – see the plan in Figure 14.12 – will aim to achieve a more integrative approach, with a structured interface between the three elements of the exercise. The present, simplest means of integration is to allow this process to take place in the minds of the participants, as they experience the different perspectives on the case . However, this is a haphazard process that relies heavily upon participants' ability to reflect and learn from their experiences. Each methodology allows people to 'play with' the situation in a different way; using each methodology allows people to 'play with' the situation in a different way and brings about a different transformation of 'inputs' into 'outputs'. So, system dynamics allows experimentation that shows how the feedback structure of the situation, in terms of interacting resources and policies, determines performance over time; drama theory shows what agreements and alliances may be secured by the adjustment of negotiating positions; and scenario planning shows what choices and policies seem appropriate in the light of future trends and uncertainties. A structured interface would require participants to make explicit the outputs of each phase and use them as a context (as 'input') for another phase: for instance, to specify and subsequently work within the negotiated outcomes of the drama theory phase when doing the scenario planning; or to reconsider positions on issues in the drama theory phase in light of simulated performance from the system dynamics phase. Ideally, methodology deployment would be a continuous, iterative process with the possibility of moving flexibly between one perspective and another, and so testing the contingencies of different outputs. However, within the confines of a taught course module a more foreshortened, linear design is the most likely compromise.

From the Teaching Context to the Organisational Context

It is our view that the strategic development process as a whole can often be strengthened more by the use of a portfolio of the approaches that have been described in this book than by the use of just one isolated method or framework. However, we are advocating a targeted and informed use of multi-methodology to support strategy rehearsal. Consider again the task of rehearsing strategy as depicted in Figure 14.13, an excerpt from the strategic development process described in Chapter 1. Here models of the organisation are devised to test the feasibility of strategic initiatives, both before and during implementation. In this picture we can distinguish two modes of rehearsal. Both involve a learning cycle of creating strategic initiatives and critically assessing them. But the aspects of organisational change being rehearsed are different and so are the methods to be used. Some modelling approaches, like system dynamics, are particularly suited to testing strategic and operational feasibility – whether or not strategic initiatives are likely to work given the internal operating constraints and capabilities of the firm and the external industry and competitive environment. Other modelling approaches, like drama theory, are particularly suited to testing political feasibility – whether or not stakeholders will buy-in to strategic initiatives and support them (or at least not obstruct them). In our view the assessment of political feasibility is distinct from the assessment of strategic and operational feasibility and in this sense the use of system dynamics and drama theory in 'Fishing for Strategy' are complementary ways of thinking about the complexity of change in real organisations. Scenario planning enriches these endogenous models of change by focusing attention on uncertainties in the external environment that can modify, sometimes radically, accepted structural or political constraints. For example, the Flatfish scenario exercise in the first

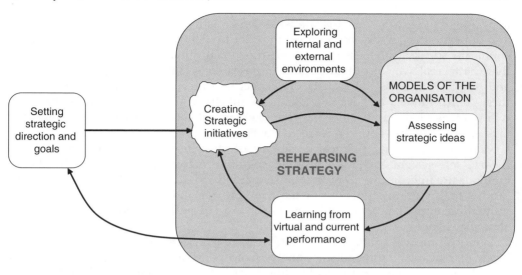

Figure 14.13. Rehearsing Strategy with Models

iteration of 'Fishing for Strategy' identified fish farming as an important 'uncertainty' in the future of fisheries. Rapid growth of fish farms would almost certainly change the nature of political interaction among the stakeholders identified in the immersive drama and also the long-term structural dynamics of natural fisheries identified in Fish Banks. In fact, this possibility led to the development of a new system dynamics model on 'future fisheries' by a Warwick MSc student as a dissertation project (Mori, 2005). The dissertation involved extending the simple fisheries model behind Fish Banks (as shown in Figure 14.4) to incorporate fish farming and then simulating alternative futures for an industry containing both natural and farmed fish stocks.

As noted at the beginning of this chapter, we were opportunistic and pragmatic in making use of approaches with which we were especially familiar. Nevertheless, we feel that our particular experience with these three approaches led us to some generalisable insights into multi-methodology that provide a suitable conclusion to our reported work. We feel that problem structuring and modelling methods from both the OR and strategy fields can be usefully classified according to their ability to support the two modes of rehearsal identified above: one for testing strategic and operational feasibility and the other for testing political feasibility.

Methods for testing strategic and operational feasibility of strategic initiatives include system dynamics, the resource-based view of the firm, SWOT and the Five Forces framework. System dynamics and the resource-based view look inside rival firms to understand what they are capable of achieving given their endowment of strategic resources, established operating policies and feedback structure. The Five Forces framework looks at industry structure (rivals along the supply chain, barriers to entry, technology and regulatory trends) to identify the likely intensity of competition facing a firm as it executes strategy. SWOT combines both internal appraisal of the firm's strengths and weaknesses with external assessment of threats and opportunities in the environment in order to identify feasible strategies. Philosophically speaking all these methods are functionalist in that they implicitly assume there is a 'real world' out there that imposes constraints on strategic initiatives and limits what firms can realistically expect to achieve. The principal purpose of these 'hard' models and frameworks is to anticipate whether strategic initiatives will work as planned, whether they are likely to fall short of strategic goals and to take appropriate pre-emptive corrective action.

Methods for testing political feasibility of strategic initiatives include drama theory, soft systems methodology and cognitive mapping. Philosophically these methods are interpretive. They recognise that individuals and different stakeholder groups may view the purpose of the firm and the industry differently and that mutual accommodation of conflicting views is an essential ingredient of successful strategic change.

In much practical strategic development there is a need and opportunity for both types of rehearsal – functionalist analysis of operational and strategic feasibility as well as interpretive analysis of political feasibility. Which approach to use then returns to the pragmatic criteria identified by Mingers (2001), as summarised in Figures 14.1 and 14.2. But we believe it is important for both modellers and managers to be aware which mode of rehearsal they are adopting and the kinds of strategic pitfalls most readily found in the chosen mode. For example, a system dynamics model is most likely to add benefit in situations where the outcome of a known and agreed strategic initiative is unclear and depends on effective coordination across functions, as in the liquid soap example in Chapter 7. An immersive drama is most likely to add benefit in situations where conflict about the strategic direction or goals of an organisation stand in the way of effective collaboration among the stakeholders.

Sometimes it will be possible to run both functionalist and interpretive modes in parallel. We think that true multi-methodology rehearsal is rare due to the combination of scarce time and skills involved. Nevertheless, such work can be valuable if indeed it sheds light on complementary aspects of operational, strategic and political feasibility. We would point the interested reader to, for instance, Ormerod's (2001) description of a large multi-methodological intervention.

The Way Forward

The authors believe that the exercise described here has implications for the use of strategy and problem-structuring methods in management education and development, where stronger theoretical underpinnings will enhance the validity of activities such as scenario planning, role playing and modelling. We would call for further action research, with a focus on supporting people in thinking about the future and engaging in strategic conversations. We would also encourage researchers with relevant experience across a range of backgrounds, e.g. those operational researchers with relevant modelling skills, to engage in cross-disciplinary research which addresses the role of models in conversations about contested futures.

REFERENCES

Bennett, P.G. (1985) 'On linking approaches to decision aiding: issues and prospects', *Journal of the Operational Research Society*, **36**, 659–669.

Gordon, H.S. (1954) 'The economic theory of a common-property resource: the fishery', *Journal of Political Economy*, **62**, 124–142.

Kunc, M.H. & Morecroft, J.D.W. (2006) 'Competitive dynamics and gaming simulation. Lessons from a fishing industry simulator', *Journal of the Operational Research Society* (forthcoming), available online July 2006.

Meadows, D.H., Fiddaman, T. & Shannon, D. (2001) *Fish Banks, Ltd. A Micro-computer Assisted Group Simulation that Teaches Principles of Sustainable Management of Renewable Natural Resources*, 3rd edn. Laboratory for Interactive Learning, University of New Hampshire: Durham, NH.

Mingers, J. (2001) 'Multimethodology – mixing and matching methods'. In: Rosenhead, J. & Mingers, J. (eds), *Rational Analysis for a Problematic World Revisited*. John Wiley & Sons: Chichester; 289–309.

Mingers, J. & Gill, A. (eds) (1997) *Multimethodology: Theory and Practice of Combining Management Science Methodologies*. John Wiley & Sons: Chichester.

Mori, Y. (2005) 'Future fisheries – extending a simple fisheries model to incorporate fish farming', MSc dissertation in Management Science and Operational Research, University of Warwick, September.

Moxnes, E. (1998) 'Not only the tragedy of the commons: misperceptions of bioeconomics', *Management Science*, **44**, 1234–1248.

Ormerod, R. (2001) 'Mixing methods in practice'. In: Rosenhead, J. & Mingers, J. (eds), *Rational Analysis for a Problematic World Revisited*. John Wiley & Sons: Chichester; 311–335.

Rosenhead, J. & Mingers, J. (eds) (2001) *Rational Analysis for a Problematic World Revisited*. John Wiley & Sons: Chichester.

Weihrich, H. (1993) 'Daimler-Benz's move towards the next century with the TOWS matrix', *European Business Review*, **93**(1).

Author Index

Subject Index